MANAGEMENT
AND
ORGANIZATIONAL
BEHAVIOR

ESSENTIALS

John R. Schermerhorn, Jr.
Ohio University

New York • C o • Singapore

This book is dedicated to my mother and father.

ACQUISITIONS EDITOR—Petra Sellers
MARKETING MANAGER—Leslie Hines
PRODUCTION EDITOR—Jeanine Furino
DESIGNER—Dawn Stanley
ASSISTANT EDITOR—Ellen Ford
MANUFACTURING COORDINATOR—Dorothy Sinclair
ILLUSTRATION COORDINATOR—Rosa Bryant

This book was set in 10/12 Century Old Style by Achorn Graphics and printed and bound by
R.R. Donnelly & Sons, Inc. The cover was printed by New England Book Components.

Recognizing the importance of preserving what has been written, it is a
policy of John Wiley & Sons, Inc. to have books of enduring value published
in the United States printed on acid-free paper, and we exert our best
efforts to that end.

Library of Congress Cataloging-in-Publication Data

Schermerhorn, John R.
  Management and organizational behavior essentials / John R.
Schermerhorn, Jr.
      p.   cm.
  Includes index.
  ISBN 0-471-13308-6 (pbk. : alk. paper)
  1. Organizational behavior. I. Title.
HD58.7.S339   1996
658.4—dc20
                                              95-37720
                                                  CIP

Printed in the United States of America

10 9 8 7 6 5 4 3 2 1

PREFACE

Management and Organizational Behavior Essentials offers the opportunity for its readers to introduce themselves to management and organizational behavior in an efficient yet useful way. It is designed with application in mind. The material is presented with a strong managerial theme and with sensitivity to the many significant changes taking place in the environment at large. The book respects the implications of these changes for organizations, for managers, and for all workers in contemporary society. The environmental context, workforce diversity, the global economy, quality and competitive advantage, and managerial ethics are core integrating themes. With a solid foundation in the disciplines of management and organizational behavior, *MOBE* tries to help its readers to both understand the essential theories and gain insights into how they can be used to achieve high-performance and high quality of life workplaces.

This first edition of *Management and Organizational Behavior Essentials* is designed as a professional book with open page layouts, crisp figures, and clear text. Study questions open each chapter to orient the reader; they also anchor the point-by-point summaries at the end of each chapter. Figures within chapters clarify concepts; while special "Effective Manager" boxes highlight managerial applications. Finally, an end-of-book glossary is helpful for reviewing key terms and their definitions.

MOBE is a compact book that brings the essentials of management and organizational behavior to the reader's attention. It is useful in a wide variety of course formats, and can easily be linked with an instructor's personal selection of supporting readings, cases, exercises, and other supplementary materials. I believe this book can help meet the needs of many instructors who want to integrate the introductory studies of management and organizational behavior, and do so in a way that allows students to avoid the costs of larger and more traditional textbooks. In the spirit of mutual inquiry and in support of education for the workplaces of tomorrow, I am pleased to offer to you this first edition of *Management and Organizational Behavior Essentials.*

John Schermerhorn
Athens, Ohio

Acknowledgments

Management and Organizational Behavior Essentials has benefitted from the reviews and contributions of the following management educators whose reviews of draft versions helped improve the finished manuscript: Mel Schnake, Valdosta State University and Michael Stevens, University of Texas/El Paso.

My very special thanks go to Ellen Ford for her assistance in managing the many development and production details in her role as Assistant Editor at Wiley; to Executive Editor Whitney Blake who committed to the book; much thanks to Acquisitions Editor Petra Sellers; and to a supportive and professional Wiley team that helped create the book in a timely and high quality fashion: Leslie Hines, Marketing Manager; Jeanine Furino, Production Editor; Dorothy Sinclair, Manufacturing Coordinator; Dawn Stanley, Designer; and Rosa Bryant, Illustration Coordinator.

BRIEF CONTENTS

C O N T E N T S

CHAPTER 3   INTERNATIONAL MANAGEMENT AND THE GLOBAL ECONOMY   30

CHAPTER 4 MANAGING WITH ETHICS AND SOCIAL RESPONSIBILITY 47

PART II
THE MANAGEMENT FUNCTIONS

CHAPTER 5 PLANNING—SETTING DIRECTION 63

CHAPTER **6** ORGANIZING—CREATING STRUCTURES   81

CHAPTER **7**   LEADING—INSPIRING EFFORT   98

CHAPTER **8**   CONTROLLING—ENSURING RESULTS   114

PART III
MANAGING INDIVIDUALS AND GROUPS

CHAPTER **10**   MOTIVATING—REWARDS AND REINFORCEMENT   144

CHAPTER **11**   DESIGNING WORK SYSTEMS—JOBS AND WORK SCHEDULES   161

PART IV
MANAGING THE PROCESSES OF ORGANIZATIONAL BEHAVIOR

CHAPTER 15   INFLUENCING—USING POWER   223

PART V
MANAGING HIGH PERFORMANCE SYSTEMS

CHAPTER **18**   PLANNED CHANGE AND CONTINUOUS IMPROVEMENT   263

MANAGEMENT
AND
ORGANIZATIONAL
BEHAVIOR

ESSENTIALS

1

MANAGEMENT AND

ORGANIZATIONAL BEHAVIOR

As you read Chapter 1, keep in mind these study questions:

- Who are managers and what do they do?

- What is the management process?

- What is organizational behavior?

- What are the challenges of management and organizational behavior today?

The new workplace is concerned with total quality, customer service, competitive advantage, productivity, quality of work life, and more—and it is already here in many organizations. It must come soon to others, or pressing forces of competition and social change will trap them in a spiral of decline and disarray. As described in *Fortune:* "Call it whatever you like—reengineering, restructuring, transformation, flattening, downsizing, rightsizing, a quest for global competitiveness—it's real, it's radical, and it's arriving every day at a company near you . . . The revolution feels something like this: scary, guilty, painful, liberating, disorienting, exhilarating, empowering, frustrating, fulfilling, confusing, challenging. In other words, it feels very much like chaos."[1] Yes, indeed, the path toward the future is exciting and unpredictable. The important forces of this decade will continue to grow in pace and complexity as we move toward the twenty-first century; new forces will surely emerge to join them. Reading and learning from this new book, *Management and Organizational Behavior Essentials,* can help you look forward with confidence to a career in our challenging environment.

Managers and Management

Formally defined, an **organization** is a collection of people working together to achieve a common purpose, with that purpose being to produce goods and/or services that satisfy the needs of customers or clients. A **manager** is responsible for the work performance of one or more other people in an organization. The job title will vary (supervisor, team leader, division head, administrator, vice president, and so on), but a manager is always someone to whom others report. These other people, usually called direct reports or subordinates, and their managers are the important and essential human resources of organizations. They use material resources like information, technology, raw materials, facilities, and money to produce the goods and services that the organization offers to its customers.

What Is Management?

Every manager's job entails a key responsibility: to help an organization achieve high performance through the utilization of all its resources, both human and mate-

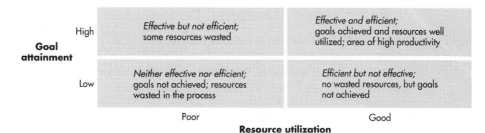

	Poor	Good
High	*Effective but not efficient; some resources wasted*	*Effective and efficient; goals achieved and resources well utilized; area of high productivity*
Low	*Neither effective nor efficient; goals not achieved; resources wasted in the process*	*Efficient but not effective; no wasted resources, but goals not achieved*

Figure 1.1 Performance effectiveness, performance efficiency, and managerial success.

rial. This is accomplished through the process of **management**—formally defined as planning, organizing, leading, and controlling the use of resources to accomplish performance goals.[2] According to the well-known management theorist Henry Mintzberg, being a manager in this sense is a most important job:

> No job is more vital to our society than that of the manager. It is the manager who determines whether our social institutions serve us well or whether they squander our talents and resources. It is time to strip away the folklore about managerial work, and time to study it realistically so that we can begin the difficult task of making significant improvement in its performance.[3]

What Do Managers Do?

Effective managers utilize organizational resources in ways that result in *both* high performance outcomes *and* high levels of satisfaction among people doing the required work. This dual concern for performance and satisfaction is a central theme in the new workplace. In respect to performance, two criteria are shown in Figure 1.1. **Performance effectiveness** is a measure of task output or goal accomplishment. If you are a manufacturing supervisor, performance effectiveness means that your work unit meets its daily production targets in terms of quantity and quality of outputs. **Performance efficiency** is a measure of the resource cost associated with goal accomplishment. Cost of labor is a common efficiency measure; others include equipment utilization, facilities maintenance, and returns on capital investment. The most efficient production supervisor, for example, is one who operates daily at minimum cost of materials and labor. As highlighted in Figure 1.1, true managerial success involves both performance effectiveness in goal attainment and performance efficiency in resource utilization.

In respect to satisfaction, the term **quality of work life** (QWL) is frequently used as an indicator of the overall quality of human experiences in the workplace. Managers are expected to achieve high performance outcomes while maintaining a high quality of work life for those doing the required work. The QWL concept expresses a true respect for people in their work environments and involves such things as adequate and fair pay for jobs well done, safe and healthy working conditions, opportunities to learn and use new skills, room to grow and progress in a career, and protection of individual rights.

Productivity and Managerial Performance

Productivity is defined as a summary measure of the quantity and quality of work performance with resource utilization considered. It can be measured at the individual, group, or organization level and is maximized when high performance is achieved at low cost. Figure 1.1 shows this as a combination of performance effectiveness and performance efficiency. Of course, people—the human resources in the workplace—count, too. Productivity and a high quality of work life can and should go hand-in-hand.

Perhaps no productivity themes are stronger today than quality and service. Today's consumers expect quality products and good customer service. Organizations that fail to deliver them are left struggling in our highly competitive environments. **Total quality management,** or TQM for short, is a popular current theme that will recur throughout this book. It means managing with an organization-wide commitment to continuous improvement of work processes and product quality, and to totally meeting customer needs.

Levels of Managers

Top managers set major performance objectives and are responsible for results achieved by the organization as a whole or one of its significant parts. Common job titles at this level include chief executive officer, chief operating officer, president, and vice-president. These senior managers or executives should pay special attention to the external environment, be alert to potential long-run problems and opportunities, and be able to develop ways of dealing with them.

Middle managers report to top managers and develop plans to implement higher-level objectives, while overseeing the work of several units as these plans are implemented. Examples include clinic directors in hospitals, deans in universities, and division managers, plant managers, and branch sales managers in businesses. Middle managers emphasize teamwork and communication as they help coordinate multiple activities.

First-line managers commonly hold job titles such as supervisor, department head, and team leader. These managers pursue short-term performance objectives consistent with the plans of middle and top management. They are people to whom front-line or nonmanagerial workers report, and most of us get our first managerial experience at this level. The Effective Manager 1.1 offers advice on being a good supervisor.

Types of Managers

Line managers are responsible for work activities that make a direct contribution to the organization's outputs. The president, retail manager, and department supervisors of a local department store all have line responsibilities, because their jobs are directly related to the sales operations of the store. **Staff managers** use technical expertise to advise and support line workers. In a department store, the director of human resources and comptroller would have staff responsibilities.

THE EFFECTIVE MANAGER 1.1

Eight Responsibilities of a Supervisor

1. Plan and schedule work daily, weekly, monthly.
2. Clarify tasks and gather ideas for improvement.
3. Appraise performance and counsel subordinates.
4. Recommend pay increases and new assignments.
5. Inform subordinates about performance goals and expectations.
6. Inform higher level managers about work-unit needs and accomplishments.
7. Recruit, select, train, and develop workers to meet performance standards.
8. Encourage and maintain high enthusiasm for work.

In business, **functional managers** have responsibility for a single area of activity, such as finance, marketing, production, personnel, accounting, or sales. **General managers** are responsible for more complex units that include many functional areas. An example is a plant manager who oversees many separate functions, including purchasing, manufacturing, warehousing, sales, personnel, and accounting. In nonprofit or public sector organizations, managers are often called **administrators,** and they hold job titles such as hospital administrator, public administrator, city administrator, and human-service administrator.

The Management Process

Success in any level or type of management position requires a capability to recognize problems and opportunities, make good decisions, and take appropriate action. This is done through the four basic management functions depicted in Figure 1.2: planning, organizing, leading, and controlling.

Planning is the process of setting performance objectives and determining what actions need to be taken to accomplish them. For example, Corning Inc.'s top management once grew concerned about a high quit rate among female managers. Noting many complaints of an "inhospitable environment," CEO Jamie Houghton set a planning objective to increase Corning's commitment to women.[4]

Organizing is the process of defining tasks, allocating resources, and arranging coordinated work activities to implement plans. Continuing with the Corning example, eleven senior Corning executives were formed into a quality improvement team to deal with the complaints of female employees. They learned that sexual harassment was an important concern. A committee was formed to develop procedures for dealing with sexual harassment cases, and training workshops were designed to increase employee awareness of gender-related issues.

Leading is the process of arousing people's enthusiasm to work hard and direct their efforts to fulfill plans and accomplish objectives. At Corning, leadership in the management of diversity comes from the top. Houghton started an affirmative

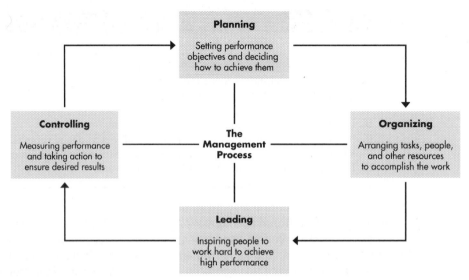

Figure 1.2 The four functions of management: planning, organizing, leading, and controlling.

action program for women and minorities and encouraged others to help women and minorities advance more quickly in the corporate structure. When Controller Richard B. Klein sensed an uneasiness among white male managers in his department, he also took the lead. Meetings were held to review and discuss Corning's new affirmative action plans. Klein said this was initially very threatening.

Controlling is the process of measuring work performance, comparing results to objectives, and taking corrective action as needed. Through controlling managers maintain active contact with people in the course of their work, gather and interpret reports on performance, and use this for constructive change. CEO Houghton was pleased when Corning was praised by the New York advocacy group, Catalyst, for its "commitment to women." But he was also aware that the firm's success in valuing diversity was still incomplete. He said, "Do we still have a lot of discrimination? Sure. Is there still sexual harassment? Yes." He explained that antiharassment and other efforts must continue, admitting, "It's a slow process."

Managerial Roles and Activities

Mintzberg suggests that daily managerial work involves a set of roles that good managers are able to perform very well. These roles fall into three categories: (1) *interpersonal roles* involve interactions with persons inside and outside the work unit; (2) *informational roles* involve the giving, receiving, and analyzing of information; (3) *decisional roles* involve using information to make decisions to solve problems or address opportunities.[5] Fulfilling these managerial roles is often a demanding and stressful job. Researchers describe these common attributes of managerial work:

- Managers work long hours.

- Managers work at an intense pace.

- Managers work at fragmented and varied tasks.

- Managers work with many communication media.

- Managers work largely through interpersonal relationships.[6]

Managerial Agendas and Networks

John Kotter, another management scholar and consultant, has found that two activities are critical to a general manager's success.[7] First, through *agenda setting* good managers develop action priorities that include short-term and long-term objectives and plans. These agendas are usually incomplete and loosely connected in the beginning, but become more specific as the manager continually gleans information while working. They are kept in mind and are "played out" whenever opportunities arise. Second, managers implement their agendas by working successfully with a variety of people. This is made possible by *networking,* the process of building and maintaining positive relationships with people whose help may someday be needed. The interpersonal networks or "trade routes" through which managers fulfill their responsibilities include peers, subordinates, and superiors from inside the organization, as well as relevant outsiders.

Managerial Skills and Competencies

A skill is an ability to translate knowledge into action that results in desired performance. The essential managerial skills are described by Robert Katz as technical, human, and conceptual.[8] Although each skill is necessary for all managers, its relative importance may vary by level of managerial responsibility.

A **technical skill** is the ability to use a special proficiency or expertise to perform particular tasks. Accountants, engineers, market researchers, and computer scientists, for example, possess technical skills. Technical skills tend to be most important at lower levels of managerial responsibility. The ability to work well in cooperation with other persons is a **human skill.** A manager with good human skills has a high degree of self-awareness and the capacity to understand or empathize with the feelings of others. Human skills are consistently important across all the managerial levels. The ability to think analytically to view situations broadly and solve problems for the benefit of everyone concerned is a **conceptual skill.** As managers move to ever-higher responsibilities, the conceptual skills gain in relative importance to technical skills.

A **managerial competency** is a skill or personal characteristic that contributes to high performance in a management job.[9] Several such competencies have been implied in prior discussions, including those related to planning, organizing, leading, and controlling workplace affairs and the information-gathering and decision-making

> **THE EFFECTIVE MANAGER 1.2**
>
> Personal Competencies for Managerial Success
>
> - **Leadership**—ability to influence others to perform tasks
> - **Self-objectivity**—ability to realistically evaluate oneself
> - **Analytic thinking**—ability to interpret and explain patterns in information
> - **Behavioral flexibility**—ability to modify personal behavior to reach a goal
> - **Oral communication**—ability to clearly express ideas in oral presentations
> - **Written communication**—ability to clearly express one's ideas in writing
> - **Personal impact**—ability to create good impression and instill confidence

activities that underlie them. The Effective Manager 1.2 identifies additional skills and personal characteristics considered important by the American Assembly of Collegiate Schools of Business (AACSB).[10]

Organizational Behavior

The prior discussion of managerial skills and competencies sets the stage for an introduction to the scientific discipline known as **organizational behavior.** Defined formally as the study of individual and group behavior in organizations, "OB" is an important body of knowledge for managers.[11] It provides a set of concepts and a vocabulary for describing and analyzing human behavior in organizations. For example, OB is very interested in job satisfaction and the attitudes people hold toward their work and work settings. OB also provides theories and frameworks that help explain and predict that behavior. For example, OB offers theories on how job designs affect job satisfaction and performance. And OB provides insights into techniques and applications useful for moving human behavior in organizations in particular directions. For example, OB suggests ways of designing jobs to achieve higher levels of performance and satisfaction for the specific individuals asked to do them.

Scientific Foundations of Organizational Behavior

Organizational behavior has several distinguishing characteristics as a field of study. To begin, it is an *interdisciplinary body of knowledge,* having strong ties to the fields of psychology, sociology, and anthropology as well as with economics and political science. Unlike these disciplines, however, OB specifically *studies human behavior in organizations.* Like its companion disciplines, OB *uses scientific methods* for research and theory building. The knowledge base of organizational behavior is being developed with solid research methods, controlled and systematic data collection, and verifiable explanations.

As a scientific discipline, furthermore, OB has a *focus on applications* that can have very practical benefits in improving performance, satisfaction, and quality of work life. In this respect, OB adopts a *contingency orientation* that rejects "one best way" solutions. Rather, OB researchers try to identify how different situations can be understood and dealt with best. Important here is a further interest in *individual differences,* the recognition of diversity and the desire to find ways to fully respect and utilize diversity in organizational workforces. This closely relates also to OB's *humanistic orientation,* one that conveys ultimate respect for people as human beings, and for their attitudes, feelings, talents, and contributions in work settings. Although OB ultimately seeks to improve the performance of organizations, its commitment is to do so in ways that always respect the people involved and allow them to achieve satisfaction from their work.

Learning about Organizational Behavior

Understanding organizational behavior can help you master the challenges of managing in the dynamic environment described in the chapter opening. Importantly, though, your learning about management and organizational behavior should only begin with this book and your formal course. You must commit to **life-long learning**—the process of continuously learning from your work experiences.

Life-long learning must be viewed as a personal responsibility and an essential foundation for long-term career success. It can be pursued through day-to-day experiences, conversations with co-workers and friends, time spent with mentors, attendance at training seminars and workshops, reading books and periodicals, and staying informed through the mass media. Life-long learning opportunities are there for everyone, but they must be utilized to have an impact. As management consultant Tom Peters says, "Students: Remember that (1) education is the *only* ticket to success and (2) it doesn't stop with the last certificate you pick up. Education is the 'big game' in the globally interdependent economy."[12]

Management and Organizational Behavior Today

Any study of management and organizational behavior must be grounded in full awareness of the complex and shifting demands of our dynamic environment. The successful twenty-first-century manager will understand the forces of change affecting the new workplace and will develop the personal capabilities to master them in a positive manner.

An Environment of Change

This book is going to cover many aspects of the changing nature of the modern organization, the new workplace, and the emerging role of managers and management. For now, four key points are worth noting as a backdrop to the chapters that follow.[13]

1. **The workforce is changing.** The watchwords of the day include *workforce diversity, workforce skills,* and *workforce values.*[14] New managers must be prepared to deal well with a multicultural workforce composed of people from different ethnic and racial backgrounds, of different genders and age, of different lifestyle preferences, and of different value sets. They must also be prepared to deal with workers whose skills may not match the demands of new technologies and changing workplace tasks. And they must be prepared to deal with a dynamic society in which family values, environmental concerns, and the very concept of *career* are changing.

2. **Customer expectations are changing.** In today's complex society, only organizations that are able to deliver what customers want in terms of *quality, service,* and *cost* will prosper. This is the age of total quality management, defined earlier as management dedicated to ensuring that an organization and all of its members operate with commitments to continuous improvement and totally meeting customer needs. The new manager must value quality, value customers, and personally do things that add value to the organization's ability to meet customers' needs.

3. **Organizations are changing.** They are changing now and they will continue to change in order to survive and prosper in a complex environment. We see organizations facing the pressures of *restructuring,* the *global economy,* and ever-present developments in *information and technologies.* New managers work in organizations that are unrelenting in the quests for productivity gains, innovation, and competitive advantage in the marketplace. Some of the terms heard now in the executive suites include *reengineering, network organizations,* and *virtual corporations.* Without a doubt, the new manager must be comfortable working in and with organizations operating in new and different ways.

4. **Managers must change, too.** The directions are clear; the future is now; but, in order to succeed, the new manager must be willing to step forward and make the changes necessary to secure it. Indeed, the very term *manager* is being questioned by some consultants and authors.[15] They believe that the changing nature of organizations in the new workplace may make the term *coordinator,* or perhaps *coach* or *facilitator,* a more apt description of the role. Regardless of the term used, however, the message is the same. The successful manager of tomorrow will make the behavioral and attitudinal adjustments necessary to succeed in very dynamic times.

Personal Career Development

In his book *No Easy Victories,* John Gardner speaks of a special challenge. Read his words twice in the following quotation—once as written, then once again substituting the word *manager* for "leader" and *organization* for "society."

> Leaders have a significant role in creating the state of mind that is the society. They can serve as symbols of the moral unity of the society. They

can express the values that hold the society together. Most important, they can conceive and articulate goals that lift people out of their petty preoccupations, carry them above the conflicts that tear a society apart, and unite them in the pursuit of objectives worthy of their best efforts.[16]

Managers are the keys to organizational productivity. Productivity, in turn, is the key to economic development and growth. Without a doubt, managers of the twenty-first century will have to excel as never before to meet the expectations held of them and of the organizations they lead.[17] And inescapably, managerial leadership today is complicated. *New* managerial outlooks and managerial competencies appropriate to the *new* workplace are requirements for future success. New managers will succeed in turbulent times only through continuous improvement. Rapid environmental change means rapid obsolescence of one's skills and competencies, unless diligent efforts are made to update and maintain them.

The situation and challenges just described should have strong personal meaning and implications, most specifically with respect to what it means to pursue and succeed in a career. Consider this point by former corporate CEO and college president, Ralph Sorenson: "It is the *ability to make things happen* that most distinguishes the successful manager from the mediocre or unsuccessful one. . . . The most cherished manager is the one who says 'I can do it,' and then does."[18] "Do it," Sorenson says. "Of course," you may quickly answer. But don't forget that the twenty-first century manager must also have the ability to do the *right* things—the things that really count. These will be things that add value to the organization's goods and/or services, things that make a real difference in performance results.

MOBE: A Framework for Career Success

Management and Organizational Behavior Essentials introduces the study of management and organizational behavior, along with its many implications for the new workplace. My goal as the author is straightforward: I would like to set the stage for you to serve successfully as a high-performing and respected manager in the work settings of your choice. The accompanying memorandum to the reader offers some advice on how this book might be used to best advantage as a learning instrument. To help you become better acquainted with the foundations for success, the book is organized into five major parts. Each part covers core concepts, basic theories, and key applications relating to a major management and organizational behavior topic. The parts are organized in a logical fashion that allows the instructor flexibility in choosing part and/or chapter combinations to best fit the course design.

Part I, Introduction, deals with the environment and context within which modern managers must operate. Key topics include competitive advantage, quality operations and other general environment themes, the global economy, and ethics and social responsibility. Part II, The Management Functions, introduces planning, organizing, leading, and controlling as basic managerial responsibilities. Part III, Managing Individuals and Groups, focuses specifically on the day-to-day managerial essentials of valuing diversity, motivating others, designing work systems, and

Memorandum

To: The Reader
From: Professor John Schermerhorn
Subject: <u>Management and Organizational Behavior Essentials</u>

By content and design this book, <u>MOBE</u> for short, is written for
serious students who want to better understand the essentials
of management and organizational behavior. It is also written
in a way that tries to make the material accessible to you in a
compact and easy-to-read fashion that fits well with the goals of
an introductory-level university course.

Special features that can help you best understand the material
and prepare for examinations include the following: <u>Study
Questions</u> open every chapter and not only provide an
overview of the chapter, but also tie in with the section
headings and chapter summaries. <u>Section Headings</u> highlight
the major themes in each chapter. You will see that they match
the study questions. If you understand the guiding questions
beforehand, it will be easier to study the material. <u>The Effective
Manager boxes</u> identify useful ways to immediately apply a
concept or theory being discussed in the text. <u>In Summary</u>
ends the chapter by summarizing major points in a question-
and-answer format linked back to the study questions. <u>The
Glossary</u> lists key terms and definitions at the end of the book
and serves as a resource for review purposes.

I urge you to use these features as you read and study this
book. In addition, please remember that the issues, concepts,
theories, and insights you are reading about apply to
organizations of all types and sizes. Your learning about
management and organizational behavior will be maximized if
it is active; that is, you should be willing to experiment by
applying new ideas to your current experiences. Ultimately,
<u>MOBE</u> can help you become familiar with the essentials of
management and organizational behavior while focusing on
the important theory-into-practice applications. This should
strengthen your career portfolio.

building teams. Part IV, Managing the Processes of Organizational Behavior, examines the managerial activities of decision making, communicating, influencing, and negotiating. Finally, Part V, Managing High Performance Systems, offers additional insights into the essentials of human resource management and the processes of planned change and continuous improvement.

In Summary

Who are managers and what do they do?

- Organizations are collections of people working together to achieve a common purpose.
- In organizations, managers are responsible for the work performance of others.
- Management is the process of planning, organizing, leading, and controlling the use of resources.
- Managers should strive for both performance effectiveness in terms of goal accomplishment and performance efficiency in terms of resource utilization.
- Managers today are expected to achieve high productivity and practice total quality management.

What is the management process?

- The management process consists of the four functions of management: planning, organizing, leading, and controlling.
- Planning sets the directions; organizing mobilizes resources and systems; leading inspires work efforts; and controlling ensures results.
- Managerial work is intense and stressful, and it places a great emphasis on the ability to perform well in interpersonal, informational, and decision-making roles.
- Good managers create and maintain interpersonal networks that facilitate the accomplishment of task agendas.
- Managers utilize a variety of technical, human, and conceptual skills, as well as supporting personal characteristics.

What is organizational behavior?

- Organizational behavior (OB) is formally defined as the study of individuals and groups in organizations.
- With roots in the allied behavioral sciences, OB is an applied discipline that takes a contingency approach to people and organizations.
- OB is an academic discipline built on scientific foundations and focused on helping organizations and their members achieve high levels of performance with satisfaction.

- Learning about organizational behavior should be continuous; one of the best sources of experiential learning is in the workplace and on the job.

What are the challenges of management and organizational behavior today?

- In an environment of change, the old ways of managing just aren't good enough anymore; new thinking is required by those who want to lead the organizations of tomorrow.
- The workforce is changing; customer expectations are changing; organizations are changing; managers must change, too.
- Managers of the twenty-first century will succeed only by being alert, sensitive, hard working, and willing to learn continuously.

THE CHANGING

ENVIRONMENT

OF ORGANIZATIONS

As you read Chapter 2, keep in mind these study questions:

- What is in the external environment of organizations?

- What environmental themes challenge today's managers?

- How can customer service and product quality create competitive advantage?

- How can operations management create competitive advantage?

The year 2000 is on the horizon. Once a benchmark for science-fiction writers, the coming of the twenty-first century now presents new challenges for organizations and their managers. Success, not just survival, must be achieved in a world of intense competition, continued globalization, and rapid technological change. Even today's most successful organizations cannot afford to rest on past laurels. IBM and General Motors are two examples of businesses whose executives have learned this lesson the hard way. Once considered pillars of success, they have struggled in recent years to come to terms with competitive industries, discerning customers, and diverse workforces. Even now, many wonder if managers in these firms—and others like them—have really mastered the challenges of operating successfully in a complex, changing, and highly demanding environment.

The Environment of Organizations

Organizations, as shown in Figure 2.1, can be viewed as **open systems** that interact with their environments in the continual process of transforming resource inputs into product outputs of finished goods and/or services. The external environment is a critical source of both resources and customer feedback in this view of organizations. Good relationships with suppliers help to ensure a smooth flow of needed resources; satisfied customers help maintain demand for the goods and/or services produced, and provide the basis for obtaining the resources needed to stay in business. Thus, the customer or client truly reigns supreme. Effective managers, accordingly, understand the many components of their environments, deal successfully with them, and remain alert to spot changes over time.

General Environment

The **general environment** consists of the background conditions in the external environment that can substantially influence the operations of an organization. This portion of the environment forms a general context for managerial decision making and includes these important factors.

- **Economic conditions** general state of the economy in terms of inflation, income levels, gross domestic product, unemployment, and related indicators of economic health

Figure 2.1   The organization viewed as an open system.

- **Sociocultural conditions** general state of prevailing social values on such matters as human rights and environment, trends in education and related social institutions, as well as demographic patterns

- **Legal–political conditions** general state of the prevailing philosophy and objectives of the political party or parties running the government, as well as laws and government regulations

- **Technological conditions** general state of the development and availability of technology in the environment, including scientific advancements

- **Natural environment conditions** general state of nature and conditions of the natural or physical environment, including levels of environmentalism

Specific Environment

The **specific environment** consists of the actual organizations, groups, and people with whom an organization must interact in order to survive and prosper. These are environmental elements of direct consequence to the organization as it operates day-to-day. Sometimes called the *task environment,* this environment is very different for each organization, varying according to its unique operating domain and circumstances. Important elements in an organization's specific environment include:

- **Customers** specific consumer or client groups, individuals, and organizations that purchase the organization's goods and/or use its services

- **Suppliers** specific providers of the human, information, and financial resources and raw materials needed by the organization to operate

- **Competitors** specific organizations that offer the same or similar goods and services to the same consumer or client groups

- **Regulators** specific government agencies and representatives, at the local, state, and national levels, that enforce laws and regulations affecting the organization's operations

Environment and Competitive Advantage

Attention in dealing with challenging environments is increasingly focused on the concept of **competitive advantage.** This is a *distinctive competency* that sets an organization apart from its competitors and gives it an advantage over them in the marketplace. Ultimately, the management process and the many challenges of achieving competitive advantage must be framed in the major environmental issues of the day—understanding the global economy, valuing workforce diversity, performing with ethics and social responsibility, harnessing new technologies, respecting the natural environment, and recognizing the demands of twenty-first-century management. Without proper attention to these critical forces, it is unlikely that any organization can prosper over the long run. By contrast, those managers who do lead their organizations in enlightened ways are likely to experience the many rewards of operational success—and personal satisfaction.

The Economy

No organization, business or otherwise, is immune from the influences of the economy. Especially today, competition for customers and scarce resources is intense and unforgiving. This is an era of *economic transitions*—at the global, national, and local levels. Managers must help their organizations compete for advantage in times of economic *decline* as well as economic growth. Clearly, the ebbs and flows of economic forces in the general environment directly impact the prosperity of organizations and the careers of their members.

Harvard scholar and consultant Michael Porter talks about not only the competitive advantage of companies (see Chapter 5) but also the competitive advantage of nations as they seek prosperity in worldwide networks of trade and commerce.[1] Both concepts reflect dramatic, important developments taking place in our increasingly global economy. Today's managers must be informed about the global economy; they cannot ignore what others are doing. Not long ago American quality pioneer Joseph M. Juran challenged a Japanese audience with this prediction: America will bounce back in business competitiveness and the words *Made in America* will once again symbolize world-class quality.[2] There seems little doubt today that Juran's prediction is coming true. Corporate leaders know now that a commitment to quality leads to lower costs, higher productivity, and sustainable success. Chapter 3 is devoted to the many issues and opportunities associated with managing in a global economy.

Sociocultural Issues

A major theme of the decade involves the controversies and opportunities of dealing positively with individual differences. The best managers understand that talented and diligent workers are essential to long-term competitive advantage. It is their commitment and effort in using an organization's resources that will determine eventual levels of performance accomplishment. Managers must make good decisions when recruiting and selecting workers, and they must create and maintain the work conditions within which these workers can achieve the highest levels of productivity. But importantly, too, they must do so in a labor market that is undergoing fundamental changes in its cultural and demographic complexities.

This is the age of *multiculturalism* and *workforce diversity.* Managers must be prepared to respect "alternative cultures" and "value diversity" in managing people so as to achieve the highest levels of task performance and job satisfaction. The effective manager of today knows how to create positive work environments in which the cultural and demographic diversity of members helps to create competitive advantage.[3] This challenge—to understand and value diversity—will be addressed again and again throughout this book. Themes of current attention include meeting the needs of an aging workforce, helping employees deal with work and family conflicts, better integrating minorities in the workforce, and improving education and skills for disadvantaged workers.[4]

Legal–Political Concerns

Managers today must pursue competitive advantage within demanding legal boundaries and in full compliance with public expectations for ethical and socially responsible behavior. Most employees in the United States today, for example, work with legal protection relating to union membership, fair employment practices, and occupational health and safety, among other matters. Managers must understand and respect these legal constraints when making day-to-day human resource management decisions. Importantly, too, this legal environment influences operations in many other ways, including consumer protection, individual rights, protection of the natural environment, and the like. Not only are managers required to understand the many local–state–federal laws affecting such matters, they must also understand and deal with the government agencies that monitor compliance with them. And organizations operating internationally face even more complications because the laws and regulations governing business practices vary from one country to the next.

In this challenging arena of legal–political concerns, lawmakers, government officials, and corporate leaders face many common pressures. The public increasingly expects that representatives of all three groups will work together to help solve the critical social problems and needs of the times. Businesses, especially, are expected to meet high standards of *corporate social responsibility;* employees of all organizations, public and private, are expected to meet high standards of *ethical conduct.*

The issue of quality of education is a timely case-in-point. When asked in a worldwide *Harvard Business Review* survey to identify the most important social issue affecting their organizations, executive respondents chose "quality of education."[5] Most also supported the position that businesses should take an active role in efforts to improve the quality of education in their countries. In a separate survey of 360 American companies conducted by Towers Perrin, it was found that the average manufacturer interviews six job applicants for each one accepted. Among the reasons for rejecting applicants, quality-of-education issues were highly evident: "inadequate reading and writing skills" ranked second, "deficient calculation skills" ranked fourth, and "poor verbal skills" ranked fifth.[6] In towns and cities across the United

States, concerned citizens are asking legitimate questions regarding the social responsibilities of employers not only to help deal with the educational deficiencies of their workers, but also to assist in the development of high-quality schools in the communities in which they operate.

Many other social issues call for the attention of both business and government. Legal–political concerns of the day include problems of alcoholism and drug addiction, crime in the cities, urban and rural poverty, and pressures of work and parenting in a complex society. On the last matter—work and parenting—it is noteworthy that the *Harvard Business Review* survey consensus was that work can and should be good for families, but that it takes special organizational support. Among the important directions in this regard are child care at the work site and flexible work arrangements. All of these issues and more are discussed in chapters to come.

Information and Technology

"Cyberspace," reads the title from a *Business Week* article discussing electronic mail, the Internet, virtual shopping malls, electronic commerce, and more. If the article were written a few months later, it would contain still more—technology is changing this fast.

We now live and work in the age of information technology: It is a key theme of the day. The growing impact of computers and related technologies on manufacturing is discussed later in the chapter; we know from everyday living that the broader impact is growing as well. It traces from the streetside ATM machines to computerized service at the local video store to the all-automatic gasoline pumps to the scanners in the grocery store check-out lines to the computers on office desktops. And it traces to ever more, always more in this rapidly developing aspect of our environment.

Take a cruise on the *information superhighway,* where a vast array of databases from the Internet and World-Wide Web are made available to anyone with a computer and a modem. Children ask their parents for subscriptions to online communication services; access to the Internet is increasingly easy and indispensable for personal and business uses. One wonders what the future will bring into the home via the telephone line; one wonders what the world of work will be like as computers and information technology continue to exert their influence on manufacturing and services. One knows for sure that competitive advantage through technology will be a driving theme in organizations for many years to come.

Natural Environment

Respecting and protecting the natural environment for future generations is a significant theme today. **Environmentalism** may be defined as the expression and demonstration of public concern for conditions of the natural or physical environment.[7] Recent history is replete with examples of environmental catastrophes, actual or imminent, that capture public attention. Our planet suffers from actual and potential *ecological damage* from toxic waste, acid rain, global warming, reduced biodiversity, and related phenomena; it also suffers from industrial accidents, such as the

Exxon Valdez oil spill in Alaska and the Chernobyl nuclear disaster in the Ukraine.[8] But not only are concerned citizens worried about the impact of abuses and accidents on the natural environment, they more broadly sponsor the goals of environmental respect and conservation among individuals and organizations.

These calls are being heard, although perhaps not fast enough for some. In the *Harvard Business Review* survey discussed earlier, environmental issues ranked as the next highest social priority after education among respondents. The consensus in the *HBR* survey was that business should take an active role in helping solve the environmental problems now facing societies around the globe. Progressive business and government leaders recognize that a substantial number of the world's industries rely on natural resources for their product bases—oil and gas, forest products, and metals, for example. They also know that the rest of the world relies on the natural environment as a continuing source of fuel, and they understand the great potential for *green marketing,* involving the sale of environment-friendly products. Furthermore, they understand the growing pressures on manufacturers to design for the environment—that is, to design products that satisfy the criteria of the "three Rs": *r*educe the number of parts, *r*euse parts, and *r*ecycle parts.[9] But even still, strong calls are still being heard for leadership in education, government, and business to do more to support and advance societal commitments to environmentalist values. Concerns for the natural environment will certainly continue to grow in importance in the future.

Competitive Advantage Through Quality

If managing for high performance and competitive advantage is the theme of the day, *quality* is its watchword. The achievement of quality objectives is more and more considered a universal criterion of organizational performance, in manufacturing and service industries alike. The competitive demands of a global economy are an important force in this race toward total quality operations. Many countries have adopted quality standards set by the International Standards Organization in Geneva, Switzerland. Businesses that want to compete in the world marketplace are increasingly expected to have **ISO certification.** To gain such certification, they must ensure quality in all operations and then undergo a rigorous outside assessment to determine whether or not they meet ISO standards. Increasingly, the ISO "stamp of approval" is viewed as a necessity in international business.

Total Quality Management

The term *total quality management* (TQM) is used to describe the process of making quality principles part of the organization's strategic objectives, applying them to all aspects of operations, committing to continuous improvement, and striving to meet customers' needs by doing things right the first time. First introduced in Chapter 1, TQM is often associated with the work of quality pioneers W. Edwards Deming and Joseph M. Juran, whose ideas have been popular in Japan since the early 1950s.[10]

The growing commitment to total quality operations in the United States is now evidenced by the Malcolm Baldridge National Quality Awards. The following list of award criteria indicates the full extent of the day-to-day commitment that is essential to total quality management.

- Top executives incorporate quality values into day-to-day management.
- The organization works with suppliers to improve quality of their goods and/ or services.
- The organization trains workers in quality techniques and has systems ensuring high-quality products.
- The organization's products are as good as or better than those of its competitors.
- The organization meets customers' needs and wants, and gets customer satisfaction ratings equal to or better than those of competitors.
- The organization's quality system yields concrete results such as increased market share and lower product-cycle times.[11]

Deming's Path to Quality

In 1951 Deming was invited to Japan to explain quality-control techniques that had been developed in the United States. The result was a life-long relationship epitomized in the Deming prize for quality control. This annual award is so important in Japan that it is broadcast on national television. "When Deming spoke," we might say, "the Japanese listened." The principles he taught the Japanese were straightforward, and they worked: tally defects, analyze and trace them to the source, make corrections, and keep a record of what happens afterward.

Deming's path to quality follows the basic proposition that the cause of a quality problem may be some component of the production and operations processes, like an employee or a machine, or it may be internal to the system itself. If it is caused by an employee, that person should be retrained or replaced. Likewise, a faulty machine should be adjusted or replaced. If the cause lies within the system, blaming an employee only causes frustration. Instead, the system must be analyzed and constructively changed. Today, many American companies are following Deming's quality guidelines in their quests for competitive advantage. Deming's advice is summarized in the fourteen points shown in The Effective Manager 2.1.[12]

Quality and Continuous Improvement

Employee involvement in the search for quality solutions is an important aspect of the TQM processes just illustrated.[13] It is closely tied to the emphasis in TQM on **continuous improvement**—the attempt to maintain the quality momentum over time by always looking for new ways to incrementally improve upon current performance. A basic philosophy of total quality management is that one can never be satisfied; something always can and should be improved upon.

> ### THE EFFECTIVE MANAGER 2.1
>
> #### Deming's Fourteen Points to Quality
>
> 1. Create a consistency of purpose in the organization to innovate, put resources into research and education, and put resources into maintaining equipment and new production aids.
> 2. Learn a new philosophy of quality to improve every system.
> 3. Require statistical evidence of process control and eliminate financial goals and quotas.
> 4. Require statistical evidence of control in purchasing parts; this will mean dealing with fewer suppliers.
> 5. Use statistical methods to isolate the sources of trouble.
> 6. Institute modern on-the-job training.
> 7. Improve supervision to develop inspired leaders.
> 8. Drive out fear and instill learning.
> 9. Break down barriers between departments.
> 10. Eliminate numerical goals and slogans.
> 11. Constantly revamp work methods.
> 12. Institute massive training programs for employees in statistical methods.
> 13. Retrain people in new skills.
> 14. Create a structure that will push, every day, on the above thirteen points.

One way to combine employee involvement and continuous improvement is through the popular **quality circle** concept, discussed in Chapter 12 as a type of worker involvement group.[14] A quality circle is a group of workers (usually no more than ten) who meet regularly to discuss ways to improve the quality of their products or services. Their objective is to assume responsibility for quality and apply every member's full creative potential to ensure that it is achieved. Such worker empowerment can result in cost-savings from improved quality and greater customer satisfaction. It can also improve morale and commitment, as the following remarks from quality circle members indicate: "This is the best thing the company has done in fifteen years. . . . The program proves that supervisors have no monopoly on brains. . . . It gives me more pride in my work."[15]

Through quality circles and related quality management techniques, continuous improvement can be made a part of everyday operations. Later in the book, *benchmarking* will be discussed as a useful planning technique (see Chapter 5). It involves identifying other "high performance" organizations or subunits, and then systematically comparing them to one's own ways of doing things. Total quality operations use benchmarking to gain insights for ongoing performance improvements. Total quality operations also focus on **cycle times**—the elapsed time between receipt of an order and delivery of the finished product. The objective here is to find ways to more quickly develop new products, reduce costs, raise quality, and increase customer loyalty. Kim Seridan, CEO of Avalon Software in Tucson, said, "Competition today is a race to improve. It's not the big companies that eat the small; it's the fast that eat the slow."[16]

Quality and Customer Service

All too often it seems, customer service is the missing link in the quest for productivity and competitive advantage. Customers and clients are putting today's organizations to a very stiff test. They demand high-quality goods and services; anything less is unacceptable. And in an increasingly competitive economy, organizations that can't meet quality standards are suffering greatly. The "flawed Pentium chip fiasco" faced by Intel is but one example. When this highly regarded company balked at replacing its defective Pentium chips, customers were unrelenting in their complaints. Eventually, as it should be, the customers won; Intel agreed to replace the chips without any questions asked.

Real customer service lies at the heart of efforts to create competitive advantage for organizations. Any company that can turn customer or client contacts into positive experiences can expect them to return again and again as members of a base of loyal and satisfied customers. Moreover, these customers will refer others to the company. Key operating objectives for an organization seeking competitive advantage through improved customer service and quality are to provide every customer with (1) high-quality goods and services, (2) low-cost goods and services, (3) short waiting times for goods and services, and (4) goods and services meeting unique individual needs.[17]

Yes indeed, the environmental pressure is on all managers to help organizations achieve productivity while meeting customer quality standards. A *Harvard Business Review* survey reports that American business leaders rank customer service and product quality as the first and second most important goals in the success of their organizations.[18] But reaching these goals isn't easy, and it isn't guaranteed—a manager's good intentions notwithstanding. To meet the quality challenge, organizations must find out what customers expect and then give it to them. This simple prescription is the heart of any comprehensive approach to productivity development and quality improvement in organizations.

Customers can be internal or external. **External customers** are the ones we normally think about in this context. They are the ultimate consumer of goods or services produced. **Internal customers,** by contrast, are found within the organization. They are individuals or groups who use or otherwise depend on the results of another person's or group's work in order to do their own jobs well. Edward Fuchs, director of the Quality Excellence Center at AT&T Bell Laboratories, says, "Whatever your job is, you've got a supplier and a customer." Your supplier has a responsibility to deliver a high-quality product to you; in turn, you have a responsibility to deliver a high-quality product to the next person in the workflow process.[19]

Operations Management and Competitive Advantage

The branch of management theory specifically concerned with the activities and decisions through which organizations transform resource inputs into product outputs is **operations management.** The product outputs can be either goods or services, and effective operations management is a concern of both manufacturing and service organizations. The resource inputs, or factors of production, include the wide variety of materials, technologies, capital, information, and people needed to create finished goods or services. The *transformation process,* in turn, is the actual set of operations or activities through which various resources are utilized to create a finished product of value to a customer or client in the organization's external environment. It is here that operations management exerts its principal influence on the organization's accomplishments.

Operations management today is increasingly viewed in a strategic perspective, and with close attention to the demands of productivity, quality, and competitive advantage just discussed.[20] The "value-added" notion is very important to operations management. *If* operations add value to the original cost of resource inputs, *then:* (1) a business organization can earn a profit—that is, sell a product for more than the cost of making it (e.g., fast-food restaurant meals); or, (2) a nonprofit organization can add wealth to society—that is, provide a public service that is worth more than its cost (e.g., fire protection in a community). To achieve such ends, the operations of manufacturing and service organizations must be well managed. This will ideally ensure that all resources—human and material—are combined in the right way and at the right time in order to create a high-quality product at minimum cost. Among the operations management issues of strategic importance to the creation and maintenance of competitive advantage in dynamic environments are product design, technology utilization, organization design, and human resource utilization.

Product Design

A timely and important issue in strategic operations management is product design. We are all aware of design differences among products—be they cars, stereos, clothes, watches, or whatever. But what might not be recognized is that design makes a difference in how things are produced, *and* at what level of cost and quality. A "good" design has eye appeal to the customer *and* is easy to manufacture.

Progressive manufacturers now emphasize *design for manufacturing.* This means that products are styled to lower production costs and smooth the way toward high-quality results in all aspects of the manufacturing processes. Simplicity counts. These manufacturers want products to be safe, readily identified, and straightforward to use. *Computer-assisted design* (CAD) allows for styling to be developed on the computer and then tested via simulation for its manufacturing implications. Teamwork is bringing better coordination between engineering, production, marketing, and other functional areas at all steps in the design process.

One of the newer developments in this area involves *design for disassembly,* or DFD. This trend in production has the goal of designing products with maximum attention to how its component parts will be reused at the end of its product life. This trend is apparent in automobile manufacturing where automakers are using more recyclable parts. Environmentalism as it relates to the costs and hazards of waste disposal is stimulating DFD interests in other industries. Computer makers (with Hewlett-Packard an acknowledged leader, for example) are starting to do more in terms of taking back obsolete machines, disassembling them, and then recycling the parts.

Technology Utilization

Another important strategic direction in operations management—and one that poses great payoffs in competitive advantage—is the utilization of technology. This is the age of *lean production,* where new technologies and streamlined systems allow work to be performed with fewer workers and smaller inventories. This is also the age of *flexible manufacturing,* wherein manufacturing processes can be changed quickly and efficiently to produce different products or modifications of existing ones. Production efficiencies are maintained while the special needs of some customers—such as a small order—are being met. This is also the age when we soon look forward to *agile manufacturing* and the advent of *mass customization,* where individualized products are made quickly and with the production efficiencies once associated only with mass production of uniform products.[21]

Modern production systems utilize computer-based technologies to better integrate various aspects of manufacturing and to allow for modifications to be made in a quick and cost-efficient fashion. For example, an IBM plant in Charlotte, North Carolina, has workers building twenty-seven different products at any one time, from bar-code scanners to fiber-optics connectors. Computers at each workstation assist in coordinating the work flow and even give advice on assembly operations when asked.[22]

Organization Design

Along with the many changes in technology have come new designs for the organization of manufacturing and service operations. Chapter 6 discusses how organizations can be structured to best advantage in a dynamic environment. Blending the best of technology with the full potential of people is a cornerstone of such organization design efforts. Among the organizing trends to be discussed in other chapters are the growing use of *cross-functional task forces* and other similar arrangements to bring people from different parts of an organization into closer working coordination; greater employee participation through *job enrichment* for individual workers; and the increased emphasis on *self-managing teams* and *autonomous work groups* for groups of workers.

Many of the emerging approaches to organization design require new thinking by the managers who staff them. Management support for new work arrangements and worker roles is critical if organization design is to be fully utilized as a source of competitive advantage. Flexibility and adaptability are important, as is worker empowerment, to make the decisions and commitment necessary to best serve quality and service objectives. "The traditional American bureaucratic command-and-control style of management must be replaced," said Paul H. O'Neill, chairperson of Aluminum Company of America.[23] Increasingly, it is.

The concept of the "upside-down pyramid" as described in Figure 2.2 reflects a new way of looking at organizations. The operating workers are at the top of the pyramid and they are supported in their work efforts by managers located at the bottom. The implications of this figure are most dramatic for day-to-day operations in manufacturing or service operations, and this theme recurs throughout the book.

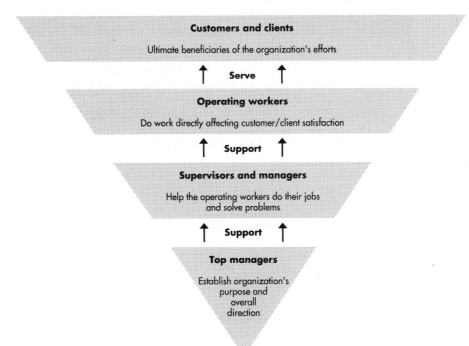

Figure 2.2   The upside-down pyramid may change the shape of tomorrow's organizations.

From this point of view the individual worker is a value-added worker, someone who must do something that creates eventual value for the organization's customer or client; the managers who support the workers are value-added managers who must clearly and substantially help them do so. The customer reigns supreme in the figure; the worker is at the top of the organizational pyramid and is devoted to serving the customer, and does so with the support of managers located at the lower levels of the upside-down pyramid.

Human Resource Utilization

Worker involvement and empowerment are critical ingredients in the new workplace. Full human resource utilization increasingly means changing the way work gets done in organizations by cutting out unnecessary layers of management and pushing decision making authority to the point where the best information exists— with the operating workers. As important as product design, technology utilization, and organization design may be, the human resource remains an irreplaceable part of the productivity–quality–competitive advantage chain. With full human resource utilization, creativity and responsibility can substantially raise performance ceilings.

"Training," George Fisher, former CEO of Motorola, said, is a "key element of a quality program." At Motorola, more than $60 million is spent each year on training, something Fisher referred to as "one of our soundest investments."[24] This invest-

---

THE EFFECTIVE MANAGER 2.2

How People Can Improve Competitive Advantage

- **Teamwork counts**—Get the right people working together. Avoid the "functional" traps; make people work together across boundaries.
- **Training counts**—Make sure everyone on the team knows what it takes to work smoothly in a group. Train continuously for teamwork success.
- **Empowerment counts**—Give people the power to make a competitive difference. Help them feel and act responsible for always improving customer service and product quality.
- **Rewards count**—Tie incentive compensation and rewards to performance results. Focus performance standards on customer feedback and quality, not just quantity goals.

---

ment is, of course, in the firm's human resources. Throughout this book, people are viewed as the key to an organization's performance success. Hiring capable people, training and developing these people so they stay that way, and providing them with a supportive and motivating work environment are indispensable keys to good management—whether the setting is Vermont Teddy Bear, GM's Saturn operation, Motorola, or any other progressive organization in modern society.

Importantly, people and technology can and should work together for improved productivity—and competitive advantage. The concept of *sociotechnical systems,* where people and machines are effectively integrated into high-performing units, is important. Today's workers often need advanced technical skills to work with the new technology, and they almost always need good interpersonal skills in working with others in more flexible and adaptive structures. Operating success is increasingly determined not just by having the best technology and structures in place, but by having a workforce that can and will utilize them to best competitive advantage. It rests, as suggested in The Effective Manager 2.2, on the organization's ability to mobilize fully the diversity of individual talents available in its workforce.

In Summary

What is in the external environment of organizations?

- Organizations are open systems that interact with their environments to obtain resource inputs that are transformed into product outputs.
- The external environment of organizations consists of both general and specific components.
- The general environment includes background conditions that influence the organization.
- Forces in the general environment include economic, sociocultural, legal–political, technological, and natural environment conditions.

- The specific environment consists of the actual organizations, groups, and people that an organization deals with.
- Forces in the specific environment consist of suppliers, customers, competitors, regulators, and pressure groups.

What environmental themes challenge today's managers?

- The major themes of the decade are workforce diversity, the global economy, ethics, and social responsibility.
- Organizations whose managers successfully tap workforce diversity will develop distinct advantages over those unable to do so.
- Organizations whose managers understand the global economy and its ever-expanding implications will be better positioned for future success.
- Organizations whose managers operate daily with a commitment to high ethical standards and social responsibility will be respected by society at large.
- Good managers not only perform the four management functions well, they do so with a sensitivity to the challenges of diversity, globalization, the natural environment, and social responsibility.

How can customer service and product quality create competitive advantage?

- Competitive advantage in a dynamic environment means offering a unique product or process in a way that makes it hard for competitors to duplicate organizational performance in the marketplace.
- Any organization must develop and maintain a loyal customer or client base; customer service and product quality are the foundations of competitive advantage.
- Customer service and product quality "add value" to goods or services by making them more attractive to the people who pay for and consume them.
- Management approaches based on total quality management are committed to meeting customers' needs—on time, the first time, and all the time.

How can operations management create competitive advantage?

- Operations management is specifically concerned with the activities and decisions through which organizations transform resource inputs into product outputs.
- Today, operations management is increasingly viewed in a strategic perspective, and with close attention to the demands of productivity, quality, and competitive advantage.
- Major issues in strategic operations management include product design, technology utilization, organization design, and human resource utilization.

INTERNATIONAL

MANAGEMENT AND

THE GLOBAL ECONOMY

As you read Chapter 3, keep in mind these study questions:

- What is the global economy?

- What are the strategies for conducting international business?

- Why are multinational corporations (MNCs) important?

- How does environment influence international operations?

- How does management apply across cultures?

There is no doubt about it. We are global citizens in an international community. Twenty-four hours a day and in vivid full-color depiction, television brings us the joys and the despairs of the world. We were able to witness both the induction of Nelson Mandela as the president of South Africa and the destruction of war-torn Rwanda. Improved transportation has also effectively shrunk the globe. A supersonic Concorde flies from New York to London in just over three hours; one can board a plane in Chicago and get off in Sydney or Singapore in less than a day's time. In addition, economic developments around the world continue to change our lives. Think about how many of your favorite consumer products are made in other countries—or made locally by foreign firms. It is difficult to buy a car that is completely "made in America;" Sony owns CBS Records and Columbia Pictures; McDonald's runs highly popular restaurants in Moscow, Budapest, and Beijing; and the astute American investor closely follows news from London, Tokyo, and other financial centers.

The Global Economy

We live in a special time in history when every informed citizen must have a high international awareness. Too much of social and political significance is happening in the world today for anyone to stay uninformed. We also work in a day and age when a new breed of manager is moving to center stage. This is someone informed about international developments, transnational in outlook, and competent in working across cultures. This is the age of a **global economy,** one based on *worldwide* interdependence of resource supplies, product markets, and business competition.

The "New" Europe

The European Union (EU) is a grouping of fifteen western European and Scandinavian countries that have agreed to support mutual economic growth by removing barriers that previously limited cross-border trade and business development. At least ten eastern European countries are also seeking to join. Members of the EU are linked through political and economic ties, including favorable trade and customs laws. The competitive implications are far-reaching. Businesses in each member country have access to a market of more than 320 million consumers. This compares to 220 million in the United States and 120 million in Japan. Workers, goods and services, and investments are supposed to flow freely across national boundaries of the members. Overall, EU-based companies have expanded regional business opportunities and may improve their positions with foreign competitors in their local markets.

In these and other ways the EU is putting the rest of the world on notice that European business is a force to be reckoned with in the global economy. The collapse of communism in the former U.S.S.R. and nations formerly dominated by it has added another dynamic element to the European scene. Business is making strong gains in Poland, Hungary, and the Czech Republic. Western businesses are also responding to opportunities in such diverse places as Belarus, Kazakhstan, and Khirgizia. But the traumas of divisive civil and ethnic strife in many parts of the region still hamper development and add to the risk for foreign investors.

The Americas

The United States, Canada, and Mexico have also joined together in a free trade agreement—the **North American Free Trade Agreement,** or NAFTA. This agreement largely frees the flow of goods and services, workers, and investments within a region with more potential consumers than its European rival, the EU.[1] Getting approval of NAFTA from all three governments was not easy. Whereas Canadian firms worried about domination by U.S. manufacturers, U.S. politicians were concerned about the potential loss of jobs to Mexico. Some calls were made for more *protectionism,* or government legislation and support to protect domestic industries from foreign competition. Mexicans feared that free trade would bring a further intrusion of U.S. culture and values, but Americans complained that Mexican businesses did not operate by the same social standards—particularly in respect to environmental protection and the use of child labor. Often at issue were controversies over *maquiladoras,* foreign manufacturing plants allowed to operate in Mexico with special privileges in return for employing Mexican labor. They are allowed to import materials, components, and equipment duty-free, assemble them into finished products, and export the products with duty paid only on the value added in Mexico.

Even with its recent problems, Mexico is highly regarded for its business and economic potential, and similar optimism extends to the countries of Central and South America. Many of these countries are cutting tariffs, updating their economic policies, and welcoming foreign investors. The significance of these developments is great. Peter Drucker once remarked that "Latin America holds the key to the U.S. trade deficit."[2]

Asia and the Pacific Rim

Fortune magazine has called Asia a "mega-market" and notes its "growing power" in the world economy.[3] This does not refer to just Japan, China, and the "four Tigers" of South Korea, Hong Kong, Taiwan, and Singapore. In Southeast Asia, growth in the economies of Malaysia, Thailand, and Indonesia is already significant; the Philippines is making progress; and Vietnam is gaining attention.

Wherever you travel or do business in Asia and the Pacific Rim, *opportunity* is a watchword. By 2000, Pacific Rim economies are expected to be larger than those of the current EU. Indeed, the *Asian Free Trade Association* (AFTA) is gaining prominence as a regional economic alliance. Member countries already represent a third of the global marketplace, including being the world's top market for cars and telecommunications equipment. Furthermore, it's not just low-cost labor that attracts businesses to Asia; the growing availability of highly skilled "brainpower" is also on the list of advantages. India, with a growing economy and the second largest population in the world, is gaining a world-class reputation for the strength of its software industry.

Developments in China continue to perplex many outside observers. The country's economic relations remain complicated by complaints about human rights violations, use of prison labor for export products, and poor protection of foreign copyrights and intellectual property, among others. Amidst it all, China has become a major export power whose manufacturing plants supply many major retailers such as Wal-Mart, Kmart, and Sears. And many large firms—including RJR Nabisco, Coca-Cola, Procter & Gamble, and H.J. Heinz—are quietly starting to penetrate China's vast markets (estimated at 1.2 billion customers) with products manufactured there. China's importance in the global economy will surely increase in the future.

Of course, in the Pacific Rim Japan's economic power is ever-present. Japanese companies account for a large majority of *Fortune*'s "Pac Rim 150"—an annual listing of the largest Asian firms. But sprinkled among the list can be found a number of emerging world-class competitors from other Asian countries—Samsung (South Korea), Sime-Darby (Malaysia), and Siam Cement (Thailand), to name but three. These and other firms like them are led by progressive managers who intend to compete successfully in the global economy.

Africa

Africa is certainly a continent in the news, but amid the mayhem that is often depicted by the media stands a continent that beckons international business. Although foreign business interests tend to stay away from trouble spots like Sudan and Zaire, they are focusing increased attention on countries in southern Africa, Ghana, and Kenya. For example, Owens-Corning has opened a plant in Botswana, PepsiCo is back in South Africa, and McDonald's is now open in Casablanca.[4] Yet it must be recognized that the rates of economic growth in Sub-Saharan Africa are among the lowest in the world, and the region suffers from an increasing number of poor people. The poverty problems in Africa most likely cannot be solved without sustained assistance from the industrialized countries, including business investments and foreign aid.[5]

Post-apartheid South Africa, undergoing political revival, is experiencing economic recovery and is proving highly attractive to outside investors. U.S. investments in the country are up sharply since Nelson Mandela became the first president to head the country as a nonsegregated democracy. Secretary of Commerce Ron Brown said during a trade mission there: "The trade and investment opportunities emerging in the new South Africa represent enormous potential for African American entrepreneurs."[6] The American government is allocating more than $275 million

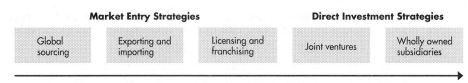

Figure 3.1   Five common forms of international business—from market entry to direct investment strategies.

to help finance U.S.-linked business development in South Africa, and African American entrepreneurs are expected to benefit.

Strategies of International Business

As the operations of organizations large and small more frequently span national boundaries, managers must rise to many new challenges in the new workplace. An **international business** conducts for-profit transactions of goods and services across national boundaries. The reasons for going international include:

- **Profits** Global operations offer profit potential.
- **New markets** Global operations offer new locations to sell products.
- **Raw materials** Global operations offer access to needed raw materials.
- **Financial capital** Global operations offer access to needed financial resources.
- **Lower labor costs** Global operations offer lower costs of labor.

Five common forms of international business are shown in Figure 3.1. Included among these are *market entry strategies,* involving the sale of goods and/or services to foreign markets, and *direct investment strategies,* involving actual ownership rights in foreign operations.

Global Sourcing

A common first step into international business, **global sourcing** is the process of manufacturing and/or purchasing components around the world and then assembling them into a final product. It is an international division of labor in which activities are performed in countries where they can be done well at the lowest cost. Global sourcing for Ford cars assembled in the United States, for example, might mean that Ford has its windshields, instrument panels, seats, and fuel tanks made in Mexico and the electronics for its anti-lock braking systems made in Germany.

THE EFFECTIVE MANAGER 3.1

Checklist for Joint Ventures

- Choose a foreign partner whose activities relate closely to your business.
- Choose a foreign partner with a strong local workforce.
- Choose a foreign partner large enough to offer future expansion possibilities.
- Choose a foreign partner with a strong local market for its own products.
- Choose a foreign partner with good profit potential.
- Choose a foreign partner in sound financial standing.

Exporting and Importing

A second form of international business involves **exporting,** selling locally made products in foreign markets and/or **importing,** buying foreign-made products and selling them in domestic markets. Because the growth of export industries creates local jobs, governments often offer special advice and assistance to businesses that are trying to develop or expand their export markets. Many U.S. policymakers look to export industries, large and small, as one way to correct trade imbalances.

Licensing and Franchising

A foreign firm may pay a fee and enter a **licensing agreement** giving it the rights to make or sell another company's products. This international business approach typically grants access to a unique manufacturing technology, special patent, or trademark rights held by the licensor. It is one way to transfer technology from one country to another. **Franchising** is a form of licensing in which the licensee buys the complete "package" of support needed to open a particular business. As in domestic franchising agreements, firms like McDonald's and KFC sell facility designs, equipment, product ingredients and recipes, and management systems to foreign investors while retaining certain product and operating controls.

Joint Ventures

To establish a presence in a foreign country many firms enter into **joint ventures** or co-ownership of business operations. This form of international business may be established by equity purchases or direct investments by a foreign partner in a local operation; it may also involve the creation of an entirely new business by a foreign and local partner. As "strategic alliances," international joint ventures are viewed as ways to gain through cooperation things that otherwise would be difficult to achieve through independent actions. The outside or foreign partner often gains new markets and the assistance of a local partner who understands them; the local partner often gains new technology as well as opportunities for its employees to learn new skills. The Effective Manager 3.1 offers guidelines for joint venture operations.[7]

Wholly Owned Subsidiaries

A **wholly owned subsidiary** is an operation completely owned by another firm. Like joint ventures, foreign subsidiaries may be formed through direct investment in start-up operations or through equity purchases in existing ones. When making such investments, foreign firms are clearly taking a business risk. They must be confident that they possess the expertise needed to manage and conduct business affairs successfully in the new environment. This is where prior experience gained by joint ventures can prove very beneficial.

Multinational Corporations (MNCs)

Many companies do business abroad, but a true **multinational corporation (MNC)** is a business firm with extensive international operations in more than one foreign country. Examples include General Electric and AT&T from the United States, Nippon Telegraph & Telephone and Toyota Motor of Japan, and Bavarian Motor Works (BMW) of Germany. At a time when resource supplies, product flows, and labor markets increasingly span national boundaries, the actions of MNCs are influential in the global economy. A 1992 United Nations report notes that MNCs held one-third of the world's productive assets and controlled 70 percent of world trade; more than 90 percent of these firms, furthermore, are based in the Northern Hemisphere.[8] Also important on the world scene are **multinational organizations (MNOs).** These are organizations like the International Red Cross, the United Nations, and the World Bank, whose nonprofit missions and operations span the globe.

The typical MNC operates in many countries, but is controlled from one home or host country—Ford, British Petroleum, and Sony are well-known examples. Although they are true multinationals, these companies and others like them still have strong national identifications. *Transnational corporations* or *global corporations* are MNCs that strive to operate worldwide on a borderless basis and without being identified with one national "home." They view the entire world as the domain for acquiring resources, locating production facilities, and marketing goods and services. Nestle is a good example. How many people would know that the firm is actually a registered Swiss company?

MNC–Host Country Relations

Ideally, both the MNCs and the countries that "host" their foreign operations should mutually benefit from the relationship. The potential benefits of MNCs to their host countries include bigger tax bases, more employment, technology transfer, capital expansion, introduction of special industries, and the development of local resources. But things can go wrong in host country–MNC relations. You might have heard about the tragedy in 1984 in Bhopal, India, when deadly poisonous gas leaked into the city from a Union Carbide subsidiary. You probably don't know that a U.S. federal judge once ruled that a North Carolina carpet mill couldn't be prevented from exporting to Africa rugs that didn't meet U.S. flammability standards. These are but two examples of how the activities of MNCs may be contrary to the interests of their host countries. Other host country complaints are that MNCs can extract excessive profits, dominate the local economy, interfere with the local government, hire the most talented local workers, and fail to transfer advanced technologies.[9]

Of course, MNCs sometimes feel exploited as well in their relations with host countries. Consider the misfortunes of some joint ventures in China, where major cultural, political, and economic differences confront the foreign investor.[10] Profits have proved elusive for many foreign partners and, even when made, government restrictions make it difficult to take profits out of the country. Other complaints include having difficulty getting raw materials or having to buy them at inflated prices, and to pay above-market prices for labor and services. This was the experience of Chrysler in starting its Beijing Jeep operation. The company had to stop assembling vehicles for one two-month period because the Chinese government refused to allocate the foreign exchange needed by the factory to buy component parts abroad. The problem was not resolved until the company appealed directly to China's premier.[11]

An MNC may also encounter difficulties in the home country in which it is head-quartered and from which its global operations are directed. This point is especially true as MNCs become more global and transnational in operations. Common home-country criticisms of MNCs focus on the loss of jobs to cheaper foreign labor markets, the shifting of capital investments abroad, and corrupt practices in foreign settings.

Ethical Concerns and MNCs

The last item on the prior list deserves special attention. The subject of foreign corrupt practices is a source of continuing controversy in the United States and for the managers of its MNCs. In 1977 the Foreign Corrupt Practices Act became law. This act made it illegal for firms and their managers to engage in a variety of "corrupt" practices overseas, including giving bribes and excessive commissions to foreign officials in return for business favors. This law specifically bans payoffs to foreign officials to obtain or keep business; provides punishments for executives who know about or are involved in such activities; and requires detailed accounting records for international business transactions. Critics think the law fails to recognize the reality of business as practiced in many foreign nations. They complain that American companies are at a competitive disadvantage because they can't offer the same "deals" as competitors from other countries can—and that locals might expect as standard business practice.

Environmental Influences on Global Operations

The changes taking place in the global economy are continuous and dramatic. MNCs are growing in number and becoming more truly global in character. More countries are joining forces to create regional economic powers. But many uncertainties remain as businesses and nations strive for competitive advantage in dynamic times.

Economic, Legal–Political, and Educational Differences

To operate successfully in the global economy, managers must recognize and understand many differences in economic, political, and educational systems.

Economic Differences   The nations of the world share many economic concerns, needs, and problems, but economic differences must also be recognized. These differences become more of a factor as regional economic cooperation increases. Perhaps most significant today are the great difficulties former communist nations are facing as they try to shift toward *free-market economies* that operate under capitalism and laws of supply and demand. Russia, Poland, and Estonia, for example, used to operate with *central-planning economies.* That is, the central government made basic economic decisions for an entire nation. Such decisions largely determined allocations of raw materials, set product or service output quotas, regulated wages and prices, and even distributed qualified personnel among alternative employers. Now these countries are struggling to establish viable free-market economies like those common to the United Kingdom, Canada, the United States, and other industrialized nations. New governments in these countries face controversies of rising prices, unemployment, business competition, and the challenges of **privatization**—the selling of state-owned enterprises into private ownership.

Among the worldwide economic issues, the *General Agreement on Trade and Tariffs* (GATT) deserves special attention. This is an international accord in which member nations agree to negotiations and the reduction of tariffs and trade restrictions. As illustrated by the most recent Uruguay Round of negotiations, however, dealings are often complicated because many GATT nations, like the United States, face internal political dilemmas relating to the challenges of seeking freer international trade while still protecting domestic industries.

Legal–Political Differences   Most countries display one of two broad extremes in governing political systems—democratic versus totalitarian governments.[12] Free elections and representative assemblies in *democratic systems* establish government with open participation by the society as a whole. In *totalitarian systems,* by contrast, representation in government is restricted through dictatorship or single-party rule. Both types of government are common in the world today, and international business is complicated by the differing operating constraints and risks they pose. The ultimate fear is that a host country, due to a change in government or political leadership, will expropriate, or take full ownership, of all foreign assets without payment. **Political risk** is the risk of losing one's investment in or managerial control over a foreign asset due to political changes in the host country. In general, the major threats of political risk come from social unrest, armed conflicts and military disruptions, shifting government systems through elections or forced takeovers, and changing government laws and policies on the operations of an economy.

Government laws also vary widely, and organizations are expected to abide by the laws of the host country in which they are operating. The more host country laws differ, the more difficult and complex it is for international businesses to adapt to local ways. In the United States, Japanese businesses must worry about antitrust issues that prevent competitors from regularly talking to one another—which is common practice in Japan. They also must deal with a variety of special laws dealing with occupational health and safety, equal employment opportunity, and other matters—all different constraints than they find at home. Other common legal problems in international business involve incorporation practices and business ownership; negotiating and implementing contracts with foreign parties; protecting patents, trademarks, and copyrights; and handling foreign exchange restrictions. The complications of legal differences can be significant and often unforeseen.

Educational Differences   An indispensable rule of thumb for staffing international operations is stated this way by one successful international business owner: "Hire competent locals, use competent locals, and listen to competent locals." But as educational systems vary from one country to the next, the availability of human resources to meet an organization's needs also varies. *Harvard Business Review*'s World Leadership Survey indicates that business executives in many parts of the world are worried about actual or potential "human resource deficits."[13] They recognize that problems of illiteracy and a lack of appropriate skills in the available workforce can compromise operations. Increasingly, they also recognize the broader social challenge this poses to organizations to become more actively involved in education and training to help build supplies of qualified labor. Informed managers everywhere are leading their organizations in the direction of greater investments in educational systems, training programs, and family-friendly workplaces to support human resource development.

Cultural Differences

Culture is the shared set of beliefs, values, and patterns of behavior common to a group of people. Anyone who has visited another country knows that cultural differences exist, but you don't even need to leave the country to find them. *Culture shock,* the confusion and discomfort a person experiences when in an unfamiliar culture, is a reminder that many of these differences must be mastered just to travel comfortably. But the important business and managerial implications of sociocultural differences must also be understood. For example, an American exporter once went to see a Saudi Arabian official in Riyadh. He sat in the office with crossed legs and the sole of his shoe exposed. He passed documents to the host using his left hand—which Muslims consider unclean—and refused to accept coffee when it was offered—suggesting criticism of the Saudi's hospitality. The price for these cultural miscues was the loss of a $10 million contract to a Korean better versed in Arab ways.[14]

Local customs vary in too many ways for most of us to become true experts in the many foreign cultures. But there are things we can do to minimize culture shock

---

THE EFFECTIVE MANAGER 3.2

Stages in Adjusting to a New Culture

1. **Confusion**—First contacts with the new culture leave you anxious, uncomfortable, and needing information and advice.
2. **Small victories**—Continued interactions bring some "success" and your confidence grows in handling daily affairs.
3. **The honeymoon**—In this time of wonderment, cultural immersion, and infatuation with local things, you view things most positively.
4. **Irritation and anger**—The negatives overtake the positives, and the new culture becomes a target of your criticism.
5. **Reality**—During this time of rebalancing, you are able to enjoy the new culture while recognizing its less desirable elements.

---

and conduct business abroad. The Effective Manager 3.2 suggests that self-awareness and reasonable cross-cultural sensitivity are the basic building blocks of success. Additional requirements include a willingness to deal with differences in areas such as language, use of space, time orientation, and religion.[15]

Language   Not only does language vary around the world—there are close to three thousand languages and dialects spoken today—but the same language (such as English) can vary in usage from one country to the next (such as from the United States to England to Australia). Although it isn't always possible to know a local language, such as Hungarian, it is increasingly common in business dealings to find some common second language in which to communicate—often English, French, German, or Spanish. Good foreign language training is increasingly critical for the truly global manager.

Space   The use of space varies among cultures. Arabs and many Latin Americans, for example, prefer to communicate at much closer distances than the standard American practice. Misunderstandings are possible if one businessperson moves back as another moves forward to close the interpersonal distance between them. Some cultures of the world also value space more highly than others. Americans tend to value large *and* private office space; the Japanese are highly efficient in using space; even executive offices are likely to be shared in major corporations.

Time Orientation   Time orientation is different in many cultures. Mexicans, for example, specify *hora Americana* on invitations if they want guests to appear at the appointed time; otherwise, it may be impolite to arrive punctually for a scheduled appointment. The anthropologist Edward T. Hall describes **monochronic cultures** in which people tend to do one thing at a time, such as schedule a meeting and give the visitor one's undivided attention for the allotted time.[16] This is standard American business practice. In **polychronic cultures,** by contrast, time is used to accomplish many different things at once. The American visitor to an Egyptian client may be frustrated by continued interruptions as people flow in and out of the office and various transactions are made.

Religion   Finally, religion is important. It is a major influence on many people's lives, and its impact may extend to business practices regarding dress, food, and interpersonal behavior. Religion can also be the source of ethical and moral teaching, with associated personal and institutional implications. In general, the traveler and businessperson should be sensitive to the rituals, holy days, and other expectations associated with religions in foreign countries. When working with Muslims, it should be remembered that the Islamic holy month of Ramadan is a dawn-to-dusk time of fasting; interest-free Islamic banks operate within guidelines set forth in the holy Koran.

Use of Contracts   Cultures vary in their use of contracts and agreements. In the United States, a contract is viewed as a final and binding statement of agreements. In other parts of the world, including the People's Republic of China, it may be viewed as more of a starting point; once in place, it will continue to emerge and be modified as the parties work together over time. McDonald's found this out in the extreme when the Chinese government threatened to take over the firm's leased building in downtown Beijing and make room for a development project. In the United States, contracts are expected to be in writing; requesting a written agreement from an Indonesian Muslim who has given his word may be quite disrespectful.

Dimensions of National Cultures

Geert Hofstede, a Dutch scholar and international management consultant, studied personnel from a U.S.-based MNC operating in forty countries.[17] His research offers one framework for understanding the management implications of broad differences in national cultures. Figure 3.2 shows how selected countries rank on the five dimensions Hofstede now uses to describe the values of national cultures:[18]

- **Power distance**   the degree to which a society accepts the unequal distribution of power in organizations
- **Uncertainty avoidance**   the degree to which a society tolerates risk and situational uncertainties
- **Individualism–collectivism**   the degree to which a society emphasizes individual self-interests, versus the collective values of groups
- **Masculinity–femininity**   the degree to which a society emphasizes assertiveness and material concerns, versus greater concern for human relationships and feelings
- **Short-term–long-term orientation**   the degree to which a society emphasizes future considerations, versus greater concerns for the past and present

Hofstede's framework helps identify some of the managerial implications of cultural differences. For example, workers from high power-distance cultures like Singapore can be expected to show great respect to people in authority. In high

from the framework we can see that

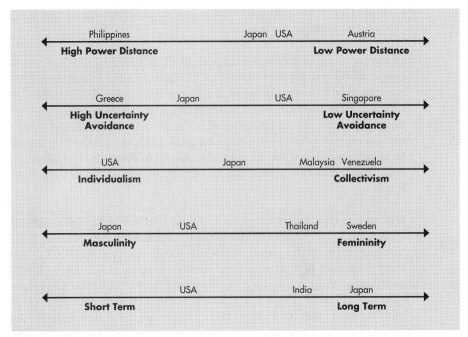

Figure 3.2 How sample countries compare on Hofstede's dimensions of national culture.

uncertainty-avoidance cultures, employment practices that increase job security are likely to be favored. In highly individualistic societies—the United States ranked as the most individualistic country in Hofstede's sample—workers may be expected to emphasize self-interests more than group loyalty. Outsiders may find that the workplace in more masculine societies, such as Japan, displays more rigid gender stereotypes. And corporate strategies of businesses in more long-term cultures are likely to be just that—more long-term oriented.

Management Across Cultures

The four management functions—planning, organizing, leading, and controlling—all apply in the complex international arena we have been discussing. Yet, as Hofstede's framework should suggest, they must be applied "appropriately" from one country and culture to the next. Competition and the global economy have given rise to the *global manager*—someone comfortable with cultural diversity, quick to find opportunities in unfamiliar settings, and able to marshal economic, social, technological, and other forces for the benefit of the organization. Global managers, simply put, apply the management functions successfully across borders.

Comparative management is the study of how management practices systematically differ from one country and/or culture to the next. A good illustration of developments in comparative management contrasts American and Japanese management practices.[19]

Do American Management Theories Apply Abroad?

U.S. management practices frequently have been used as models by managers from other nations. However, a significant question is: "Do American theories apply abroad?" Hofstede believes they do not apply universally.[20] He thinks that many of these theories are ethnocentric and fail to take into account cultural differences. For example, he argues that the American emphasis on participation in leadership (see Chapter 13) reflects the culture's moderate stance on power distance. National cultures with lower scores, such as Sweden and Israel, are characterized by even more "democratic" leadership initiatives. France and some Asian countries with higher power-distance scores seem less concerned with participative leadership.

Hofstede also points out that the motivation theories (see Chapter 14) of American scholars are value-laden, with an emphasis on individual performance. Hofstede considers this viewpoint consistent with the high individualism found in Anglo-American countries such as the United States, Canada, and the United Kingdom. Elsewhere, where values are more collectivist, the theories may be less applicable. Even a common value, such as the desire for increased humanization of work, may lead in different management directions. Until recently, U.S. practices largely emphasized broadening jobs to enrich them for *individual* workers. Elsewhere in the world, such as in Sweden, the emphasis has been on broadening jobs for *groups* of workers. As interest in more teamwork grows in the United States and elsewhere, a lingering question remains as to how well this practice fits highly individualistic cultures.

What Are the Lessons of Japanese Management?

Theory Z, by William Ouchi, and *The Art of Japanese Management,* by Richard Tanner Pascale and Anthony G. Athos, were among the first books calling attention to the possible link between unique Japanese management practices and business success.[21] Much of the early attention focused on the working relationships between Japanese employers and their employees. An important foundation of this relationship is shared loyalty—loyalty of the organization to the needs of the individual employee, and individual loyalty to the objectives of the organization. More specifically, researchers have characterized Japanese management along the following lines.[22]

1. **Lifetime employment** Many Japanese intend to work an entire career for one employer. Both the organization and the individual are expected to grow and mature together over time.

2. **Job rotation and broad career experience** Japanese managers tend to rotate through many jobs. They emphasize gaining broad experiences, not just specialized skills. They accept gradual career advancement and try to become well informed about the organization as a whole.

3. **Shared information** Japanese firms emphasize information sharing at all levels of responsibility. This includes information on performance objectives and accomplishments and on proposed activities and problems. The interpersonal networks built through job rotation are helpful.

4. **Collective decision making** Japanese managers like to make group decisions that spread responsibility for results and create a team feeling. In the *ringi* system, agreement is gained from individuals or groups affected by a decision well *before* any actions are implemented.

5. **Quality emphasis** Japanese firms emphasize product quality and *kaizen,* or quest for continuous improvement. Everyone is expected to produce high-quality work and to work with others to solve quality problems and advance quality objectives.

Theory Z identifies a management framework used by successful American firms that follow the Japanese example. However, the lessons of Japanese management practices aren't simple ones. And as Hofstede would surely suggest, the learning must allow for important cultural differences between Japan and the United States. Interestingly, as Japan's society experiences changes, its managers now face what some fear is a declining work ethic among the youth.[23] Like their Western counterparts (or *gaijin*), the new breed of Japanese worker (the *shinjinru* or "new people") seem somewhat less obedient, more willing to switch employers, and more interested in leisure pursuits.

Recent observers also note the role of **keiretsu** in Japanese business success. These are long-term industry alliances or business groups that link together various businesses—manufacturers, suppliers, and finance companies—for common interests. The companies involved often own stock in one another; boards of directors may overlap; and it is common to do business with one another on a preferential basis. This practice is criticized by outsiders as a potential trade barrier that makes it hard for them to do business in Japan—a theme most recently voiced by American trade representatives in their dispute with Japan over its domestic automobile markets. It is also criticized as a source of unfair competition in the ways that Japanese firms operate in other countries—like the antitrust-conscious United States. For example, Tenneco executives were dismayed when Mazda USA stopped buying its products and shifted orders to a *keiretsu* firm that had just set up a plant in Kentucky. On the topic of doing business with suppliers, one unnamed Japanese auto executive said: "First choice is a *keiretsu* company, second is a Japanese supplier, third is a local company.[24]

Global Management Learning

We live at a fortunate time, when managers around the world are realizing they have much to share with and learn from one another. This point is evident in the words of Kenichi Ohmae, noted Japanese management consultant and author of *The Borderless World:*

Companies can learn from one another, particularly from other excellent companies, both at home and abroad. The industrialized world is becoming increasingly homogeneous in terms of customer needs and social infrastructure, and only truly excellent companies can compete effectively in the global marketplace.[25]

Yes, we do have a lot to learn from one another. Yet it must be learned in full appreciation of the constraints and opportunities of different cultures and environments. Like the American management practices before them, Japanese approaches and those from other cultures must be studied and adapted for local use only carefully. This applies to the way management is practiced in Mexico, Korea, Indonesia, Hungary, or any other part of the world. As Hofstede states:

> Disregard of other cultures is a luxury only the strong can afford. . . . [The] consequent increase in cultural awareness represents an intellectual and spiritual gain. And as far as management theories go, cultural relativism is an idea whose time has come.[26]

The best approach to comparative management is to be alert, open, inquiring, and always cautious. It is important to identify both the potential merits of management practices found in other countries *and* the ways cultural variables may affect their success or failure when applied elsewhere. We can and should be looking for new ideas to stimulate change and innovation. But we should hesitate to accept any practice, no matter how well it appears to work somewhere else, as a universal prescription to action. Indeed, the goal of comparative management studies is not to provide definitive answers but to help develop creative and critical thinking about the way managers around the world do things—and about whether or not they can and should be doing them better.

In Summary

What is the global economy?

- International management is practiced in organizations—small or large, for-profit and nonprofit, that operate or conduct business in more than one country.
- International management is challenged by the global economy in which the diverse countries of the world are increasingly interdependent in resource supplies, product markets, and business competition.
- The global economy is strongly influenced by regional developments that involve more economic integration in Europe, North America, and Asia.

What are the strategies for conducting international business?

- Five forms of international business are: global sourcing, exporting and importing, licensing and franchising, joint ventures, and wholly owned subsidiaries.
- A firm's financial and managerial involvement in international business increases as one moves from global sourcing toward wholly owned subsidiaries.

- Market entry strategies like global sourcing and exporting are common for firms wanting to get started internationally.
- Direct investment strategies to establish joint ventures or wholly owned subsidiaries in foreign countries are even deeper commitments to international operations increases.

Why are multinational corporations (MNCs) important?

- A multinational corporation, MNC, is a business with extensive operations in more than one foreign country.
- True MNCs are global firms with worldwide missions and strategies that earn a substantial part of their revenues abroad.
- MNCs are extremely important in the global economy, and offer broader tax bases, new technologies, employment opportunities, and other benefits to their host countries.
- MNCs can also disadvantage host countries by interfering in local government, extracting excessive profits, and dominating the local economy, among other things.
- U.S. MNCs are prohibited by law from engaging in corrupt practices in their overseas' operations.

How does environment influence international operations?

- International operations are affected by a country's specific economic, legal–political, and educational systems, as well as by the dimensions of popular culture, including language, space, time, religion, and the meaning of contracts.
- International operations are affected by differences in national cultures as described by Hofstede's five dimensions of power distance, uncertainty avoidance, individualism–collectivism, masculinity–femininity, and long-term–short-term orientation.

How does management apply across cultures?

- The management functions must always be appropriately used—that is, they must be applied with sensitivity to the local situation.
- American management theories of motivation, leadership, and organizational design must be used with an understanding that they were developed in a culture tending toward moderate power distance and high individualism.
- Japanese management practices, with an emphasis on long-term employment, consensus decision making, teamwork, and quality control, have been a major influence in recent years.
- Comparative management research is extending studies of management to countries of the former Soviet Union, central Europe, and other places, as well as continuing interest in Japan, South Korea, China, and other countries of the Pacific Rim.

MANAGING WITH ETHICS AND SOCIAL RESPONSIBILITY

As you read Chapter 4, keep in mind these study questions:

- What is ethical behavior?

- What forces influence managerial ethics?

- How can high ethical standards be maintained?

- What is corporate social responsibility?

- How does government regulate business?

"You are powerful people. You can make this world a better place where business decisions and methods take account of right and wrong as well as profitability.... You must take a stand on important issues: the environment and ecology, affirmative action, sexual harassment, racism and sexism, the arms race, poverty, the obligations of the affluent West to its less-well-off sisters and brothers elsewhere."[1] These words were spoken by Desmond Tutu, archbishop of Capetown, South Africa. Although speaking to the corporate leaders of the world at large, Tutu's comments seem applicable to managers working at all levels in organizations everywhere. At issue in his comments is a challenge that will be addressed throughout this book: An organization's quest for high performance should always be led by managers who act ethically and in a socially responsible fashion.

What Is Ethical Behavior?

For our purposes, *ethics* can be defined as the code of moral principles that sets standards of good or bad, right or wrong, in one's conduct and thereby guides the behavior of a person or group.[2] In concept, the purpose of ethics is to establish principles of behavior that help people make choices among alternative courses of action. In practice, **ethical behavior** is what is accepted as "good" and "right" as opposed to "bad" or "wrong" in a social context.

Law, Values, and Ethical Behavior

There is clearly a legal component to ethical behavior; that is, any behavior considered ethical should also be legal in a just and fair society. This does not mean, however, that simply because an action is not illegal it is necessarily ethical. Just living up to the "letter of the law" is not sufficient to guarantee that one's actions are ethical. Is it ethical, for example, to take longer than necessary to do a job? To make personal telephone calls on company time? To call in sick to take a day off for leisure? To fail to report rule violations by a co-worker?

None of these acts are strictly illegal, but many people would consider one or more of them to be unethical. Indeed, most ethical problems arise when people are asked to do or find themselves about to do something that violates their personal conscience. For some of them, if the act is legal, they proceed with confidence. For others, however, the ethical test goes beyond the legality of the act; it extends to personal **values**—the underlying beliefs and attitudes that help determine individual behavior. To the extent that values vary among people, we can expect different interpretations of what behavior is ethical or unethical in a given situation.

Four Views of Ethical Behavior

Over the years, four views of how alternative norms or values may guide someone's approach to ethical behavior have been identified:

- **Utilitarian view** Ethical behavior delivers the greatest good to the greatest number of people.
- **Individualism view** Ethical behavior is that which best serves long-term self-interests.
- **Moral-rights view** Ethical behavior is that which respects fundamental human rights shared by all.
- **Justice view** Ethical behavior is impartial, fair, and equitable in treating people.[3]

Behavior that would be considered ethical under a **utilitarian view** is that which delivers the greatest good to the greatest number of people. With foundations in the work of nineteenth-century philosopher John Stuart Mill, this is a results-oriented point of view that tries to assess the moral implications of decisions in terms of their consequences. Business decision makers, for example, are inclined to use profits, efficiency, and other performance criteria to judge what is best for the most people. A manager might make a utilitarian decision to cut 30 percent of a plant's workforce in order to keep the plant profitable, and save jobs for the remaining 70 percent.

The **individualism view** of ethical behavior is based on the belief that one's primary commitment is to the advancement of *long-term* self-interests. If self-interests are pursued from a long-term view, the argument goes, things like lying and cheating for short-term gain should not be tolerated because if one person does it, everyone will do it, and no one's long-term interests will be served. The individualism view is supposed to promote honesty and integrity. But in business practice it may result in a *pecuniary ethic,* described by one observer as the tendency to "push the law to its outer limits" and "run roughshod over other individuals to achieve one's objectives."[4]

Ethical behavior under a **moral-rights view** is that which respects and protects the fundamental rights of people. From the teachings of John Locke and Thomas Jefferson, for example, the rights of all people to life, liberty, and fair treatment under the law are considered inviolate. In organizations today, this concept extends to ensuring that employee rights such as these are always protected: right to privacy, due process, free speech, free consent, health and safety, and freedom of conscience.

The **justice view** of moral behavior is based on the belief that ethical decisions treat people impartially and fairly according to guiding rules and standards. This approach evaluates the ethical aspects of any decision on the degree to which it is "equitable" for everyone affected. One justice issue in organizations is *procedural justice*—the degree to which policies and rules are fairly administered. For example, does a sexual harassment charge receive the same full hearing if levied against a senior executive instead of a shop-level supervisor? Another issue is *distributive justice*—the degree to which people are treated the same regardless of individual characteristics based on ethnicity, race, gender, age, or other particularistic criteria. For example, does a woman with the same qualifications and experience as a man receive the same pay for doing the same job?

Managerial Ethics

A classic quote states: "Ethical business is good business." The same can be said for all persons and institutions in all aspects of society. Ethical managerial behavior conforms not only to law, but also to a broader set of moral principles common to society.[5] Managers who act ethically can have a positive impact on other people in the workplace *and* on the social good performed by their organizations. Managers who fail to do so make it more difficult for their organizations to perform in moral and socially acceptable ways.

Ethical Dilemmas Faced by Managers

Ethical dilemmas are situations forcing people to decide on a course of action that, although offering the potential of personal or organizational benefit or both, may be considered potentially unethical. These are situations where actions must be taken but there is no clear consensus on what is right and wrong. The burden is on the individual to make good choices. One engineering manager sums it up this way: "I define an unethical situation as one in which I have to do something I don't feel good about."[6]

In a survey of *Harvard Business Review* subscribers, most of the ethical dilemmas reported by managers involved conflicts with superiors, customers, and subordinates.[7] The most frequent issues related to honesty in advertising and communications with top management, clients, and government agencies. Problems in dealing with special gifts, entertainment, and kickbacks were also reported. Significantly, the managers' bosses were singled out as sometimes pressuring their subordinates to engage in such unethical activities as supporting incorrect viewpoints, signing false documents, overlooking a boss's wrongdoings, and doing business with a boss's friends. While you consider the potential difficulties of these situations, test yourself with this short case originally presented to this same sample of managers. What would you do?

> *The Case of the Foreign Payment:* The minister of a foreign nation asks you to pay a $200,000 consulting fee. In return for the money, the minister promises special assistance in obtaining a $100-million contract that would produce at least a $5-million profit for your company. The contract will probably go to a foreign competitor if not won by you.

Among the *HBR* subscribers responding to this case, 42 percent said they would refuse to pay; 22 percent would pay, but consider it unethical; 36 percent would pay and consider it ethical in the foreign context.

Rationalizations for Unethical Behavior

Why might otherwise reasonable people act unethically? Think about the possible examples—placing bids using insider information, paying bribes to obtain foreign business, falsifying expense account bills, and so on. "Why," you should be asking, "do people do things like this?" There are at least four common rationalizations that may be used to justify such misconduct.[8]

Upon doing something that might be considered unethical, a rationalizer says, *"It's not really illegal."* This expresses a mistaken belief that one's behavior is acceptable, especially in ambiguous situations. When dealing with "shady" or "borderline" situations in which you or someone else is having a hard time precisely defining right from wrong, the answer is quite simple: When in doubt about a decision to be made or an action to be taken, don't do it.

Another common statement by a rationalizer is: *"It's in everyone's best interest."* This response involves the mistaken belief that because someone benefits from the behavior, the behavior is also in the individual's or the organization's best interests. Overcoming this rationalization depends in part on the ability to look beyond short-run results to address longer-term implications and to look beyond results in general to the *ways* in which they are obtained.

Sometimes rationalizers tell themselves, *"No one will ever know about it."* They mistakenly believe that a questionable behavior is really "safe" and will never be found out or made public. Unless it is discovered, the argument implies no crime was really committed. Lack of accountability, unrealistic pressures to perform, and a boss who prefers "not to know" can all reinforce such thinking. In this case, the best deterrent is to make sure that everyone knows that wrongdoing will be punished and to apply the punishment whenever wrongdoing is discovered.

Finally, rationalizers may proceed with a questionable action because of a mistaken belief that *"the organization will stand behind me."* This is misperceived loyalty. The individual is caught up in a sense of obligation to the organization and believes that the organization's best interests stand above all others. In return, the individual believes that top managers will condone the behavior and protect the individual from harm. But loyalty to the organization is not an acceptable excuse for misconduct. Everyone should be taught by management example and clear performance expectations that organizational loyalty should not stand above the law and social morality.

Factors Affecting Managerial Ethics

It is almost too easy to confront ethical dilemmas in the safety of a textbook or a college classroom. In practice, a manager is often challenged to choose ethical

Figure 4.1 Factors influencing ethical managerial behavior: the person, organization, and environment.

courses of action in situations where the pressures may be contradictory and great. Increased awareness of factors influencing managerial ethics may help you deal better with them in the future. Figure 4.1 shows these influences emanating from the (1) manager, (2) organization, and (3) environment.

Managerial ethics are affected by the personal experiences and background of the manager. Family influences, religious values, personal standards, and personal needs—financial and otherwise—will help determine a manager's ethical conduct in any given circumstance. Managers who lack a strong and consistent set of personal ethics will find that their decisions vary from situation to situation as they strive to maximize self-interests. Managers who operate with strong *ethical frameworks*—personal rules or strategies for ethical decision making, will be more consistent and confident because choices are made against a stable set of ethical standards. For example, at B & O, Great Britain's leading retailer of do-it-yourself products, marketing director Bill Whiting was caught off-guard when a newspaper reporter asked how much and what kinds of tropical hardwoods the company sold. Whiting didn't know the answers, but he didn't take long to find out. Then he ended up leading an environmental policy review that resulted in B & O's refusal to stock any more wood from unknown sources. Says Whiting: "There comes a time when the community feels that an industry's policy is no longer acceptable."[9]

The organization is another important influence on managerial ethics. We noted earlier that a person's immediate supervisor can have an important effect on the employee's behavior. Just exactly what a supervisor requests, and which actions are rewarded or punished, can certainly affect an individual's decisions and actions. The expectations and reinforcement provided by peers and group norms are likely to have similar impact. Policy statements and written rules, of course, are very important in establishing an ethical climate for the organization as a whole. At the Body Shop, founder Anita Roddick created an eleven-point charter to guide the company's employees: "Honesty, integrity and caring form the foundations of the company and should flow through everything we do—we will demonstrate our care for the world in which we live by respecting fellow human beings, by not harming animals, by preserving our forests."[10]

Organizations operate in external environments composed of competitors, government laws and regulations, and social norms and values among others. Laws interpret social values to define appropriate behaviors for organizations and their members; regulations help governments monitor these behaviors and keep them within acceptable standards. The climate of competition in an industry also sets a standard of behavior for those who hope to prosper within it. Sometimes the pressures of competition contribute further to the ethical dilemmas of managers. Former American Airlines president Robert Crandall once telephoned Howard Putnam, then president of now-defunct Braniff Airlines. Both companies were suffering from money-losing competition on routes from their home base of Dallas. A portion of their conversation follows.

Putnam: Do you have a suggestion for me?
Crandall: Yes. . . . Raise your fares 20 percent. I'll raise mine the next morning.
Putnam: Robert, we—
Crandall: You'll make more money and I will, too.
Putnam: We can't talk about pricing.
Crandall: Oh, Howard. We can talk about anything we want to talk about.

The U.S. Justice Department disagreed. It alleged that Crandall's suggestion of a 20 percent fare increase amounted to an illegal attempt to monopolize airline routes. The suit was later settled when Crandall agreed to curtail future discussions with competitors about fares.[11]

Maintaining High Ethical Standards

Progressive organizations support a variety of ways for maintaining high ethical standards in workplace affairs. Some of the most important efforts in this area involve ethics training, whistleblower protection, top management support, formal codes of ethics, and strong ethical cultures.

Ethics Training

Ethics training—in the form of structured programs to help participants understand the ethical aspects of decision making—is designed to help people incorporate high ethical standards into their daily behaviors. Many college curricula now include courses on ethics, and seminars on this topic are popular in the corporate world. But it is important to keep the purpose of ethics training in perspective. An executive at Chemical Bank put it this way: "We aren't teaching people right from wrong— we assume they know that. We aren't giving people moral courage to do what is right—they should be able to do that anyhow. We focus on dilemmas."[12] Many of these dilemmas arise as a result of the time pressures of decisions. Most ethics training is designed to help people deal with ethical issues while under pressure and to avoid the four common rationalizations for unethical behavior that were discussed earlier.

THE EFFECTIVE MANAGER 4.1

Checklist for Making Ethical Decisions

Step 1. Recognize the ethical dilemma.
Step 2. Get the facts.
Step 3. Identify your options.
Step 4. Test each option:
    Is it legal?
    Is it right?
    Is it beneficial?
Step 5. Decide which option to follow.
Step 6. Double-check your decision by asking:
    "How would I feel if my family finds out about my decision?"
    "How would I feel if my decision is printed in the local newspaper?"
Step 7. Take action.

The Effective Manager 4.1 presents a seven-step checklist for making ethical decisions when confronting an ethical dilemma.[13] Notice Step 6 in particular; it suggests a way of double-checking a decision *before* implementation to determine the degree to which you are prepared to live with it publicly. This is perhaps the strongest test of all for the consistency of a decision with one's personal ethical standards.

Whistleblower Protection

Agnes Connolly pressed her employer to report two toxic chemical accidents, as she believed the law required; Dave Jones reported that his company was using unqualified suppliers in the construction of a nuclear power plant; Margaret Newsham revealed that her firm was allowing workers to do personal business while on government contracts; Herman Cohen charged that the American Society for the Prevention of Cruelty to Animals (ASPCA) in New York was mistreating animals.[14] They were **whistleblowers**—people who expose the misdeeds of others in organizations in an attempt to preserve ethical standards and protect against wasteful, harmful, or illegal acts. All four were fired from their jobs. Indeed, whistleblowers face the risks of impaired career progress and other forms of organizational retaliation up to and including termination.[15]

Recently, federal and state laws have offered whistleblowers some defense against "retaliatory discharge." But although signs indicate that the courts are growing supportive of whistleblowers, legal protection can still be inadequate. Laws vary from state to state, and federal laws protect mainly government workers. Futhermore, even with legal protection, potential whistleblowers might find it hard to expose unethical behavior in the workplace. Some organizational barriers to whistleblowing include strict chain of command—making it hard to bypass the boss; strong work-group identities—encouraging loyalty and self-censorship; and ambiguous priorities—making it hard to distinguish right from wrong.[16]

THE EFFECTIVE MANAGER 4.2

"Do" and "Don't" Tips for Whistleblowers

- *Do* make sure you really understand what is happening and that your allegation is absolutely correct.
- *Don't* assume that you are automatically protected by law—federal or state.
- *Do* talk to an attorney to ensure that your rights will be protected and proper procedures followed.
- *Don't* talk first to the media.
- *Do* keep accurate records to document your case; keep copies outside of your office.
- *Don't* act in anticipation of a big financial windfall if you end up being fired.[18]

In the attempt to remove these and other barriers to the exposure of unethical behaviors, some organizations have formally appointed staff members to serve as "ethics advisors"; others have set up formal staff units to process reported infractions. One novel proposal goes so far as to suggest the convening of *moral quality circles* to help create shared commitments for everyone to work at their moral best.[17] Some tentative guidelines on whistleblowing are provided in The Effective Manager 4.2.

Top Management Support

An individual worker may be honest and of high moral character, but examples set by supervisors and higher-level managers might cause the worker to overlook the unethical practices of others, or even to adopt some. Top managers have the power to shape an organization's policies and set its moral tone as well. They also have a major responsibility to use this power well. They can and should serve as models of appropriate ethical behavior for the entire organization. Not only must their day-to-day behavior be the epitome of high ethical conduct, top managers must also communicate similar expectations throughout the organization—and reinforce positive results. Unfortunately, communication from the top may subtly suggest that it does not want to know about deceptive or illegal practices among employees. And, if top management is known to use organizational resources for personal pleasures, lower-level employees may expect to do likewise.

Every manager is in a position to influence subordinates. All managers must act as good ethical role models and set an ethical tone for their areas of responsibility. Care must be taken to do so in a positive and informed manner. The important supervisory act of setting goals and communicating performance expectations is a good case in point. A surprising 64 percent of 238 executives in one study, for example, reported feeling under pressure to compromise personal standards to achieve company goals. A *Fortune* survey reported that 34 percent of its respondents felt a company president can create an ethical climate by setting reasonable goals "so that subordinates are not pressured into unethical actions."[19] Clearly, a supervisor may unknowingly encourage unethical practices by exerting *too* much pressure for the accomplishment of goals that are *too* difficult.

Formal Codes of Ethics

Formal **codes of ethics**—that is, official, written guidelines on how to behave in situations prone to create ethical dilemmas—are found in such professions as engineering, medicine, law, and public accounting. The codes try to ensure that individual behavior is consistent with the historical and shared norms of the professional group. The National Association of Accountants has a formal code of ethics to guide internal accountants working for corporate employers. Among other things, the code requires an accountant to report to company superiors any improper behavior that may be observed. Association officials think the code gives management accountants a standard to point to if asked to "cook the books" or overlook accounting abuses.[20]

Most codes of ethical conduct identify expected behaviors in terms of general organizational citizenship, the avoidance of illegal or improper acts in one's work, and good relationships with customers. In a related survey of companies with written codes, the items most frequently addressed included: workforce diversity, bribes and kickbacks, political contributions, honesty of books or records, customer/supplier relationships, and confidentiality of corporate information.[21]

Although interest in codes of ethical conduct is growing, it must be remembered that the codes have limits; they cannot cover all situations and they do not ensure universal ethical conduct. The value of any formal code of ethics still rests on the underlying human resource foundations of the organization—its managers and other employees. There is no replacement for effective hiring practices that staff the organization with honest and moral people to do the work. And there is no replacement for having these people led by committed managers who are willing to set the examples and expectations, and then act as positive role models to ensure desired results.

Corporate Social Responsibility

It is now time to shift our interest in ethical behavior from the level of the individual to the organization. **Corporate social responsibility** is defined as an obligation of the organization to act in ways that serve both its own interests and the interests of its many external publics. These publics are considered *stakeholders*—the persons and groups who are affected in one way or another by the behavior of an organization. They are people affected by the organization's performance—and who may be affected in one way or another by its commitment to social responsibility.

Contrasting Views on Social Responsibility

In academic and public policy circles, two contrasting views of corporate social responsibility prevail: the classical view and the socioeconomic view.[22] The *classical view* holds that management's only responsibility in running a business is to maximize profits. This narrow "stockholder" model is supported by Milton Friedman, a respected free-market economist, who argues: "Few trends could so thoroughly undermine the very foundations of our free society as the acceptance by corporate officials of social responsibility other than to make as much money for their stockholders as possible."[23] Among the arguments of this viewpoint *against* corporate social responsibility are: loss of profits, increased costs, dilution of purpose, and lack of business accountability to the public.

In contrast, the *socioeconomic view* holds that any organization must be concerned for the broader social welfare, and not just for corporate profits. This broad-based "stakeholder" model is supported by Paul Samuelson, another distinguished economist. He states: "A large corporation these days not only may engage in social responsibility, it had damn well better try to do so."[24] Among the arguments *for* social responsibility are: Longer-run profits, better public image, better environment, less need for government regulation, businesses have the resources, and businesses have the ethical obligation.

Today, there is little doubt that the public at large expects businesses and other organizations to act with genuine social responsibility. Indeed, the demands of our complex social and economic climate all point toward ever-increasing expectations that organizations will integrate expanded social responsibility into their core values and daily activities. The appearance in some firms of new vice-presidents of the environment is but one among many testimonies to this fact. These comments by Keith Davis, a respected management theorist, sum it up best:

> Society wants business as well as all other major institutions to assume significant social responsibility. Social responsibility has become the hallmark of a mature, global organization. . . . The business which vacillates or chooses not to enter the arena of social responsibility may find that it gradually will sink into customer and public disfavor.[25]

Evaluating Corporate Social Performance

There are many action domains in which social responsibility can be pursued by business firms and other types of organizations. These include concerns for ecology and environmental quality, truth in lending and consumer protection, aid to education, service to community needs, employment practices affecting minorities, progressive labor relations and employee assistance, and general corporate philanthropy, among others.

At the organizational level, a **social audit** can be used at regular intervals to assess systematically and report on an organization's resource commitments and action accomplishments in these and other areas of social performance. You might think of social audits as attempts to assess the social performance of organizations, much as accounting audits assess their performance in a financial sense. A popular model for evaluating corporate social performance in a social audit or less formal assessment includes these four criteria, in increasing order of socially responsible activity:

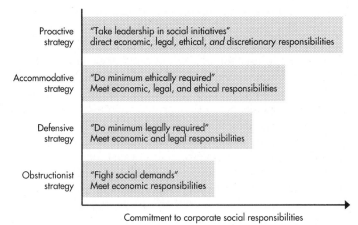

Proactive strategy — "Take leadership in social initiatives" direct economic, legal, ethical, *and* discretionary responsibilities

Accommodative strategy — "Do minimum ethically required" Meet economic, legal, and ethical responsibilities

Defensive strategy — "Do minimum legally required" Meet economic and legal responsibilities

Obstructionist strategy — "Fight social demands" Meet economic responsibilities

Commitment to corporate social responsibilities

Figure 4.2 Four strategies of corporate social responsibility—from "obstructionist" to "proactive" behavior.

1. Is the organization's *economic* responsibility met?
2. Is the organization's *legal* responsibility met?
3. Is the organization's *ethical* responsibility met?
4. Is the organization's *discretionary* responsibility met?[26]

An organization is meeting its *economic responsibility* when it earns a profit through the provision of goods and services desired by customers. *Legal responsibility* is fulfilled when an organization operates within the law and according to the requirements of various external regulations. Ideally, economic responsibilities are met in a legally responsible manner. An organization meets its *ethical responsibility* when its actions voluntarily conform not only to legal expectations, but also to the broader values and moral expectations of society. The highest level of social performance comes through the satisfaction of an organization's *discretionary responsibility.* Here, the organization voluntarily moves beyond basic economic, legal, and ethical expectations to provide leadership in advancing the well-being of individuals, communities, and society as a whole. In today's global economy, a growing sense of community responsibility is finding its place in the strategies of many international businesses.

A Continuum of Social Responsibility Strategies

Figure 4.2 describes different degrees of commitment by organizations to their social responsibilities. Generally speaking, an **obstructionist strategy** reflects mainly economic priorities; social demands lying outside the organization's perceived self-interests are resisted. If the organization is criticized for wrongdoings, it can be expected to deny the claims. A **defensive strategy** of social responsibility seeks to protect the organization by doing the minimum legally required to satisfy expectations. Corporate behavior at this level conforms only to legal requirements and competitive market pressures. If criticized, intentional wrongdoing is likely to be denied, but a legally acceptable response will also be made. An organization following a defensive strategy will probably meet the criterion of legal responsibility, but often only because of outside pressure—even to the point of whistleblowing.

Organizations pursuing an **accommodative strategy** accept their social responsibilities. They try to satisfy criteria of economic, legal, and ethical responsibility. Corporate behavior at this level is congruent with society's prevailing norms, values, and expectations, but it may only be so at times because of outside pressures. All-too-frequent examples are the responses of oil firms to clean up major ocean spills. While they are happy to "accommodate" when a spill occurs, they are quite slow in taking preventative measures in the first place.

Finally, the **proactive strategy** is designed to meet all the criteria of social performance, including discretionary performance. Corporate behavior at this level takes preventative action to avoid adverse social impacts from company activities, and it even anticipates or takes the lead in identifying and responding to emerging social issues. A growing number of progressive organizations, such as Levi Strauss, are pursuing proactive strategies.

Government Regulation of Business

If organizations do not act responsibly on their own, governments will often pass laws and establish regulating agencies in attempts to control their behavior in certain areas. It may not be too farfetched to say that behind every piece of legislation—national, state, or local—is a government agency charged with the responsibility of monitoring and ensuring compliance with its mandates. You know these agencies best by their acronyms—the FAA (Federal Aviation Administration), EPA (Environmental Protection Agency), OSHA (Occupational Safety and Health Administration), and FDA (Food and Drug Administration), among many others.

As with the underlying legislation itself, the activities of government agencies are often subject to criticism. Public outcries to "dismantle the bureaucracy" and/or "deregulate business" reflect concerns that specific agencies and their supportive legislation are not functional. Many times an agency's interpretation of a law or its manner of seeking compliance are criticized, not the law itself.

The Complex Legal Environment

Government regulations are an important influence on all organizations; the legal environment of business is particularly complex. Although many laws and regulations are certainly beneficial, business executives often complain that others are overly burdensome. Specific concerns are that regulations increase costs by creating the need for increased paperwork and staff to maintain compliance and by diverting managerial attention from important productivity concerns.

Major laws are behind many key social-responsibility areas. Managers must stay informed about new and pending laws, as well as existing ones. Yet, when we hear or read about such regulations in the news, the reports can be negative; that is, we hear either business complaints about the costs of compliance with the laws or public outcries over spectacular business violations. As a reminder of the positive sides of state and federal legislation, consider four areas in which the U.S. government takes an active role in regulating business affairs.

1. **Occupational safety and health** The Occupational Safety and Health Act of 1970 firmly established that the federal government was concerned about worker health and safety on the job. Even though some complain that the regulations are still not strong enough, the act continues to influence the concerns of employers and government policymakers for worker safety.

2. **Fair labor practices** Legislation and regulations that prohibit discrimination in labor practices will be discussed in Chapter 17. The Equal Employment Opportunity Act of 1972 and related regulations are designed to reduce barriers to employment based on race, gender, age, national origin, and marital status.

3. **Consumer protection** The Consumer Product Safety Act of 1972 gives government authority to examine and force a business to withdraw from sale any product that it feels is hazardous to the consumer. Children's toys and flammable fabrics are among the great range of products affected by such regulation.

4. **Environmental protection** Several antipollution acts, beginning with the Air Pollution Control Act of 1962, are designed to eliminate careless pollution of the air, water, and land.

Ethics, Social Responsibility, and Managerial Performance

Trends in the evolution of social values point to increasing demands that managerial decisions reflect ethical as well as high performance standards. Today's managers—and those of tomorrow—must accept personal responsibility for doing the "right" things. Broad social and moral criteria must be used to examine the interests of multiple stakeholders in a dynamic and complex environment. Decisions must be made and problems solved with ethical considerations standing side-by-side with high performance objectives—be they individual, group, or organizational. Indeed, the point that profits and social responsibility can go hand-in-hand is being confirmed in new and creative ways.

As public demands grow for organizations to be held more accountable for ethical and social performance, as well as economic performance, the manager stands once again in the middle. It is the manager whose decisions affect quality-of-life outcomes in critical boundaries—between people and organizations, and between organizations and their environments. This book will focus your attention on achieving performance objectives with a commitment to high ethical standards and social responsibility. This concept should become a core value guiding your study of management and organizational behavior. It should also guide your approach to the practice of management throughout your work career. Simply put, there is no reason that high ethical standards and social responsibility cannot be maintained by every manager in the quest for high performance at work.

In Summary

What is ethical behavior?

- Ethical behavior is that which is accepted as "good" or "right" as opposed to "bad" or "wrong."
- Simply because an action is not illegal does not necessarily make it ethical in a given situation.
- Because values vary, the question of "What is ethical behavior?" may be answered differently by different people.
- Four ways of thinking about ethical behavior are the utilitarian, individualism, moral-rights, and justice views.

What forces influence managerial ethics?

- When managers act ethically they can have a positive impact on other people in the workplace *and* on the social good performed by their organizations.
- An ethical dilemma occurs when someone must decide whether or not to pursue a course of action that, although offering the potential of personal or organizational benefit or both, may be considered potentially unethical.
- Managers report that their ethical dilemmas often involve conflicts with superiors, customers, and subordinates over such matters as honesty in advertising and communications, as well as pressure from their bosses for doing unethical things.
- Common rationalizations for unethical behavior include believing the behavior is not illegal, is in everyone's best interests, will never be noticed, and will be supported by the organization.
- Managerial ethics are influenced by personal, organizational, and environmental factors.

How can high ethical standards be maintained?

- Ethics training in the form of courses and training programs helps people better deal with ethical dilemmas in the workplace.
- Whistleblowers expose the unethical acts of others in organizations, even while facing career risks for doing so.
- Top management sets an ethical tone for the organization as a whole, and all managers are responsible for acting as positive models of appropriate ethical behavior.

- Written codes of ethical conduct are used increasingly to formally state an organization's expectations of its employees regarding ethical conduct in workplace affairs.

What is corporate social responsibility?

- Corporate social responsibility is an obligation of the organization to act in ways that serve both its own interests and the interests of its many external publics, often called stakeholders.
- Criteria for evaluating corporate social performance include economic, legal, ethical, and discretionary responsibilities.
- Corporate strategies in response to social demands include obstruction, defense, accommodation, and proaction, with more progressive organizations taking proactive stances.

How does government regulate business?

- Government agencies are charged with monitoring and ensuring compliance with the mandates of law.
- Managers must be well informed about existing and pending legislation in a variety of areas—including environmental protections and other quality-of-life concerns.
- Trends in social values include ever-increasing demands that managerial decisions reflect ethical as well as high performance standards.
- For every manager, all decisions made and actions taken should allow his or her performance accountability to be met by high ethical standards and socially responsible means.

PLANNING:

SETTING DIRECTION

As you read Chapter 5, keep in mind these study questions:

- What is planning as a management function?

- How can managers plan effectively?

- What is strategic management?

- How do managers formulate strategies?

- How do managers implement strategies?

The process of management involves looking ahead, making plans, and then helping people take the actions needed to accomplish them. Simply put, *planning* is an essential and inescapable managerial responsibility. This principle holds true for all managers working in organizations of all types and sizes. Consider the retailing industry, where a fascinating story continues to unfold as Wal-Mart, Kmart, Sears, Target, and others battle for consumers, both at home and in the global marketplace. Who will survive and prosper? Success will come to those whose managers have clear visions of what needs to be done and whose organizational systems help make those visions reality. Many careers will rise or fall on the quality of *strategic thinking*—the ability to look ahead, understand a dynamic environment, and effectively position one's organization or subunit for continued success in changing times.

Planning as a Management Function

The first of the four basic managerial functions, **planning** is formally defined as a process of setting objectives and making plans to accomplish them. *Objectives* are the specific results that one wishes to achieve; *plans* are action statements that describe how the objectives will be accomplished. Planning initiates the management process and sets the stage for further managerial efforts at organizing (allocating and arranging resources to accomplish essential tasks), leading (guiding the efforts of human resources to ensure high levels of task accomplishment), and controlling (monitoring task accomplishments and taking necessary corrective action). The Effective Manager 5.1 describes five steps in the planning process.

Types of Plans Used by Managers

Managers work with different types of plans. First, plans vary by time frame. A rule of thumb is that *short-range plans* cover one year or less, *intermediate-range plans* cover one to two years, and *long-range plans* cover two to five years or more. Planning objectives will be more specific in short-range plans and more open-ended when addressing the long term. Organizations need plans of all lengths.

Second, plans differ in the scope or breadth of activities they represent. **Strategic plans** address long-term needs and set comprehensive action directions for the entire organization or major subunit. They help managers allocate resources to achieve the best possible long-term results. **Operational plans,** sometimes called *tactical*

THE EFFECTIVE MANAGER 5.1

The Planning Process

1. **Define your objectives**—Know where you want to go; be specific enough that you will know you have arrived when you get there or how far off the mark you are at various points along the way.
2. **Determine where you stand in terms of your objectives**—Evaluate accomplishments versus desired results; analyze strengths and weaknesses in terms of being able to meet future objectives.
3. **Develop your premises regarding future conditions**—Identify and analyze things that may help or hinder accomplishment of objectives; generate alternative "scenarios" of how these factors may develop in the future.
4. **Create plans for accomplishing objectives**—Choose most likely scenario; list and evaluate action alternatives for accomplishing objectives; select courses of action to achieve your objectives.
5. **Implement the action plan and evaluate results**—Do what the plan requires, and carefully evaluate results to ensure accomplishment of objectives; follow through by planning and taking corrective actions as needed.

---

plans, are more limited in scope and define what needs to be done to implement strategic plans. Typical operational plans in a business firm might include:

- **Production plans** dealing with the methods and technology needed by people in their work
- **Financial plans** dealing with the money required to support various operations
- **Facilities plans** dealing with facilities and layouts required to support task activities
- **Marketing plans** dealing with the requirements of selling and distributing goods or services
- **Human resource plans** dealing with recruitment, selection, and placement of people into various jobs

Third, plans vary according to frequency or repetitiveness of use. *Standing plans* are ongoing guidelines for action. Designed to cover recurring situations, they guide behavior in common directions over time. A **policy** is a standing-use plan that communicates broad guidelines for making decisions and taking action. In human resource matters, for example, policies often cover hiring, termination, layoffs, smoking, alcohol and drug abuse, employee discipline, illness, and related issues.[1] With the demographic changes now taking place in the workforce, many organizations are finding it necessary to update their human resource policies and to develop new ones. This addition to the policy of one major corporation is a case in point.

Sexual harassment related to one's job is a violation of the sex discrimination coverage of Title VII of the Civil Rights Act of 1964. It's also a violation of the company's policy. . . . Sexual harassment will not be tolerated in any form, whether committed by supervisors, other employees or non-employees. Any individual found violating this policy can be subject to disciplinary action up to and including termination, and possibly prosecution by the victim.

Procedures or **rules** are standing plans that describe what actions are to be taken in support of policies. They communicate precise guidelines to help ensure that daily actions and decisions are consistent with organizational values, strategies, and objectives, such as on the sexual harassment issue. They are often found in employee handbooks or manuals that outline SOPs—standard operating procedures.

Single-use plans are used only once to meet the needs of unique situations. An example is a **budget** that commits resources to specific activities, projects, or programs. Budgets are powerful management tools that allocate scarce resources among multiple and often competing uses. Managers are expected to achieve performance objectives while remaining within budget. In *zero-based budgeting,* all projects compete anew for available funds. The intent is for managers to totally reconsider their priorities, objectives, and activities at the start of each new budget cycle. It is used by businesses, government agencies, and other types of organizations to help ensure that only the most desirable programs receive funding.

Approaches to Planning

Planning may be approached in different ways.[2] *Inside-out planning* focuses on trying to do the best at what you are already doing; *outside-in planning* involves analysis of the external environment and making internal adjustments necessary to exploit the opportunities and minimize the problems it offers. In most settings, planning should combine the two approaches to best advantage. In general, inside-out planning is more appropriate when you like what you and/or others are already doing, but want to do it better. The planning objective in this case is to determine *how* to do it better. It is more appropriate to use outside-in planning when you want to find a unique niche for your activities—that is, to do something no one else is doing. The planning objective here is to find the niche you can exploit to best advantage.

There is also a difference between *top-down planning*—where top management sets the broad objectives and then allows lower levels to make plans within these constraints, and *bottom-up planning*—where plans are developed at lower levels without such constraints and are then sequentially passed up the hierarchy to top-management levels. Again, both approaches have advantages and disadvantages. When followed to the extreme, bottom-up planning may fail to result in an integrated, overall direction for the organization as a whole. This occurs when multiple plans from various subsystems reflect uncoordinated or even conflicting action directions. But a major advantage of this approach is a strong sense of commitment and ownership among those involved in the planning at lower levels. Pure top-down planning, on the other hand, sometimes fails on just this latter point.

The best planning probably begins at the top, but then proceeds in a way that allows serious inputs from all levels. That is, managers are well advised to begin the planning process by communicating to all concerned the basic planning assumptions—who we are, what we want to be, and what the future is expected to hold. They should seek inputs on these and related planning issues from all levels in the organization. They should suggest some action alternatives and be open to others' suggestions. They should let people from all levels comment on the relative merits and demerits of the ideas. And finally, they should work hard at each stage to get commitments from people throughout the organization whose support will be critical in implementing the eventual plan of action.

Contingency Planning

The more uncertain the planning environment, the more likely that one's original assumptions, predictions, and intentions may prove to be in error. Unexpected problems and events frequently occur. When they do, plans might have to be changed. In general, it is better to anticipate that things might not go as expected and be prepared with alternative action plans than to be caught by surprise. **Contingency planning** involves identifying alternative courses of action that can be implemented if and when an original plan becomes inappropriate due to changing circumstances. The key is early identification of possible shifts in future events that could affect current plans. Sometimes this is accomplished simply by good forward-thinking by managers and/or staff planners. Other times, it is assisted by a "devil's advocate" method, where people are formally assigned to develop worst-case scenarios of future events. By looking ahead in this fashion, contingency planning allows for quick action when preselected "trigger points" indicate that an existing plan is no longer desirable.

Foundations of Good Planning

Planning is not all that managers do, but it is an extremely important anchor point for the entire management process. Good planning can go far in helping managers organize, lead, and control organizations to achieve productivity. The benefits of planning are maximized when managers truly understand the planning process and work hard to implement it well. Important foundations of good plans are forecasting, scenario planning, benchmarking, participation and involvement, and the use of staff planners.

Forecasting

Forecasting is the process of making assumptions about what will happen in the future.[3] All good plans involve forecasts, either implicit or explicit. Periodicals such as *Business Week* and *Fortune* regularly report a variety of forecasts for economic conditions, interest rates, unemployment, and trade deficits, among other issues. Some are based on *qualitative forecasting,* which uses expert opinions to predict the future. In this case, a single person of special expertise or reputation or panels of experts may be consulted. By contrast, *quantitative forecasting* uses mathematical and statistical analyses of data banks to predict future events. In the final analysis, however, forecasting always relies on human judgment. Even the results of highly sophisticated quantitative approaches still require interpretation. Importantly, it should be remembered that forecasting is not planning. Planning is a more comprehensive activity that involves deciding what to do about the implications of forecasts once they are made.

Use of Scenarios

A long-term version of contingency planning, **scenario planning,** involves identifying several alternative future *scenarios* or states of affairs that may occur.[4] Plans are then made to deal with each should it actually happen. Identifying different possible scenarios ahead of time helps organizations operate more flexibly in dynamic environments. Royal Dutch/Shell, for example, has been doing scenario planning for many years. While recognizing that planning scenarios are never inclusive of all future possibilities, the firm's group planning coordinator, Peter Hadfield, said: "They're there to condition the organization to think" and helps the firm remain better prepared than its competitors for "future shocks."[5]

Benchmarking

Another important influence on the success or failure of planning relates to the frame of reference used as a starting point. All too often, planners have only a limited awareness of what is happening outside the immediate work setting. Successful planning must challenge the status quo; it cannot simply accept things the way they are. One way to do this is through **benchmarking,** a technique that makes use of external comparisons to better evaluate one's current performance and identify possible actions for the future. The purpose of benchmarking is to find out what others— people and organizations—are doing very well, and to plan how to incorporate these ideas into one's own operations. This powerful planning technique is increasingly popular in today's competitive business world. It is a way for progressive companies to learn from other "excellent" companies, not just competitors. It allows them to thoroughly analyze and compare all aspects of the production process for efficiencies and opportunities for innovation.

Participation and Involvement

Participation is a very key word in planning. **Participative planning** actively includes in the planning process as many of the people as possible who will be affected by the resulting plans and/or will be asked to help implement them. Participation can increase the creativity and information available for planning. It can also increase the understanding, acceptance, and commitment of people to final plans. Indeed, for the most part, planning should not be an individual activity. It should be organized and accomplished in a participative manner, which builds commitment at each

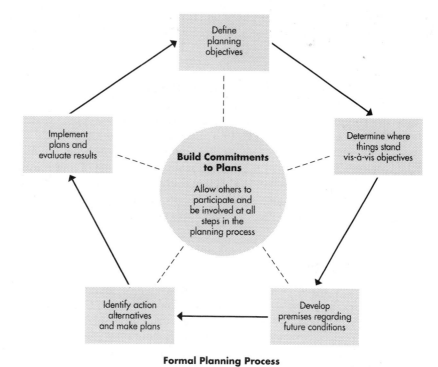

Formal Planning Process

Figure 5.1 How participation and involvement build commitment to the planning process.

step among all those whose support and efforts may be needed to actually implement the final plans.

Figure 5.1 highlights the importance of participation in all phases of the planning process. To build and enact the best plans, proper attention must be given to genuine involvement of others during all planning steps. Even though this process may initially take more time to formulate plans, it may ease the actual implementation and improve final results.

Use of Staff Planners

As the planning needs of organizations grow, there is a corresponding need to increase the sophistication of the overall planning system itself. In some cases *staff planners* are employed to take responsibility for leading and coordinating the planning system for the total organization or for one of its major components. These planners should be skilled in all steps of the formal planning process, as well as in using the participative, benchmarking, and scenario planning approaches just discussed. One trend in organizations today is to de-emphasize the role of large staff planning groups and to place greater emphasis on participation and involvement of line managers in the planning process. At General Electric, CEO Jack Welch carefully limits the size of the firm's planning staff. He helped dismantle a large planning group that emphasized voluminous written reports. Now, GE employs only a few planners whose responsibilities are limited to advising line managers.[6]

Strategies and Strategic Management

A **strategy** is a comprehensive plan of action that sets a critical direction and guides the allocation of resources to achieve long-term organizational objectives. It is an action focus that represents a "best guess" regarding what must be done to ensure continuing prosperity for the organization or any one of its subsystems. In practice, choosing a strategy is a complex and even risky task. Any strategy is a choice that specifies how managers plan to move the organization in a competitive environment. Whereas good strategies thus become competitive weapons, poor ones can be great disadvantages.

Levels of Strategy

There are three prominent levels of strategies found in organizations: corporate strategy, business strategy, and functional strategy. **Corporate strategy** concerns the organization as a whole. It answers the strategic question: "What business or businesses should we be in?" The purpose of corporate strategy is to set direction and guide resource allocations for the total enterprise. In organizations that have multiple product and/or service divisions, like GE for example, corporate strategy identifies the major areas of business in which a company intends to compete. Typical strategic decisions at this level relate to the use of resources for acquisitions, new business development, divestitures, and the like.

Business strategy is the strategy for a single business unit or product line. The selection of a business strategy involves answering the strategic question: "How are we going to compete for customers in this business and industry?" Typical business strategy decisions include choices about product/service mix, facilities locations, and new technologies. In single-business enterprises, business strategy is the same as corporate strategy; in diversified firms, there will be separate business strategies for each product or service division. The term *strategic business unit* (SBU) is often used to describe such divisions when they operate with separate missions within a larger enterprise.

Functional strategy guides activities within a specific functional area of operations. Within a typical business, the functions of marketing, manufacturing, finance, human resources, and research and development illustrate this level of strategy. The strategic question to be answered in selecting functional strategies becomes: "How can we best apply functional expertise to support the business-level strategy?"

Grand or Master Strategies

There are four grand or master strategies used at the corporate and business levels.[7] **Growth strategies** seek an increase in size and the expansion of current operations. They are popular, in part, because growth is necessary for long-run survival in some industries. McDonald's, for example, pursues a highly aggressive growth strategy nationally and globally; Wal-Mart pursues aggressive growth nationally and is just starting to branch out abroad. Many managers equate growth with effectiveness, although this is not necessarily true.

There are different ways to pursue growth. Some organizations try to grow internally through *concentration*—that is, by using existing strengths in new and productive ways, without taking the risks of great shifts in direction. This can be done through market development, product development, and innovation. Other organizations pursue growth through *diversification*—the acquisition of new businesses in related or unrelated areas, or investment in new ventures. Although diversification makes it possible for a business to grow, it can also bring the complications of operating in new and unfamiliar business areas. Common diversification strategies include horizontal integration, vertical integration, conglomerate diversification, and joint ventures.

Retrenchment strategies, sometimes called *defensive strategies,* reduce the scale of operations in order to gain efficiency and improve performance. Such decisions can be difficult for managers to make. Retrenchment, at least on the surface, seems to be an admission of failure and is viewed by many as a last resort. But today, retrenchment strategies have taken on new legitimacy. In an effort to refocus its energies on its core business strengths in photography and electronic imaging, for example, Eastman Kodak sold unrelated businesses acquired in an earlier diversification program. These included a household-products unit making the Lysol brand and other cleaners.[8]

Retrenchment by turnaround is a strategy of "downsizing" to reduce costs and "restructuring" to improve operating efficiency. Retrenchment by divestiture involves selling parts of the organization to cut costs, improve operating efficiency, and/or return to business areas of traditional strength. Finally, liquidation is the closing down of operations through complete sale of assets or declaration of bankruptcy.

A **stability strategy** maintains the current course of action without commitment to any major operating changes. Stability is typically pursued when an organization is already doing very well in a receptive environment, when "low risk" is important to decision makers, and/or when time is needed to consolidate strengths after a period of involvement with one or more other strategies. This is not a "do nothing" approach, however. It is a useful and important strategy that simply seeks to continue, for good reasons, an existing pattern of operations. For example, when Carl Schmitt founded University National Bank & Trust Company in Florida, he operated within strict geographical limits. This strategy slowed the pressure for a too-early and too-quick growth rate, and allowed the bank to become established on a solid footing.[9]

A **combination strategy** simultaneously employs more than one of the other strategies. It often reflects different strategic approaches among subsystems. For example, a conglomerate such as GE may seek growth overall, but it may do so by pursuing growth in some divisions, stability in others, and retrenchment in still others. Combination strategies are common in complex organizations operating in dynamic and highly competitive environments.

The Strategic Management Process

Formally defined, **strategic management** is the process of creating and implementing strategies to ensure long-term organizational success.[10] The first responsibility is for *strategy formulation,* the process of analyzing the current situation, selecting strategies that seem to best fit the organization's needs, and making plans to pursue those strategies. Strategies may be formulated by the entrepreneurial insight of one person, as the by-product of management responses to problems, or through systematic planning and analysis. Once strategies are created, they must be acted upon successfully to achieve the desired results. The second responsibility is for *strategy implementation,* the process of putting strategies into action. All organizational systems and the other management functions—organizing, leading, and controlling—must be well applied to support and reinforce strategies. All of this, in turn, requires the strong commitment of organization members. Getting this commitment through participative planning is part of the strategic management challenge.

Strategy Formulation

Strategies should be formulated with a clear understanding of organizational mission and objectives. The **mission** of any organization may be described as its reason for existence; it reflects the organization's basic purpose as a supplier of goods or services to society. In today's quality-conscious and highly competitive environments, this reason for existence must be directly centered on serving the needs of customers or clients. After all, their satisfaction and continued support are the ultimate keys to organizational survival. *Mission statements* are typically found in such formal documents as annual reports, charters, and information brochures. They identify the domains in which the organization intends to operate, and they provide frameworks for the allocation of scarce resources.[11] For example, Xerox now calls itself "The Document Company." This broadens its domain beyond being just a copy machine maker and opens new competitive opportunities in information technology. But with this clear sense of purpose, the firm is unlikely to repeat past mistakes of investing in unrelated businesses such as insurance and financial services.

Operating objectives are key and specific results that organizations seek to achieve as part of their mission commitment. They are shorter-term targets against which actual performance results can be measured to indicate the success and/or failure of existing strategies. Common operating objectives for businesses include:[12]

- **Profitability** producing at a net profit in business
- **Market share** gaining and holding a specific share of a product market
- **Human talent** recruiting and maintaining a high-quality workforce
- **Financial health** acquiring financial capital and earning positive returns
- **Cost efficiency** using resources well to operate at low cost
- **Product quality** producing high-quality goods or services

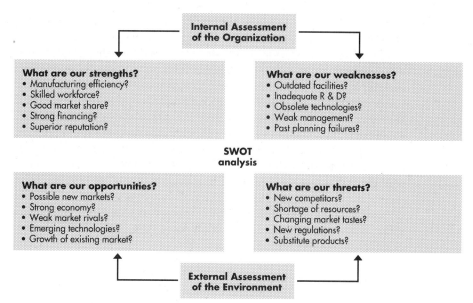

Figure 5.2   SWOT analysis: assessing organizational *S*trengths and *W*eaknesses, and environmental *O*pportunities and *T*hreats.

- **Innovation** achieving a desired level of new product or process development
- **Social responsibility** making a positive contribution to society

SWOT Analysis

A useful technique for formulating strategies consistent with organizational mission and objectives is the **SWOT analysis.** It involves the analysis of organizational *s*trengths and *w*eaknesses, as well as environmental *o*pportunities and *t*hreats. A SWOT analysis should provide a realistic understanding of the organization in relationship to its environment. It should also assist in the creation of strategies that take maximum advantage of strengths and opportunities while minimizing weaknesses and threats.

The SWOT analysis, as shown in Figure 5.2, begins with an internal appraisal of the organization's strengths and weaknesses. When done well, such an analysis helps establish a realistic basis for the formulation of strategies at all levels. A major strategic management goal at this point is to identify *distinctive competencies,* or special strengths, that do or can give the organization a competitive advantage in its operating domain. Of the many possible sources of distinctive competency, the figure highlights technology, human resources, manufacturing approaches, management talent, and financial strength, among others. Organizational weaknesses, of course, are the other side of the picture. They can also be found in the same or related areas.

The second part of a SWOT analysis involves the analysis of environmental opportunities and threats. Given the intended direction as clarified in an organization's mission statement, it is necessary to assess how actual—and future—environmental conditions may affect its accomplishment. Broadly speaking, good strategic management is based on understanding the influences of the environment as discussed in Chapter 2. These influences include the general environmental factors of economic, sociocultural, legal–political, and technological conditions; they also include the specific environmental influences of an organization's customers, competitors, resource suppliers, and regulators, among others. All strategic management, whether addressing the needs of an entire organization or one of its subcomponents, must be consistent with both short-run and long-run environmental challenges. As external conditions change, their potential implications for strategy formulation and implementation also change. This requires constant vigilance on the part of managers, and the ability to interpret environmental trends correctly and use this understanding to make successful strategies and action plans. The O and the T cannot be neglected in a SWOT analysis.

Portfolio Planning

Strategy formulation at the corporate level focuses on the creation of competitive strategies that make the best overall use of organizational resources. This means that strategies must be selected in ways that balance resource utilization among a variety of possible internal applications. One way to do this is through the *portfolio planning approach,* which is similar to how an individual chooses among alternative stocks to create a personal investment portfolio. The goal of a portfolio strategy is to identify a mix of investments that best serve organizational objectives.[13] It is most useful for addressing corporate-level strategy in multibusiness or multiproduct situations. The approach can help managers decide on how the major grand strategies of growth, retrenchment, and stability should be applied.

Figure 5.3 summarizes a popular portfolio planning approach offered by the Boston Consulting Group, called the **BCG matrix.** This approach ties strategy formulation to an analysis of business opportunities according to market growth rate and market share.[14] As shown in the figure, this comparison results in four possibilities: stars, question marks, cash cows, and dogs.

Stars have high market shares in high-growth industries. They produce large profits through substantial penetration in expanding markets. The preferred strategy for stars is growth, and further investments in them are recommended. *Question marks* have low market shares in high-growth industries. They do not produce much profit but compete in rapidly growing markets. They are the source of difficult strategic decisions. The preferred strategy is growth, but the investments are risky. Only the most promising question marks should be targeted for growth; others become retrenchment candidates.

Cash cows have high market shares in low-growth industries. They produce large profits and a strong cash flow. Because the markets offer little growth opportunity, the preferred strategy is stability or modest growth. "Cows" should be "milked" to generate cash that can be used to support needed investments in stars and question marks. *Dogs* have low market shares in low-growth industries. They do not produce

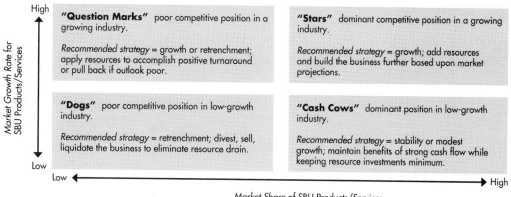

Market Growth Rate for SBU Products/Services

High

"Question Marks" poor competitive position in a growing industry.

Recommended strategy = growth or retrenchment; apply resources to accomplish positive turnaround or pull back if outlook poor.

"Stars" dominant competitive position in a growing industry.

Recommended strategy = growth; add resources and build the business further based upon market projections.

"Dogs" poor competitive position in low-growth industry.

Recommended strategy = retrenchment; divest, sell, liquidate the business to eliminate resource drain.

"Cash Cows" dominant position in low-growth industry.

Recommended strategy = stability or modest growth; maintain benefits of strong cash flow while keeping resource investments minimum.

Low

Low ← → High

Market Share of SBU Products/Services

"SBU" = Strategic Business Unit

Figure 5.3 Alternative strategies within the BCG Matrix: a portfolio model for strategic planning.

much profit, and they show little potential for future improvement. The preferred strategy for dogs is to retrench by divestiture.

Although it can oversimplify a complex decision situation, the portfolio planning approach is a useful strategic planning tool. Its major appeal rests largely on helping managers focus attention on the comparative strengths and weaknesses of multiple businesses and/or products. At GE, for example, diversity must be well managed to create the right portfolio of businesses at any point in time. GE's senior executives seek to do this by rating key businesses in their industries, and then concentrating resources on those businesses with the highest ratings.

Porter's Competitive Model

Michael Porter, management consultant and scholar, criticizes the portfolio approaches for leading corporate strategists into unwarranted diversification. His *competitive model* is a popular alternative that gives specific attention to the organization's current and potential competitive environment.[15] This approach is especially helpful in formulating business-level strategies.

Porter's approach begins with an analysis of an organization's competitive environment, as described in Figure 5.4. The relevant forces are the threats of new entrants, bargaining power of suppliers, bargaining power of buyers, threats of substitute products or services, and rivalry or jockeying for position among industry firms. Porter believes that these forces govern the state of industry competition, which must be properly addressed if organizational decision makers are to formulate effective strategies.

A good SWOT analysis, from Porter's perspective, begins by examining the competitive forces in an organization's environment. This provides a frame of reference for further assessment of organizational strengths and weaknesses. Then, strategies can be chosen that give the organization a "strategic advantage" relative to its com-

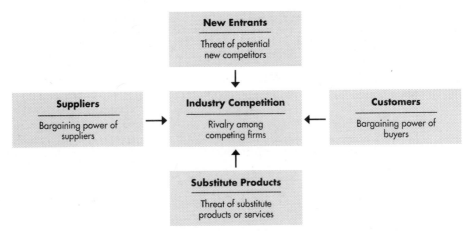

Figure 5.4 Michael Porter's model of the strategic forces affecting industry competition.

petitors. Porter identifies three *generic strategies* that organizations can pursue to gain this strategic advantage:

- **Differentiation**—trying to distinguish one's products from those of the competition
- **Cost leadership**—using cost minimization to operate more efficiently than competitors
- **Focus**—concentrating on serving one special market or customer group

Organizations pursuing a **differentiation strategy** seek competitive advantage through uniqueness. They try to develop goods and services that are clearly different from those made available by the competition. The objective is to attract customers who become loyal to the organization's products and uninterested in those of competitors. This strategy requires organizational strengths in marketing, research and development, technological leadership, and creativity. It is highly dependent for its success on continuing customer perceptions of product quality and uniqueness.

A second generic strategy in Porter's approach is based on control. Organizations pursuing a **cost leadership strategy** seek lower costs than their competitors by improving on the efficiency of production, distribution, and other organizational systems. The objective is to have the lowest costs in the industry and therefore achieve profits above the industry averages. This strategy requires tight cost and managerial controls, as well as products that are easy to manufacture or provide. Of course, quality must not be sacrificed in the process. Wal-Mart, for example, aims to keep its costs so low that it can always offer customers the lowest prices and still make a reasonable profit. Most discount retailers operate with 18–20 percent gross margins; Wal-Mart accepts half of that and still makes the same or higher returns.[16]

Organizations pursuing a **focus strategy** concentrate attention on a special market segment and try to serve its needs better than anyone else. The objective is to serve the targeted market better through concentration of organizational resources and expertise on a particular customer group, geographical region, or product or service line. This should also help develop strength through differentiation or cost leadership, or both. Importantly, the strategy requires a *willingness* to "focus" and the ability to use resources to special advantage in a single area.

Strategy Implementation

No strategy, no matter how well formulated, can achieve its desired result if it is not properly implemented. Effective strategy implementation depends on commitment to truly comprehensive strategic management. All managers must support and lead strategy implementation within their areas of supervisory responsibility.

Importantly, not all strategies are clearly formulated at one point in time and then implemented step-by-step. They take shape, change, and develop over time as modest adjustments to past patterns. James Brian Quinn calls this a process of *logical incrementalism,* whereby incremental changes in strategy occur as managers learn from experience.[17] Then too, effective managers must have the capacity for *strategic opportunism,* or the ability to stay focused on long-term objectives while still remaining flexible enough to master short-run problems and opportunities as they occur.[18] In this sense, consultant Robert H. Waterman Jr. notes that top managers at the best organizations "sense opportunity where others can't . . . act while others hesitate, and demur when others plunge."[19]

Such reasoning has led Mintzberg to identify what he calls *emergent strategies*— strategies that develop progressively over time as "streams" of decisions made by managers as they learn from and respond to work situations.[20] There is an important element of craftsmanship here that Mintzberg worries may be overlooked by managers who choose and discard strategies in rapid succession while using the formal planning models. He also believes that incremental, emergent strategic planning allows managers and organizations to become really good at implementing strategies, not just formulating them.

The best point of departure for a manager who wants to minimize the risk of these and other implementation problems is to start with a good strategy. The Effective Manager 5.2 offers useful guidelines on how to double-check a strategy.[21]

THE EFFECTIVE MANAGER 5.2

How to Double-check a Strategy

Check 1: Is the strategy consistent with organizational purpose and mission?
Check 2: Is the strategy feasible given organizational strengths and weaknesses?
Check 3: Is the strategy responsive to environmental opportunities and threats?
Check 4: Does the strategy offer a sustainable competitive advantage?
Check 5: Is the "risk" in the strategy a reasonable risk?
Check 6: Does the strategy have an appropriate time horizon?
Check 7: Is the strategy flexible enough?

In order to successfully put strategies into action the entire organization and all of its resources must be mobilized in support of them. This, in effect, involves the complete management process of planning, organizing, leading, and controlling the use of resources to achieve organizational objectives. We can use the case of Eastman Kodak to illustrate how organizational systems and practices must be aligned with strategies in order to achieve the desired results.

> After some years of mixed results, Eastman Kodak's new CEO, George Fisher, redirected the company with a focus strategy. He decided that Kodak should be in the "imaging" business and that it should divest unrelated businesses previously purchased, such as those in health and household products. To implement this strategy, a change in *organization structure* was made to create a digital imaging division that brought all relevant talent and resources together. Increased attention was given to *human resource management* by recruiting fresh talent and *leadership* was reinvigorated to improve morale. To better meet competitive pressures, *control systems* were upgraded to build in greater accountability for performance results, especially quality improvements, reduced cycle times, and reduced operating costs. Money gained by selling unrelated businesses was reinvested in *research and development* to support the new strategy. All of this was accomplished with an ever-present drive for increased *customer focus.*[22]

In Summary

What is planning as a management function?

- Planning, the process of setting performance objectives and making action plans to accomplish them, sets the stage for the other management functions—organizing, leading, and controlling.

- The steps in the planning process are (1) define your objectives, (2) determine where you stand in terms of the objectives, (3) develop your premises regarding future conditions, (4) identify and choose among alternative ways of accomplishing objectives, and (5) implement action plans and evaluate results.

- Short-range plans tend to cover a year or less, while long-range plans extend to five years or more.

- Strategic plans set critical long-range directions; operational plans help to implement strategic plans.

- Standing plans, such as policies and procedures, are used over and over again; single-use plans like budgets are established for a specific purpose and time frame.

- Inside-out planning looks at internal strengths and tries to improve what is already being done; outside-in planning looks for opportunities in the external environment.
- Top-down planning helps maintain direction; bottom-up planning builds commitment.
- Contingency planning identifies alternative courses of action that can be implemented if and when circumstances change in certain ways over time.

How can managers plan effectively?

- Forecasting, or predicting what will happen in the future, is a planning aid but not a planning substitute.
- Scenario planning through the use of alternative versions of the future is a useful form of contingency planning.
- Planning through benchmarking, or identifying the special strengths and accomplishments of others, utilizes external comparisons to identify desirable action directions.
- Participation and involvement open the planning process to valuable inputs from people whose efforts are essential to effective implementation of plans.
- Specialized staff planners can help with planning details, although care must be taken to make sure they work well with line personnel.

What is strategic management?

- Strategic management is the process of creating and implementing strategies to achieve long-term objectives.
- Corporate strategy sets the direction for an entire organization; business strategy sets the direction for a business division or product/service line; functional strategy sets the direction for the operational support of business and corporate strategies.
- The four grand or master strategies are growth to pursue expansion, retrenchment to scale back operations, stability to maintain the status quo, and combination to utilize various aspects of growth, retrenchment, and stability.

How do managers formulate strategies?

- Strategies must support organizational mission and objectives.
- Operating objectives, such as profitability and product quality, are specific end results that the organization seeks to achieve as part of its mission commitment.
- A SWOT analysis specifically examines the *s*trengths and *w*eaknesses of the organization, and the *o*pportunities and *t*hreats in its environment.
- The BCG matrix is a portfolio approach to strategy formulation that classifies businesses or product lines as stars, question marks, cash cows, or dogs.

- Porter's competitive model of strategy formulation identifies the major strategic options as differentiation, cost leadership, and focus.

How do managers implement strategies?

- All managers are responsible for strategic management within their areas of supervisory responsibility.
- All management practices and systems—including the functions of planning, organizing, leading, and controlling—must be mobilized to support strategy implementation.
- Many strategies are incremental and emergent, developing progressively over time as managers learn from experience.

ORGANIZING:

CREATING STRUCTURES

As you read Chapter 6, keep in mind these study questions:

- What is organizing as a management function?

- What are the major types of organization structures?

- What organizing trends are changing the modern workplace?

- What are the essentials of organizational design?

- Why is the culture of an organization important?

The new workplace is here, and one of its characteristics is a renewed concern for the human side of management. More and more organizations are changing their structures and updating operations in the quest for improved teamwork, more creativity, shorter cycle times, higher quality, better customer service, and increased overall productivity. Enlightened managers are realizing that they need more flexible organizations that can deliver high-quality products and services while supporting the internal cooperation needed to create future performance. The organizing approaches that are used to deal with complex environmental challenges are multiple and varied. And they should be. Organizations are different, they operate in different settings, and they are faced with widely varying problems and opportunities. Good managers understand these differences and help build organizations that deal well with them. Although there is no one best way to manage, there are many insights available from theory and practice as to how one may organize systems to best implement action plans.

Organizing as a Management Function

Organizing is the process of defining work tasks and arranging together people and other resources to best perform them. Once plans are created, the manager's job is to organize things so that they can be properly implemented. Planning sets the directions; organizing creates the systems to turn plans into performance results. When done well, organizing should clarify who is supposed to do what, identify who is in charge of whom, and establish official channels for communication.

Organization Structure

Formally defined, an organization's **structure** is the system or network of communication and authority that links people and groups together as they perform important tasks. It is the way in which the various parts of an organization are arranged to both divide up the work to be done and coordinate performance results. A "good" structure does both of these things well and is an important asset to an organization.[1] *Restructuring,* a term you frequently hear about, refers to changing an organization's structure in an attempt to improve performance.

You may know the concept of structure best in the form of an *organization chart*—

THE EFFECTIVE MANAGER 6.1

What You Can Learn from an Organization Chart

- **Division of work**—Positions and titles indicate major work responsibilities.
- **Supervisory relationships**—Lines between positions show who reports to whom.
- **Communication channels**—Lines between positions show formal channels of communication.
- **Major Subunits**—Positions reporting to a common manager represent departments or divisions.
- **Levels of management**—Vertical layers show the management levels in an organization.

---

a diagram of how jobs and reporting relationships are arranged within an organization.[2] A typical organization chart shows the official view of how the organization is intended to function. The Effective Manager 6.1 identifies some of the things that you can learn by reviewing an organization chart.

Informal Structures

Behind every formal structure typically lies an **informal structure**—a set of unofficial working relationships among organizational members. Whereas the formal structure officially designates who reports to whom, the informal structure is based upon who actually talks to and interacts regularly with whom.[3] In the latter, people can often find ways to get jobs done easier and in a more timely fashion. Informal structures also help people to communicate with one another, support and protect one another, and satisfy needs for social interaction.

On the negative side, the unofficial and informal structures may work against the best interests of the organization as a whole. They can be susceptible to rumor, breed resistance to change, and even divert work efforts from important objectives. People left out of informal groupings, that is, the "outsiders," may feel less a part of daily activities and become dissatisfied with their work. American executives at some Japanese firms, for example, find the existence of a *shadow cabinet* particularly irritating. This is an informal group of Japanese managers who hold the real power to get things done in the firms, regardless of the job titles given to non-Japanese managers. Members of these informal groups converse in Japanese, and may make important decisions when together after work hours and during social occasions.[4]

Types of Organization Structures

The traditional approaches to organization structure are largely vertical or pyramid in form. They include what are commonly called the functional, divisional, and ma-

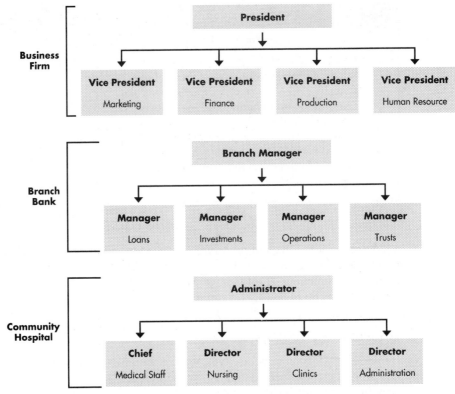

Figure 6.1 Functional structures in a business firm, hospital, and bank.

trix structures. Newer approaches are more horizontal in character and include the team and network structures.

Functional Structures

In **functional structures,** people with similar skills and responsibilities for similar tasks are placed together in formal groups. The example in Figure 6.1 shows common functional departments of a business—marketing, finance, production, and human resources. In this functional structure, all manufacturing problems are the responsibility of the production vice-president, marketing problems are the province of the marketing vice-president, and so on. Figure 6.1 also shows how functional departmentalization may be used in other types of organizations, such as schools and hospitals.

Functional structures typically work well for smaller and less complex organizations dealing with only one or a few products or services. They also work best in relatively stable environments that allow organizations to pursue consistent strategies. The major potential *advantages* include:

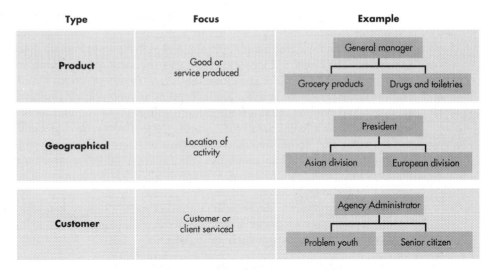

Type	Focus	Example
Product	Good or service produced	General manager → Grocery products / Drugs and toiletries
Geographical	Location of activity	President → Asian division / European division
Customer	Customer or client serviced	Agency Administrator → Problem youth / Senior citizen

Figure 6.2 Divisional structures based on product, geography, and customer.

Adv.

- economies of scale with efficient use of resources
- task assignments consistent with technical training
- high-quality technical problem solving
- in-depth training and skill development within functions
- clear-cut career paths within functions

The potential *disadvantages* of functional structures include poor communication and coordination across functions, having too many decisions referred upward in the hierarchy, a loss of clear responsibility for product or service delivery, and slow innovation in response to environmental changes. One of the most serious disadvantages occurs when members of functional departments become overspecialized, develop self-centered, narrow viewpoints, and lose the total system perspective. Failure to communicate and extend support across department lines is common in such situations. This often slows decision making because problems must be referred up the hierarchy for resolution.

Divisional Structures

A second organizational alternative is the **divisional structure.** It groups together people with diverse skills and tasks who work on the same product, serve similar customers, and/or operate in the same geographical region. Shown in Figure 6.2, such structures are useful in complex situations where organizations are pursuing diversified strategies or operating in different competitive environments. They can also help organizations meet pressures for innovation and change in dynamic environments—something functional structures often have difficulty doing. As shown in the figure, divisional structures can be created along product, area, and client distinctions.

Product structures group together jobs and activities working on a single product or service. They clearly focus expertise and tie costs, profits, problems, and successes to points of product accountability. *Area structures* group together jobs and activities being performed in the same location or geographical region. This focuses expertise and accountability on the unique cultures and requirements of particular regions, such as a major area of the world. *Customer structures* group together jobs and activities that serve the same customers or clients. The major appeal of these structures is the ability to serve the special needs of different customer groups. Banks, for example, use them to give separate attention to commercial and consumer customers for loans.

Divisional structures are popular among organizations with diverse operations cutting across many products, areas, and customers. Organizations using them hope to gain potential *advantages* such as:

- greater flexibility in responding to environmental changes
- improved coordination across functional departments
- clear points of responsibility for product or service delivery
- expertise focused on specific customers, products, and regions
- easier growth or reduction in size by adding or deleting divisions

The divisional structures also have potential *disadvantages*. They may reduce economies of scale, disperse technical competency and expertise, and even create unhealthy rivalries among operating units. They may also increase costs by duplicating resources and efforts across divisions and causing an overemphasis on divisional versus organizational goals.

Matrix Structures

The **matrix structure** uses permanent cross-functional teams to combine the technical strengths of functional structures with the integrating potential of divisional structures.[5] As shown in Figure 6.3, workers in a matrix structure belong to at least two formal groups at the same time—a functional group and a product or project group. Within each group, the individual is accountable to a manager or team leader. Thus, the matrix organization is sometimes referred to as a "two-boss" structure.

The matrix approach grew out of developments in the U.S. aerospace industry. It has now gained a strong foothold elsewhere in the workplace, with applications in such diverse settings as manufacturing (e.g., aerospace, electronics, and pharmaceuticals), service (e.g., banking, brokerage, and retailing), professional (e.g., accounting, advertising, and law), and nonprofit (e.g., city, state, and federal agencies, hospitals, and universities). There is growing awareness that matrix structures can help manage the complexity of multinational corporations. The flexibility offered by the matrix concept can help accommodate cross-national differences as well as allow for multiple product, program, or project orientations. Matrix structures are often

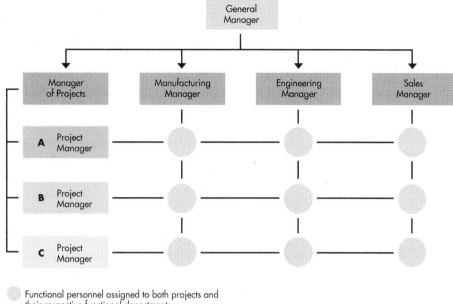

Functional personnel assigned to both projects and
their respective functional departments

Figure 6.3 Matrix structure in a small multiproject business firm.

found in organizations pursuing growth strategies in dynamic and complex environments.

The potential *advantages* of matrix structures include:

- **More interfunctional cooperation** The matrix provides a way of coordinating different functional contributions to serve specific program needs.
- **Flexibility** The matrix makes it easier to add, remove, and change the focus of teams to reflect new program directions, or basic changes in business size.
- **Customer service** The customer or client of a matrix structure always has a program manager available to respond to questions, provide status reports, and address problems.
- **Better accountability** The matrix clearly identifies program managers who can be held accountable for performance results; this helps top managers stay informed about what is going on, and why.
- **Improved decision making** The matrix forces decision making and problem solving down to the team level, where the best information exists.
- **Improved strategic management** The matrix helps keep top managers free of routine decisions and enables them to devote their time to more strategic management concerns.

Like the other organization structures discussed so far, the matrix also has potential *disadvantages*. They include power struggles, which may result from the two-boss system. Team members may become too focused on themselves and develop "groupitis," losing sight of important program goals. And, the matrix often creates increased costs as overhead rises in the form of extra salaries for program managers.

Team Structures

By formally utilizing project teams, matrix structures are part of the shift away from the more vertical functional and divisional structures. The **team structure** takes things a step further. Here, permanent and temporary teams are created to improve lateral relations and solve problems throughout an organization.[6] The use of *cross-functional teams* composed of members from different functional departments is particularly important. Members of these teams work together as needed to solve problems and explore opportunities. But they still retain their full-time functional work assignments and formally report to higher-level managers or supervisors in that capacity.

The goal of any team-based structure is to harness the intellectual and problem-solving potential of human resources at all levels of the organization, and to allow people to share knowledge and experience to gain competitive advantage. Under the guidance of a team leader, appointed or elected, each team should conduct its task with an emphasis on group decision making and consensus. For example, a research team at Polaroid Corporation developed a new medical imaging system called Helios in three years, when most had predicted it would take six. A Polaroid senior executive commented: "Our researchers are not any smarter, but by working together they get the value of each other's intelligence almost instantaneously."[7]

Team structures offer the potential *advantages* of helping to break down barriers among operating departments. They can boost morale as people from different parts of an organization get to know more about one another and each person's work responsibilities. Because the teams focus shared knowledge and expertise on specific problems, they can also improve the speed and quality of decisions in many situations. Potential *disadvantages* may arise from conflicting loyalties among members having both team and functional assignments. By its very nature, furthermore, the team structure requires that organization members spend a lot of time in meetings. How well this time is spent often depends on the quality of interpersonal relations, group dynamics, and leadership on a team.

Network Structures

Organizations using a **network structure** consist of a central core that is linked through "networks" with outside suppliers of essential business services.[8] These networks, in the form of strategic alliances and business contracts, allow the organization to operate without having to "own" all of its supporting functions. They are accessed as needed through the networks.

For example, consider how a mail-order company selling lawn and deck furniture through a catalog may be organized as a network structure. The firm itself is very small, consisting of relatively few full-time employees working from a central headquarters. Beyond that, it is structured as a series of business relationships. Merchandise is designed on contract with a furniture design firm; its manufacture and packaging are contracted to "off-shore" companies; stock is maintained and shipped from a contract warehouse; and all of the accounting and financial details are managed on contract with an outside firm. The quarterly catalog is designed, printed, and mailed as a strategic alliance with two other firms selling different home furnishings of a related price appeal.

An important foundation for the success of this type of creative organization lies with developments in information technology. Electronic computer networks greatly facilitate the links necessary for a network structure to function effectively, even across great distances. This is one of a network structure's potential *advantages,* flexibility in responding to changing conditions. It also allows organizations to operate as smaller and less complex basic systems. This reduces overhead and increases efficiency even while maintaining extensive operations. The potential *disadvantages* rest mainly with the complexities of "network management," a task that must be well handled to maintain the integrity of the total system. The greater the network complexity, the greater the chance for control problems. And if one part of the network breaks down or fails to deliver, the entire system suffers.

Organizing Trends in the Modern Workplace

It is more and more common to hear references to the *upside-down pyramid* first introduced in Chapter 2. In this view of an organization, managers are at the bottom supporting the work of nonmanagerial employees who are on the top and directly serve the needs of customers. While this is more of a concept than an accurate depiction of an organization chart, the thinking is fundamental to new directions in organizing the modern workplace. Under pressure for change, organization structures are becoming more horizontal and less rigid; they are becoming more open to various forms of employee participation and involvement—developments highlighted many times in this book for their significance.

Shorter Chains of Command

A typical organization chart shows the **chain of command,** or line of authority that vertically links all persons with successively higher levels of management. When organizations grow in size they tend to get taller, as more and more levels of management are added. This increases overhead costs; it increases distance in communication, understanding, and access between top and bottom levels; and it can greatly slow decision making. These are all reasons why "tall" organizations with many levels of management are often criticized for inefficiencies and poor productivity. The *current trend* is to streamline structures by cutting unnecessary levels of management.

THE EFFECTIVE MANAGER 6.2

What Delegation Involves

Step 1: The manager assigns responsibility.—The manager explains what work or duties someone is expected to do. This creates responsibility—the obligation of the other person to perform assigned tasks.

Step 2: The manager grants authority to act.—Along with the assigned task, the right to take necessary actions (spend money, direct the work of others, use resources) is granted to the other person. This is what is meant by authority—the right to act in ways needed to carry out the assigned tasks.

Step 3: The manager creates accountability.—In accepting an assignment, a person takes on a direct obligation to the manager to complete the job as agreed upon. This is accountability—the requirement to answer to the manager for performance results.

Less Unity of Command

A classical management principle called *unity of command* states that each person in an organization should report to one and only one supervisor. This is supposed to avoid the confusion of people receiving work directions from more than one source. However, one of the central elements of the matrix structure—the "two-boss" system—clearly violates unity of command. Whereas the classical advice is to avoid creating multiple reporting relationships, the matrix concept creates them by design. It does so in the attempt to improve lateral relations and teamwork on special programs or projects. Unity of command is also less predominant in team structures emphasizing cross-functional teams and task forces. Clearly, the *current trend* is for less, not more, unity of command.

Wider Spans of Control

The **span of control** is number of people reporting directly to a manager. When span of control is narrow, only a few people are under a manager's immediate supervision; a "wide" span of control indicates that the manager supervises many people. Organizations with wider spans of control tend to be flatter and have few levels of management; those with narrow spans of control tend to be taller and have many levels of management. Narrow spans of control tend to increase overhead costs; wider spans of control not only reduce these costs, but also offer workers less direct supervision and more independence.[9] The *current trend* is for managers to take responsibility for larger numbers of subordinates who are allowed to operate with less direct supervision.

More Delegation and Empowerment

All managers must decide what work they should do themselves and what should be left for others. At issue here is **delegation**—the process of distributing and entrusting work to others, as explained in The Effective Manager 6.2. The failure to delegate is a common management mistake. Whether it is due to a lack of trust in others or to a manager's inflexibility in the way things get done, failure to delegate can be damaging. It overloads the manager with work that could be done by others; it also denies others many opportunities to fully utilize their talents and gain satisfaction. When done properly, however, delegation leads to *empowerment,* an increasingly popular theme in today's workplace. Effective delegation is empowering and allows others to do their jobs in the best possible ways. The benefits include more satisfaction for the individual, and, frequently, a job better done.[10] The *current trend* is for managers to delegate more and find more ways to empower others.

Decentralization with Centralization

A question frequently asked by managers is: "Should most decisions be made at the top levels of an organization, or should they be dispersed by extensive delegation throughout all levels of management?" The former approach is referred to as **centralization;** the latter is called **decentralization.** The traditional pyramid form of organization gives the impression of a highly centralized structure, although decentralization is implicit in current trends toward shorter chains of command, wider spans of control, more delegation, and increased empowerment. But it doesn't have to be an "either–or" choice. Developments in information technology increasingly make it possible for organizations to provide more decentralization without giving up centralized control.[11] Computer reporting systems can keep managers better and more immediately informed about a wider range of day-to-day performance matters than ever before. This makes it possible for them to allow others to make more decisions, while remaining confident that the information systems will alert them quickly if something goes wrong. The *current trend* is for decentralization and centralization to work together in organizations.

Reduced Staff Component

The most common role of staff personnel in organizations is to provide expert advice and assistance to line personnel. But in some cases, the size of an organization's support staff grows to the point where it costs more in administrative overhead than it is worth. This is why staff cutbacks are common in downsizing and other turnaround efforts. In the quest for productivity, organizations are being restructured to minimize the size of the staff component and to empower line personnel with as much freedom to act as possible. The *current trend* is toward reduced size of staff.

Essentials of Organizational Design

Organizational design is the process of choosing and implementing structures that meet the needs of an organization or subunit. The ultimate purpose of organizational design is to put into place structures that facilitate the implementation of strategies to accomplish key objectives.

Bureaucratic Organizations

Any discussion of organizational design necessarily begins with a look at **bureaucracy,** first described by the German sociologist Max Weber as an ideal form of organization based on a clear-cut division of labor, strict hierarchy of authority, formal rules and procedures, and promotion based on competency.[12] Bureaucratic organizations are supposed to be orderly, fair, and highly efficient.

Many people view bureaucracies and bureaucrats in a negative sense. Simply put, such organizations can be too rigid and formal.[13] By relying heavily on rules and procedures, they can be slow to respond to changing environments. Bureaucracies can also become unwieldy as organizations grow large. Too many levels in the hierarchy of authority can cause higher managers to lose touch with lower-level operations. Overspecialization of jobs can reduce employee initiative and creativity as workers conform to rules instead of reaching out in new directions.

Instead of viewing all bureaucratic structures as inevitably flawed, the contingency approach to organizational design asks some critical questions. When is a bureaucratic form a good choice for an organization? What alternatives exist when it is not a good choice? A basis for answering these questions rests in research conducted in England during the early 1960s by Tom Burns and George Stalker. After investigating twenty manufacturing firms, Burns and Stalker concluded that two quite different organizational forms could be successful, depending on the nature of a firm's external environment. A more bureaucratic form, which Burns and Stalker called *mechanistic,* thrived when the environment was stable; it experienced difficulty when the environment was rapidly changing and uncertain. In dynamic situations, a much less bureaucratic form, called *organic,* performed best.[14] Figure 6.4 portrays these two approaches as opposite extremes on a continuum of organizational design alternatives.

Adaptive Organizations

In her book *The Change Masters,* Rosabeth Moss Kanter notes that the ability to respond quickly to shifting challenges in today's rapidly changing environment often distinguishes successful organizations from less successful ones. Specifically, Kanter states:

> The organizations now emerging as successful will be, above all, flexible; they will need to be able to bring particular resources together quickly, on the basis of short-term recognition of new requirements and the necessary capacities to deal with them. . . . The balance between static plans— which appear to reduce the need for effective reaction—and structural flexibility needs to shift toward the latter.[15]

In many settings, the limits of bureaucracy are increasingly apparent, and adjustments in organizational design are being made. Enlightened managers are reconfiguring organizations into more organic forms that emphasize flexibility and speed, without losing sight of important performance objectives. The organizational design trend is toward more **adaptive organizations** that operate with a minimum of bu-

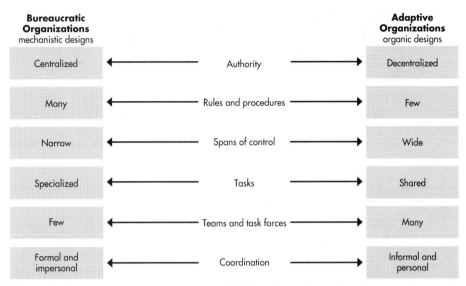

Bureaucratic Organizations mechanistic designs		Adaptive Organizations organic designs
Centralized	Authority	Decentralized
Many	Rules and procedures	Few
Narrow	Spans of control	Wide
Specialized	Tasks	Shared
Few	Teams and task forces	Many
Formal and impersonal	Coordination	Informal and personal

Figure 6.4   A continuum of organizational design alternatives: from bureaucratic to adaptive organizations.

reaucratic features and with cultures that encourage worker empowerment and participation.[16] Often, adaptive organizations are based on the team structures and network structures described earlier in this chapter.

The Nature of Organizational Culture

Culture is a popular word in management these days. Important differences in national cultures were introduced in Chapter 3 on managing in a global economy. Now it is time to talk about **organizational culture,** defined by noted scholar and consultant Edgar Schein as the system of shared beliefs and values that develops within an organization and guides the behavior of its members.[17] Sometimes called the *corporate culture,* this aspect of the organization can give important meaning and direction to the day-to-day behaviors of its members. It serves as a background force and has the potential to shape behavior, reinforce common beliefs, and encourage members to apply their efforts to accomplish important organizational objectives.

Organizational culture, in this sense, can become a major competitive advantage—*if* it supports strategy and *if* it is properly aligned with challenges in the organization's environment. Managing organizational culture on these terms is a formidable but important task.

What "Strong" Cultures Can Do

Some scholars and consultants, like Peter Drucker, worry that focusing attention on organizational culture has become the latest management fad.[18] On the other side of the issue stand many others like Schein, Terrence Deal and Alan Kennedy, and Ralph Kilmann, who consider culture an essential part of organizational success.[19] While it is clear that culture is not the sole determinant of what happens in organizations, it is an important influence on what they accomplish. *Strong cultures* have a clear influence on the behavior of organizational members. They commit and reinforce members to do things for and with one another that are considered to be in the best interests of organizational objectives. Dysfunctional behaviors are discouraged. When strong cultures have the desired effects, functional behaviors become the rule. The best organizations have strong cultures that allow for adaptability and continuous improvement in all areas of operations.[20]

Levels of Organizational Culture

Broadly stated, there are two levels of culture in organizations—the "observable" culture and the "core" culture.[21] *Observable culture* is what one sees and hears when walking around an organization—as a visitor, a customer, or an employee. It can be seen in the way people dress at work, how they arrange their offices, how they behave toward one another, and how they talk about and treat their customers. More specifically, it is found in the following elements of daily workplace affairs.

- **Stories** oral histories and tales, told and retold among members, about dramatic sagas and incidents in the life of the organization
- **Heroes** the people singled out for special attention, and whose accomplishments are recognized with praise and admiration among members, including founders and role models
- **Rites and rituals** the ceremonies and meetings, planned and spontaneous, that celebrate important occasions and performance accomplishments
- **Symbols** the special use of language and other nonverbal expressions to communicate important themes of organizational life.[22]

At the foundation of what one directly observes daily in an organization lies a second level of culture—the reason why things are this way. This is the *core culture*. It consists of *values,* or underlying beliefs, that influence behavior and actually give rise to the aspects of observable culture just described. Values are essential to strong culture organizations and are often widely publicized in formal statements of corporate mission and purpose. Core organizational values typically emphasize special themes such as performance excellence, innovation, social responsibility and ethics, worker involvement, and quality of work life.

Symbolic Management and Organizational Culture

Management of the core culture involves establishing and maintaining appropriate values. While this responsibility is most often considered at the level of the entire organization, the same point can be made for any manager in his or her work unit. Like the organization as a whole, the work unit will have a culture. How well this culture serves key work-unit objectives will partly depend on the influence of guiding values. Good managers—at any level in the organization—work hard to set and communicate core values as the foundation of a strong and positive culture.

In addition to making clear the existence of core values, managers must continue to communicate and reinforce them through the observable culture. A vast pool of symbols can and should be used to keep core values visible in day-to-day operations. Indeed, more and more attention is now being given to the concept of a **symbolic manager,** someone who uses symbols well to establish and maintain a desired organizational culture. Symbolic managers talk the "language" of the organization. They use spoken and written words to describe people, events, and even the competition in ways that reinforce and communicate a desired culture. *Language metaphors,* the use of positive examples from another context, are very powerful in this regard. For example, newly hired workers at Disney World and Disneyland are counseled to always think of themselves as more than employees: they are key "members of the cast" and they work "on stage." After all, they are told, this isn't just any business, this is an "entertainment" business.

Good symbolic managers tell key *stories* over and over again, and they encourage others to tell them. They often refer to the "founding story" about an entrepreneur whose personal values set a key tone for the enterprise. The stories told by symbolic managers often tell about organizational *heroes,* past and present, whose performances exemplify core values. Heroes are regularly identified and publicized in strong culture organizations as role models for others to follow. This can occur during highly symbolic *rites and rituals* that glorify the performance of the organization and its members. Such ceremonies may be as simple as a spontaneous public congratulation of a work group that exceeded its quality goals, or as formal as mass meetings called to announce major organizational accomplishments.

In Summary

What is organizing as a management function?

- Organizing is the process of creating an organization by defining tasks and bringing people and resources together to accomplish them.

- Structure is the system of communication and authority that links people together as they perform important tasks.

- An organization chart depicts the formal structure of how an organization is officially supposed to operate.

- The informal structure consists of unofficial working relationships among organizational members.

What are the major types of organization structures?

- All organizational structures have advantages and disadvantages; managers must choose and modify structures to best fit situational needs.

- In functional structures, people with similar skills who perform similar activities work together under a common manager.
- Divisional structures, based on product, area, or customer, group together people who work on a similar product, work in the same geographical region, or serve the same customers.
- A matrix structure combines the functional and divisional approaches to create permanent cross-functional project teams.
- Team structures create cross-functional teams and task forces to improve lateral relations and improve problem-solving at all levels of an organization.
- Network structures include systems of contracted services and strategic alliances clustered around a "core" business or organizational center.

What organizing trends are changing the modern workplace?

- The traditional organizational pyramid, arranged vertically and with top-down command and control, is giving way to more horizontal structures and the "upside-down pyramid" with an emphasis on employee involvement and customer service.
- Many organizations are finding that they can operate with shorter chains of command, less unity of command, and larger spans of control.
- The emphasis in more organizations today is on effective delegation and empowerment at all levels of work responsibility.
- Decentralization with centralization, supported by advances in computers and information technology, is occurring in more organizations.
- With an emphasis on empowerment and operating efficiency, many organizations are reducing the size of their staff components and allowing line personnel more operating authority.

What are the essentials of organizational design?

- Organizational design is the process of choosing and implementing appropriate structures for their organizations or subunits.
- The contingency view of organizational design seeks to match organizations with situational demands.
- Mechanistic organizational designs are bureaucratic in nature and perform best in stable environments.
- Organic organizational designs are less adaptive in nature, more flexible and open in the way they operate, and perform best in more uncertain environments.

Why is the culture of an organization important?

- The organizational or corporate culture establishes a personality for the organization as a whole and has a strong influence on the behavior of members.

- The observable culture is found in the rites, rituals, stories, heroes, and symbols of the organization.
- The core culture consists of the shared values that underlie the organization.
- In organizations with strong cultures, members behave with shared understandings that support accomplishment of important organizational objectives.
- Symbolic managers are good at building shared values and using stories, ceremonies, heroes, and language to reinforce these values in daily affairs.

L E A D I N G :

INSPIRING EFFORT

As you read Chapter 7, keep in mind these study questions:

- What is effective managerial leadership?

- What are important leadership traits?

- What are important leadership behaviors?

- What can be learned from contingency theories of leadership?

- What is transformational leadership?

T he chapter is about a centuries-old question: "What is leac̄ ship?" In the context of a management book, it inquires even more specifically into the nature of leadership as a managerial responsibility. But here already, the difficulty begins. The very terms themselves, *manager* and *leader,* are at issue. Warren Bennis, a respected leadership scholar and consultant, claims that too many American corporations are "overmanaged and underled"; Grace Hooper, another management expert and the first woman admiral in the U.S. Navy, says: "You manage things; you lead people."[1] There is no doubt that in today's complex workplace managers must be leaders. The situation, the people, the organization, demand it. The substantial challenge, however, is to fill this important organizational role. Developing your capabilities to succeed as a leader and learning how to help others to do the same, therefore, is one of your most significant personal and professional challenges. Let this chapter begin your systematic commitment to developing your leadership capacity.

Leading as a Management Function

A glance at the shelves in your local bookstore will quickly confirm that **leadership**—the process of inspiring others to work hard to accomplish important tasks—is one of the most popular management topics. It is also one of the four functions that constitute the management process. Planning sets the direction and objectives; organizing brings the resources together to turn plans into action; *leading* builds the commitments and enthusiasm needed for people to apply their talents fully to help accomplish plans; and controlling makes sure things turn out right.

Leadership and Vision

Vision has been identified as an essential ingredient of effective leadership. The term is generally used to describe someone who has a clear sense of the future and the actions needed to get there—successfully. The Effective Manager 7.1 offers five principles for meeting the challenges of visionary leadership.[2] Note that the suggestions go beyond a manager's responsibilities for making long-term plans and drafting budgets. They go beyond putting structures in place and assigning people jobs. And they go beyond making sure that results are consistent with the original plan. *Leadership with vision* means doing all these things and more. It means beginning with a

---

THE EFFECTIVE MANAGER 7.1

Five Principles of Visionary Leadership

1. **Challenge the process**—Be a pioneer—encourage innovation and ideas.
2. **Be enthusiastic**—Inspire others through your actions to share the vision.
3. **Help others to act**—Be a team player and support others' efforts and talents.
4. **Set the example**—Provide a consistent role model for others.
5. **Celebrate achievements**—Use emotion to rally hearts as well as minds.

---

clear vision, communicating that vision to all concerned, and motivating and inspiring people to pursue the vision in their daily work. Doing this, quite frankly, may be the ultimate test for managers in dynamic leadership settings around the world.

Leadership by Empowerment

A manager leads in a top-down fashion as the "boss" of a work unit, "chair" of a task force, or "head" of a project team. Success in any of these roles is consistent with the vertical form of organizations as described in the last chapter. But as we noted there also, top-down leadership alone is increasingly insufficient today to guarantee managerial success in the new workplace. Something more is needed—something that includes opportunities for *empowerment,* defined previously as giving people at all levels of work responsibility the power to act and make relevant decisions on their own. The use of empowerment is a broad-based approach to leadership devoted to helping every person working in every job to use his or her knowledge and judgment to make a real difference in daily workplace affairs. It occurs in organizations where top management truly empowers others by supporting initiative, respecting individual talents, and sharing power at all levels of operations. In today's changing work environments, managerial success depends on the willingness and skill to exercise leadership through empowerment.

Leadership in Practice

Leadership with vision and leadership by empowerment are concepts that sound good on paper. They are much harder to accomplish through personal behavior and actual practice. As a preface to the coming look at leadership research and theory, it is useful to ponder this description of leadership from someone who is widely recognized for his personal leadership accomplishments.

> At Herman Miller, Inc., the Michigan-based office furniture maker considered a model of innovation and management excellence, an essential component of leadership is a belief in people. Max DePree, the firm's chairperson and son of its founder, says that he learned from his father the value of leadership based on respect for others and a respect for diversity. He tells the story of a millwright who worked for his father. The millwright

held an important job in the plant. He was responsible for keeping all of the machines supplied with power from a central boiler. When the man died, DePree's father, wishing to express his sympathy to the family, went to their home. There he listened as the widow read some beautiful poetry, which, he was surprised to learn, had been written by the millwright. To this day, DePree says, he and his father still wonder: "Was he a poet who did millwright's work, or was he a millwright who wrote poetry?"

The question can never be answered, but DePree states the lesson of the story this way: "It is fundamental that leaders endorse a concept of persons. This begins with an understanding of the diversity of people's gifts, and talents, and skills." According to DePree, when we recognize the unique qualities of others, we become less inclined to believe that we alone know what is best. By valuing diversity, not only do we learn what may be needed to provide people with meaningful work and opportunities, we also benefit by allowing everyone's contribution to have an influence on the organization. Under DePree's leadership, and using techniques such as participative ownership and teamwork, Herman Miller has achieved ranking as one of *Fortune*'s "most admired" American corporations.[3]

Perhaps this glimpse into Max DePree's approach to leadership at Herman Miller, Inc. has stimulated you to think seriously about the many demands of serving as a manager and leader in the new workplace. Managerial success demands the capacity to excel, and to help others to excel, in all aspects of leadership. Understanding this challenge is one thing; meeting it is quite another. For centuries people have recognized that some people perform very well as leaders, while others do not. The question is: "Why?"

Leadership Traits

An early branch of leadership research focused attention on personal **traits,** or relatively stable and enduring characteristics, as the keys to leadership success.[4] The research goal was to find a set of universal traits that separate effective and ineffective leaders. Given such a list, it would be easy to select for leadership positions only those people whose characteristics match the profile and who would therefore surely succeed.

Overall, researchers have been unable to isolate a definitive profile of traits that separate leaders from nonleaders. The results of many years of research can be summarized as follows. Physical traits such as a person's height, weight, physique, and appearance make *no* difference in determining leadership success. On the other hand, "followers" do appear to admire certain things about leaders. In one study of more than 3,400 managers, the most respected leaders were described as honest, competent, forward-looking, inspiring, and credible.[5] Such positive feelings may enhance a leader's effectiveness, particularly in respect to creating vision and a sense of

P TO

empowerment, as previously discussed. Among the personal traits now considered important as foundations for leadership success are:

- **Drive** initiative, high energy, and desire for achievement
- **Motivation** desire to lead and influence others to reach common goals
- **Honesty and integrity** truthful in dealings with others; consistency in words and deeds
- **Self-confidence** decisive and confident in oneself and in dealings with others
- **Intelligence** able to gather, integrate, and interpret complex information
- **Knowledge** a good understanding of the organization, its industry, and technical task requirements
- **Flexibility** willing and able to adapt to changing demands[6]

Leadership Behaviors

Whereas certain traits may help leaders take effective action or develop useful skills, mere possession of the traits alone is not a guarantee of leadership success. There is more to it than one's personal attributes. Leadership success ultimately depends on actions taken and results achieved. Accordingly, a second historical branch of leadership research focuses on a leader's behavior vis-à-vis followers as the key determinant of leadership success. Central to this research direction is the notion of **leadership style**—a recurring pattern of behaviors exhibited by a leader. Although all leadership involves the use of power to influence others, leaders may vary in the styles they use to accomplish desired results. Leader-behavior research identifies alternative leadership styles and tries to determine which ones work best. This goal has a strong practical appeal. If one "best" style can be identified, it should be possible to train people how to use it to achieve leadership success.

Beginning in the 1940s, the work of scholars at Ohio State University and the University of Michigan was important in examining leader behavior.[7] Although the terminologies varied, leaders were described along two alternative dimensions—concern for task and concern for people. *Concern for task* is sometimes referred to as initiating structure, job-centeredness, and task orientation; *concern for people* is sometimes called consideration, employee-centeredness, and relationship orientation. Regardless of the terminology, however, the behaviors exhibited by leaders with these two concerns are quite clear. A leader high in concern for task or initiating structure tends to behave this way:

- plans and defines work to be done
- assigns task responsibilities
- sets clear work standards
- urges task completion
- monitors performance results

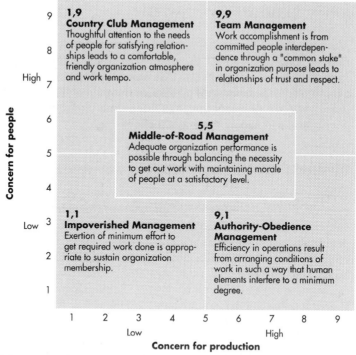

Figure 7.1 The Leadership Grid®. From Robert R. Blake and Anne Adams McCanse, *Leadership Dilemmas—Grid Solutions* (Houston: Gulf, 1991), p. 29. Copyright © 1991, by Scientific Methods, Inc. Reproduced by permission of the owners.

By contrast, a leader high in concern for people or consideration tends to behave this way:

- acts warm and supportive toward followers
- develops social rapport with followers
- respects the feelings of followers
- is sensitive to followers' needs
- shows trust in followers

The results of research on leader behaviors at first suggested that followers of people-oriented leaders would be more productive and satisfied than those working for task-oriented leaders. Later results, however, suggested that truly effective leaders were high in both concern for people and concern for task. One of the popular versions of this conclusion is the Blake and Mouton managerial grid shown in Figure 7.1. The grid refers to someone high on both of these dimensions as a "team" leader, somewhat similar to the participative leadership style previously described.[8] This is a manager who shares decisions with subordinates, encourages participation, and supports the teamwork needed for high levels of task accomplishment. In today's terminology, this could also be a manager who "empowers" others.

Contingency Leadership

Although the trait and leader-behavior approaches are useful, many leadership theorists no longer search for the one list of traits or the single best leadership style. Instead, they focus on a broader question: "When and under what circumstances is a particular leadership style preferable to others?" This is the essence of the *contingency approach* to leadership—an attempt to understand the conditions for leadership success in widely varying situations.

Fiedler's Contingency Model

A prominent contingency leadership theory was developed by Fred Fiedler on the premise that good leadership depends on a match between leadership style and situational demands.[9] Leadership style is measured on what Fiedler calls the *least-preferred coworker scale* that describes a person's tendencies toward either task-motivated or relationship-motivated leadership. This either–or concept is important. Fiedler believes that leadership style is part of one's personality; therefore, it is relatively enduring and difficult to change. Rather than trying to train a task-motivated leader to be relationship-motivated, or vice versa, Fiedler suggests that the key to leadership success is putting the existing styles to work in situations for which they are good "fits."

In Fiedler's theory the amount of control a situation allows the leader is a critical issue in determining the correct style–situation fit. Three contingency variables are used to diagnose situational control. The *quality of leader–member relations* (good or poor) measures the degree to which the group supports the leader. The *degree of task structure* (high or low) measures the extent to which task goals, procedures, and guidelines are clearly spelled out. The *amount of position power* (strong or weak) measures the degree to which the position gives the leader power to reward and punish subordinates.

Figure 7.2 shows eight leadership situations resulting from different combinations of these variables. They range from the most favorable of high-situational control (good leader–member relations, high task structure, strong position power) to the least favorable of low-situational control (poor leader–member relations, low task structure, weak position power). The figure also summarizes Fiedler's research, showing that neither the task-oriented nor the relationship-oriented leadership style is effective all of the time. Instead, each style appears best when used in the right situation. A task-oriented leader will be most successful in either very favorable (high control) or very unfavorable (low control) situations; a relationship-oriented leader will be most successful in situations of moderate control.

Hersey–Blanchard Situational Theory

The Hersey–Blanchard situational leadership theory suggests that successful leaders adjust their styles depending on the readiness of followers to perform in a given situation.[10] "Readiness," in this sense, is based on how able, willing, and confi-

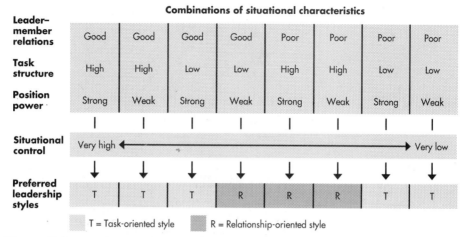

Combinations of situational characteristics

Leader–member relations	Good	Good	Good	Good	Poor	Poor	Poor	Poor
Task structure	High	High	Low	Low	High	High	Low	Low
Position power	Strong	Weak	Strong	Weak	Strong	Weak	Strong	Weak

| Situational control | Very high ← | | | | | | → Very low |

| Preferred leadership styles | T | T | T | R | R | R | T | T |

    T = Task-oriented style   R = Relationship-oriented style

Figure 7.2 Matching leadership style and situation: Summary predictions from Fiedler's contingency theory.

dent followers are in performing required tasks. As shown in Figure 7.3, the possible leadership styles resulting from different combinations of task-oriented and relationship-oriented behaviors are:

- **Delegating** allowing the group to make and take responsibility for task decisions; a low-task, low-relationship style
- **Participating** emphasizing shared ideas and participative decisions on task directions; a low-task, high-relationship style
- **Selling** explaining task directions in a supportive and persuasive way; a high-task, high-relationship style
- **Telling** giving specific task directions and closely supervising work; a high-task, low-relationship style

Managers using this model must be able to implement the alternative leadership styles as needed. The delegating style works best in high-readiness situations of able, willing, and confident followers; the telling style works best at the other extreme of low readiness. In between, the participating style is recommended for low to moderate readiness, and the selling style for moderate to high readiness. Hersey and Blanchard further believe that leadership styles can and should be adjusted as followers in a given situation change over time. The model also implies that if the correct styles are used in lower readiness situations, followers will "mature" and grow in ability, willingness, and confidence. Not only is this a positive result in itself, but it also allows the leader to become less directive.

House's Path–Goal Theory

A third contingency leadership approach is the path–goal theory advanced by Robert House.[11] This theory suggests that an effective leader is one who clarifies paths

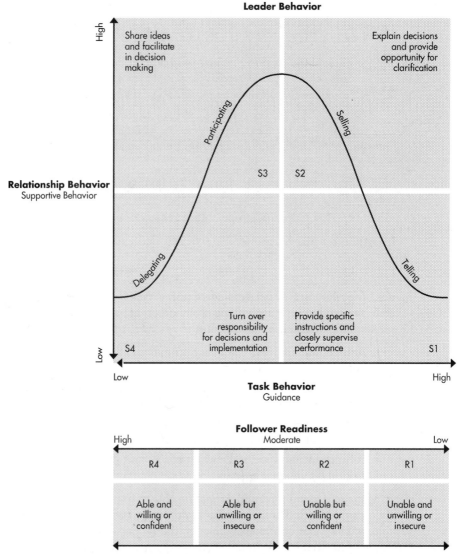

Figure 7.3 Essentials of the Hersey–Blanchard model of situational leadership. Source: Paul Hersey and Kenneth H. Blanchard, *Management of Organizational Behavior* (Englewood Cliffs, N.J.: Prentice-Hall, 1988), p. 171. Used by permission.

through which followers can achieve both task-related and personal goals. A good leader helps people progress along these paths, removes any barriers, and provides appropriate rewards for task accomplishment. House identifies four leadership styles that may be used in this "path–goal" sense.

- **Directive leadership** letting subordinates know what is expected; giving directions on what to do and how; scheduling work to be done; maintaining definite standards of performance; clarifying the leader's role in the group

- **Supportive leadership** doing things to make work more pleasant; treating group members as equals; being friendly and approachable; showing concern for the well-being of subordinates
- **Achievement-oriented leadership** setting challenging goals; expecting the highest levels of performance; emphasizing continuous improvement in performance; displaying confidence in meeting high standards
- **Participative leadership** involving subordinates in decision making; consulting with subordinates; asking for suggestions from subordinates; using these suggestions when making a decision

The path–goal leadership theory advises managers to use leadership styles that complement the needs of situations. An effective path–goal leader *adds value* by contributing things that are missing from the situation or that need strengthening; the leader specifically avoids redundant behaviors. For example, someone who feels unsure how to perform a task is likely to be grateful for a manager's directive leadership; someone working in a structured assembly-line job, by contrast, is likely to resent it.

Continuing research on path–goal theory suggests the following: When job assignments are unclear, the effective manager provides directive leadership to clarify task objectives and expected rewards. When worker self-confidence is low, the effective manager provides supportive leadership to clarify individual abilities and offers needed task assistance. When performance incentives are poor, the effective manager provides participative leadership to identify individual needs and appropriate rewards. When task challenge is insufficient, the effective manager provides achievement-oriented leadership to clarify job challenges and raise performance aspirations.[12]

Path–goal theory also recognizes what some theorists call **substitutes for leadership**.[13] These are aspects of the work setting and the people involved that can reduce the need for a leader's personal involvement. In effect, they make leadership from the outside unnecessary because leadership is already built into the situation. When substitutes are present, managers should avoid redundant leadership behaviors and concentrate on things that truly require outside attention. Possible substitutes for leadership include: *subordinate characteristics*—ability, experience, and independence; *task characteristics*—routineness and availability of feedback; and *organizational characteristics*—clarity of plans and formalization of rules and procedures.

Vroom–Jago Leader Participation Theory

The Vroom–Jago theory of leader participation is designed to help a leader choose the best decision-making method for any problem situation. The alternatives include the individual or authority decision, the consultative decision, or the group or consensus decision.[14]

An **authority decision** is one made by the manager and then communicated to the group. No input is asked of group members other than to provide specific information on request. A **consultative decision** is made by the manager after asking

---

THE EFFECTIVE MANAGER 7.2

Six Guidelines for Consensus

1. Present a clear and logical position; help others understand your point of view.
2. Listen to what others have to say; don't blindly argue your point of view.
3. Get everyone involved in discussion; actively seek out alternative points of view.
4. Don't change your mind just to avoid conflict; do yield to better and more logical positions.
5. Don't suggest "voting" or "compromise" to resolve differences; try to achieve a true agreement.
6. Don't settle for a "win–lose" situation; in a stalemate, push for more options to be considered.

---

group members for information, advice, or opinion. In some cases group members are consulted individually; in others the consultation occurs during a meeting of the group as a whole. In a **group decision** all members participate in making a decision and work with the manager to achieve consensus on the course of action to be taken. The Effective Manager 7.2 gives tips on how to achieve consensus.[15] Importantly, the consensus approach to decision making is a form of empowerment. It is successful to the extent that each member is ultimately able to accept the logic and feasibility of the final group decision. Complete unanimity is not the goal. Instead, consensus is achieved when any dissenting member is able to say, for example: "I understand what most of you would like to do. I personally would not do that, but I think that you understand what my alternative would be. I have had sufficient opportunity to sway you to my point of view, but clearly have not been able to do so. Therefore, I will gladly go along with what most of you wish to do."[16]

A single contingency notion underlies the Vroom–Jago leader participation model: Effective leadership results when the decision method used correctly matches the characteristics of the problem to be solved. There will be times when each of the three decision methods is most appropriate. In general, managers are advised to use participation and make more group decisions when:

- They lack sufficient information to solve a problem by themselves.
- The problem is unclear and help is needed to clarify the situation.
- Acceptance of the decision by others is necessary for its implementation.
- Adequate time is available to allow for true participation.

On the other hand, the model suggests that managers can use authority and make more individual decisions when:

- They personally have the expertise needed to solve the problem.
- They are confident and capable of acting alone.
- Others are likely to accept the decision they make.
- Little or no time is available for discussion.

For a manager who wants to be successful at leading through participation, therefore, the challenge is twofold: (1) knowing when each decision method is the best approach; and (2) implementing each well when needed. Managing the "group" aspects of decision making will be addressed again in Chapter 12 on building teams and Chapter 13 on decision making.

Charisma, Transformational Leadership, and Beyond

Current trends in leadership thinking seek to integrate and extend the insights discussed so far in this chapter. **Transactional leadership** is a term often used to describe the approach of managers who apply the insights of both the leader behavior and contingency theories, particularly the path–goal theory. Through a variety of task-oriented and/or people-oriented "transactions" with followers, the leader adjusts tasks, rewards, and structures to help followers meet their needs while working to accomplish organizational objectives.[17]

But transactional leadership meets only part of an organization's leadership requirements. Today's dynamic times demand something more. This is the era of *superleaders*—leaders who, through vision and strength of personality, have a truly inspirational impact on others.[18] Their leadership efforts result in followers not just meeting performance expectations, but performing *above and beyond* them. These are **charismatic leaders,** ones who develop special leader–follower relationships and inspire their followers in extraordinary ways. The presence of charismatic leadership is reflected in followers who are enthusiastic about the leader and his or her ideas, work very hard to support them, remain loyal and devoted, and seek superior performance accomplishments.[19]

What is Transformational Leadership?

The term **transformational leadership** describes someone who uses charisma and related personal qualities to raise aspirations and shift people and systems to new and higher-level performance patterns.[20] Transformational leadership is inspirational leadership that influences followers to achieve extraordinary performance, often in the context of large-scale organizational change. Transformational leaders get followers to do things different from and far beyond what they originally anticipated being willing or able to do. The special qualities of transformational leaders include:

- **Vision** having ideas and a clear sense of direction, communicating them to others, and developing excitement about working hard to accomplish shared "dreams"

- **Charisma** arousing others' enthusiasm, faith, loyalty, pride, and trust in themselves through the power of personal reference and appeals to emotion

- **Symbolism** identifying "heroes," offering special rewards, and holding spontaneous and planned ceremonies to celebrate excellence and high achievement

- **Empowerment** helping others to develop and perform, removing performance obstacles, sharing responsibilities, and delegating truly challenging work
- **Intellectual stimulation** gaining the involvement of others by creating awareness of problems and stirring their imagination to create high-quality solutions
- **Integrity** being honest and credible, acting consistently out of personal conviction; above all, meeting commitments by following through[21]

The notion of transformational leadership offers a distinct challenge to managers. It says that it is not enough to be able to possess leadership traits, know the alternative leadership behaviors, and understand leadership contingencies. Beyond such foundations of transactional leadership, the manager must also lead in an inspirational way and with a compelling personality. The charismatic and transformational leader provides a strong aura of vision and contagious enthusiasm that substantially raises the confidence, aspirations, and commitments of followers. This leader arouses followers to be more highly dedicated, more satisfied with their work, and more willing to put forth extra efforts to achieve success in challenging times.

Gender and Leadership

One of the leadership themes of continuing interest deals with the question of whether or not gender influences leadership effectiveness.[22] To state the bottom line: The evidence clearly supports that both women and men can be effective leaders. Interestingly enough, some emerging results indicate that women and men may tend, generally speaking, to use somewhat different styles in their work. Women may be more prone to behaviors typically considered democratic and participative—such as showing respect for others, caring for others, and sharing power and information with others. This style is sometimes referred to as *interactive leadership,* focusing on the building of consensus and good interpersonal relations through communication and involvement. Men, by contrast, may be more transactional in their leadership tendencies. They are prone to more directive and assertive behaviors that use the authority of a leadership position in a traditional "command and control" sense.

Given the emphasis on shared power, involvement, communication, cooperation, and participation in the new form of organizations of today, these results are provocative. Gender issues aside, the interactive leadership style seems to be an excellent fit with the demands of a diverse workforce and the new workplace. Regardless of whether the relevant behaviors are displayed by women or men, it seems clear that future leadership success will rest more often on one's capacity to lead through positive relationships and empowerment than through aloofness and authority.

Good "Old-Fashioned" Leadership

Peter Drucker offers another very pragmatic approach to leadership in the new workplace. It is based on what he refers to as a good "old-fashioned" view of the plain hard work it takes to be a successful leader. Consider, for example, his description of a telephone conversation with a potential consulting client—the human resource vice-president of a big bank. "We'd want you to run a seminar for us on how one acquires charisma," she said. Drucker's response caught her by surprise. He told the VP that there's more to leadership than the popular emphasis on personal qualities that offer a sense of personal "dash" or charisma. In fact, he said, "Leadership . . . is work."[23]

Drucker's observations on leadership offer a useful complement to the transformational leadership ideas just discussed. He identifies these three essentials of leadership. The first is *defining and establishing a sense of mission.* A good leader sets the goals, priorities, and standards. A good leader keeps them all clear and visible and maintains them. In Drucker's words, "The leader's first task is to be the trumpet that sounds a clear sound." The second essential is *accepting leadership as a responsibility rather than a rank.* Good leaders surround themselves with talented people. They are not afraid to develop strong and capable subordinates. And they do not blame others when things go wrong. As Drucker says, "The buck stops here" is still a good adage. The third essential is *earning and maintaining the trust of others.* The key here is the leader's personal integrity. The followers of good leaders trust the leader, even if they do not necessarily like him or her. This means they believe the leader means what is being said and that actions will be consistent with what is being said. Using Drucker's words once again: "Effective leadership . . . is not based on being clever; it is based primarily on being consistent."[24]

Ethical Aspects of Leadership

Firmly embedded in the concept of transformational leadership and good old-fashioned leadership is *integrity*—the leader's honesty, credibility, and consistency in putting values into action. Leaders have an undeniable responsibility to set high ethical standards to guide the behavior of followers. For managers, the ethical aspects of leadership are important and everyday concerns.

Concerned about what he perceives as a lack of momentum in organizational life, John Gardner talks about the "moral aspects" of leadership.[25] "Most people in most organizations most of the time," he writes, "are more stale than they know, more bored than they care to admit." Leaders, according to Gardner, have a moral obligation to supply the necessary spark to awaken the potential of each individual—to urge each person "to take the initiative in performing leaderlike acts." He points out that high expectations tend to generate high performance. It is the leader's job to remove "obstacles to our effective functioning—to help individuals see and pursue shared purposes." Gardner's *moral leadership* view is based on a premise that people who "own" their jobs will naturally outperform those who feel they are outsiders. Good managers, accordingly, should instill a sense of ownership by being the kind of leaders who are truly willing to let others do their best. Once again, the words of Max DePree at Herman Miller provide a useful final reminder on the responsibilities and challenges of leadership: "Nobody is common," DePree says. "Everybody has a right to be an insider."[26]

In Summary

What is effective managerial leadership?

- Leadership is the process of inspiring others to work hard to accomplish important tasks.
- An effective leader influences other people to work enthusiastically in support of organizational performance objectives.
- Not all leaders are good managers; not all managers are good leaders, even though they should be.
- Vision is increasingly considered to be an essential ingredient of effective leadership. Visionary leaders are able to communicate their vision to others and build commitments to perform the work required to fulfill it.
- Leadership by empowerment, allowing others to make job-related decisions, is a consistent theme of the new workplace.

What are important leadership traits?

- Researchers have been unable to identify a definitive list of traits that always separates effective leaders from ineffective ones.
- Recent developments suggest that followers do admire certain leadership qualities, including honesty, competency, and credibility.
- Personal traits now considered important as foundations for leadership success include drive, motivation, integrity, self-confidence, intelligence, knowledge, and flexibility.

What are important leadership behaviors?

- Research on leader behaviors focuses on alternative leadership styles, or recurring patterns of their impact on followers.
- Two primary dimensions of leadership behavior are recognized—concern for task or initiating structure, and concern for people or consideration.
- A leader high in concern for task emphasizes getting work done through behaviors that define and clarify tasks and control results.
- A leader high in concern for people emphasizes helping people to feel good through behaviors that show respect, communicate sensitivity, and develop social rapport.
- The Blake and Mouton leadership grid suggests that the best leaders are good at both task-oriented and people-oriented behaviors.

What can be learned from contingency theories of leadership?

- Contingency leadership approaches point out that no one leadership style always works best; rather, style must match or "fit" the demands of a situation.

- Fiedler's contingency theory describes how situational differences in task structure, position power, and leader–member relations influence which leadership style works best.
- House's path–goal theory points out that leaders should add value to situations by responding with supportive, directive, achievement-oriented, and/or participative styles as needed.
- The Hersey–Blanchard situational theories recommend using task- and people-oriented behaviors, depending on the "maturity" of the group a manager is attempting to lead.
- The Vroom–Jago leader participation theory advises leaders to choose different decision-making methods appropriate to the problems they are trying to resolve.

What is transformational leadership?

- Charismatic leadership is truly inspirational in raising the aspirations of followers to extraordinary levels of achievement.
- Transactional leadership focuses on tasks, rewards, and structures to influence follower behavior; transformational leaders use charisma and related qualities to inspire extraordinary efforts in support of innovation and large-scale change.
- An interactive leadership style emphasizing communication, involvement, and interpersonal respect is sometimes associated with women and is highly consistent with the demands of the new workplace.
- All leaders should commit to the highest ethical standards in their personal behavior; they should fulfill the responsibility of what John Gardner calls the "moral aspects" of leadership.

CONTROLLING:

ENSURING RESULTS

As you read Chapter 8, keep in mind these study questions:

- What is the control process?

- How do managerial controls work?

- What organizational systems assist in control?

- How do information systems facilitate control?

- How does operations management facilitate control?

Keep in touch. Stay informed. Be in control. These are im~~.~~ tant responsibilities for every manager. But *control* is one those words like *power*. If you aren't careful when it is used, it has a negative connotation. Yet control plays a positive and necessary role in the management process. To have things "under control" at work is good; for things to be "out of control" generally is bad. Today, being in control is increasingly tied to advances in computer and information technologies. Futurist Alvin Toffler considers the speed of decision making to be a major asset—"speed to market," "quick response," "fast cycle time," and "time-based competition" are hot topics in many executive suites; technology and operations control are mainstream concerns.[1] This chapter introduces the fundamentals of controlling as a basic managerial responsibility and an important key to sustained organizational performance.

Controlling as a Management Function

Formally defined, *controlling* is the process of monitoring performance and taking action to ensure desired results. As the fourth management function, its purpose is straightforward—to make sure that actual performance meets or surpasses objectives. Planning sets the directions and allocates resources; organizing brings people and material resources together to do the work; leading inspires people to best utilize these resources; *controlling* sees to it that the right things happen, in the right way, and at the right time.

The Control Process

The control process involves four steps. The first is planning, that is, *establishing performance objectives and standards*. Performance objectives should be both defined and associated with specific measurement standards for determining how well they are accomplished. *Output standards* measure performance results in terms of quantity, quality, cost, or time. Examples include percentage error rate, dollar deviation from budgeted expenditures, and the number of units produced or customers serviced in a time period. *Input standards* measure the work efforts that go into a performance task. They are used in situations where actual performance outputs are difficult or expensive to measure. Examples include conformance to rules and procedures, efficiency in the use of resources, and work attendance or punctuality.

The second step in the control process is the all-important act of *measuring actual*

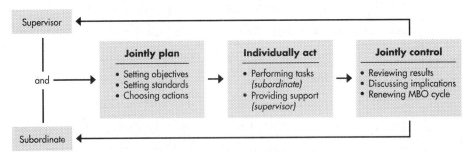

Figure 8.1   The management by objectives (MBO) process: an integrated planning and controlling system.

performance. The task here is to measure accurately the performance outcomes achieved (under output standards) and/or the performance inputs applied (under input standards). This measurement must be accurate enough to spot important differences between what is really taking place and what was originally intended according to plan. A common management failure is an unwillingness or inability to specifically measure the performance accomplishments of people at work.

The third step is *comparing actual performance with objectives and standards.* This comparison of actual performance with desired performance establishes the need for action. A good way to remember this step is the *control equation:*

$$\text{Need for Action} = \text{Desired performance} - \text{Actual performance}.$$

The fourth step in the control process involves *taking necessary action* to correct or improve the situation. Two types of action situations are important to recognize. A *problem situation* is one in which actual performance is less than desired. This indicates a need for corrective action to restore performance to the desired level. Equally important is the exception signaled when actual performance is above standard. This is an *opportunity situation.* The need for action is to discover why desired performance was exceeded and learn what can be done to continue this higher level of accomplishment in the future. It is also a chance to review established objectives and standards to determine if they should be improved.

Management by Objectives

A basic premise of the control process is that planning and controlling must work together. One way to accomplish this in direct supervisor–subordinate relationships is through a technique known as **management by objectives,** or MBO.[2] Formally defined, MBO is a process of joint objective setting between a supervisor and subordinate. The process is described in Figure 8.1, with important emphasis on the point that the supervisor and subordinate jointly establish plans and jointly control results.

MBO is a form of employee involvement and participation that results in a formal agreement with a supervisor regarding (1) the subordinate's performance objectives for a given time period, (2) the plans through which they will be accomplished, (3) standards for measuring whether or not they have been accomplished, and

(4) procedures for reviewing results. MBO offers the advantages of clearly focusing the subordinate's task efforts, specifying a timetable for them, and giving the supervisor a framework for providing needed work support. Because the process involves direct, face-to-face communication, MBO also fosters understanding between supervisor and subordinate about performance objectives and standards.

The nature of the performance objectives and the way in which they are established can have a major impact on how well MBO works. *Improvement objectives* document desires to improve performance in a specific way and in respect to a specific factor. An example is: "To reduce quality rejects by 10 percent." *Personal development objectives* pertain to personal growth activities, often those resulting in expanded job knowledge or skills. An example is: "To learn the latest spreadsheet package for personal computers." Some MBO contracts also include *maintenance objectives,* which formally express intentions to maintain performance at an existing level. In all cases, good performance objectives are written, are formally agreed to by both the supervisor and subordinate, and meet these criteria:

- targets a key result to be accomplished
- identifies a date for achieving results
- offers a realistic and attainable challenge
- specifies clear and measurable results

One of the more difficult aspects of MBO relates to the last point—the desire to have performance objectives stated as specifically and as quantitatively as possible. Ideally, this occurs as agreement on a measurable end product; for example: "To reduce housekeeping supply costs by 5 percent by the end of the fiscal year." But some jobs, particularly managerial ones, involve performance areas that are hard to quantify. Rather than abandon MBO in such cases, it is often possible to agree on performance objectives stated as verifiable work activities. Accomplishment of the activities indicates progress under the performance objective. An example is: "To improve communications with my subordinates in the next three months by holding weekly group meetings." While it is difficult to measure "improved communications," the holding of weekly group meetings can be documented easily.

The Effective Manager 8.1 offers six steps on how to make sure MBO succeeds in practice. The steps convey the key ingredient of participation discussed earlier. This advice is not lost on many of today's best managers. Although they might call what they are doing by different names, the common thread is consistent with the MBO concept—hire the best people, work with them to set challenging performance objectives, give them the best possible support, and hold them accountable for results.

How Do Managerial Controls Work?

The three major types of managerial controls—feedforward, concurrent, and feedback—are shown in Figure 8.2. Each addresses a different part of the input-

---

THE EFFECTIVE MANAGER 8.1

Steps to Successful MBO

- **Step 1**—An individual lists suggested key performance objectives, along with target dates for accomplishing them.
- **Step 2**—These objectives are reviewed jointly by the individual and his or her supervisor, and both parties agree on the objectives and target dates.
- **Step 3**—The individual and supervisor meet each month to review progress and make revisions or update objectives as needed.
- **Step 4**—At the end of six months, the individual prepares a performance report listing major accomplishments and commenting on any discrepancies between expected and actual results.
- **Step 5**—This report, or self-appraisal, is discussed with the supervisor.
- **Step 6**—A new set of objectives is established for the next six months, following the process as described in Step 1. Then the MBO cycle begins anew.

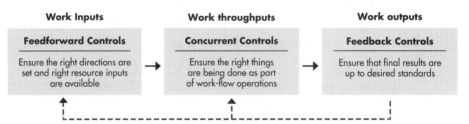

Figure 8.2   Three types of controls: feedforward, concurrent, and feedback.

throughput-output cycle of organizational activities.[3] **Feedforward controls,** also called preliminary controls, are done before work begins. They are designed to anticipate potential problems and take preventative action to avoid their occurrence. At McDonald's, for example, preliminary control of food ingredients plays an important role in the company's ability to meet its quality objectives in meal services. For instance, the company requires that suppliers of its hamburger buns produce them to exact specifications, covering everything from texture to uniformity of color.[4]

Concurrent controls focus on what happens during the work process. Sometimes called steering controls, they monitor operations and activities to make sure that things are being done correctly. Ideally, they ask and answer the question: "What can we do to improve things before we finish?" At McDonald's, shift leaders exercise concurrent control through direct supervision. They constantly observe what is taking place even while helping out with the work. They are trained to intervene immediately when something is not done right and to correct things on the spot. Detailed instruction manuals that specify, for example, which machine or part of the facility is to be cleaned each day of the week also "steer" workers in the right directions as their jobs are performed.

Feedback controls, also called postaction controls, take place after an action is completed. They ask the question: "Now that we are finished, how well did we do?" Restaurants ask how you liked a meal—after it is eaten; a final exam grade tells you how well you performed—after the course is over; a final budget summary informs managers of any cost overruns—after a project is completed. In these ways, feedback controls can be used to better plan future activities. They are also used to formally document accomplishments for administrative purposes, such as performance appraisal. McDonald's employees at each location never know when a corporate evaluator may stop in to sample the food and the service. When this happens, though, the evaluator provides feedback with the goal of helping to further improve operations.

Organizational Systems and Control

Control in the workplace can be approached from two different directions.[5] *Internal control* occurs when motivated individuals and groups exercise self-control in the performance of their job responsibilities. The trend toward more empowerment and participation, reflected in the earlier discussion of MBO, is bringing renewed emphasis on the importance and power of internal control. Its potential is enhanced when capable people have clear performance objectives, the right resources, and supportive work environments that treat them with respect and consideration. *External control,* by contrast, occurs through outside guidance and supervision. It is exercised when managers take direct action to control the behavior of others; it is also found in organizational systems of administrative controls, compensation and benefits, and employee discipline.

Administrative Controls

The day-to-day implementation of the management process establishes a framework for administrative effective control. *Control via strategy and objectives* occurs when work behaviors are initially directed toward the right end results. When performance goals are clearly set and understood, lack of performance due to poor direction in one's work is less likely to occur. *Control via policies and procedures* operates in similar ways. To the extent that good policies and procedures exist to guide behavior, it is more likely that organizational members will act uniformly on important matters. Learning from past experience and incorporating that learning into future strategies, objectives, policies, and procedures is an important element of effective control in organizations.

Control via work structures involves giving people jobs that are well designed and properly linked to organizational work flows and operations. *Control via organization culture* occurs in similar fashion when shared values and continuous mutual reinforcement support individual performance efforts. *Control via performance norms* occurs as group members support leadership initiatives and work hard to accomplish them. When a manager exercises leadership to help develop and sustain positive performance norms and a supportive organizational culture, this leadership facilitates control. When a manager exercises leadership to design jobs and structures, create a supportive organizational culture, and develop high performance aspirations, he or she is also facilitating control.

Compensation and Benefit Systems

In order to hire the best possible workers and to maintain a highly qualified workforce, organizations should offer *attractive base compensation* in the form of market-competitive salaries or hourly wages. This is important from a control standpoint, since the more capable a person is the more self-control you can expect them to exercise. If you get the right people into jobs in the first place, you can save costs and boost productivity over the long run. When the compensation is uncompetitive, it is more difficult to build and keep a staff of highly competent workers. The less capable the workforce, the greater the likelihood of performance problems and the greater the burden on external controls.

The fringe benefits component in the total compensation package is also important. In today's era of rising costs and workforce diversity, however, meeting fringe benefit demands—all the way from health insurance, to pension plans, to child and elder care—is an increasingly challenging task. More and more employers are trying to manage benefits spending as a way to control costs and boost productivity. Many are asking employees to pay a greater share of fringe benefit costs—an unpopular move with employees and with labor unions. A substantial proportion of union strikes, for example, involve concerns for workers' health care coverage.[6] One current trend is toward more *flexible benefits,* where employees are allowed to choose a set of benefits best meeting personal needs, while remaining within cost limits set by the employer.

Employee Discipline Systems

Absenteeism, tardiness, sloppy work—and even more extreme misbehaviors such as falsifying records, sexual harassment, and embezzlement—all are examples of behaviors that can and should be formally addressed in employee discipline systems. **Discipline** can be defined as a form of control that takes place by influencing behavior through reprimand. Ideally, all discipline is handled in a fair, consistent, and systematic way.

Progressive discipline ties reprimands to the severity and frequency of the employee's infractions. Under such a system, penalties vary according to how significant a disruptive behavior is and how often it occurs. For example, the progressive-discipline guidelines for the employees of one university state: "The level of disciplinary action shall increase with the level of severity of behavior engaged in and based on whether the conduct is of a repetitive nature."[7] In this particular case, the ultimate penalty of "discharge" is reserved for the most severe behaviors (e.g., any felony crime) or for continual infractions of a less severe nature (e.g., being continually late for work and failing to respond to a series of written reprimands and/or suspensions).

The goal of a progressive discipline system is to achieve compliance with organi-

---

THE EFFECTIVE MANAGER 8.2

Hot Stove Rules of Discipline

- **A reprimand should be immediate**—A hot stove burns the first time you touch it.
- **A reprimand should be directed toward someone's actions, not their personality**—A hot stove doesn't hold grudges, doesn't try to humiliate people, and doesn't accept excuses.
- **A reprimand should be consistently applied**—A hot stove burns anyone who touches it, and it does so every time.
- **A reprimand should be informative**—A hot stove lets a person know what to do to avoid getting burned in the future—"Don't touch."
- **A reprimand should occur in a supportive setting**—A hot stove conveys warmth but also operates with an inflexible rule—"Don't touch."
- **A reprimand should support realistic rules**—The don't-touch-a-hot-stove rule isn't a power play, a whim, or emotion of the moment; it is a necessary rule of reason.

---

zational expectations through the least extreme reprimand possible. In general, a good starting point for properly handling day-to-day disciplinary situations is the advice, based on the "hot stove" analogy, offered in The Effective Manager 8.2: "When a stove is hot, don't touch it"; when this rule is violated, you get burned—immediately, consistently, but usually not beyond the point of repair.[8]

Management Information and Control

Information is the foundation of managerial control. Any control system requires communication of the *right* information at the *right* time and among the *right* people if it is to function effectively. People must know what is expected of them in terms of task performance. Managers and other decision makers must have useful information regarding performance results if they are to make plans, provide support, and take other appropriate actions. Although the settings and applications differ widely, new managers are exploring new ways of using information and technology to help workers meet high performance standards.

Management Information Systems

A **management information system,** or MIS, collects, organizes, and distributes data in such a way that it meets the information needs of managers. It does so by getting the right information into the hands of the right people on a timely and cost-efficient basis. Good MISs greatly facilitate each of the management functions, but they are especially beneficial when it comes to planning and controlling. More and more today, these systems are supported by the latest in computer technology. For example, at C.R. England, a long-haul refrigerated trucking company in Salt Lake City, Utah, a computerized information system monitors more than five hundred aspects of organizational performance. The system tracks everything from billing accuracy to arrival times to driver satisfaction with company maintenance on their vehicles. Pay bonuses and extra vacation days are awarded based on driver performance on such goals as safety and fuel consumption. Says CEO Dan England: "Our view was, if we could measure it, we could manage it."[9]

Continuing advances in microelectronics bring about almost weekly changes in both computer technology and its role in organizations. Today's managers have wonderful advantages in desktop and laptop computing that handles a wide variety of information-based jobs, including writing, calculating, storing, organizing, and analyzing data, drawing graphs, and transmitting messages. Most recently, the use of high-speed modems brings to these same desktops access to a growing information gateway to the world—the Internet and what is commonly called the *information superhighway.*

Among the developments in computerized MIS, *decision-support systems* allow users to interact directly with a computer to create information helpful in making decisions to solve complex and sometimes unstructured problems. Decision-support systems are now available to assist in such business decisions as mergers and acquisitions, plant expansions, new product developments, and stock portfolio management, among many others. An advancement that is proving increasingly useful is the area of *group decision-support systems,* or GDSS. A GDSS is an interactive computer-based information system that facilitates group work at solving complex and unstructured problems. GDSS software, called *groupware,* is a system for computer-mediated meetings. It facilitates information exchange, group decision making, work scheduling, and other forms of group support, whether the members are geographically proximate or distant from one another. The computer-mediated group meeting is being referred to as the *virtual meeting.*

One of the advantages of groupware and virtual meetings is that group members tend to focus more intently on data displayed on their computers or a common screen. This can help overcome the problem of "dueling egos," wherein people concentrate more on the people making points than on the substance of the points themselves. Of course, disadvantages may occur with GDSS as group members lose personal touch with one another, are unable to read nonverbal messages, and miss the shared exuberance of spontaneous and creative thinking.

Information systems that meet the special needs of senior management are called *executive information systems.* They support a variety of operational and strategic decisions. Distinguishing features of an EIS include the emphasis on multicolor displays of charts and graphs, big-screen projections for conference use, and easy-to-use, touch-sensitive monitors or mouses instead of keyboards for computer control. Some EIS programs even color-code exceptions to help executives focus on trouble spots and opportunities. Furthermore, this new data-rich environment allows executives to probe more deeply and quickly than ever before through the levels of an organization and to review data on day-to-day operations.

Another development in information technology relates to continuing progress in the area of *artificial intelligence.* This is a field of study concerned with building computer systems with the capabilities to reason the way people do, even to the point of dealing with ambiguities and difficult issues of judgment. The managerial applications of artificial intelligence lie in the realm of *expert systems*—software systems that mimic the thinking of human experts and, in so doing, offer consistent "expert" decision-making advice to the user.[10] Most expert systems currently in use are "rule-based" and use a complicated set of "if . . . then" rules to help users analyze problems. They are appearing in a wide variety of settings, such as business, government services, health care, and more. One complaint about their use is that they can "deskill" work by requiring the employee to know less because the computer does more.[11] But their advocates point out that they help users concentrate their attention and problem-solving skills on more complex matters.

Information Technology and the New Workplace

There is no doubt that information technology is dramatically changing the way information flows and is utilized in organizations. More information about more things is being made available to more people in organizations more quickly than ever before. One of the most evident examples of the everyday impact of information technology lies with **office automation,** the use of computers and related technologies to facilitate operations typical of the office environment. Take a moment to consider this view of the "electronic" office.

> People work at *smart stations* supported by computers that allow sophisticated voice, image, text, and other data handling operations. *Voice messaging* utilizes the voice recognition capabilities of computers to take dictation, answer the telephone, and relay messages. *Databases* are easily accessed to prepare and analyze reports. Once finished, documents drafted via word processing are stored for later retrieval and/or sent via *electronic mail* or *facsimile transmission* to others. Standard filing cabinets are few, and little paper is found. Mail arrives and is routed to its destination via computer; it gets posted on *electronic bulletin boards* to be prioritized and accessed according to importance. Telephone calls are received at the workstation, which can accept and store voice messages for later retrieval. *Computer conferencing* and *videoconferencing* are commonplace, and people work with one another every day over great distances, without ever being personally face-to-face.

This isn't fantasy; it's real. Progressive organizations are doing all they can to utilize computers and information technology to streamline work, improve operating efficiencies, and make overall performance improvements.[12] As organizations become more "virtual" and "network" oriented (see Chapter 6), the use of computerized linkages will expand even further. Some are already developing *enterprise-wide networks* where the total enterprise is fully integrated through computer-communication links. In the near future it will be possible, for example, for a field salesperson to pass on a customer's suggestion for a product modification via electronic mail. This mail will arrive at the computer used by a product designer at company headquarters. After working on computer designs for the product, the designer can pass on the new prototype simultaneously to engineering, manufacturing, finance, and marketing for their preliminary analyses. The results may be pooled through a GDSS to allow further consideration of the prototype's business potential.

Operations Management and Control

Control is an essential element in the operations management process (see Chapter 2), where the emphasis is always on utilizing people, resources, and technology to best advantage. Among the most important points of attention in operations control, furthermore, are purchasing management, inventory management, project management, and statistical quality control.

Purchasing Management

In today's economy the rising costs of materials seem to be a fact of life. Given the importance of all forms of cost control to organizations, the power of the purchasing function is rising also. Senior executives are recognizing that purchasing management is a productivity tool. Cost control for an organization, just as for any consumer, involves watching what it pays for what it buys. Some executives, including those at AT&T, think the purchasing function is one of the most important aspects of business.[13]

Among the purchasing management approaches now being tried, these trends seem evident. In order to *leverage buying power,* more organizations are centralizing purchasing to allow buying in volume. They are committing to a *small number of suppliers* with whom they can negotiate special contracts, gain quality assurances, and get preferred service. They are also finding ways to work together in *supplier–purchaser partnerships* to operate in ways that allow each partner to contain costs. An example is the relationship between Arrow Electronics, a New York-based parts supplier, and Bailey Controls, its Ohio-based customer. Arrow keeps a warehouse in Bailey's factory, and stocks it according to Bailey's bi-monthly order forecasts. Bailey provides the space; Arrow does the rest. Bailey lowers its purchasing costs and gains preferred service; Arrow gains an exclusive supplier contract and more sales volume.[14]

Inventory Management

Inventory is the amount of materials or products kept in storage. It is common for organizations to maintain inventories of raw materials, work in process, and finished goods. Organizations keep inventories to maintain flexibility in their production/operations processes, smooth out periods of excess or undercapacity, meet periods of unusual demand, and/or achieve economies from large-scale purchases. Because inventories can represent major resource investments, they must be well managed. The basic objective of inventory control is to make sure that inventory is neither too large nor too small for the tasks at hand.

The **economic order quantity** (EOQ) is a method of inventory control that involves ordering a fixed number of items every time an inventory level falls to a predetermined point. When this point is reached a decision is automatically made, more and more frequently by computer, to place a standard order. The best example is the supermarket, where hundreds of daily orders are routinely made on this basis. These standard order sizes are calculated according to a mathematical formula and the entire process is likely computerized.

A popular development in inventory control involves **just-in-time scheduling,** or JIT. These systems, which were popularized by the productivity of Japanese industry, involve attempts to reduce costs and improve workflows by scheduling materials to arrive at a workstation or facility "just in time" to be used. This approach to inventory control involves minimizing carrying costs and maintaining almost no inventories by ordering or producing only as needed. It usually occurs in extremely small lots, possibly even on a unit-by-unit basis. This can cut down carrying costs of inventories, maximize the use of space, and even contribute to improved quality of results. For example, *kanban* is a Japanese word for the piece of paper that accompanies, for example, a bin of parts in a camera factory. When a worker first takes parts from a new bin, the *kanban* is routed back to the supplier and serves as an order for new parts.

The JIT technique is simple and effective. Richard J. Schonberger, noted consultant in operations management, says that the just-in-time approach may be the most important productivity-enhancing management innovation since the turn of the century.[15] All this is true, he says, merely because the system allows production and purchasing to be done in small quantities and no earlier than necessary for use. But JIT can also add important discipline to the production process and further support the use of teamwork. In the absence of backup inventories, materials scheduling must be done well, materials must be of usable quality when they arrive, and the workers must continually strive to use them well in the ongoing production process.

Materials requirements planning is an integrated inventory planning and control system that is also popular in complex manufacturing and service operations. MRP, as it is called, is a computer-based technique for ensuring that the right materials and component parts are always available as needed at each stage of the production process—for example, each stage in automobile assembly. An MRP computer system is able to ensure a smooth and efficient flow of materials and components to meet the requirements of manufacturing and service schedules. It is also able to make updates as changes in master schedules are made. MRP not only handles the inventory elements, but also updates schedules and resources when rush orders are received.

MRP is a powerful managerial tool that quickly increases in complexity when applied to operations that involve many different component parts, such as the new Boeing 777 airplane. Fortunately, computers make MRP easy and readily supply managers with good information that helps anticipate materials needs, analyze lead times, release purchase orders, and plan production runs in accord with the master schedule. A further development in this area, **manufacturing resources planning,** or MRPII, extends control of resources into all aspects of operations. The system links production schedules with purchasing, accounting, sales, engineering, market-

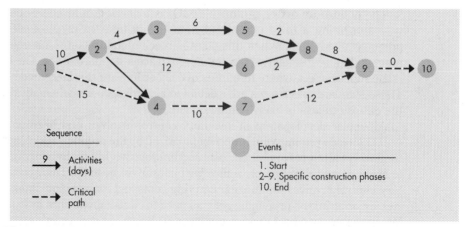

Figure 8.3 A PERT diagram showing the critical path for a construction project.

ing, finance, and other business functions. Using complex software, MRPII collects and analyzes data through all stages of operations to support a broad array of managerial decisions—cost accounting, plant maintenance, distribution planning, and many other areas. Because MRPII integrates so many functions, it adds considerable efficiency to the operations planning and control process. It allows for better utilization of financial and human resources, as well as the physical plant and equipment.

Project Management

The term *project* is used to describe an entire set of actions needed to create single products (goods or services) that are not complete until many—perhaps hundreds—of individual tasks are finished in a particular sequence. An example would be the production of a nuclear submarine, or the construction of an athletic stadium. *Project management,* in these and other settings, is the responsibility of making sure that various activities are completed on time, in the order specified, and with a level of quality sufficient to guarantee the success of the final product.

Among the techniques used to facilitate project management is the **program evaluation and review technique,** PERT, which identifies and controls the many separate events required to complete a project. The use of *PERT diagrams* such as the one shown in Figure 8.3 is common in project management. The diagrams chart the relationships among various phases of a project, with key activities being identified according to anticipated time requirements. The model makes it possible to plan for effective completion of a project by ensuring that activities on all paths get done in proper sequence and on time. The path requiring the longest time to accomplish is designated the *critical path.* Any delays encountered in this path will lengthen the entire project and, most likely, increase costs.

Statistical Quality Control

Every organization should be concerned with the quality of its outputs. **Quality control** involves the process of checking products or services to ensure that they meet certain standards. The purpose of quality control is to ensure that the finished good or service produced by an organization is of high standards. The process of quality control, however, is applied to all aspects of production and operations from the selection of raw materials and supplies right down to the last task performed on the finished good or service. Properly done, quality control improves productivity by reducing waste on the input side and reducing rejects on the output side. More and more frequently these days, the emphasis is on *total quality management,* as already discussed earlier in this book.

One foundation of any quality improvement program is *statistical quality control.* To illustrate how the process might work, consider the case of an engine crankshaft for an automobile. These crankshafts are first molded, then machined to the correct dimensions. Because of variation in the parts, wear on the equipment, and differences among the skills of machine operators, not all crankshafts will have exactly the same dimensions after machining. That's not totally bad in itself because the crankshaft will still perform properly as long as its dimensions are within certain limits. For instance, the diameter at a certain point on a crankshaft should be 1.28 inches; the part will still function if the diameter is between 1.26 inches (the lower control limit) and 1.30 inches (the upper control limit).

The quality of these crankshafts might be checked by measuring each one as it is completed. If the diameter of a crankshaft is within the upper and lower control limits, it passes; otherwise it fails and must be reworked. An occasional crankshaft falling outside the limits would not be cause for managerial concern, it would simply be rejected. However, several rejects might mean the machining process is out of control and requires correction.

This same concept can be extended to very large operations by using statistical concepts to set upper and lower control limits and monitor performance in respect to them. In such cases, instead of checking every part, batches of a product or service are checked by taking a random sample from each. This is called inspection by statistical sampling. Because of the inherent difficulty of carefully inspecting every raw-material input or product/service output, most quality control is accomplished via statistical sampling procedures. The information made available for managerial control is of equal significance and is more efficient in larger and more complex operations.

In Summary

What is the control process?

- Controlling, the fourth management function, is the process of monitoring performance and taking corrective action as needed.
- The four steps in the control process are: (1) establish performance objectives, (2) measure actual performance, (3) compare results with objectives, and (4) take necessary action to resolve problems or to take advantage of special opportunities.

- Management by objectives, MBO, is a process through which supervisors work with their subordinates to jointly set performance goals and jointly review performance results.
- MBO can be effectively used by managers as an integrated approach to planning and controlling.

How do managerial controls work?

- Feedforward controls, also called preliminary controls, are accomplished before a work activity begins.
- Feedforward control ensures that directions are clear and that the right resources are available to accomplish them.
- Concurrent controls, sometimes called steering controls, monitor ongoing operations and activities to make sure that things are being done correctly.
- Concurrent control allows for corrective actions to be taken while the work is being done.
- Feedback controls, also called postaction controls, take place after an action is completed and focus on end results.
- Feedback control is based on the question: "Now that we are finished, how well did we do?"

What organizational systems assist in control?

- Internal control occurs through individual responsibility for one's work; external control is accomplished through personal supervision and the use of formal administrative systems.
- Administrative control is facilitated by the management functions of planning, organizing, and leading.
- An organization's compensation and benefits system assists in control by helping to attract and retain a high-quality workforce.
- Discipline is the process of influencing behavior through reprimand.
- Progressive discipline links reprimands to the severity and frequency of inappropriate behavior.

How do information systems facilitate control?

- A management information system, or MIS, collects, organizes, stores, and distributes data in a way that meets the information needs of managers.
- Most management information systems are now computerized and able to store, analyze, and present large amounts of data in easy-to-use fashion for managers.
- Decision-support systems provide information and help managers make decisions to solve complex problems; group-decision support systems utilize

groupware to allow for computer-mediated collaboration among group members.

- Executive information systems are designed to help meet the information and decision-making needs of senior managers.

How does operations management facilitate control?

- Operations management can improve control by assisting in the management of purchasing, inventories, and projects, as well as with statistical quality control.
- The economic order quantity (EOQ) method controls inventories by ordering a fixed number of items every time inventory level falls to a predetermined point.
- The program evaluation review technique (PERT) is a means of controlling many separate events over the time frame of a complex project.
- Just-in-time scheduling (JIT) attempts to reduce costs and improve workflows by scheduling materials to arrive at a workstation or facility "just in time" to be used.
- Statistical quality control uses mathematical techniques and statistical sampling to check products or services to ensure that they meet certain standards.

VALUING DIVERSITY:

INDIVIDUAL DIFFERENCES

As you read Chapter 9, keep in mind these study questions:

- What is workforce diversity?

- What are individual differences?

- What is perception?

- What are multicultural organizations?

*W*orkforce diversity* is here to stay. Managers must be prepared to value diversity and respect individual differences in today's complex work environments. The best managers create positive work settings in which diversity boosts productivity and competitive advantage. This challenge—to value diversity and respect individual differences—is raised again and again throughout this book. Dr. Renee Lerche knows it firsthand. In her position as director of training, education, and development at Ford, Dr. Lerche oversees and develops training programs worldwide and helps in hiring thousands of workers. Her commitment to diversity includes the beliefs that "diversity should be about inclusion . . . we should be looking at making all of our people better."[1] Lerche admits that senior management at Ford is almost all men. But she is one of three women on an executive committee drafting ways to remove barriers to advancement by women and minorities. In all this Dr. Lerche respects the advice of her father, a union organizer. "I can remember being a little girl and being told I was going to get a doctorate," she says. "You've got to achieve," her father told her.

Managers and Workforce Diversity

It used to be that most managers dealt with a fairly uniform workforce consisting mostly of white males. Times have changed. More than half of the U.S. workforce is now composed of women, minorities, and immigrants. White, native-born male workers are a statistical minority and will continue to be so at least well into the next century.[2] In this context, the term **workforce diversity** describes demographic differences—principally in respect to age, gender, race, national origin, and physical characteristics—that help to differentiate individual members of the workforce. Today, managers in all settings are being asked to achieve high productivity and create high quality-of-work-life environments for a workforce that is increasingly diverse.

Trends in Workforce Diversity

When published in 1987 by the Hudson Institute, *Workforce 2000: Work and Workers for the 21st Century* created an immediate stir in business circles, among government policymakers, and in the public eye.[3] It called attention to the following demographic trends in the U.S. workforce that could have important management and social policy implications by the year 2000.

- The size of the workforce is growing more slowly.
- The available pool of younger workers is shrinking.
- The average age of workers is rising.
- More women are entering the workforce.
- The proportion of ethnic minorities in the workforce is increasing.
- The proportion of immigrants in the workforce is increasing.

Valuing Diversity

A subsequent follow-up study by Towers Perrin and the Hudson Institute confirmed that these trends are being felt in the American workplace.[4] With younger workers in shorter supply, with more women employed, and with more workers from single-parent or two-career households, for example, employers are feeling the pressure to be more family friendly. Many progressive employers are expanding their support for worker needs to include children's day-care and elder-care services, more flexible work scheduling, better parental leave policies, and other related programs.

Yes, increased diversity in the workplace reinforces the importance of fair employment practices. It also offers potential performance gains for those employers who can successfully tap the talents of a diverse workforce.[5] A female vice-president at Avon sets the goals when she calls managing diversity "a question of consciously creating an environment where *everyone* has an equal shot at contributing, participating, and most of all, advancing."[6] But, even though the goal of valuing diversity may be clear, bias and misunderstanding are still limiting factors in too many settings.[7] They can take the form of **prejudice,** the display of negative, irrational attitudes toward individuals because of their minority group identity. They can also take the form of **discrimination,** where prejudice results in actual disadvantage to minorities by denying them full benefits of organizational membership.

Consider what some call the **glass-ceiling effect,** where an invisible barrier may prevent women and minority workers from rising above a certain level of organizational responsibility.[8] Not long ago, the glass ceiling of cultural and other barriers limiting the advancement of women and minorities into the management was the target of a study by the U.S. Department of Labor. The study of ninety-four large employers found that although 37 percent of the workforce was female and 16 percent minority, only 7 percent of their executives were women and 3 percent were minorities.[9] When confronted with the data, nine of the companies signed affirmative action agreements to improve advancement opportunities for minorities and to end discriminatory practices. This attack on the glass ceiling proceeds on many fronts and in a growing number of organizations. But even as the U.S. workforce grows more diverse, one fact remains clear—top management jobs are still held disproportionately by white men. Indeed, the lack of advancement opportunity in larger corporate enterprises is one reason cited for the growth in smaller business ownership by women and minorities.

THE EFFECTIVE MANAGER 9.1

Abilities and Skills for Twenty-first Century Managers

- **Social objectivity**—ability to act free of racial, ethnic, gender, and other biases
- **Inner work standards**—ability to set and meet high personal work goals
- **Introspection**—ability to learn from experience and self-study
- **Adaptability**—ability to modify personal behavior to reach a goal
- **Entrepreneurism**—ability to spot and take advantage of opportunities
- **Stamina**—ability to sustain long work hours
- **Self confidence**—ability to be consistently decisive

Individual Differences

Because diversity is now a fact of organizational life, managers must master the challenges of fully understanding what researchers call **individual differences**—the demographic, competency, and personality characteristics that make each person a unique human being. In this respect, the concept of individual differences requires managers to focus on what one diversity consultant refers to as "enabling every member of your workforce to perform to his or her potential."[10] While easily said, this may not be easy for some to do—especially those generations of managers used to dealing with more homogeneous work groups in more traditional work settings. Today's managers must be more broadly informed and capable in recognizing and dealing with individual differences based on abilities and skills, demographics, personality factors, and values and attitudes.

Abilities and Skills

Ability, the capacity to do a particular task well, is a cornerstone of performance in any job. And it plays a key role in the management process. An inescapable responsibility of all managers is to staff the jobs under their supervision with people who have the abilities needed to perform at the highest possible levels of achievement. Closely related to this is supporting job incumbents with the training and development opportunities needed to maintain their abilities over time. In today's environment of change and high technology, a commitment to employee training and development is essential to organizational success. A common productivity loss in organizations is the untapped or underutilized potential of capable employees who are not given the opportunities to develop their abilities to full advantage.

Skills are well-developed task competencies. By way of example, The Effective Manager 9.1 reviews selected competencies that a twenty-first century manager should possess, adding further to those already described in Chapter 1 (Effective Manager 1.2). Both listings are opportunities for you to do a skills and abilities "self-check" from a personal and professional development perspective.[11]

Demographics

Age, gender, and racial or cultural differences are among the most common demographic characteristics considered in respect to workforce diversity. Each is a potential source of prejudice and discrimination as previously discussed, and each may be the source of perceptual distortions to be discussed in the next section. Here, we should simply recognize that there is no consistent evidence that task competency varies on any demographic criterion. Indeed, in the United States, a core foundation of laws protects individuals against discrimination in employment based on demographic factors. Among these, the Civil Rights Act of 1964, the Civil Rights Act Amendments of 1991, and the Equal Employment Opportunity Act of 1972 stand out for their guarantees of individual liberties in the form of **equal employment opportunity** (EEO)—the right to employment without regard to race, color, national origin, religion, or gender. EEO is federally enforced by the Equal Employment Opportunity Commission (EEOC) and generally applies to all public and private organizations employing fifteen or more people. Virtually everyone is accorded this legal protection. The Age Discrimination Act of 1981 gives it to people between the ages of 40 and 70; the Americans with Disabilities Act of 1990 extends such protection to the disabled.

As a general rule, the various statutes on employment discrimination do not restrict the employer's right to establish *bona fide occupational qualifications.* These are criteria for employment that can be clearly justified as being related to a person's capacity to perform a job. However, in order to prevent a man from becoming an airline flight attendant or a woman from becoming a pilot, for example, an airline recruiter would have to prove that a person of that gender could not do the job in question.

EEO legislation helps guarantee people's rights as employees to fair treatment in all aspects of human resource management and staffing. As a manager, it requires you to act in accordance with the principles of equal opportunity. Failure to do so is not only unjustified in a free society, it can also be a very expensive mistake. When discrimination is encountered, legal charges can be filed and court action taken to resolve complaints. Three female employees of Evelth Mines in Minnesota, for example, charged in court that they were subject to illegal sexual harassment by having to deal with obscene graffiti, sexually explicit pictures, and sexual comments from male co-workers. Furthermore, they claimed that this created a hostile work environment that helped perpetuate beliefs that mining was not "women's work."[12]

Personalities

When it comes to **personality,** the term is typically defined to include the enduring and relatively stable profile of traits that make each person unique in the eyes of others. Among the facets of personality that are often considered important to management and organizational behavior are cognitive style, locus of control, and machiavellianism.

The issue of **cognitive style** deals with the way people gather, process, and inter-

Sensation–thinking types—tend to be thorough, logical and sensitive to details; they are practical, dependable, and applied in dealing with problems.	Intuitive–thinking types—tend to be independant, critical, and insightful; they are creative, spontaneous, and full of ideas in dealing with problems.
Sensation–feeling types—tend to be dedicated, conscientious, and respon-sible; they are methodical and pragmatic in dealing with problems.	Intuitive–feeling types—tend to be social and charismatic; they are people–oriented, helpful, and participative in dealing with problems.

Figure 9.1   Personality dimensions on the Myers–Briggs Type Indicator.

pret information for decision-making purposes. Importantly, people of different cog-nitive styles may have difficulty working well together in problem-solving situations and in various types of group activities. By being more aware of the differences, however, it is expected that accommodations and adjustments can be made to better deal with this aspect of individual differences. One popular instrument used to mea-sure alternative cognitive styles and to help develop this sensitivity is the Myers–Briggs Type Indicator, or MBTI.[13] As noted in Figure 9.1, individuals with different dominant tendencies on the MBTI can also be expected to display quite different behaviors in problem-solving and decision-making situations.

Another important personality dimension is the **locus of control,** or degree to which a person believes it is their own behavior that most influences what happens to them. According to researchers, some people tend to be *internals* who believe they are largely in control of their own fates or destinies. Others, by contrast, are *externals* who believe they are mainly controlled by outside forces or events over which they have very little control.[14] The two personalities tend to have quite differ-ent implications in the workplace. Externals can be expected to be more outgoing and social, and perhaps even more inclined toward managerial positions. Internals can be expected to be more introverted, less prone to interpersonal relationships, and perhaps more conforming in their work behaviors.

The sixteenth century classic *The Prince* by Nicolo Machiavelli gives rise to an additional personality dimension relevant to the management and organizational be-havior.[15] In the book, Machiavelli offers insight and advice on the acquisition and use of power. Today, we use the term **machiavellianism** to describe the personality of someone inclined toward manipulation and political control of other people. Re-searchers refer to the *high-Mach* personality as one comfortable in unstructured situations with room open to negotiate and maneuver to obtain resources; a high-Mach person may be expected to do whatever is necessary to get what he or she wants.[16] The *low-Mach* personality is more comfortable in structured situations with

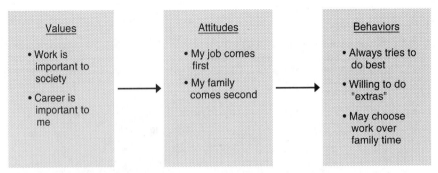

Figure 9.2 The relationship among values, attitudes, and work-related behaviors.

clear expectations for behavior; a low-Mach personality is less likely to seek personal gains at whatever costs to others.

Values and Attitudes

Formally defined, **values** are broad beliefs, preferences, viewpoints, and inclinations forming a person's approach to the surrounding world.[17] One recent description of work-related values notes that individuals may vary in their basic inclinations toward achievement, concern for others, honesty, and fairness.[18] The sources of individual values tend to lie in the combined influences of family, friends, teachers, and others with whom someone is closely associated. Values also derive from culture and experiences, with important foundations set in one's early childhood.

In contrast to values, **attitudes** are more specific "likes" and "dislikes" that result in predispositions to behave in certain ways toward other people, objects, and events. Of course, a most important work-related attitude is *job satisfaction,* the degree to which an individual feels positively or negatively about various aspects of the job. It represents the personal meaning or perceived *quality* of one's job and associated work experiences. It may also help predict the occurrence of important workplace behaviors such as tendencies to work hard or not, to be absent or not, and to be helpful or not to others. More specifically, job satisfaction often reflects attitudes toward such aspects of one's work as pay, tasks, supervision, co-workers, and advancement opportunities.

Figure 9.2 offers one view of the relationship between values, attitudes, and workplace behavior. In the figure, a person values work as an important part of his or her self-fulfillment. This value is linked to the attitude that "work comes first—family comes second." This leads to tendencies to work long hours, work weekends, and, in general, give priority to work rather than family commitments.

Perception and Individual Differences

Perception is the process through which people receive and interpret information from the environment. It is the way we form impressions about ourselves, other people, and daily life experiences, and the way we process information into the decisions that ultimately guide our actions. Perception acts as a screen or filter through which information must pass before it has an impact on individual decisions and actions. Depending on individual values, needs, cultural background, and other circumstances of the moment, information will pass through this screen with varying interpretations and degrees of accuracy. Perception, simply put, may obscure individual differences and cause errors in the way we view other people.

The "bottom line" in understanding the importance of perception to the process of management is that people can perceive the same things quite differently. In this time of cultural and workforce diversity, great value is placed on respect for individual differences. Yet, four common perceptual distortions—stereotypes, halo effects, selective perceptions, and projections—can obscure individual differences and prevent us from drawing accurate impressions of a person or situation. To the extent that our perceptions are biased and inaccurate, furthermore, the decisions we make and the way we deal with people and events will be negatively affected.

Stereotypes

A **stereotype** occurs when an individual is identified with a group or category, and then oversimplified attributes associated with the group or category are assigned to the individual in question. Common stereotypes are those of young people, old people, teachers, students, union members, males, and females, among others. The phenomenon, in each case, is the same: A person is classified into a group on the basis of one piece of information—age, for example. Characteristics commonly associated with the group (e.g., "Young people do not respect authority") are then assigned to the individual. But, what is generalized about the group might or might not be true about the individual.

Stereotypes based on such factors as gender, age, and race can, and unfortunately still do, bias perceptions of people in some work settings.[19] The glass ceiling, mentioned earlier in this book as an invisible barrier to career advancement, still exists in some places. Although employment barriers caused by *gender stereotypes* are falling, women, for example, may still suffer from false impressions and biases tied to them. Consider these examples of how the behavior of female workers may be misinterpreted in comparison to their male counterparts.

> **Case #1** *He's* having lunch with the boss. (Interpretation: He's on his way up.) *She's* having lunch with the boss. (Interpretation: They must be having an affair.)
>
> **Case #2** *He's* talking with coworkers. (Interpretation: He's discussing a new deal.) *She's* talking with coworkers. (Interpretation: She's gossiping.)[20]

Age stereotypes also exist in the workplace. The following examples show how the inappropriate use of age stereotypes by managers may place older workers at a disadvantage in various work situations.

> **Case #1** Someone must be promoted to fill an important challenging job. *Impact of age stereotype:* Manager assumes older workers lack creativity, are cautious, and tend to avoid risk; the older worker is not selected for promotion.

Case #2 An older individual requests reassignment to a job requiring substantial physical strength. *Impact of age stereotype:* Manager assumes older workers are weak because their physical strength has declined with age; the older worker is asked to withdraw the request for transfer.[21]

The presence of *racial stereotypes* can still confound the sensibilities and opportunities of the workplace. When it comes to "glass ceilings," for example, questions can be raised on the slow progress of African American managers into America's corporate mainstream. Their numbers in the executive ranks remain disappointingly low, despite clear advances over the past two decades.

Halo Effects

A **halo effect** occurs when one attribute is used to develop an overall impression of a person or situation. This involves generalization from only one attribute to the total person or event. When meeting a new person, for example, the halo effect may cause one trait, such as a pleasant smile, to result in a positive first impression. By contrast, a particular hairstyle or manner of dressing may create a negative reaction.

Halo effects cause the same problem for managers as do stereotypes—that is, individual differences become obscured. This is especially significant in respect to a manager's view of subordinates' work performance. One factor, such as a person's punctuality, may become the "halo" for a positive overall performance evaluation. But just as it is not correct to assume that anyone who comes to work early is necessarily a good performer, occasional lateness should not be equated with poor overall performance. Even though the general conclusion seems to make sense, it may or may not be true in a given circumstance. The manager's job is to get accurate impressions and not allow halo effects to result in biased performance evaluations.

Selective Perception

Selective perception is the tendency to single out for attention those aspects of a situation or person that reinforce or appear consistent with one's existing beliefs, values, or needs. What this often means in an organization is that people from different departments or functions tend to see things from their own points of view—and tend *not* to recognize other points of view.

Like the other perceptual distortions just discussed, selective perception can bias the way a manager deals with specific situations and people. One way to reduce its impact is to gather additional opinions from others. This adds multiple perceptions to the singular point of view of the manager. When the alternative perceptions prove contradictory, efforts should be made to check one's original impression to create the most appropriate basis for decision making and action.

Projection

Projection is the assignment of personal attributes to other individuals. A classic projection error is assuming other persons share our needs, desires, and values.

Suppose, for example, that you enjoy a lot of responsibility and challenge in your work. Suppose, too, that you are the newly appointed supervisor of people whose work seems dull and routine. You move quickly to redesign their jobs by adding more responsibility and challenge. This might not be a good decision. Instead of designing the subordinates' jobs to best fit their needs, you have designed their jobs to fit yours. In fact, your subordinates may be quite satisfied and productive doing jobs that, to you, seem routine. By projecting your desires onto others, you might inadvertently draw the wrong impressions and make erroneous decisions. This tendency can be controlled by self-awareness and by a willingness to empathize with others and to try to see things from their points of view.

Perception and Attribution

Another perceptual tendency is identified by *attribution theory,* or the study of the ways in which people assign causes to or interpret the reasons for people's behaviors. Consider the case of a poor-performing subordinate. Is a performance deficiency due to some internal weakness or failure of the individual as a person? Or, is it due to some external deficiency or failure in the environment? In this example *attribution error* may lead the manager to blame a subordinate's poor performance on internal causes such as a lack of skills or insufficient motivation. The manager's response, in turn, may be to offer training (to improve skills) or to offer rewards or threaten punishment (to improve motivation). However, the actual causes of the poor performance may be external to the individual, resting instead with the work environment. Perhaps we have a very capable person who lacks the goals, technology, resources, or other support needed to use his or her talents to maximum advantage. In this case, skills training is not needed and the motivation to work hard is already there. The missing element is outside support—something the manager might readily provide, *if* the need is recognized. Unless the manager is on guard against attribution errors, however, the opportunity to improve performance by providing better support is likely to be missed.

Multicultural Organizations

Workforce diversity and individual differences are real; they are facts of organizational life. There is no reason why progressive managers and organizations cannot respect and, indeed, utilize the rich potential of diversity to gain competitive advantage and achieve high performance results. But standing in contrast to this ideal concept of "valuing diversity" are the forces of *ethnocentrism,* the tendency of people to consider their own cultures and ways superior to any and all others. We know the concept best as it applies across the boundaries of national cultures. But ethnocentrism is just as much of a threat inside organizations. Like nations, organizations contain *subcultures* or *co-cultures.* These are the cultures common to groups of people with similar values and beliefs based on shared personal characteristics.

```
THE EFFECTIVE MANAGER 9.2
```
Characteristics of the Multicultural Organization

- **Pluralism**—Members of both minority cultures and majority cultures are influential in setting key values and policies.
- **Structural integration**—Minority-culture members are well-represented in jobs at all levels and in all functional responsibilities.
- **Informal network integration**—Various forms of mentoring and support groups assist in the career development of minority-culture members.
- **Absence of prejudice and discrimination**—A variety of training and task-force activities continually address the need to eliminate culture-group biases.
- **Minimum intergroup conflict**—Diversity does not lead to destructive conflicts between members of majority cultures and minority cultures.

Organizations contain subcultures formed around occupational, ethnic, racial, gender, age, and other groupings. In order to meet the goals of valuing diversity and respecting individual differences in these settings, people must be comfortable working together across subculture borders. They must be able to avoid the everyday pitfalls of ethnocentrism. Increasingly, the term **multicultural organization** is used to describe an organization that is internally rich in diversity that operates in every way in full respect for individual differences and subculture differences. The directions in which organizations should be moving in this respect are shown in The Effective Manager 9.2.[22]

Occupational Subcultures

In his book *Clash of Cultures,* Joseph Raelin discusses how "salaried professionals"—lawyers, scientists, engineers, accountants, and the like—may be members of occupational subcultures that must be understood by the people who manage them.[23] In particular, he suggests that professionals have needs for work autonomy that may conflict with traditional management methods of top-down direction and control. Unless these needs are recognized and dealt with properly, salaried professionals may prove difficult to integrate into the culture of the larger organization.

Ethnic and Racial Subcultures

Hofstede's research, as reported in Chapter 3, helps us understand some ethnic cultures based on how values may vary across national boundaries.[24] But this is just a starting point for understanding differences in ethnic cultures. It is a broad-brush view that must be supplemented by other understandings gained through direct contact, personal commitment, and genuine openness in dealing with people of different ethnic backgrounds. Hofstede's framework is a useful beginning for those active in international business relationships. It may also help managers gain initial insights for dealing with immigrant groups in the domestic workforce.

As imprecise as our understanding of ethnic subcultures may be, things seem even less clear on matters of race. Although references are often made to "African American," "Asian American," and "Anglo" or "Caucasian" cultures, one has to wonder: Do members of *racial subcultures* have a framework for understanding the culture of one another? And if we in management are ready to admit that improved cross-cultural understandings can help people work better across national boundaries, why can't improved cross-cultural understandings help people from different racial subcultures work better together?

Generational Subcultures

We live at a time when the general population in many countries is aging and the "graying" of the workforce is a recognized phenomenon. But the influence of *generational subcultures* at work is more subtle than young–old issues alone. Raelin, for example, describes "generational gaps" among people who grew up during different periods of history and whose values have thus evolved under very different influences. He notes that the "defiant '60s kids"—those who were teens in the 1960s—have strong needs to experience participative decision making. They may have difficulty working today with higher-level managers whose values were set in the 1950s and who may be more inclined toward hierarchy and top-down operations. It is interesting to ponder how the '90s kids—often called the "Generation Xers"—will do in the future when working with managers of the 1960s and 1970s subcultures.[25]

Gender Subcultures

The issues of gender and the glass-ceiling effect linked to gender discrimination continue to complicate the workplace. Some research shows that when men work together, a male group culture forms. It typically has a competitive atmosphere rich in sports metaphors; and where the games and stories deal with winning and losing in various situations.[26] When women work together, a rather different group culture may form—one involving more personal relationships and an emphasis on collaboration. We can reasonably ask: What happens when *gender subcultures* mix in the organization? What happens when a representative of one gender subculture is placed in charge of people from the other? Women are still underrepresented in many management capacities, especially in top management ranks. If men primarily control this level of operations, isn't it likely that resulting organizational practices—even corporate cultures—will reflect values and ways of the majority male subculture? Answers to these and related questions are still needed as progressive managers address gender issues in the workplace.

People in organizations must avoid the pitfalls of negative cultural clashes based on gender or any other factors. As times change, progressive managers must help their organizations to develop along multicultural lines. There is no reason why organizations cannot identify core values and encourage common work directions while still respecting individual and subculture differences.

In Summary

What is workforce diversity?

- Workforce diversity is the pattern of demographic differences in respect to age, gender, race, national origin, and other characteristics that help to differentiate individual members of the workforce.

- Demographic changes in the workforce are having an important impact on the management of organizations today.

- The best organizations and managers value diversity and respect individuals for their talents and potential.

- Unfortunately, prejudice and discrimination still exist in the workplace; the glass-ceiling effect refers to an invisible barrier that may limit the career advancement of minority-group members in certain situations.

What are individual differences?

- Individual differences are personal characteristics that make each person unique.

- Individual differences relevant to management and organizational behavior include abilities and skills, demographics, personality factors, and values and attitudes.

What is perception?

- Perception is the process through which people receive and process information from their environments.

- Inaccurate perceptions obscure individual differences and cause errors in the way people view one another and situations.

- Stereotypes, based, for example, on age or gender, generalize assumed group characteristics to an individual.

- Halo effects generalize from one attribute of an individual to an overall evaluation of the person.

- Selective perception sees only those aspects of a person or situation that are consistent with one's personal viewpoints or expectations.

- Projection assumes that others have similar needs, desires, and values to one's own.

- Attribution error is the tendency to make incorrect judgments when evaluating other people's behavior.

What are multicultural organizations?

- A multicultural organization is rich in internal diversity and operates with respect for individual differences and subcultural differences.
- Important subcultures or co-cultures in organizations include those based on occupations, race and ethnicity, age, and gender, among other possibilities.

10

MOTIVATING: REWARDS

AND REINFORCEMENT

As you read Chapter 10, keep in mind these study questions:

- How does motivation influence performance?

- What are the different types of individual needs?

- What are the insights of process theories of motivation?

- What role does reinforcement play in motivation?

- How does compensation influence motivation?

W hy do some people outperform others in their work? What can be done to ensure that maximum performance is achieved by every employee? These questions are, or should be, asked by managers in all work settings, and they will continue to be important in our dynamic environment. Good answers rest on a foundation of respect for people, with all their talents and diversity, as human resources of organizations. Managers in progressive organizations already know this; their leadership approaches reflect an awareness that "productivity through people" is a key ingredient for long-term success. The corporate philosophy of Dana Corporation is a well-known example. It states, in part: "We are dedicated to the belief that our people are our most important asset. We will encourage all of them to contribute and to grow to the limit of their desire and ability. We believe people respond to recognition, freedom to contribute, opportunity to grow, and to fair compensation."[1]

Motivation and Rewards

The term **motivation** is used in management theory to describe forces within the individual that account for the level, direction, and persistence of *effort* expended at work. Simply put, a highly motivated person works hard at a job; an unmotivated person does not. A manager who leads through motivation does so by creating conditions under which other people with whom the manager works feel inspired to work hard. Obviously, a highly motivated workforce is indispensable if high performance outcomes are to be consistently achieved in organizations.

A **reward** is formally defined as a work outcome of positive value to the individual. A motivational work setting is rich in rewards for people whose performance accomplishments help meet organizational objectives. There are two basic types of rewards available to people at work—extrinsic and intrinsic rewards. **Extrinsic rewards** are externally administered. They are valued outcomes given to someone by another person—typically, a supervisor or higher-level manager. Common examples of extrinsic rewards available in the workplace are incentive pay, promotion, time off, special assignments, office fixtures, benefits, awards, verbal praise, and the like. In all cases, the motivational stimulus of extrinsic rewards originates *outside* the individual.[2]

Intrinsic rewards, or *natural rewards,* are self-administered. They occur "naturally" as a person performs a task. They are, in this sense, built directly into the job itself. The major sources of intrinsic rewards are the feelings of competency, personal development, and self-control people experience in their work.[3] The motivational stimulus of intrinsic rewards is therefore *internal* and does not depend on the actions of some other person. In the next chapter on work systems, both job enrichment and self-managing work teams are described as ways of creating opportunities for internal feelings of accomplishment. Informed managers understand the value of intrinsic rewards and take every effort to encourage "motivation from within."[4]

If used well, both extrinsic and intrinsic rewards can help managers lead effectively through motivation. To do so, however, managers must: (1) respect diversity and individual differences; (2) clearly understand what people want from work; and (3) create and distribute rewards to satisfy these needs while serving the organization's performance interests. The motivation theories with insights to these objectives fall into three main categories, with each having slightly different implications for the management of individual performance at work.

- **Content theories** try to help managers understand human needs and how people with different needs may respond to different work situations
- **Process theories** try to help managers understand how people give meaning to rewards and the work opportunities available to achieve them
- **Reinforcement theory** tries to help managers understand how people's behavior is influenced by its environmental consequences

Content Theories of Motivation

The content theories of motivation explain behavior and attitudes at work based upon individual **needs.** These are physiological or psychological deficiencies that people feel some compulsion to eliminate. Although each of the following theories discusses a slightly different set of needs, all agree that needs cause tensions that influence attitudes and behavior. Good managers establish conditions in which people can satisfy important needs through their work. They also eliminate from the work setting those things that block or interfere with need satisfaction.

Hierarchy of Needs Theory

Abraham Maslow describes a hierarchy of human needs involving the five levels shown in Figure 10.1—physiological, safety, social, esteem, and self-actualization needs. In this hierarchy, the **lower-order needs** include physiological, safety, and social concerns; the **higher-order needs** include esteem and self-actualization.[5] While lower-order needs are concerns for a person's social and physical well-being, the higher-order needs represent a person's desires for psychological development and growth.

Maslow's theory is based on two underlying principles. First is the *deficit principle*—a satisfied need is not a motivator of behavior. People act to satisfy "deprived" needs, those for which a satisfaction "deficit" exists. Second is the *progression principle*—the five needs exist in a hierarchy of prepotency. A need at any

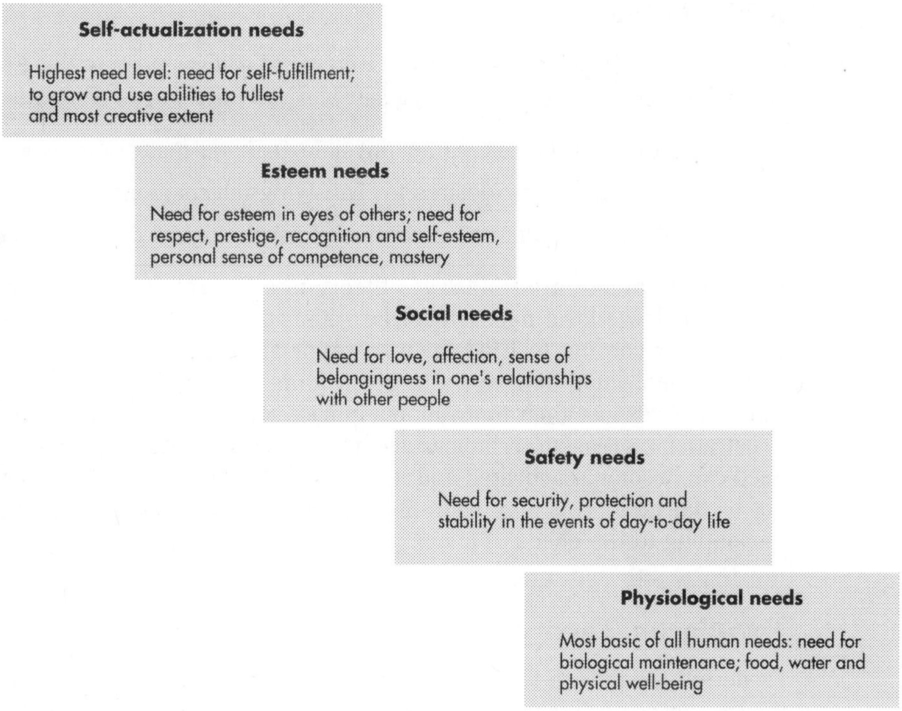

Self-actualization needs

Highest need level: need for self-fulfillment;
to grow and use abilities to fullest
and most creative extent

Esteem needs

Need for esteem in eyes of others; need for
respect, prestige, recognition and self-esteem,
personal sense of competence, mastery

Social needs

Need for love, affection, sense of
belongingness in one's relationships
with other people

Safety needs

Need for security, protection and
stability in the events of day-to-day life

Physiological needs

Most basic of all human needs: need for
biological maintenance; food, water and
physical well-being

Figure 10.1 Maslow's hierarchy of needs: things people want from their work.

level only becomes activated once the next lower-level need has been satisfied. According to Maslow, people try to satisfy the five needs in sequence. They are expected to advance step by step up the hierarchy in their search for need satisfactions. Along the way, a deprived need dominates individual attention and determines behavior until it is satisfied. Then, the next higher-level need is activated, and progression up the hierarchy occurs. At the level of self-actualization, the deficit and progression principles cease to operate. The more this need is satisfied, the stronger it grows. According to Maslow, a person should continue to be motivated by opportunities for self-fulfillment as long as the other needs remain satisfied.

Although research has not verified the strict deficit and progression principles just presented, Maslow's ideas are very helpful for understanding the needs of people at work and for determining what can be done to satisfy them. His theory advises managers to recognize that deprived needs will dominate the attention of people at work and may negatively influence their attitudes and behaviors. By the same token, providing opportunities for need satisfaction may have positive motivational consequences. Figure 10.1 also gives some examples of how managers can use Maslow's ideas to better meet the needs of their subordinates. Notice that the higher-order self-actualization needs are served entirely by intrinsic rewards. The esteem needs are served by both intrinsic and extrinsic rewards. Lower-order needs are served solely by extrinsic rewards.

ERG Theory

One of the most popular efforts to build on Maslow's work is the ERG theory by Clayton Alderfer.[6] His theory collapses Maslow's five needs categories into three:

- **Existence needs** desires for physiological and material well-being
- **Relatedness needs** desires for satisfying interpersonal relationships
- **Growth needs** desires for continued psychological growth and development

ERG theory differs from Maslow's theory in other respects. Alderfer does not assume that lower-level needs must be satisfied before higher-level needs become activated. According to ERG theory, any or all of these three types of needs can influence individual behavior at a given time. Alderfer also does not assume that satisfied needs lose their motivational impact. Rather, ERG theory contains a unique "frustration-regression" principle, according to which an already-satisfied lower-level need can become reactivated and influence behavior when a higher-level need cannot be satisfied. This approach offers an additional means for understanding and responding to the needs of people at work.

Two-Factor Theory

Frederick Herzberg's two-factor theory was developed from a pattern identified in the responses of almost four thousand people to questions about their work.[7] When questioned about what "turned them on," they tended to identify things relating to the nature of the job itself. Herzberg calls these **satisfier factors.** When questioned about what "turned them off," they tended to identify things relating more to the work setting. Herzberg calls these *hygiene factors.*

Beginning with the hygiene factors, the two-factor theory considers them to be sources of *job dissatisfaction* and to be derived from aspects of the *job context.* That is, dissatisfiers are considered more likely to be a part of the work setting than the nature of the work itself. They include such things as working conditions, interpersonal relations, organizational policies and administration, technical quality of supervision, and base wage or salary. Herzberg indicates, furthermore, that improving on these hygiene factors, such as adding piped-in music or implementing a no-smoking policy, can make people less dissatisfied with these background aspects of their work, but it will not directly improve job satisfaction. That, he claims, is controlled by an entirely different set of factors and must be addressed by a very different set of managerial initiatives.

To really improve job satisfaction, Herzberg advises that a manager's attention must be shifted away from concerns for hygiene factors and toward the satisfier factors. These are part of *job content;* they deal with what people actually do in their work; and they directly affect *job satisfaction.* By making improvements in what people are asked to do in their jobs, Herzberg suggests that job satisfaction and performance can be raised. The important satisfier factors include such things as sense of achievement, feelings of recognition, sense of responsibility, opportunity for advancement, and feelings of personal growth.

Herzberg's two-factor theory is a useful reminder that there are two important aspects of all jobs: (1) what people do in terms of job tasks—job content, and (2) the work setting in which they do it—job context.[8] His advice to managers is twofold: always correct poor hygiene to eliminate any sources of job dissatisfaction in the work unit; and build satisfier factors into job content to maximize opportunities for job satisfaction. The two-factor theory cautions managers not to expect too much by way of performance and satisfaction improvements from investments only in such things as special office fixtures, attractive lounges for breaks, and even high base salaries. Rather, it reminds managers that true job satisfaction begins with the nature of the job itself. It directs attention toward such things as responsibility and opportunity for personal growth and development, factors consistent with the job enrichment and self-managing team concepts to be examined in the next chapter.

Acquired-Needs Theory

In the late 1940s, David McClelland and his colleagues began experimenting with the Thematic Apperception Test (TAT) as a way of examining human needs. The TAT asks people to view pictures and write stories about what they see. The stories are then content analyzed for themes that display individual needs.[9] From this research, McClelland identified three needs that are central to his approach to motivation. **Need for Achievement** (nAch) is the desire to do something better or more efficiently, to solve problems, or to master complex tasks. **Need for Power** (nPower) is the desire to control other people, to influence their behavior, or to be responsible for them. **Need for Affiliation** (nAff) is the desire to establish and maintain friendly and warm relations with other people.

According to McClelland, people acquire or develop these needs over time as a result of individual life experiences. In addition, he associates each need with a distinct set of work preferences. Managers are encouraged to recognize the strength of each need in themselves and in other people. Attempts can then be made to create work environments responsive to them. For example, people high in *need for achievement* like to put their competencies to work; they take moderate risks in competitive situations; they are willing to work alone; and they believe the success of a task serves as its own reward. As a result, a person high in nAch generally has these work preferences: work that involves individual responsibility for results, work that involves achievable but challenging goals, and work that provides feedback on performance.

Effective managers may reasonably be expected to be high in nAch. But while an achievement orientation is certainly important, the issue is more complex. In a study of executive careers, for example, McClelland reports that people high in need for achievement advanced quickly in technical fields where individual skills and creativity were required. But their careers tended to peak rather early. Those who advanced to senior management displayed a broader profile of needs that seemed more consistent with higher-level responsibilities. He concludes that success in top management is not based on a concern for individual achievement alone. It requires broader interests that also relate to the needs for power and affiliation.

People high in *need for power* are motivated to behave in ways that have a clear impact on other people and events. They enjoy being in control of a situation and being recognized for this responsibility. A high nPower person has work preferences that include: work that involves control over others, work that has an impact on people and events, and work that brings public recognition and attention.

McClelland distinguishes between two forms of the power need. The need for *personal* power is exploitative and involves manipulation for the pure sake of personal gratification. It is not successful in management. The second form, need for *social* power, is the positive face of power. It is essential to leadership and managerial success. Successful top managers are comfortable with power and enjoy the ability and responsibility to influence other persons' behaviors. But they do so in a socially responsible way that is directed toward organizational rather than personal objectives.

Finally, McClelland notes that people high in *need for affiliation* seek companionship, social approval, and satisfying interpersonal relationships. Their work preferences involve special interest in work that involves interpersonal relationships, work that provides for companionship, and work that brings social approval.

McClelland further suggests that people very high in nAff alone may not make the best managers. For these managers, desires for social approval and friendship may complicate managerial decision making. There are times when managers must decide and act in ways that other persons are likely to disagree with and even resent. To the extent that high nAff interferes with someone's ability to make these decisions, managerial effectiveness will be sacrificed. Thus, the successful executive (in McClelland's view) is likely to possess a high need for social power that is greater than an otherwise strong need for affiliation.

Questions and Answers on Individual Needs

Although the terminology varies, there is a lot of common ground in the theories just presented. Their insights can and should be used together to best understand human needs. By way of further summary, let's pose and answer some common questions about individual needs at work.[10]

"How many different individual needs are there?" Research has not yet identified a perfect list of individual needs at work. But, as a manager, you can use the ideas of Maslow, Alderfer, and McClelland for better understanding the various needs that people may bring with them to the work setting.

"Can a work outcome or reward satisfy more than one need?" Yes, work outcomes or rewards can satisfy more than one need. Pay is a good example. It is a source of performance feedback for the high-need achiever. It can be a source of personal security for someone with strong existence needs. It can also be used indirectly to obtain things that satisfy social and ego needs.

"Is there a hierarchy of needs?" Research does not support the precise five-step hierarchy of needs postulated by Maslow. It seems more legitimate to view human needs as operating in a flexible hierarchy, such as the one in Alderfer's ERG theory. However, it is useful to distinguish between the motivational properties of lower-order and higher-order needs.

"How important are the various needs?" Research is inconclusive as to the importance of different needs. Individuals vary widely in this regard. They may also value needs differently at different times, and at different ages or career stages. This is another reason why managers should use the insights of all the content theories to best understand the differing needs of people at work.

Process Theories of Motivation

Although the details vary, each of the content theories considers managers to be responsible for allocating rewards so that individuals find opportunities to satisfy important needs on the job. Another set of motivation theories deals with the thought processes that underlie individual responses to work situations.

Equity Theory

Equity theory is a process theory of motivation known best through the work of J. Stacy Adams.[11] The essence of the theory is that perceived inequity is a motivating state—that is, when people believe that they have been inequitably treated in comparison to others, they will try to eliminate the discomfort and restore a sense of equity to the situation. This sense of inequity, furthermore, is based on the following *equity comparison:*

$$\frac{\text{Individual's rewards}}{\text{Individual's efforts}} \textit{ compared with } \frac{\text{Others' rewards}}{\text{Others' efforts}}$$

Equity comparisons such as the above typically occur whenever managers allocate extrinsic rewards, especially monetary incentives or pay increases. Perceived inequities occur whenever people believe that the rewards received for their work efforts are unfair, based on the rewards other people appear to be getting. The comparison group might be co-workers, workers elsewhere in the organization, and even people employed by other organizations. Adams predicts that people will respond in one or more of the following ways to perceived inequity: change their work inputs; try to change the rewards received; use different comparison points; rationalize the inequity; or leave the situation.

The research of Adams and others, largely accomplished in the laboratory, lends some support to his predictions. People who feel overpaid—that is, who perceive *positive inequity*—have been found to increase the quantity or quality of their work. Those who feel underpaid—that is, who perceive *negative inequity*—tend to reduce their work efforts to compensate for the missing rewards; that is, they are less motivated to work hard in the future. The research is most conclusive in respect to felt negative inequity. It obviously represents a condition that most managers would want to avoid.

Equity theory reminds us that the way rewards are perceived by their recipients will largely determine how they impact satisfaction and performance. Because feelings of inequity are based on individual perceptions, it is not the reward's absolute value or what a manager thinks that counts. It is what the recipients think that determines motivational outcomes. Rewards perceived as equitable should have a positive result; those perceived as inequitable may create dissatisfaction and reduced performance.

Thus, it is not enough for a manager simply to give rewards. The entire process, including dealing with the way rewards are perceived by recipients, must be well managed. Ultimately, it is the manager's responsibility to ensure that any negative consequences of the equity comparison are avoided, or at least minimized, when rewards are allocated. Informed managers recognize that equity comparisons are likely whenever especially visible rewards such as pay or promotions are allocated. They anticipate felt negative inequities, particularly as co-workers may compare one another's rewards and performance accomplishments. Prepared managers carefully communicate the intended value of the reward being given, an appraisal of the performance on which it is based, and appropriate comparison points.

Expectancy Theory

Victor Vroom's expectancy theory asks a central question: What determines a person's willingness to work hard at important tasks?[12] This question, of course, constitutes the heart of a manager's interest in any motivation theory. In response expectancy theory offers the logic: "People will do what they can do when they want to." More specifically, Vroom suggests that a manager must understand the importance of these three expectancy factors:

- **Expectancy** a person's belief that working hard will result in a desired level of task performance being achieved (this is sometimes called effort–performance expectancy)

- **Instrumentality** a person's belief that successful performance will be followed by rewards and other potential outcomes (this is sometimes called performance–outcome expectancy)

- **Valence** the value a person assigns to the possible rewards and other work-related outcomes

Expectancy theory posits that motivation (M), expectancy (E), instrumentality (I), and valence (V) are related to one another in a multiplicative fashion: $M = E \times I \times V$. In other words, motivation is determined by expectancy times instrumentality times valence. The multiplier effect has important managerial implications. Mathematically speaking, a zero at any location on the right side of the equation (that is for E, I, or V) will result in zero motivation. Managers are thus advised to act in ways that maximize all three components of the motivation equation—expectancy, instrumentality, and valence; not one can be left unattended.

Suppose, for example, that a manager is wondering whether the prospect of earning a promotion will be motivational to a subordinate. A typical assumption is that people will be motivated to work hard to earn a promotion. But is this necessarily true? Expectancy theory predicts that a person's motivation to work hard in the

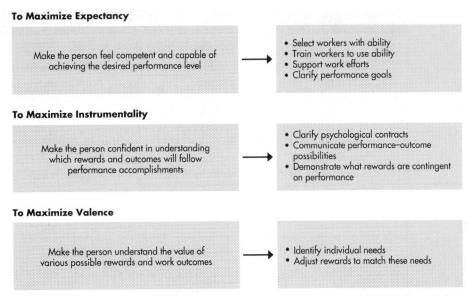

Figure 10.2 Managerial implications of expectancy theory: understanding and responding to the individual's point of view.

prospect of earning a promotion will be low if any one or more of these three conditions apply. First, *if expectancy is low, motivation will suffer.* The person might feel that he or she cannot achieve the performance level necessary to get promoted. So, why try? Second, *if instrumentality is low, motivation will suffer.* The person may lack confidence that a high level of task performance will result in being promoted. So, why try? Third, *if valence is low, motivation will suffer.* The person may place little value on receiving a promotion. It simply isn't much of a reward. So, once again, why try?

Expectancy theory makes managers aware of such issues. It can help them better understand and respond to different points of view in the workplace. As shown in Figure 10.2, this includes working with each individual and trying to maximize their expectancies, instrumentalities, and valences in ways that support organizational objectives. Stated a bit differently, a manager should create a work environment within which task efforts serving the organization's needs are also viewed by subordinates as paths toward highly desirable rewards.

Goal-Setting Theory

Task goals, in the form of clear and desirable performance targets, form the basis of Edwin Locke's goal-setting theory.[13] The theory's basic premise is that task goals can be highly motivating—*if* they are properly set and *if* they are well-managed. Goals can give direction to people in their work. Goals can clarify performance expectations between a superior and subordinate, between co-workers, and between levels of authority in an organization. Goals can establish a frame of reference for task

THE EFFECTIVE MANAGER 10.1

How to Make Goal-Setting Work for You

- **Set specific goals**—They lead to higher performance than more generally stated ones, such as "Do your best."
- **Set challenging goals**—As long as they are viewed as realistic and attainable, more difficult goals lead to higher performance than do easy goals.
- **Build goal acceptance and commitment**—People work harder toward goals that they accept and believe in; they tend to resist goals that seem forced on them.
- **Clarify goal priorities**—Make sure that expectations are clear as to which goals should be accomplished first, and why.
- **Reward goal accomplishment**—Don't let positive accomplishments pass unnoticed; reward people for doing what they set out to do.

feedback. In these and related ways, Locke believes goal setting can enhance individual work performance and job satisfaction.

Research by Locke and his associates indicates, however, that these benefits are realized only when a manager works with subordinates to set the *right* goals in the *right* ways. The key issues and principles in managing the goal-setting process are described in The Effective Manager 10.1.

Participation clearly plays an important role in the goal-setting process. This is the degree to which the person expected to do the work is involved in setting the performance goals. Participation can be a great source of satisfaction for the individuals involved and can also contribute to higher performance. Research indicates that this is most likely to occur when the participation (1) allows for increased understanding of specific and difficult goals, and (2) provides for greater acceptance and commitment to them. Managers should also be aware of participation options. It might not always be possible to allow others to select exactly *which* goals need to be pursued. But it might be possible to allow them to help determine *how* to best pursue the goals. In some settings, furthermore, the constraints of time and other factors may not allow for participation. But, research suggests that people will accept and commit to imposed goals if the people assigning them are trusted, and if the recipients believe they will be adequately supported in attempts to achieve them.

The concept of management by objectives (MBO), introduced in Chapter 5 on planning, is a good illustration of a participative approach to goal setting. As a process of *joint* goal setting by supervisors and subordinates, MBO helps to unlock the motivational power of goal-setting theory.

Reinforcement Theory of Motivation

The content and process theories use cognitive explanations of behavior. They are concerned with explaining "why" people do things in terms of satisfying needs, resolving felt inequities, and/or pursuing positive expectancies and task goals. Reinforcement theory, by contrast, views human behavior as determined by its environmental consequences.[14] Instead of looking within the individual to explain motivation and behavior, it focuses on the external environment and the consequences it holds for the individual. The basic premises of the theory are based on *Thorndike's law of effect:* Behavior that results in a pleasant outcome is likely to be repeated; behavior that results in an unpleasant outcome is not likely to be repeated.[15]

Reinforcement Strategies

The noted psychologist B. F. Skinner popularized the concept of **operant conditioning,** the process of applying the law of effect to control behavior by manipulating its consequences.[16] You may think of operant conditioning as learning, such as to walk, by reinforcement, such as being praised by parents at every step. **Organizational behavior modification,** or *OB Mod* for short, is a term that describes the application of operant conditioning techniques to influence human behavior in the workplace.[17] Its goal is to systematically reinforce desirable work behavior and discourage undesirable work behavior. The four basic OB Mod or reinforcement strategies are:

- **Positive reinforcement** This increases the frequency of or strengthens desirable behavior by making a pleasant consequence contingent upon its occurrence. *Example:* A manager nods to express approval to a subordinate making a useful comment during a staff meeting.
- **Negative reinforcement** This increases the frequency of or strengthens desirable behavior by making the avoidance of an unpleasant consequence contingent upon its occurrence. *Example:* A manager who has been nagging a worker every day about tardiness does not nag when the worker comes to work on time one day.
- **Punishment** This decreases the frequency of or eliminates an undesirable behavior by making an unpleasant consequence contingent upon its occurrence. *Example:* A manager docks the pay of an employee who reports late for work one day.
- **Extinction** This decreases the frequency of or eliminates an undesirable behavior by making the removal of a pleasant consequence contingent upon its occurrence. *Example:* A manager observes that a disruptive employee is receiving social approval from co-workers. The manager counsels co-workers to stop giving this approval.

Positive Reinforcement

Among the OB Mod strategies, positive reinforcement is most important. It must be a central part of any manager's motivational strategy. In order to properly accomplish positive reinforcement, two laws must be understood: the laws of contingent reinforcement and immediate reinforcement.[18] The *law of contingent reinforcement* states:

> ### THE EFFECTIVE MANAGER 10.2
>
> Guidelines for Positive Reinforcement . . . And Punishment
>
> *For Positive Reinforcement:*
> - Clearly identify desired work behaviors.
> - Maintain a diverse inventory of rewards.
> - Inform everyone of what must be done to get rewards.
> - Recognize individual differences in allocating rewards.
> - Follow the laws of immediate reinforcement and contingent reinforcement.
>
> *For Punishment:*
> - Tell the person what is being done wrong.
> - Tell the person what is being done right.
> - Make the punishment match the behavior.
> - Administer the punishment in private.
> - Follow the laws of immediate reinforcement and contingent reinforcement.

In order for a reward to have maximum reinforcing value, it must be delivered only if the desired behavior is exhibited. The *law of immediate reinforcement* states: The more immediate the delivery of a reward after the occurrence of a desirable behavior, the greater the reinforcing value of the reward.

Taken together, these two laws suggest that managers should give rewards as immediately as possible, and contingent on desired behavior. Only then will they have maximum impact as positive reinforcers in the work setting. Managers should take full advantage of the everyday value and power of these laws as they pursue positive reinforcement. They should also apply them to **shaping,** the creation of a new behavior by the positive reinforcement of successive approximations to the desired behavior. Several useful guidelines for positive reinforcement are presented in The Effective Manager 10.2.

The timing of positive reinforcement can also make a difference in its impact. Continuous reinforcement administers a reward each time a desired behavior occurs; intermittent reinforcement rewards behavior only periodically. In general, a manager can expect that: (1) continuous reinforcement will draw forth a desired behavior more quickly than intermittent reinforcement, and (2) behavior acquired under an intermittent schedule will be more permanent than behavior acquired under a continuous schedule. To succeed with a shaping strategy, for example, reinforcement should be given on a continuous basis until the desired behavior is achieved. Then an intermittent schedule should be used to maintain the behavior at the new level.

Punishment

Punishment is a means of eliminating undesirable behavior by administering an unpleasant consequence upon the occurrence of that behavior. To punish an employee, a manager may deny the individual a valued reward, such as verbal praise or merit pay, or the manager may administer an adversive or obnoxious stimulus, such as a verbal reprimand or pay reduction. Like positive reinforcement, punishment can be done poorly or it can be done well. Once again, The Effective Manager 10.2 offers guidance on handling punishment as a reinforcement strategy. Remember, too, that punishment can be combined with positive reinforcement.

Ethical Issues

Testimony to the potential payoffs associated with the use of reinforcement techniques in work settings includes many success stories of improved safety and decreased absenteeism and tardiness, as well as higher productivity.[19] Some critics argue that such positive results may be due only to the fact that specific performance goals were clarified, as in goal-setting theory, and workers were held individually accountable for results.[20] Important also are debates over the ethics of controlling human behavior. From the manager's standpoint, there is concern that using operant conditioning principles ignores the individuality of people, restricts their freedom of choice, and ignores the fact that people can be motivated by things other than externally administered rewards.

Advocates of the reinforcement orientation attack the problem straight on. They agree that it involves the control of behavior. But they argue that behavior control is an irrevocable part of every manager's job. It is inevitable that managers use power and influence the behavior of other people at work. In fact, this influence must be done well if the manager's challenge is to be met successfully. The real question may be not whether it is ethical to control behavior, but whether it is ethical *not* to control behavior well enough that the goals of both the organization and the individual are well served. Thus, even as research continues, the value of reinforcement techniques seems confirmed. This is especially true when they are combined with the insights of the other motivation theories discussed in this chapter.

Motivation and Compensation

Of the many managerial issues in motivation, perhaps none receives as much attention as the special case of compensation. And among the current trends and developments, pay for performance, incentive compensation schemes, and pay for knowledge deserve a special look.[21]

Pay for Performance

In general, the success of any pay-for-performance system rests with its ability to link pay to performance in a clear and credible way. This means that pay is allocated in a performance-contingent and equitable manner. Formally defined, **merit pay** is a system of awarding increases in base compensation based on some measure of individual performance. By allocating pay increases and other important rewards on a merit basis, managers hope to recognize high performers for their achievements and encourage similar and even greater accomplishments in the future. Managers also hope to remind low performers of their lack of achievement and encourage them to do better in the future.

The pay for performance concept is closely tied to equity, expectancy, and reinforcement theories of motivation. To make the necessary link between compensation and motivation, however, "performance" must be agreed-upon, measurable, and well-defined—things that are often difficult to accomplish in actual practice. Thus, managing pay-for-performance systems can be a great challenge to managers.

Incentive Compensation Systems

An alternative approach to motivation and compensation ties monetary incentives to important performance contributions. This may include bonuses, profit-sharing, and related schemes applied to individuals, groups, or both.[22]

Bonus pay plans provide bonuses to employees based on the accomplishment of performance targets or some other extraordinary contribution, such as an idea for a work improvement. Bonuses traditionally have been most common at the executive level, but they are now being used more extensively in many settings. And they can be applied to individuals or groups. At Corning Glass Works, for example, individual achievements may be rewarded by on-the-spot bonuses of 3 to 6 percent of someone's pay. Peter Maier, director of risk management and prevention for the firm, gave about 40 percent of his subordinates individual bonuses in a year. He says: "If someone has done a spiffy job, you need to recognize them."[23]

Profit-sharing plans distribute to some or all employees a proportion of net profits earned by the organization during a stated performance period. The exact amount varies according to the level of profits and each person's base compensation level. For example, at Vatex America, CEO Jerry Gorde instituted a profit-sharing program to help "democratize the work environment" in his $9 million T-shirt and sweatshirt manufacturing firm. The program distributes 10 percent of pre-tax profits to employees each month, and an additional amount at the end of the year. The exact share depends on an individual's monthly attendance, tardiness, and performance as rated by supervisors.[24]

Gain-sharing plans extend the profit-sharing concept by allowing groups of employees to share in any savings or "gains" realized through their efforts to reduce costs and increase productivity. Specific formulas are used to calculate both the performance contributions and gain-sharing awards. A classic example is the *Scanlon Plan,* which usually results in 75 percent of gains being distributed to workers and 25 percent being kept by the company.

Employee stock ownership plans involve employees in ownership through the purchase of stock in the companies that employ them. While formal "ESOP" plans can be used primarily as financing schemes in the business arena, more general stock ownership by employees can be an important performance incentive. A slightly different approach to employee stock ownership operates through **stock options.** These give the option holder the right to buy stock at a future date at a fixed price. When employees hold stock options, they presumably also have an incentive to work hard to raise the price of the firm's stock in the future—at which point they can exercise their option and, in effect, buy the stock at a discount to experience a financial gain. Previously stock options were primarily used in executive compensation. Now they are being extended by some employers.

Pay for Knowledge

Beyond the examples just given, other creative pay schemes are being tried that link pay with knowledge. While varying in approach, they share the objective of raising workforce motivation and encouraging high performance through special compensation. For example, Honeywell and TRW, Inc. use **skills-based pay,** which pays workers according to the number of job-relevant skills they master. Such programs are often found in autonomous work groups or self-managing teams where part of "self-management" includes the training and certification of co-workers in job skills. Another new approach is **entrepreneurial pay,** where individuals put part of their compensation at risk in return for the rights to pursue entrepreneurial ideas within the corporate umbrella and participate in any resulting profits. AT&T encourages new venture development through such a plan. Interested employees may contribute portions of their salaries in return for opportunities to pursue new ideas, and in the prospect of future income gains.[25]

In Summary

How does motivation influence performance?

- Motivation affects the willingness of people to work hard; that is, to put forth high levels of work effort.
- Motivation is influenced by extrinsic (or external) rewards and intrinsic (or natural) rewards.
- The use of rewards by managers should respect individual diversity and reflect an understanding of content, process, and reinforcement theories of motivation.

What are the different types of individual needs?

- Maslow's hierarchy of human needs suggests a progression from lower-order physiological, safety, and social needs, to higher-order ego and self-actualization needs.
- Alderfer's ERG theory identifies existence, relatedness, and growth needs.
- Herzberg's two-factor theory points out the importance of both job content and job context factors in satisfying human needs.
- McClelland's acquired needs theory identifies the needs for achievement, affiliation, and power, all of which may influence what a person desires from work.

What are the insights of process theories of motivation?

- Adams's equity theory recognizes that social comparisons take place when rewards are distributed in the workplace.
- People who feel inequitably treated are motivated to act in ways that reduce the sense of inequity. In some cases this may mean working less hard in the future or finding an alternative job.
- Vroom's expectancy theory states that Motivation = Expectancy × Instrumentality × Valence.
- Expectancy theory encourages managers to make sure that any rewards offered for motivational purposes are achievable and desirable.
- Goal-setting theory, popularized by Edwin Locke, emphasizes the motivational power of goals.
- People tend to work hard and be most highly motivated when task goals are specific rather than ambiguous, are difficult but achievable, and are set through participatory means.

What role does reinforcement play in motivation?

- Reinforcement theory recognizes that human behavior is influenced by its environmental consequences.
- The law of effect states that behavior followed by a pleasant consequence is likely to be repeated; behavior followed by an unpleasant consequence is unlikely to be repeated.
- B. F. Skinner's work with operant conditioning, the control of behavior by manipulating its consequences, has helped apply reinforcement principles to management.
- Skinner's ideas emphasize positive reinforcement to raise the level of motivation in the workplace. When people perform or behave in desirable ways, his advice is to make sure they are positively reinforced.

How does compensation influence motivation?

- Pay-for-performance compensation schemes try to tie pay and related rewards to a worker's performance accomplishments.
- Merit pay links pay increases to individual performance accomplishments.
- Special incentive pay schemes involve gain sharing, profit sharing, and various types of bonus systems designed to encourage worker efforts to improve productivity and organizational performance.
- New directions in compensation involve skills-based pay, which encourages the development of multiple job skills, and entrepreneurial pay, which encourages entrepreneurship and innovation.

11

DESIGNING WORK SYSTEMS: JOBS AND WORK SCHEDULES

As you read Chapter 11, keep in mind these study questions:

- What is the meaning of work?

- What are the alternative job design approaches?

- How can a manager enrich jobs for individual workers?

- Why are self-managing work teams so popular today?

- How can alternative work schedules improve the workplace?

Managers in all organizations—small and large, for-profit and not-for-profit—should be seeking higher productivity through the better use of human resources. Although the approaches vary, the roles of the individual worker and the work team are critical elements in the developments taking place in progressive workplaces. All of this is especially crucial as employers struggle to come to grips with the implications of workforce diversity and the shrinking labor pool. People are less "disposable" in today's labor markets—and rightly so. The pressure is on every employer to develop human resources and use all available talents to their fullest. Unlocking the performance potential of each worker is the order of the day for the modern manager. This chapter is about work and the jobs people are asked to perform in organizations.[1] A central premise is that high performance and high quality of work life can go hand-in-hand.

The Meaning of Work

Work should involve a positive give-and-take, or exchange of values, between the individual and the organization. This sense of mutual benefit is expressed in the concept of a **psychological contract**—a person's expectations about what will be given to and received from an organization as part of the employment relationship.[2] Ideally, this exchange of values will be considered fair. A person offers *contributions,* or valued work activities, to the organization. These contributions, such as effort, time, creativity, and loyalty, are what make the individual a desirable resource for the organization. *Inducements* are things of value that the organization gives to the individual in return for these contributions. Typical inducements include pay, fringe benefits, training, and opportunities for personal growth and advancement. Such inducements should be valued by employees and make it worthwhile for them to work hard for the organization. In a healthy psychological contract, inducements and contributions are in balance.

In a sense, the rest of this chapter deals with managing psychological contracts to create a healthy "fit" among people, jobs, and organizations. The term *quality of work life,* or QWL, was first used in Chapter 1 to describe the overall quality of human experiences in the workplace. Most people spend many hours a week, and many years of their lives, at work. What happens to them at work, how they are treated, and what their work is like can influence their lives overall. QWL, simply put, is an important component in the quality of life for most of us. Thus, serving as a manager—that is, being in a position to directly influence the quality of work

Old Ways	Issue	New Ways
Taller, many management levels	**Structures**	Flatter, fewer management levels
Centralized with top management	**Authority**	Decentralized with "empowerment" at all levels
Large and diversified	**Role of staff**	Small and concentrated
Simplified and narrow; managers "think," workers "do"	**Job designs**	Multiskilled and broad; workers "think" and "do"
Important as a formal administrative unit	**Work group**	"Teams" and integrated sociotechnical systems are emphasized
Pay by job classification and individual performance	**Compensation**	Pay by skills and individual and group performance
Worker is replaceable; training limited to one job	**Training**	Worker is valuable; encouraged to learn new skills and many jobs

Figure 11.1 Trends in the changing nature of the workplace.

life of other people—is a job with high social responsibility. Figure 11.1 identifies some of the trends that are helping advance the quality of life in the modern workplace, all of which are consistent with themes already developed in this book.

Job Design Approaches

A *job* is a collection of tasks performed in support of organizational objectives. **Job design** is the process of creating or defining jobs by assigning specific work tasks to individuals and groups.

What Should Job Design Accomplish?

A good job design creates opportunities for workers to achieve both high levels of job performance and high levels of job satisfaction. Formally defined, **job performance** is the quantity and quality of task accomplishments by an individual or group at work. Performance, as is commonly said, is the "bottom line" for people at work. It is a cornerstone of productivity and it should contribute to the accomplishment of organizational objectives. Indeed, a *value-added criterion* is being used in more and more organizations to evaluate the worthwhileness of jobs and/or job holders. The performance of every job should add value to the organization's production of useful goods and/or services. If a job does not add value in this sense, corrective actions should be taken to readjust or eliminate the job, or to train or replace the worker.

Job satisfaction is the degree to which an individual feels positively or negatively about various aspects of the job. It represents the personal meaning or perceived "quality" of one's job and associated work experiences. Important aspects of a job that can influence a person's job satisfaction include pay, tasks, supervision, co-workers, the work setting, and advancement opportunities.

People at work should achieve both job performance and job satisfaction. One without the other is simply insufficient to meet the high standards of today's workplace and the trends shown in Figure 11.1. The test of a manager's skill in building value-added jobs is to discover what work means to other people, and then to create work environments that help them achieve high levels of both performance and satisfaction. Once again, this is consistent with the earlier concept of creating and maintaining a healthy psychological contract for people at work.

Alternative Job Design Strategies

Consider this short case. Datapoint Corporation manufactures a line of personal computers. Jackson White has just been employed by Datapoint. He is a competent person who enjoys interpersonal relationships. He also likes to feel helpful or stimulating to others. How do you think he will react to each of the following job designs?

Job 1 Jackson reports to a workstation on the computer assembly line. A partially assembled circuit board passes in front of him on a conveyor belt every ninety seconds. He adds two pieces to each board and lets the conveyor take the unit to the next workstation. Quality control is handled at a separate station at the end of the line. Everyone gets a ten-minute break in the morning and afternoon, and a thirty-minute lunch period. Jackson works by himself in a quiet setting.

Job 2 Jackson works on the same assembly line. Now, however, a circuit board comes to his station every twelve minutes and he performs a greater number of tasks. He adds several pieces to the board, adds a frame, and installs several electric switches. Periodically, Jackson changes stations with one of the other workers and does a different set of tasks on earlier or later stages of the same circuit board. In all other respects, the work setting is the same as in the first job described.

Job 3 Jackson is part of a team responsible for completely assembling circuit boards for the computers. The team has a weekly production quota but makes its own plans for the speed and arrangement of the required assembly processes. The team is also responsible for inspecting the quality of the finished boards and for correcting any defective units. These duties are shared among the members and are discussed at team meetings. Jackson has been selected by the team as its plant liaison. In addition to his other duties, he works with people elsewhere in the plant to resolve any production problems and achieve plant-wide quality objectives.

Job Simplification

Job simplification involves standardizing work procedures and employing people in well-defined and highly specialized tasks.[3] Simplified jobs are narrow in *job scope*—the number and variety of different tasks a person performs. Jackson White's first job on the assembly line was highly simplified. He isn't alone. Many employees around the world earn their livings working at highly simplified tasks.

The logic of job simplification is straightforward: Because the jobs don't require complex skills, workers should be easier and quicker to train, less difficult to supervise, and easy to replace if they leave. With tasks precisely and narrowly defined, furthermore, workers should become good at doing the same tasks over and over again. Things don't always work out this well in highly simplified jobs. Productivity can suffer as unhappy workers drive up costs through absenteeism and turnover, and through poor performance caused by boredom and alienation. Although simplified jobs appeal to some people, disadvantages can emerge if employees do not really want to spend their time working at repetitive tasks of narrow scope.

The most extreme form of job simplification is *automation*—the total mechanization of a job. There is also the special case of *robotics*—the use of computer-controlled machines to completely automate work tasks previously performed by hand. The use of robots in manufacturing industries is growing, particularly in Japan, which leads the world in this respect.[4] Their use in service industries is also growing: the now-familiar automatic teller machines in banks are a good example. But while automation and robotics are here to stay, with ever-increasing applications, the technology still has its limits. In service industries, for example, customers often miss the human touch when being served by a computer rather than a person.

Going back to the Datapoint case, White's social need is thwarted in Job 1, where the assembly line prevents interaction with co-workers. Thus, we would predict low job satisfaction, along with frequent absences from work and boredom that may cause a high error rate. White's overall performance could be just adequate enough to prevent him from being fired. This is hardly sufficient for a computer-maker to maintain a high performance edge in today's competitive global economy.

Job Rotation and Job Enlargement

One way to move beyond job simplification is to expand job scope by increasing the number and variety of tasks performed by a worker. This can be done through job rotation and job enlargement.

Job rotation increases task variety by periodically shifting workers among jobs involving different task assignments. While there is no absolute change in any one job, task variety is increased by switching jobs on a regular basis. Job rotation can be done on a regular schedule; it can also be done periodically or occasionally. The latter approach is often used to broaden people's understanding of jobs performed by others. This is increasingly valued as a way for managers to stay well informed about job pressures and needs of peers and subordinates alike.

Job enlargement increases task variety by combining two or more tasks that were previously assigned to separate workers into one job. Often, these are tasks

---

THE EFFECTIVE MANAGER 11.1

Job Enrichment Checklist

- **Check 1** Remove controls that limit people's discretion in their work.
- **Check 2** Grant people authority to make decisions about their work.
- **Check 3** Make people understand their accountability for results.
- **Check 4** Allow people to do "whole" tasks or complete units of work.
- **Check 5** Make performance feedback available to people doing the work.

---

done immediately before or after the work performed in the original job. *Horizontal loading*—pulling prework and/or later work stages into the job, can be used to enlarge jobs. In this job design strategy, the old job is permanently changed through the addition of new tasks.

Jackson White's second job on the modified assembly line is an example of job enlargement with occasional job rotation. Instead of doing only one task, he now does three. And he occasionally switches jobs with another worker to work on a different part of the board assembly. Because job enlargement and rotation can reduce some of the monotony in otherwise simplified jobs, we would expect an increase in White's satisfaction and performance. Satisfaction should remain only moderate, however, since the job still does not respond completely to his social needs. Although White's work quality should increase as boredom is reduced, some absenteeism is likely to keep job performance at a moderate level.

Job Enrichment

Frederick Herzberg, whose two-factor theory of motivation was discussed in Chapter 10, questions the true value of the prior job design approaches. "Why," he asks, "should a worker become motivated when one or more 'meaningless' tasks are added to previously existing ones, or when work assignments are rotated among equally 'meaningless' tasks?" By contrast, he says: "If you want people to do a good job, give them a good job to do."[5] **Job enrichment,** the practice of building more opportunities for satisfaction into a job, is the means through which he feels this end can be achieved. This job design approach tries to expand not just job scope but also job depth—the extent to which task planning and evaluating duties are performed by the individual worker rather than the supervisor. Changes designed to increase job depth are sometimes referred to as *vertical loading*. Herzberg's recommendations for enriching jobs through vertical loading are found in The Effective Manager 11.1.

There are some elements of job enrichment in Job 3, where Jackson White works in a team-assembly process. White's team is responsible for task planning and evaluation duties, as well as actual product assembly. He should respond well to the challenges of this arrangement. It provides opportunities to satisfy his social needs, and he should get added satisfaction from acting as the team's plant liaison. Higher performance and satisfaction are the predicted results.

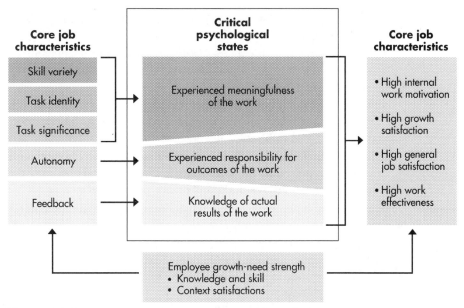

Figure 11.2   Core job characteristics and individual work outcomes in a diagnostic model of job design. Source: Reprinted by permission from J. Richard Hackman and Greg R. Oldham, *Work Redesign* (Reading, Mass.: Addison-Wesley, 1980), p. 90.

Job Enrichment Directions

The job design strategy of job enrichment is an important part of progressive changes being made in the new workplace. But modern management theory takes job enrichment a step beyond the suggestions of Frederick Herzberg. Most importantly, it adopts a contingency perspective and recognizes that job enrichment may not be good for everyone. Among the current directions in job design, the job characteristics model developed by Richard Hackman and his associates offers a way for managers to create jobs—enriched or otherwise—that best fit the needs of people and organizations.[6]

The Job Characteristics Model

The model described in Figure 11.2 offers a diagnostic approach to job enrichment. Five core job characteristics are identified as task attributes of special importance. A job that is high in the core characteristics is considered enriched; the lower a job scores on the core characteristics, the less enriched it is considered to be. The core job characteristics are:

- **Skill variety** the degree to which a job requires a variety of different activities in carrying out the work and involves the use of a number of different skills and talents of the individual
- **Task identity** the degree to which the job requires completion of a whole and

identifiable piece of work—that is, one that involves doing a job from beginning to end with a visible outcome

- **Task significance** the degree to which the job has a substantial impact on the lives or work of other people elsewhere in the organization or in the external environment
- **Autonomy** the degree to which the job gives the individual substantial freedom, independence, and discretion in scheduling the work and in determining the procedures to be used in carrying it out
- **Feedback (from the job itself)** the degree to which carrying out the work activities required by the job results in the individual obtaining direct and clear information on the results of his or her performance

According to the last figure, the diagnostic model views job satisfaction and performance as influenced by three critical psychological states of the individual: (1) experienced meaningfulness of the work; (2) experienced responsibility for the outcomes of the work; and (3) knowledge of actual results of work activities. These psychological states, in turn, are affected by the presence or absence of the five core-job characteristics.

In true contingency fashion, however, the model recognizes that the core characteristics will not affect all people in the same way. The key contingency variable is **growth-need strength**—defined in ERG theory (see Chapter 10) as the degree to which an individual desires to achieve a sense of psychological growth in his or her work. A person high in growth-need strength seeks to satisfy higher-order needs at work. In Maslow's hierarchy-of-needs theory (see also Chapter 10) these include needs for ego fulfillment and self-actualization. The expectation is that people with strong growth needs will respond positively to enriched jobs, while people with weaker job-related growth needs may have negative reactions. They might find that enriched jobs entail more responsibility than they want to deal with at work.

When job enrichment is a good job design choice, Hackman and his colleagues recommend five ways to improve the core characteristics. First, you can *form natural units of work*—make sure that the tasks people perform are logically related to one another and provide a clear and meaningful task identity. Second, you can *combine tasks*—expand job responsibilities by pulling together into one larger job a number of smaller tasks previously done by others. Third, you can *establish client relationships*—allow people to maintain contact with other persons who, as clients inside and/or outside the organization, use the results of his or her work. Fourth, you can *open feedback channels*—provide opportunities for people to receive performance feedback as they work and to learn how this performance is changing over time. Fifth, you can *practice vertical loading*—give people more control over their work by increasing authority for planning and controlling activities previously done by supervisors.

Questions and Answers on Job Enrichment

What follows are several common questions about job enrichment, along with answers.

Question: *"Is it expensive to implement job enrichment?"* Job enrichment can be costly. The cost grows as the required changes in technology, work flow, and other facilities become more complex.

Question: *"Will people demand more pay for doing enriched job?"* Herzberg believes that if people are being paid truly competitive wages (i.e., if pay dissatisfaction does not already exist), the satisfactions of performing enriched tasks will be adequate compensation for the increased work involved. But a manager must be cautious on this issue. Any job-enrichment program should be approached with due recognition that pay may be an important issue for the people involved.[7]

Question: *"What do the unions say about job enrichment?"* It is hard to speak for all unions. The following comments of one union official sound a note of caution:

> Better wages, shorter hours, vested pensions, a right to have a say in their working conditions, the right to be promoted on the basis of seniority, and all the rest. That's the kind of job enrichment that unions believe in. And I assure you that that's the kind of job enrichment that we will continue to fight for.[8]

Question: *"Should everyone's job be enriched?"* No. The people most likely to respond favorably to job enrichment are those seeking higher-order or growth-need satisfactions at work, who are not dissatisfied with hygiene factors in the job context, and who have the levels of training, education, and ability required to perform the enriched job.

Question: *"How does technology influence job enrichment?"* Some technologies may make it easier or more difficult to utilize job enrichment concepts.[9] In all cases the potential advantages of new technology must be balanced with its implications for the human factor. For example, computer-assisted design and manufacturing is changing the mix of skills needed in many industrial settings. Whereas some of the old machine operations skills are less in demand, new machine management skills are becoming more important. Job enrichment should proceed with the goal of increasing productivity through integrated *sociotechnical systems*—job designs that use technology to best advantage while still treating people with respect and allowing their human talents to be applied to the fullest potential.[10]

Work Designs for Groups and Teams

Job design principles can and should be applied to groups as well as individuals, and the role of teamwork should always be considered when managers make job design changes in their areas of work responsibility. Work teams are playing increasingly prominent roles in adaptive organizations. When properly utilized, creative work group designs not only bring people and technology together to good advantage, they can also enhance employee involvement and empowerment in the process.

Most new-form work arrangements emphasize the use of high technology, enriched jobs, and more groupwork. The possibilities are endless.

Creative Work Group Designs

Let's use the automobile industry as an example. Traditionally, automakers have operated with highly integrated assembly lines. This mass-production technology produces large numbers of cars at a relatively fast pace. But it has its disadvantages. Consider these reflections by one auto worker in the book *Rivethead: Tales from the Assembly Line.*

> The noise level was deafening. . . . When everything went just right, I had absolutely no recollection of what had transpired moments before. . . . GM [General Motors] had every right to usher me . . . past the time clocks, out the exit and point me in the general direction of nowhere. Nowhere seemed fine in a way, but it was highly doubtful that nowhere paid $12.82 an hour.[11]

But what are the alternatives? What can we do to protect workers from the alienation and frustration that often accompany simplified work in assembly-line jobs? One answer goes back to technology: Robots and high-tech automation can replace humans in some routine jobs, and this is being done. But the limits of such technology must be recognized. And when there are decisions to be made during the work process, the human resource is still unbeatable. Thus, another answer to the question goes back to job design—this time with a twist: Some jobs can be rearranged, enriched, and assigned to work teams, not individuals.

Self-Managing Work Teams

An important job design trend is toward the creation of more **self-managing work teams.** Sometimes called *autonomous work groups,* these are groups of workers whose jobs have been redesigned to create a high degree of task interdependence and who have been given authority to make many decisions about how they go about doing the required work.[12] Self-managing teams operate with participative decision making, shared tasks, and responsibility for many of the "managerial" tasks performed by supervisors in more traditional work groups. As shown in Figure 11.3, typical characteristics of a self-managing team are:

- Members are held collectively accountable for performance results.
- Members have discretion in distributing tasks within the team.
- Members have discretion in scheduling work within the team.
- Members are able to perform more than one job on the team.
- Members train one another to develop multiple job skills.
- Members evaluate one another's performance contributions.
- Members are responsible for total quality of group products.

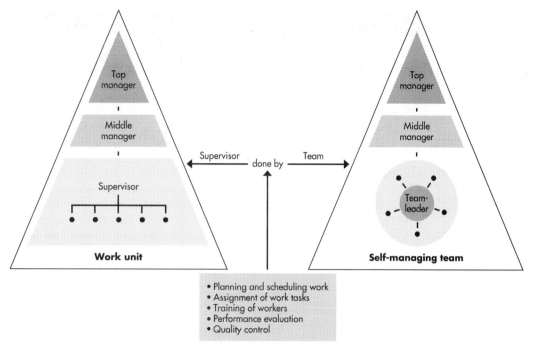

Figure 11.3 Organizational and management implications of self-managing work teams.

The structural implications of self-managing teams are also depicted in the figure. Most typically, members of a self-managing team report to higher management through a "team leader" rather than a formal supervisor. This is an important change in structure. At the extreme, the need for traditional first-level supervisors is eliminated. Each self-managing team handles the supervisory duties on its own, and each team leader handles the upward reporting relationships. Higher-level managers to whom self-managing teams report must learn to work with teams rather than individual subordinates. This can be a difficult challenge for some managers who are used to more traditional operating ways.

Positive attributes of high-performance teams are described in The Effective Manager 11.2. Among the many developments in the workplace today, continuing efforts to refine and apply the various types of creative work group and self-managing team concepts are certainly at the forefront of any progressive manager's action agendas.[13]

Alternative Work Schedules

Not only is the content of jobs changing for individuals and groups in today's workplace, the context is changing, too. Among the more significant developments is the emergence of a number of alternative ways for people to schedule their work time. This is especially important as employers deal with today's highly diverse workforce,

---

THE EFFECTIVE MANAGER 11.2

Attributes of High-Performing Work Teams

- **Participative leadership**—All members are committed to empowerment and mutual assistance.
- **Shared responsibility**—All members, not just the leader, feel responsible for performance results.
- **Clear purpose**—All members understand and support the team and its purpose.
- **Intense communication**—All members communicate in an open and trusting climate.
- **Future oriented**—All members are willing to accept change to improve performance.
- **Task focused**—All members are concerned about meeting job expectations.
- **Creative**—All members' talents and creativity are used to benefit the team.
- **Fast**—All members are willing and able to act quickly on problems and opportunities.

---

whose members have varying needs and interests. Family-friendly employers are finding that alternative work schedules can help attract and retain the best workforce. The top three reasons employers give for initiating such plans are: response to employee requests, support of corporate image, and part of a work-family assistance program.[14] It is popular in this sense to talk about a new and more flexible workplace in which alternative work schedules such as the following are made available.

The Compressed Workweek

A **compressed workweek** is any work schedule that allows a full-time job to be completed in less than the standard five days of eight-hour shifts.[15] Its most common form is the "4-40"—that is, forty hours of work accomplished in four ten-hour days. One advantage of the 4-40 schedule is that the employee receives three consecutive days off from work each week. This benefits the individual with more leisure time and lower commuting costs. The organization should also benefit from lower absenteeism and any higher performance that may result. Potential disadvantages include increased fatigue and family adjustment problems for the individual, as well as increased scheduling problems, possible customer complaints, and union-opposition problems for the organization. At USAA, a diversified financial services company, almost 75 percent of the firm's San Antonio workforce is on a four-day schedule, with some working Monday–Thursday and others working Tuesday–Friday. Company benefits include improved employee morale, lower overtime costs, less absenteeism, and less sick leave.[16]

Flexible Working Hours

The term **flexible working hours,** also called *flexitime* or *flextime,* describes any work schedule that gives employees some choice in the pattern of daily work hours.

For example, a flexible working schedule might require that employees work four hours of "core" time between 9 and 10 A.M. and 1 and 3 P.M.; this is time they *must* be at work. They are then free to choose another four work hours from "flextime" blocks. For example, employees at Blue Cross/Blue Shield in Minneapolis, work during core time of 9:30 A.M. to 3:30 P.M. They are free to schedule their remaining work day to fit personal needs.

Flexible working hours give people greater autonomy in work scheduling. Early risers may choose to come in earlier and leave earlier, while still completing an eight-hour day; late sleepers may choose to start later in the morning and leave later. In between these extremes are opportunities to attend to personal affairs, such as dental appointments, home emergencies, visits to children's school, and so on. The advantages are especially important to members of a diverse workforce. By offering flexibility, organizations can attract and hold employees with special nonwork responsibilities. Single parents with young children and employees with elder-care responsibilities are two examples. The added discretion flextime allows may also encourage workers to have more positive attitudes toward the organization.

Job Sharing

Another important development for today's workforce is **job sharing,** whereby one full-time job is split between two or more people. Job sharing often involves each person working one-half day, but it can also be done on weekly or monthly sharing arrangements.

When it is feasible for jobs to be split and shared, organizations can benefit by employing talented people who would otherwise be unable to work. The qualified specialist who is also a parent may be unable to stay away from home for a full workday but be able to work a half-day. Job sharing allows two such persons to be employed as one. While there are sometimes adjustment problems, the arrangement can be good for all concerned.

Job sharing should not be confused with a more controversial concept called *work sharing.* This is when employees in an organization that faces layoffs or terminations agree to cut back their work hours so they can all keep their jobs. Rather than losing 20 percent of a firm's workforce to temporary layoffs in an unexpected business downturn, for example, a work-sharing program would cut everyone's hours by 20 percent to keep them all employed.

Work sharing allows employers to retain trained and loyal workers, even when forced to economize temporarily by reducing labor costs. For employees whose seniority might otherwise protect them from layoff, the disadvantage is lost earnings. For those who would otherwise be terminated, however, it allows continued work—albeit with reduced earnings—with a preferred employer. Some unions endorse this concept, and it is now legal in many states. It is prohibited in others, however, because of legal complications relating to unemployment compensation and benefits.

Telecommuting

Another significant development in work scheduling is the growing popularity of *work-at-home* approaches. This includes a variety of alternatives, ranging from self-employment and entrepreneurship based at home to working for an outside employer with the freedom to spend all or part of one's work time at home. The latter approach has been greatly facilitated by the advent of the personal computer and convenient electronic communications, as well as express mail. Rather than commute to work in the traditional sense, workers can now "commute" via computer networks, "fax" machines, and express-mail delivery services. This is sometimes referred to as the *virtual office*, or mobile office arrangement.

Telecommuting describes work done at home using computers and information technology with links to the home office, central computers, external databases, and other places of work. Working at home frees the job-holder from the constraints of commuting, fixed hours, special work attire, and even direct contact with supervisors. It is especially popular among computer programmers, although it is found increasingly in such diverse areas as marketing, financial analysis, and administrative support. Telecommuting has found its place, for example, at J.C. Penney's Catalog Distribution Center. A group of part-time telemarketers use home computers to take orders by telephone. They are paid the same and treated the same as telemarketers working in the home office, and are expected to spend one day a month in the office to keep up with company operations and policies.[17]

Work-at-home and telecommuting have advantages and disadvantages. When asked what they liked about these alternatives, a survey of "homeworkers" conducted by *The Wall Street Journal* reported increased productivity, fewer distractions, being your own boss, and having more time for yourself. On the negative side, they identified working too much, having less time to yourself, difficulty in separating work and personal life, and having less time for family.[18] Other considerations for the individual are possible feelings of isolation and loss of visibility for promotion. Managers, in turn, may be required to change routines and procedures to accommodate the difficulties of supervising people from a distance.

Such problems tend to be magnified in situations where employees are forced into this work arrangement. Some employers, for example, are finding that shifting toward the virtual office can encounter problems. Whereas this mobile office concept offers such potential benefits as increased customer contacts and reduced administrative expenses, it can be resented by employees who feel unfairly treated. In some cases this resentment may entail the belief that the company saves money by shifting office costs to employees, who must work from their homes or automobiles.[19]

Part-Time Work

Another striking trend in work scheduling today also has a controversial side. **Part-time work** is work done on any schedule less than the standard forty-hour work week in which the worker is not classified as a full-time employee. Increasingly, employers are relying on *contingency workers*—part-timers and temporaries—to supplement and reduce their commitments to a permanent workforce. No longer limited to the traditional areas of clerical services, sales personnel, and unskilled labor, these workers serve an increasingly broad range of employer needs. It is now possible to hire on a part-time basis everything from executive support—such as a chief financial officer—to such special expertise as engineering, computer programming, and market research.

Because part-time or contingency workers can be easily hired, contracted, and terminated in response to changing needs, many employers like the flexibility they offer in controlling labor costs. On the other hand, some worry that temporaries lack the commitment of permanent workers; the result may be lower productivity. Perhaps the most controversial issue relates to the different treatment part-timers may receive from employers. They may be paid less than full-time counterparts, and they often fail to receive important benefits, such as health care, life insurance, pension plans, and paid vacations. When one realizes that the large majority of part-timers are women and that many of them are single parents, the implications of this point are troublesome.

In Summary

What is the meaning of work?

- Work is an exchange of values between individuals who contribute time and effort and organizations who offer monetary and other inducements in return.
- High performance and job satisfaction are most likely to occur when a person believes that his or her contributions and inducements are in balance.
- A balanced or "healthy" psychological contract is one foundation for a high quality of work life.

What are the alternative job design approaches?

- Job design is the process of creating or defining jobs by assigning specific work tasks to individuals and groups.
- Jobs should be designed for both high levels of job performance and job satisfaction by the workers.
- Job simplification creates narrow and repetitive jobs consisting of well-defined tasks with many routine operations, such as the typical assembly-line job.
- Job enlargement allows individuals to perform a broader range of simplified tasks; job rotation allows individuals to transfer among different jobs of similar skill levels on a rotating basis.
- Job enrichment gives more meaningful jobs involving more autonomy in making decisions and broader task responsibilities.

How can a manager enrich jobs for individual workers?

- The diagnostic approach to job enrichment involves analyzing jobs according to five core characteristics: skill variety, task identity, task significance, autonomy, and feedback.

- Jobs deficient on one or more of the prior "core" characteristics can be redesigned to improve their level of enrichment.
- Jobs can be enriched by forming natural work units, combining tasks, establishing client relationships, opening feedback channels, and vertically loading to allow more planning and controlling decisions by the job holder.
- Job enrichment does not work for everyone; it works best for people with a high growth-need strength, that is, the desire to achieve psychological growth in their work.

Why are self-managing work teams so popular today?

- There is a growing emphasis on the "group" or "team" as a basis for organizing work and designing jobs in all types of settings.
- Self-managing teams are groups of workers who are responsible for performing operating jobs, along with many tasks previously performed by first-level supervisors.
- Self-managing teams can allow workers to experience job enrichment, along with the many benefits of being part of a group.
- Self-managing teams can allow organizations to become more efficient by eliminating unnecessary first-line supervision.

How can alternative work schedules improve the workplace?

- Many progressive organizations are adjusting work schedules to better fit with individual needs and nonwork responsibilities.
- Flexible working hours allow people to adjust daily schedules in terms of starting and ending times.
- The compressed workweek allows forty hours to be completed in only four days' time.
- Job sharing allows two people to share one job.
- Telecommuting allows people to work at home or in mobile offices through computer links with their employers and/or customers.
- An increasing number of people work on part-time schedules; more and more organizations are using part-timers as contingency workers to minimize their commitments to full-time workforces.

12

BUILDING TEAMS:

GROUP DYNAMICS

AND TEAMWORK

As you read Chapter 12, keep in mind these study questions:

- What is the role of groups in organizations?

- What are current directions in the use of groups?

- What makes a group effective?

- What should managers understand about teamwork and group dynamics?

- How can team building increase group effectiveness?

T oday's managers are expected to create work environments within which people can achieve high performance, not only as individual contributors but also as members of work groups. Indeed, an important goal in the new workplace is to best use groups as resources. Leading through teamwork is an increasingly important managerial responsibility, but not an easy one to achieve. Just the words *group* and *team* cause both positive and negative reactions in the minds of many people. Although it is said that "two heads are better than one," we are also warned that "too many cooks spoil the broth." The true skeptic warns: "A camel is a horse put together by a committee." But against this somewhat humorous background lies a most important point: Many tasks are beyond the capabilities of people operating alone. True managerial success entails mobilizing and utilizing groups as essential human resources of organizations.

Groups in Organizations

Formally defined, a **group** is a collection of two or more people who regularly interact with one another in the pursuit of common goals.[1] And simply put, groups can be very good for both organizations and their members.[2] They can increase resources for problem solving, foster creativity and innovation, improve quality of decision making, enhance members' commitments to tasks, raise motivation through collective action, help control and discipline members, and help satisfy individual needs as organizations grow in size.

Teamwork is the process of people working together in groups to accomplish common goals.[3] When teamwork exists, organizations may gain the performance benefits of group **synergy**—the creation of a whole that is greater than the sum of its parts. The presence of synergy means that a group is using its membership resources to the fullest and is achieving through collective performance far more than could be otherwise achieved. When teamwork exists, individuals clearly gain the personal benefits of having important needs satisfied through working in and being part of a group—needs that may be harder to satisfy in the regular work setting.

The groups officially designated by the organization (those that appear on organization charts) are **formal groups.** They are specifically created to perform tasks considered essential to the accomplishment of key operating objectives. The formal work unit consisting of a manager and his or her subordinates is a *functional group;* it is a basic building block of organizations. Such groups are often called departments (e.g., market research department), teams (e.g., product assembly team), or divisions (e.g., office products division). Indeed, one way to view organizations is as interlocking networks of functional groups. Noted management scholar Rensis Likert points out that managers serve as important "linking pins" in such networks.[4] Each manager acts as a supervisor in one work group and a subordinate in another at the next higher level. In the latter, the manager interacts not only with a "boss" but also with "peers" who are in charge of other work units themselves. The resulting vertical and horizontal linkages—if well maintained—help integrate the activities and accomplishments of groups throughout an organization.

Informal groups are not official; they are part of the informal organization structure and emerge from natural or spontaneous relationships. Some form as *interest groups* in which workers band together to pursue a common cause or special position, such as a concern for poor working conditions. Some emerge as *friendship groups* that develop for a wide variety of personal reasons, including shared nonwork interests. Others emerge as *support groups* in which the members basically help one another do their jobs.

Managers should understand informal groups and try to make them work to best advantage. In particular, the relationships and connections made possible by informal groups may actually help speed the work flow or allow people to get things done in ways not possible within the formal structure. Informal groups can help satisfy the personal needs of their members—needs that otherwise may be thwarted or left unmet in the formal work setting. Among other things, members of informal groups often find that the groups offer social satisfactions, security, support, and a sense of belonging.

Directions in the Use of Groups in Organizations

Trends toward greater empowerment and more emphasis on lateral relations are having an impact on the way groups are used in organizations. The following directions are most important today.

Self-Managing Work Teams

As noted in Chapter 11, the functional group consisting of a first-level supervisor and his or her immediate subordinates is disappearing in some organizations. It is being replaced with some form of *self-managing team* whose members are empowered to perform many duties previously done by the supervisor.[5] These self-management responsibilities include planning and scheduling work, training members in various tasks, sharing tasks, meeting performance goals, ensuring high quality, and solving day-to-day operating problems. In some settings, the team's authority may even extend to "hiring" and "firing" its members when necessary. Within a self-managing team, however, the emphasis is always on participation. The leader and members are expected to work together not only to do the required work but also to determine how the work gets done. A true self-managing team empha-

---

THE EFFECTIVE MANAGER 12.1

Guidelines for Managing a Task Force

- *Select appropriate task-force members* who will be challenged by the assignment, who have the right skills, and who seem able to work well together.
- *Clearly define the purpose of the task force* to ensure that members and important outsiders know what is expected, why, and on what timetable.
- *Carefully select the task-force leader* and ensure that the leader has good interpersonal skills, can respect the ideas of others, and is willing to do what needs to be done.
- *Periodically review progress* at regular intervals to ensure that task-force members feel accountable for results and get performance feedback.

---

sizes group decision making, shared tasks, and collective responsibility. The expected advantages include better performance, decreased costs, and higher morale.

Committees and Task Forces

Two common and important types of groups used in organizations are *committees* and *task forces*. While serving somewhat different functions, each brings people together outside of their daily job assignments to work in small groups for a specific purpose. They typically operate with task agendas and are led by a designated head or chairperson who, in turn, is held accountable for committee or task force results.

A **committee** usually operates with an ongoing purpose; its membership might change over time even as the committee remains in existence. Organizations usually have a variety of permanent or standing committees dedicated to a wide variety of concerns. Many are now using cross-functional committees to improve lateral coordination. In addition, committees frequently serve as official mechanisms for different constituencies to be represented when important policies are developed or various rules and procedures are implemented in their support.

A **task force** usually operates on a more temporary basis. Its official tasks are usually very specific and time-defined.[6] Once its stated purpose has been accomplished, the task force may disband. Creativity and innovation are very important because task forces are often convened to handle particularly difficult or troublesome problems or to establish directions that will take best advantage of opportunities. Task forces can get something done quickly while still taking diverse viewpoints into account. Like committees, task forces are increasingly used to bring together people from different functions to work on common problems—such as a new-product-development task force. But to achieve the desired results, any task force must be carefully established and then well run. Some task force management guidelines are found in The Effective Manager 12.1.

Employee Involvement Groups

Another development in the use of groups in today's organizations is the formation of various types of **employee involvement groups**.[7] These are groups of workers who meet on a regular basis outside of their functional groups, with the goal of applying their expertise and attention to important workplace matters. The general purpose of all employee involvement groups is continuous improvement, but they may attack the issue from different perspectives. Using a problem-solving framework, the groups try to bring the benefits of employee participation to bear on a wide variety of performance issues and concerns. At Phillipps Corporation, an Ohio-based building materials producer, employee involvement groups are used in a "How-can-we-save-money?" program. It allows small groups of employees to work together for a week to improve Phillipps products and help cut costs. More than 150 teams a year choose to do this.[8]

A popular form of employee involvement group is the **quality circle,** a group of workers that meets regularly to discuss and plan specific ways to improve work quality.[9] Usually it consists of six to twelve members from a work area. After receiving special training in problem solving, group processes, and quality issues, members of the quality circle try to come up with suggestions that can be implemented to raise productivity through quality improvements. Quality circles became popular in U.S. industry in part as a result of their place in Japanese management practices. Along with other types of involvement groups, they are now found in organizations where empowerment and participation are valued as keys to high performance.

Virtual Teams

Another form of group that is increasingly common in today's organizations is the **virtual team,** sometimes called a *computer-mediated group* or *electronic group network.* This is a group of people who work together and solve problems through computer-based rather than face-to-face interactions. As organizations go global in operations and perspectives, computer-mediated groups can provide important advantages by allowing people from diverse locations to work and solve problems together.

Special software support, or *groupware,* for computerized meetings is also changing the way some committees, task forces, and other problem-solving groups function when they meet. Some organizations use electronic meeting rooms, in which group members sit at computer terminals. Guided by software and perhaps specially trained group facilitators, participants address problems and seek consensus on how to best deal with them. Such electronic group meetings can have problems, particularly when members' working relationships are depersonalized and some of the advantages of direct interaction are lost. But the approach has potential advantages of its own. Members of computer-mediated groups can deal collectively with issues in a time-efficient fashion and without some of the interpersonal difficulties that might otherwise occur—especially when the issues are controversial.

Group Effectiveness

An **effective group** is defined as one that achieves and maintains high levels of *both* task performance *and* member satisfaction over time. On the *performance* side, any formal group is expected to transform resource inputs (such as ideas, materials, and objects) into product outputs (such as a report, decision, service, or commodity) of some value to the organization. On the *satisfaction* side, any group should also provide for adequate human resource maintenance. This is the group's ability to maintain its interpersonal fabric and to keep its members willing and able to work well together again and again.

What Can Go Wrong in Groups?

Even though groups often prove superior to individuals in solving certain problems and accomplishing complex tasks, there is no guarantee that any group will achieve effectiveness. Managers or group members should be prepared to face four problems:

1. **Membership differences** Individual differences in personality and work style can disrupt the group.
2. **Poorly defined tasks** Unclear agendas and/or ill-defined problems can cause groups to work too long on the wrong things.
3. **Poor readiness to work** Time can be wasted because meetings lack purpose and structure, and because members come unprepared.
4. **Poor group process** Failures in communication, conflict, and decision making may limit performance and/or hurt morale.

In addition, who hasn't encountered another common group problem—**social loafing**? This is the presence of "free-riders" who slack off because responsibility is diffused in groups and others are present to do the work.[10] And who hasn't heard complaints from people heading off to attend what they would call another "time-wasting" meeting?[11]

Things don't have to be this way. In fact, they must not if the types of groups we have been discussing are to make their best contributions to organizations. Time spent by people in groups can be productive and satisfying, but getting there requires an understanding of the complex nature of groups and their internal dynamics. The first part of a manager's job in dealing with groups is knowing *when* a group is the best choice for applying human resources to a task. The second is to know *how* to work with and manage the group to best accomplish that task.

Importance of Group Inputs

Figure 12.1 shows how any group may be viewed as an open system that transforms various inputs into two key outputs, task performance and human resource maintenance—the criteria of group effectiveness. Four input factors that deserve managerial attention are the organizational setting, nature of the task, group size, and membership characteristics.[12]

The *organizational setting* can affect how group members relate to one another and apply their skills toward task accomplishment. A key issue is the amount of support provided in terms of material resources, technology, spatial arrangements, organization structures, and available rewards. The *nature of the task* is also impor-

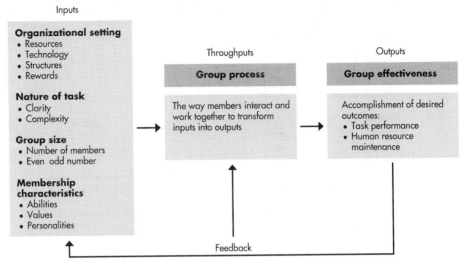

Figure 12.1   How to understand any group as an open system.

tant. It affects how well a group can focus its efforts and how intense the group process needs to be to get the job done. Clearly defined tasks make it easier for members to focus their efforts than do ill-defined ones. Complex tasks require more information exchange and intense interaction than do simpler tasks. ·

Group size affects how members work together, handle disagreements, and reach agreements. The number of potential interactions increases geometrically as groups increase in size and communications become more restricted. Groups larger than about six or seven members can be difficult to manage for creative problem solving. And, when voting, odd-numbered groups are often preferred in order to prevent ties.

In all groups, *membership characteristics* are important. The ability of members to work well together for task accomplishment depends on the blend of competencies among members. Although heterogeneity in the mix of individual skills, values, and personalities broadens the resource base of the group, it also adds complexity to members' interpersonal relationships. Recent research suggests, for example, that culturally diverse work groups have more difficulties learning how to work well together than culturally homogeneous ones. However, the diverse teams eventually prove more creative than the homogeneous ones.[13]

Understanding Teamwork and Group Dynamics

A group's ability to be effective always depends, in part, on its internal **group process.** This is the way members actually work together to transform resource inputs into group outputs. Among other things, it includes how well members communicate, make decisions, and handle conflicts as they interact. In this sense, effective groups excel at *teamwork,* defined earlier as the process of people working together in groups to accomplish common goals. They also have positive **group dynamics,** which are forces operating in groups that affect task performance and membership satisfaction.[14] When teamwork breaks down and group dynamics fail in any way, group effectiveness is compromised.

Stages of Group Development

Because newly formed groups can act quite differently from mature ones, it is helpful to recognize the maturity of groups in which you participate. A synthesis of research on small groups suggests that five distinct phases of group development are important in the life cycle of any group.[15] They are:

- **Forming** a stage of initial orientation and interpersonal testing
- **Storming** a stage of conflict over tasks and ways of operating as a group
- **Norming** a stage of consolidation around task and operating agendas
- **Performing** a stage of teamwork and focused task performance
- **Adjourning** a stage of task accomplishment and eventual disengagement

The *forming stage* involves the initial entry of individual members into a group. This is a stage of initial task orientation and interpersonal testing. As individuals come together for the first time or two, they ask a number of questions: "What can or does the group offer me?" "What will I be asked to contribute?" "Can my needs be met while I serve the task needs of the group?" People begin to identify with other members and the group itself. They are concerned about getting acquainted, establishing interpersonal relationships, discovering what is considered acceptable behavior, and learning how others perceive the group's task. This may also be a time when some members rely on or become temporarily dependent on another member who appears "powerful" or especially "knowledgeable." Such things as prior experience with group members in other contexts and individual impressions of organization philosophies, goals, and policies may also affect how members "form" together in new work groups. Difficulties in the forming stage tend to be greater in more culturally diverse groups.

The *storming stage* of group development is a period of high emotionality. Tension often emerges among members over task and interpersonal concerns. There may be periods of outright hostility and infighting. Coalitions or cliques may appear around personalities or interests. Subgroups form around areas of agreement and disagreement on group tasks or manner of operations. Conflict may develop as individuals compete to impose their preferences on others and to become influential in the group's status structure. Important changes occur as task agendas become clarified and members begin to clarify one another's interpersonal styles. Here, attention begins to shift toward obstacles that may stand in the way of task accomplishment. Efforts are made to find ways to meet group goals while also satisfying individual needs. Failure in the storming stage can be a lasting liability, whereas success in the storming stage can set a strong foundation for later group effectiveness.

Cooperation is an important theme of groups in the *norming stage*. At this stage, members of the group begin to become coordinated as a working unit and tend to operate with shared rules of conduct. The group feels a sense of leadership, with each member starting to play useful roles. Most interpersonal hostilities give way to a precarious balancing of forces as norming builds initial integration. Harmony is emphasized, but minority viewpoints may be discouraged. Members are likely to develop initial feelings of closeness, a division of labor, and a sense of shared expectations. This helps protect the group from disintegration. Holding the group together may become even more important than successful task accomplishment.

Groups in the *performing stage* are more mature, organized, and well-functioning. This is a stage of total integration in which group members are able to deal in creative ways with both complex tasks and interpersonal conflicts. The group operates with a clear and stable structure, and members are motivated by group goals. The primary challenges of groups are to continue refining the operations and relationships essential to working together as an integrated unit. Such groups need to remain coordinated with the larger organization and adapt successfully to changing conditions over time. A group that has achieved total integration will score high on the criteria of group maturity presented earlier.

The *adjourning stage* is where group members prepare for and eventually implement the group's disbandment. This stage is especially common for temporary groups that operate in the form of committees, task forces, and projects. Ideally, the group disbands with a sense that important goals have been accomplished. Members are acknowledged for their contributions and the group's overall success. This may be an emotional time, and disbandment should be managed with this possibility in mind. For members who have worked together intensely for a period of time, breaking up the close relationships may be painful. It is desirable for the group to disband with members feeling they would work with one another again sometime in the future if another need or opportunity to do so arises.

Group Norms

A **group norm** is a behavior expected of group members.[16] It is a rule or standard that guides the behavior of group members. When violated, a norm may be enforced with reprimands and other sanctions. In the extreme, violation of a norm can result in a member being expelled from a group or socially ostracized by other members. The **performance norm** is extremely important; it defines the level of work effort and performance that group members are expected to contribute. It can have positive or negative implications for group performance and organizational productivity. In general, work groups and teams with more positive performance norms tend to be more successful in accomplishing task objectives than groups with more negative performance norms. Other important group norms relate to such things as attendance, helpfulness, participation, preparedness, and innovation.

Because a group's norms are largely determined by the collective will of its members, it is difficult for a manager or designated leader simply to dictate which norms will be adopted. Instead, the concerned manager or group leader must help and encourage members to adopt norms that support important organizational objectives. Of course, the needs for norm-building vary a bit from stage to stage. During forming and storming, norms relating to membership issues such as expected attendance and levels of commitment are important. By the time the stage of performing is reached, norms relating to adaptability and change become most relevant. Things a manager can do to help create and maintain positive group norms include:

- acting as a positive role model
- reinforcing the desired behaviors with rewards
- controlling results by performance reviews and regular feedback
- training and orienting new members to adopt desired behaviors
- recruiting and selecting new members who exhibit the desired behaviors
- holding regular meetings to discuss progress and ways of improving effectiveness
- using group decision-making methods to reach agreement on appropriate behaviors[17]

Group Cohesiveness

Norms vary in the degree to which they are accepted and adhered to by group members. Conformity to norms is largely determined by the strength of **group cohesiveness**—the degree to which members are attracted to and motivated to remain part of a group. Persons in a highly cohesive group value their membership and strive to maintain positive relationships with other group members. Because of this, they also tend to follow group norms.

Highly cohesive groups are good for their members, who experience satisfaction from group identification and interpersonal relationships. But highly cohesive groups may or may not be good for organizations. It all depends on the performance norm. A basic rule of group dynamics is that the more cohesive the group, the greater the conformity of members to group norms. When the performance norm of a group is positive, high cohesion and resulting conformity to norms has a beneficial effect on productivity. This is a "best-case" situation for the organization. Competent group members work hard and reinforce one another's task accomplishments while experiencing satisfaction with the group. But when the performance norm is negative in a cohesive group, high conformity to the norm can have undesirable results. This is a worst-case situation, where productivity suffers from restricted work efforts.

To achieve and maintain the best-case scenario, managers should be skilled at influencing both group norms and cohesiveness. They will want to build and maintain cohesiveness in groups whose performance norms are positive. In order to increase cohesion, a manager can:

- induce agreement on group goals
- increase membership homogeneity
- increase interactions among members
- decrease group size
- introduce competition with other groups

- reward group rather than individual results
- provide physical isolation from other groups

Groupthink

Another, more subtle, side to group cohesiveness can sometimes work to a group's disadvantage. Members of highly cohesive groups may publicly agree with actual or suggested courses of action, while privately having serious doubts about them. Strong feelings of group loyalty can make it hard for members to criticize and evaluate one another's ideas and suggestions. Desires to hold the group together and avoid disagreement may lead to poor decision making. Psychologist Irving Janis calls this phenomenon **groupthink**—the tendency for highly cohesive groups to lose their critical evaluative capabilities.[18] The possible symptoms of groups experiencing groupthink include:

- **Illusions of group invulnerability** feeling the group is above criticism or beyond attack
- **Rationalizing unpleasant and disconfirming data** refusing to accept contradictory data or to consider alternatives thoroughly
- **Belief in inherent group morality** feeling the group is inherently "right" and above any reproach by outsiders
- **Stereotyping competitors as weak, evil, and stupid** refusing to look realistically at other groups
- **Applying direct pressure to deviants to conform to group wishes** refusing to tolerate a member who suggests the group might be wrong
- **Self-censorship by members** refusing to communicate personal concerns to the group as a whole
- **Illusions of unanimity** accepting consensus prematurely, without testing its completeness
- **Mind guarding** protecting the group from hearing disturbing ideas or viewpoints from outsiders

Groupthink can occur anywhere. In fact, Janis ties a variety of well-known historical blunders to groupthink, including the lack of preparedness of the U.S. naval forces for the Japanese attack on Pearl Harbor, the Bay of Pigs invasion under President Kennedy, and the many roads that led to the U.S. involvement in Vietnam. When and if you encounter groupthink, Janis suggests taking action along the lines shown in The Effective Manager 12.2.

Task and Maintenance Needs of Groups

Research on the social psychology of groups identifies two types of activities that are essential if group members are to work well together over time.[19] **Task activities** contribute directly to the group's performance purpose, while **maintenance activities** support the emotional life of the group as an ongoing social system.

THE EFFECTIVE MANAGER 12.2

How to Deal with Groupthink

- Assign the role of critical evaluator to each group member; encourage a sharing of viewpoints.
- Avoid, as a leader, seeming partial to one course of action; miss a meeting to allow free discussion.
- Create subgroups to work on the same problems and then share their proposed solutions.
- Have group members discuss issues with outsiders and report back on their reactions.
- Invite outside experts to observe group activities and react to group processes and decisions.
- Assign one member to play a "devil's advocate" role at each group meeting.
- Hold a "second-chance" meeting after consensus is apparently achieved to review the decision.

Although a person with formal authority, such as a chairperson or supervisor, will often handle them, the responsibility for task and maintenance activities should be shared and distributed among all group members. It is important to remember that any member can assist a group by taking actions that help satisfy its task and maintenance needs. This concept of *distributed leadership in group dynamics* thus makes every group member responsible for (1) correctly recognizing when task and/or maintenance activities are needed, and (2) responding appropriately by providing or helping others to perform them.

Figure 12.2 shows that leading through group task activities involves making an effort to define and solve problems and apply work efforts in support of task accomplishment. Without relevant task activities groups will have difficulty accomp-

Figure 12.2   Distributed or shared leadership helps a group meet its task and maintenance needs.

lishing their objectives. Leading through maintenance activities, by contrast, helps strengthen and perpetuate the group as a social system. When maintenance activities are performed well, good interpersonal relationships are achieved and the ability of the group to stay together over the longer term is ensured. The maintenance activities listed in Figure 12.2 can be performed by any group member. They can also make an important contribution to group development and effectiveness.

Both group task and maintenance activities stand in distinct contrast to the dysfunctional activities also common in everyday group affairs. As noted in the figure, these activities are self-serving to the individual member and detract from, rather than enhance, group effectiveness. Unfortunately, very few groups are immune to the display of such dysfunctional behavior by members.

Team Building for Group Effectiveness

When we think of the word *team,* sporting teams often come to mind. And we know these teams certainly have their share of problems. Members slack off or become disgruntled; some are retired or traded as a result. Even world-champion teams have losing streaks. Even the most highly talented players sometimes lose motivation, quibble with other team members, and lapse into performance slumps. When these things happen, the owners, managers, and players are apt to take corrective action to "rebuild the team" and restore what we have called group effectiveness.

Work groups are teams in a similar sense. Teams in organizations are responsible for doing things (e.g., a manufacturing team), recommending things (e.g., a quality improvement team), and running things (e.g., a management team).[20] Even the most mature work team, however, is likely to experience problems over time. When such difficulties arise, team-building activities can help. **Team building** is a sequence of planned activities used to gather and analyze data on the functioning of a group and implement constructive changes to increase its operating effectiveness.[21]

The Team-Building Process

Most systematic approaches to team building begin with sensitivity that a problem may exist or might develop within the group. Members then work together to gather and analyze data so that the problem is finally understood. Action plans are made by group members and collectively implemented. Results are evaluated in similar group fashion. Any difficulties or new problems that are discovered serve to recycle the team-building process. Consider this case-in-point as related to Figure 12.2.

> The consultant received a call from the hospital's director of personnel. He indicated that a new hospital president thought the top management team lacked cohesiveness and was not working well together as a team. The consultant agreed to facilitate a team-building activity that would include a day-long retreat at a nearby resort hotel. The process began when the consultant conducted interviews with the president and other

members of the executive group. During the retreat, the consultant reported these results to the group as a whole. She indicated that hospital goals were generally understood by all, but that they weren't clear enough to allow agreement on action priorities. Furthermore, she reported that interpersonal problems between two team members—the directors of nursing services and administration—were making it difficult for the group to work together comfortably. These and other issues were addressed by the group at the retreat. Working sometimes in small subgroups, and other times together as a whole, they agreed first of all that action should be taken to clarify the hospital's overall mission and create a priority list of objectives for the current year. Led by the president, activity on this task would involve all group members and would be targeted for completion within a month. The president asked that progress on the action plans be reviewed at each of the next three monthly executive staff meetings. Everyone agreed.

The example introduces team building as a way of assessing a work group's functioning and taking corrective action to improve group effectiveness. This can and should become a regular part of a group's continuing work routine. There are many ways to gather data on group functioning, including structured and unstructured interviews, questionnaires, group meetings, and written records. Regardless of the method used, the principle of team building requires that a careful and collaborative assessment of the group be made. All members should participate in the data-gathering process, assist in the data analysis, and collectively decide to take action to resolve or prevent problems that interfere with group effectiveness. Sometimes, team building involves sending group members to special training and development programs run by experienced group consultants. In all cases, the ultimate goal of team building is to create more and better teamwork among members of a group.

Characteristics of High-Performance Teams

High-performance teams generally have clear and motivating goals, a results-oriented structure, competent and committed members who work hard, high standards of excellence, collaborative work environments, and strong and principled leadership. The last point on this list may be the key to them all. In their book *Teamwork: What Can Go Right/What Can Go Wrong,* Carl Larson and Frank LaFasto state: "The right person in a leadership role can add tremendous value to any collective effort, even to the point of sparking the outcome with an intangible kind of magic."[22] They further point out that leaders of high-performing teams they have studied share characteristics with the *transformational leader,* which we introduced in Chapter 7.

According to Larson and LaFasto, effective team leaders establish a *clear vision of the future.* This vision serves as a goal that inspires hard work and the quest for performance excellence; it creates a sense of shared purpose. Effective team leaders help to *create change.* They are dissatisfied with the status quo, influence team members toward similar dissatisfaction, and infuse the team with the motivation to change in order to become better. Finally, effective team leaders *unleash talent.* They make sure the team is staffed with members of the right skills and abilities. And they make sure these people are highly motivated to use their talents to achieve the group's performance objectives.

Overall, leaders of high-performance teams create supportive climates in which team members know what to expect from the leader and each other, and know what the leader expects from them. They empower team members. By personal example they demonstrate the importance of setting aside self-interests to support the team's goals. Team building can and should be used to assist in all these respects. In fact, leaders of high-performance teams are most likely engaged in team building on a relatively continuous basis. Rather than looking at the process as something to be used only on a fixed schedule, and typically with an outside facilitator, they view it as an ongoing leadership responsibility.

In Summary

What is the role of groups in organizations?

- A group is a collection of people who work together to accomplish a common goal.
- Organizations operate as interlocking networks of groups, which offer many benefits to the organizations and to their members.
- Groups help organizations through synergy and task performance; they also help members to satisfy important needs.

What are current directions in the use of groups?

- Organizations are becoming more "groupy" as interest grows in better utilizing groups and work teams as organizational resources.
- Groups are important mechanisms of empowerment and participation in the workplace.
- Self-managing teams are changing the lower level of the organization by allowing group members to perform for themselves many tasks previously reserved for their supervisors.
- Committees and task forces are increasingly being used to facilitate cross-functional relations and allow special projects to be completed with creativity.
- Employee-involvement groups, such as the quality circle, are also creating opportunities for employees to provide important insights into daily problem solving.
- New developments in information technology are also making virtual teams, or computer-mediated groups, more commonplace.

What makes a group effective?

- An effective group is one that achieves high levels of both task performance and member satisfaction.
- An effective group not only performs well, but also has the quality of relationships among group members that allows for the continuation of this high performance over time.
- Groups may be viewed as open systems that depend on a variety of inputs and processes to achieve output effectiveness.
- Important group input factors include the organizational setting, nature of the task, size, and membership characteristics.

What should managers understand about teamwork and group dynamics?

- In any group, the input factors and throughput processes must be well managed.
- As a group matures through various stages of development, from forming to adjourning, it needs different support at each stage.
- Group norms are the standards or rules of conduct that influence the behavior of members.
- Group cohesion is the attractiveness of the group to its members.
- In highly cohesive groups, members tend to conform to group norms.
- The best situation for any manager is for the group to have a positive performance norm and be highly cohesive.
- A proper balance of task and maintenance activities helps groups operate effectively.

How can team building increase group effectiveness?

- Team building is a sequence of activities designed to help groups analyze their operations and performance and develop action plans for improving them.
- High-performing work teams have a clear and shared sense of purpose, as well as strong internal commitment to its accomplishment.
- The team-building process should be data-based and collaborative, involving a high level of participation by all group members.

13

DECISION MAKING:

SOLVING PROBLEMS

As you read Chapter 13, keep in mind these study questions:

- Why are decision making and problem solving important?

- How do managers find and define key problems?

- What techniques help in generating and evaluating alternative solutions?

- How do managers decide among alternative courses of action?

- What must be done to implement a solution and evaluate results?

Consider this problem situation. Lee Iacocca, as CEO of Chrysler Corporation, was once caught by surprise with a crisis situation. It all began when a few Chrysler executives were caught speeding by Missouri troopers, who later discovered the cars' odometers were disconnected. This resulted in charges that Chrysler was selling as "new" autos that had been driven up to four hundred miles by employees. Iacocca's first inclination was to defend the practice as normal quality-control testing. After reconsidering, he changed his mind. The company pleaded "no contest" and agreed to pay more than $16 million to owners of the suspect vehicles. Iacocca told a group of reporters that the company practice "went beyond dumb and reached all the way to stupid." To back up the admission, Chrysler ran full-page ads in major newspapers saying, in part, "Disconnecting odometers is a lousy idea. That's a mistake we won't make again at Chrysler. Period."[1]

Managers as Decision Makers and Problem Solvers

Not all managerial situations are as sensational as the one just described at Chrysler. But decisions—big and small, momentous and routine—make up a manager's daily work life. A **decision** is a choice among alternative courses of action for dealing with a problem. A **problem,** in turn, is a difference between an actual situation and a desired situation. That is, a problem exists whenever there is a difference between what is in a work situation and what should be.

The most obvious problem situation faced by managers is a *performance deficiency*. This occurs when actual performance is less than desired. For example, a manager faces a possible problem when turnover or absenteeism suddenly increases in the work unit, when a subordinate's daily output decreases, or when a higher executive complains about something that has been said or done. However, managers also encounter problem situations that represent *performance opportunities*. These occur when actual performance is better than anticipated or offers the potential to be so. Good managers aren't content simply to accept the status quo; they aggressively search for new ways to make performance gains.

The challenge in dealing with any problem, be it a performance deficiency or an opportunity, is to proceed with effective **problem solving**—the process of identifying a discrepancy between an actual and desired state of affairs and then acting to resolve the discrepancy.[2] As part of problem-solving, **decision making** is the process of choosing a preferred course of action from a set of alternatives. But the

194

full problem-solving process is not complete until action has been taken to do what is necessary to implement the decision and correct a performance deficiency or properly explore an opportunity.

How Managers Deal with Problems

In practice, managers exhibit three quite different styles for dealing with workplace problems. Some are *problem avoiders*. They ignore information that would otherwise signal the presence of a problem; they are inactive and do not want to deal with problems. Some are *problem solvers*. They try to solve problems when they arise; that is, they are reactive in responding to problems after they occur. And still others are *problem seekers*. They actively look for problems to solve or opportunities to explore; they are proactive in anticipating problems before they occur.

All three styles play useful roles in day-to-day management. There will be times when problem avoidance is an appropriate managerial response. And all managers, like the earlier example of Lee Iacocca, must be able to react well to solve problems when they arise unexpectedly. Ultimately, though, success at problem seeking will distinguish the exceptional managers from the merely good ones. True problem seekers are forward-thinking managers who anticipate problems and opportunities and take appropriate action to gain the advantage.

Systematic and Intuitive Thinking

Another distinction in the way managers deal with problems contrasts "systematic" with "intuitive" thinking. *Systematic thinkers* approach problems in a rational and analytical fashion. They are able to break a complex problem into smaller components and then address them in a logical and integrated fashion. They can be expected to make a plan before taking action, and then search for information to facilitate problem solving in a step-by-step fashion. This approach works best when information is readily available and there is time to collect and analyze it carefully.

Intuitive thinkers are more flexible and spontaneous than systematic thinkers, and they also may be quite creative.[3] They are likely to respond imaginatively to a problem based on a quick and broad overview of the situation and possible alternative courses of action. They can be expected to deal with many aspects of a problem at once, jump quickly from one issue to another, and consider "hunches" based on experience or spontaneous ideas. This approach tends to work best in situations of high uncertainty, where facts are limited and few precedents exist.

Managers should feel confident in applying both systematic and intuitive thinking in problem solving. But, interestingly, some employers are concerned that today's college graduates may tend to err in the direction of being too systematic in problem solving. The result, they say, is a loss of creativity in the process. When General Foods faced diminishing Sugar-Free Kool-Aid sales, someone suggested that the company invite six teams of business-school students to develop marketing plans. For a full day, students from Stanford, Michigan, Northwestern, Pennsylvania, Columbia, and Chicago universities pored over GF-supplied data. A panel of judges from General Foods and its ad agencies were disappointed; they felt the proposed

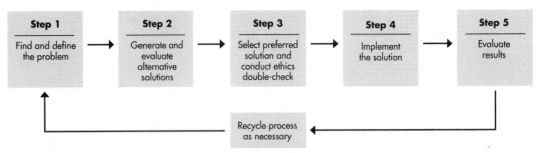

Figure 13.1   Steps in the problem-solving process.

plans lacked originality. The students were criticized for being overly concerned with the many facts and figures provided to them and not concerned enough about broader strategic issues.[4]

Multidimensional Thinking

Multidimensional thinking is the capacity to view many problems at once, in relationship to one another, and across long and short time horizons.[5] The importance of this thinking grows the higher one goes in the managerial ranks and the more general one's managerial responsibilities become. Senior managers, in particular, are described as dealing with "portfolios" of problems and opportunities consisting of multiple and interrelated issues. Good problem solving requires that these problems be "mapped" into a network that can be managed actively over time as priorities, events, and demands continuously change.

Effective managers are able to make decisions and take action in the short run but in ways that benefit longer-run objectives. Through all the daily challenges of a complex and shifting mix of problems, there is still a need to retain a sense of direction as each one is solved. The ability to do so is called *strategic opportunism*— the ability to remain focused on long-term objectives while being flexible enough to resolve short-term problems and opportunities in a timely manner.[6]

The Problem-Solving Process

Figure 13.1 describes a typical approach to managerial problem solving. The process begins with problem identification and ends with the evaluation of implemented solutions. Most importantly, it includes a built-in checkpoint to verify the ethical aspects of a decision before any action is taken. Five steps in problem solving are discussed in the remainder of this chapter:

1. Find and define the problem.
2. Generate and evaluate alternative solutions.
3. Choose a preferred solution *and* conduct the ethics double-check.
4. Implement the preferred solution.
5. Evaluate results.

Finding and Defining Problems

In the first step of the problem-solving process, the manager is concerned with finding and defining the problem. This is a stage of information gathering, information processing, and deliberation. It often begins with the appearance of *problem symptoms,* which signal the presence of a performance deficiency or opportunity. The manager's goal here is to assess a situation properly. She or he must look beyond symptoms to find out what is really wrong or how things could be improved. Special care must be taken to not just address a symptom while ignoring the true problem. Merely reprimanding a subordinate for absenteeism, for example, might never solve the underlying problem of dissatisfaction with a new job assignment.

The best managers continually search and scan the work environment for indicators of actual or potential performance deficiencies or opportunities. They are *entrepreneurial managers* who remain alert to problem-solving opportunities. For example, Peter Drucker claims that the success of Japanese firms in the market for fax machines may be due partly to the failure of American firms to seize an opportunity. The fax machine was invented in the United States, and U.S. firms had them ready to sell. But market researchers supposedly concluded that there was little demand for a product whose cost to send messages was higher than the mail.[7]

Types of Problems and Decisions

Managers face many problems in their day-to-day work. *Structured problems* are familiar, straightforward, and clear in respect to the information needed to resolve them. They can often be anticipated as common situations that regularly occur. The manager can plan ahead for them and even take actions to prevent their occurrence. When problems are structured and routine, tending to arise on a regular basis, they can be addressed through standard or prepared responses. *Programmed decisions* are solutions already known by past experience to be appropriate for the problem at hand. For example, a typical manager may expect to encounter personnel problems when making decisions on periodic staff pay raises and promotions, vacation requests, and committee assignments. Knowing that problems might occur, extra care can be taken when making the decisions, and plans can be made to handle any complaints that might arise.

Unstructured problems occur as new or unexpected situations that involve ambiguities and information deficiencies. Being unfamiliar and unanticipated, standard or programmed responses to them are not available. They require novel solutions created through *nonprogrammed decisions* specifically tailored to the situation at hand. The information requirements for defining and resolving nonroutine problems typically are high. And although computer support may assist in information processing, the decision will be made largely on the basis of human judgment. Most problems faced by higher-level managers are of this type.

Dealing with Crisis

A *crisis problem* is an unexpected problem that can lead to disaster if it is not resolved quickly. No one can avoid crises, and the public is well aware of the immensity of corporate crises in the modern world. The Tylenol poisonings of the mid-1980s, the Chernobyl nuclear plant explosion in the Ukraine, and the *Exxon Valdez* oil spill in Alaska are but a few sensational examples. Managers in more progressive organizations now anticipate that crises, unfortunately, will occur. They are installing "early-warning" crisis information systems and developing crisis-management plans in order to deal with them in the best possible ways.

The ability to handle crises may be the ultimate test of a manager's problem-solving capabilities. Unfortunately, research indicates that managers may react to a crisis by isolating themselves and trying to solve the problem alone or in a small, closed group.[8] This unfortunate tendency actually denies them access to crucial problem-solving information and assistance at the very time they are most needed. The crisis may even be accentuated if more problems are created because critical decisions are made with poor or inadequate information and from a limited perspective. Intel's initial nonresponse in 1994 to the "crisis" relating to its defective Pentium chip is a multimillion dollar case in point; the firm eventually bowed to consumer pressure and offered replacement chips.

Tips on Defining Problems

The way a problem is originally defined can have a major impact on how it is eventually resolved. Three common mistakes may occur at this critical first step in problem solving. Mistake #1 is *defining the problem too broadly or too narrowly*. To take a classic example, the problem stated as, "Build a better mousetrap" might be better defined as, "Get rid of the mice." Like the latter approach, managers should define problems to give themselves the best possible range of problem-solving options. Mistake #2 is *focusing on symptoms instead of causes*. Symptoms are indicators that problems may exist, but they shouldn't be mistaken for the problems themselves. Managers should be able to spot problem symptoms (e.g., a drop in performance). And rather than simply treating symptoms (such as disciplining someone for absenteeism), managers should be able to address their root causes (e.g., the need for training in how to use a complex new computer system). Mistake #3 is *choosing the wrong problem to deal with*. Managers should set priorities and deal with the most important problems first. They should give priority to problems that are truly solvable, and should be willing to take no action if the situation warrants.

Generating and Evaluating Alternative Solutions

Once the problem is defined, it is possible to formulate one or several possible solutions. At this stage more information is gathered, data are analyzed, and the pros and cons of alternative courses of action are identified. Creativity is important here. The better the pool of alternatives, the more likely a good solution will be achieved. Common errors must also be avoided in this stage. These errors include selecting a particular solution too quickly or choosing a convenient alternative that has damaging side effects or that is not as good as others that might be discovered with extra

---

THE EFFECTIVE MANAGER 13.1

Ten Ways to Increase Creativity

1. Look for more than one "right" answer or one "best way."
2. Avoid being too logical; let your thinking roam.
3. Challenge rules, ask *why;* don't settle for the status quo.
4. Ask "what if" questions.
5. Let ambiguity help you and others see things differently.
6. Don't be afraid of error; let trial-and-error be a path to success.
7. Take time to play and experiment; let them be paths to discovery.
8. Look outside of your specialization to find other viewpoints and perspectives.
9. Support nonconformity; let differences exist.
10. Believe in creativity, by you and others; make it a self-fulfilling prophecy.

---

effort. The involvement of others is very important at this stage. Involvement helps to maximize information and build commitment for action follow-through.

Improving Creativity

Creativity is an application of ingenuity and imagination that results in a novel approach or unique solution to a problem.[9] The greater the creativity, the more alternatives that are likely to be considered in problem solving and the greater the likelihood that they will be rigorously evaluated. Take a moment to test your creativity. Each of the following puzzles symbolizes a familiar word or phase. See if you can name each.

1. SAND 2. $\dfrac{\text{MIND}}{\text{MATTER}}$ 3. $\dfrac{0}{\begin{array}{c}\text{M.D.}\\\text{PH.D.}\\\text{D.D.}\end{array}}$ 4. $\begin{array}{c}\text{DICE}\\\text{DICE}\end{array}$

In order to solve these puzzles, you must be creative and look at things with a fresh and unrestrained eye. The correct answers are (1) "sandbox," (2) "mind over matter," (3) "three degrees below zero," and (4) "paradise." And, just as the puzzles probably look easier in retrospect, creativity is something that can be enhanced through discipline and good judgment. The Effective Manager 13.1 introduces a number of additional techniques that can be used to enhance creative thinking. All are designed to help you look at problems more creatively.

Chapter 12 discussed the importance of groups as human resources in organizations. One of their major benefits is the potential to increase creativity in the workplace. Two group techniques are particularly helpful in this respect—brainstorming and the nominal group technique.[10]

In **brainstorming,** groups of five to ten members meet to generate ideas. Brainstorming groups typically operate within strict guidelines. *All criticism is ruled out.* Judgment or evaluation of ideas must be withheld until the idea-generation process has been completed. *Freewheeling* is welcomed. The wilder or more radical the idea, the better. *Quantity is important.* The greater the number of ideas, the greater the likelihood of obtaining a superior idea. Building on one another's ideas is encouraged. Participants should suggest how ideas of others can be turned into better ideas, or how two or more ideas can be joined into still another hybrid idea.

By prohibiting criticism, brainstorming reduces fears of ridicule or failure on the part of individuals. Ideally, this results in more enthusiasm, involvement, and a freer flow of ideas among members. But there are times when group members have very different opinions and goals. The differences may be so extreme that a brainstorming meeting might deteriorate into antagonistic arguments and harmful conflicts. In such cases, a **nominal group technique** could help. This approach uses a highly structured meeting agenda to allow everyone to contribute ideas without the interference of evaluative comments by others. It allows for many alternatives to be generated and evaluated without risk of inhibitions or hostilities. The basic steps for running a nominal group are:

1. Participants are asked to work alone and respond in writing with possible solutions to a stated problem.

2. Ideas are then read aloud in round-robin fashion *without* any criticism or discussion; all ideas are recorded on a flip-chart or blackboard as they are presented.

3. Ideas are discussed and clarified in round-robin sequence, with no evaluative comments allowed.

4. Members individually and silently follow a written voting procedure that allows for all alternatives to be rated or ranked in priority order.

5. The last two are repeated as needed to further clarify the process.

Problem-Solving Environments

All managers must be prepared to make problem-solving decisions under different environmental conditions. In a *certain environment* there is sufficient information for the problem solver to know the possible alternatives and the results of each. This is an ideal condition for problem solving. The challenge is simply to study the alternatives and choose the best solution. Very few managerial problems occur in certain environments, but steps can sometimes be taken to reduce uncertainty.

In a *risk environment* the problem solver lacks complete information on action alternatives and their consequences but has some sense of the "probabilities" associated with their occurrence. A probability is the degree of likelihood (e.g., 4 chances out of 10) that an event will occur. Risk is a fairly common decision environment for managers. It is especially typical for entrepreneurs and organizations that depend on ideas and continued innovation for their success.

When information is so poor that managers are unable even to assign probabilities to the likely outcomes of known alternatives, an *uncertain environment* exists. This is the most difficult problem environment. Uncertainty forces managers to rely heavily on creativity in problem solving. It requires unique, novel, and often totally innovative alternatives to existing patterns of behavior. Groups are frequently used for problem solving in such situations. In all cases, responses to uncertainty depend greatly on intuition, educated guessing, and hunches—all of which leave considerable room for error.

Criteria for Analyzing Alternatives

The analysis of alternatives should determine how well each possible course of action deals with the problem at hand. A very basic evaluation involves **cost–benefit analysis,** the comparison of what an alternative will cost in relationship to the expected benefits. At a minimum, the *benefits* of a chosen alternative should be greater than its *costs.* Another issue typically involves *timeliness;* that is, how fast the desired outcomes are likely to be achieved. Various quantitative approaches can help in the analysis of problems. In all cases, however, the insights of quantitative analysis must be tempered with human judgment to ensure that all criteria are properly considered. This is particularly true in respect to the criterion of *ethical soundness,* which involves answering this question: How well does the alternative meet acceptable ethical criteria in the eyes of all those who have an interest in it?

Choosing Among Alternatives: Making a Decision

Once alternatives are generated and evaluated, a final choice among them must be made. This is the point of ultimate decision making. Just how this is done, and by whom, must be successfully resolved in each problem situation.

Deciding to Decide

The effective manager knows when to delegate decisions to others, how to set priorities in addressing problems, and when not to act at all. When presented with a problem, it is recommended that a manager proceed with problem solving only if each of the following questions can be answered *yes:* Is the problem significant? Is the problem solvable? Is the problem here to stay? Is this my problem to solve? Asking and answering these questions adds discipline to managerial decision making. It can also help managers avoid a potentially damaging tendency called **escalating commitment.** This is the tendency to increase effort and perhaps apply more resources to pursue a course of action that is not working.[11] In such cases, managers let the momentum of the situation overwhelm them. They are unable to "call it quits," even when experience otherwise deems that this is the most appropriate thing to do.

It takes great objectivity to avoid escalating commitments to previously chosen

---

THE EFFECTIVE MANAGER 13.2

How to Avoid the Escalation Trap

- Set advance limits on your involvement and commitments to a particular course of action; stick with these limits.
- Make your own decisions; don't follow the lead of others, since they are also prone to escalation.
- Carefully determine just why you are continuing a course of action; if there are insufficient reasons to continue, don't.
- Remind yourself of what a course of action is costing; consider the saving of such costs as a reason to discontinue.
- Watch for escalation tendencies; be on guard against their influence on both you and others involved in the course of action.

---

courses of action. The Effective Manager 13.2 contains advice on how to avoid the escalation trap. In addition, two pieces of advice are important. First, be willing to deal with negative information rather than disregard or downplay it. Second, be willing to depersonalize the situation and avoid the *hero's fallacy*—the tendency to be blind to one's own mistakes.

Deciding How to Decide

Management theory distinguishes between two major models of decision making—the classical model and the behavioral model. These are described in Figure 13.2 along with another important influence on managerial decision making—the use of judgmental heuristics.

Classical decision theory views the manager as acting in a certain world: The manager faces a clearly defined problem and knows all possible action alternatives plus their consequences. As a result, an *optimizing decision* is made. That is, the manager chooses the alternative giving the absolute best solution to the problem. The classical approach is a very rational model for managerial decision making.

Behavioral scientists question the assumptions underlying classical decision the-

Classical model
Views manager as acting with complete information in a certain environment

- Clearly defined problem
- Knowledge of all possible alternatives and
- their consequences
  Optimizing decision—
  choice of the "optimum" alternative

Administrative model
Views manager as having cognitive limitations and acting with incomplete information in risk and uncertain environments

- Problem not clearly defined
- Knowledge is limited on possible alternatives and their consequences
- Satisficing decision—
  choice of "satisfactory" alternative

Judgmental heuristics approach
Heuristics are adopted to simplify managerial problem solving

Decisions are influenced by:
- Information readily available in memory—the available heuristic
- Comparisons with similar circumstances—the representatives heuristic
- Current situation—The anchoring and adjustment heuristic

Figure 13.2   The classical, behavioral, and judgmental heuristics approaches to managerial decision making and problem solving.

ory. Perhaps best represented by the work of Herbert Simon, they recognize the existence of cognitive limitations, or limits to our human information-processing capabilities.[12] These limitations make it hard for managers to make perfectly rational decisions. They create a bounded rationality such that managerial decisions are rational only within the boundaries defined by the available information.

Behavioral decision theory, accordingly, assumes that people act only in terms of what they perceive about a given situation. Because such perceptions are frequently imperfect, the decision maker has only partial knowledge about the available action alternatives and their consequences. Consequently, the first alternative that appears to give a satisfactory resolution of the problem is likely to be chosen. Simon, who won a Nobel Prize for his work, calls this a *satisficing decision*—choosing the first satisfactory alternative that comes to your attention. This model seems especially accurate in describing how people make decisions about ambiguous problems in risky and uncertain conditions. Although this may be adequate in low-consequence cases where other factors demand more attention, caution should be exercised when satisficing is used in high-consequence decisions.

Faced with complex environments, limited information, and cognitive limitations, people tend to use simplifying strategies for decision making. The use of such strategies, called **heuristics,** can cause decision errors. An awareness of them and their potential biases can help you improve managerial decision making.[13] The *availability heuristic* occurs when people use information "readily available" from memory as a basis for assessing a current event or situation. An example is deciding not to invest in a new product based on your recollection of how well a similar new product performed in the recent past. The potential bias is that the readily available information might be fallible and might represent irrelevant factors. The new product that recently failed may have been a good idea that was released to market at the wrong time of year.

The *representativeness heuristic* occurs when people assess the likelihood of something occurring based on its similarity to a stereotyped set of occurrences. An example is deciding to hire someone for a job vacancy simply because he or she graduated from the same school attended by your last and most successful new hire. The potential bias is that the representative stereotype may fail to discriminate important and unique factors relevant to the decision. For instance, abilities and career expectations of the newly hired person may not fit job requirements.

The *anchoring and adjustment heuristic* involves making decisions based on adjustments to a previously existing value or starting point. An example is setting a new salary level for an employee by simply raising the prior year's salary by a reasonable percentage. The potential bias is that this may inappropriately bias a decision toward only incremental movement from the starting point. For instance, the individual's market value may be substantially higher than the existing salary. A simple adjustment won't keep this person from looking for another job.

Deciding Who Should Decide

In practice, three decision-making methods are important to managers. In *individual decisions,* the manager acts alone in making a decision. In *consultative decisions,* the manager gathers the advice of others before making a decision. In *group decisions,* the manager allows others to work together as a group to make a decision. All of these decision-making methods are useful. The keys are to know both when to use each and how to do each well.

In individual decisions the manager makes the choice of a preferred course of action. This decision is made alone, based on information the manager possesses, and without the participation of other people. When this method is used, a manager relies on his or her formal authority and personal expertise. The latter point is especially important: An individual decision presumes that the decision maker has sufficient information and understanding to make a "good" decision—one that satisfies the criteria for evaluating alternatives introduced earlier.

In today's complex work settings, the demands of problem solving often surpass the abilities of a single decision maker. One way of dealing with this is by involving others in consultative decisions. In this case, a manager seeks information and advice on the problem from others. This consultation may be done one-on-one or in a group setting. Based on the information received and its interpretation, the manager then makes a final choice of a preferred course of action.

Further along the scale of involvement is the group decision. Here, a manager not only consults with others, she asks them to make—or help make—a final, problem-solving decision. This is the most participative of the three methods. It is also the foundation for true employee empowerment in the workplace. Group decision making offers three potential benefits.[14] First, there is more knowledge and information available for decision making. Second, it results in better understanding of the final decision by everyone involved. Third, it results in increased acceptance of the final decision by everyone involved; participants in group problem solving are more likely to feel responsible for making the final decision work.

By the same token, group decision making has its limitations. Sometimes groups suffer from social pressure to conform. The desire to be a good member and go along with the group can lead people to conform prematurely to poor decisions. Group decision making may also fall prey to individual domination: A dominant individual may emerge and control the group's decisions. And also, the time requirements of group decisions may be a disadvantage. Groups frequently are slower to make decisions than are individuals acting alone.

Conducting the Ethics Double-Check

As mentioned earlier, any potential solution to a problem should be tested by an *ethics double-check*. This requirement is increasingly necessary to ensure that the ethical aspects of a problem are properly considered in the complex, fast-paced decision making so common in today's organizations. It is also consistent with the demanding moral standards of modern society. A willingness to pause to examine the ethics of a proposed decision might well result in both better decisions and the prevention of costly litigation. The suggested ethics double-check involves asking—and answering—these two questions: (1) "How would I feel about this decision if my family found out?" and (2) "How would I feel about this decision if it were reported in the local newspaper?"

Implementing the Solution and Evaluating Results

The final challenges in the problem-solving process are to implement the chosen solution and evaluate results. Implementation is a managerial responsibility that speaks for itself. Nothing new can or will happen unless action is taken. For problem solving to succeed, managers not only need the courage and creativity to arrive at a decision, they also need the personal willingness and the support of others to implement it.

A common implementation failure is due to the *lack of participation error*—the failure of a decision maker to adequately involve those persons whose support is necessary to ensure a decision's complete implementation. Managers who use participation wisely get the right people involved in problem solving from the beginning. Implementation typically follows quickly, smoothly, and to everyone's satisfaction. Once again, such participation is the cornerstone for broad-based worker involvement in daily organizational problem solving.

Evaluation is an often neglected but essential component in problem solving. It is a form of managerial control where actual results are compared to desired outcomes to see if a problem really has been resolved. If not, corrective action is supposed to be taken. Evaluation can reveal where modifications can be made in the original solution to improve its results over time. It can also provide important information to make "go–no go" decisions and to avoid the pitfalls of escalating commitments to previously chosen courses of action.

In any evaluation, both the positive and negative consequences of the chosen course of action should be examined. If the original solution appears inadequate, a return to earlier steps in the problem-solving process to generate a modified or new solution may be required. In this way, problem solving becomes a dynamic and ongoing activity within the management process. Evaluation is also made easier if the original goals and objectives of the proposed solution to a problem are clear and objective. Action plans that include measurable targets with timetables for their accomplishment have a built-in advantage in terms of the evaluation and control of results.

In Summary

Why are decision making and problem solving important?

- Managers make and help others to make decisions that solve important organizational problems.

- A problem is a discrepancy between an actual and desired state of affairs; problems occur as both performance deficiencies and unexplored opportunities.

- Decisions are problem-solving choices made among alternative courses of action.

- Managers who are problem seekers, and who use both systematic and intuitive thinking, are well suited for problem solving in today's challenging work settings.

- The problem-solving process begins with finding and defining a problem, and ends with implementing a preferred solution and evaluating results.

How do managers find and define key problems?

- Routine problems can be addressed through programmed decisions used over and over again.
- Nonroutine problems require nonprogrammed decisions and unique solutions to fit the situation.
- The most threatening type of problem is the crisis, which occurs unexpectedly and can lead to disaster if not handled quickly and properly.
- Common problem-solving errors include defining a problem too broadly or too narrowly and mistaking symptoms for causes.

What techniques help in generating and evaluating alternative solutions?

- Creativity, in the form of ingenuity and imagination, is an asset in decision making and problem solving.
- Individual creativity should be encouraged and developed.
- Techniques for enhancing group creativity include brainstorming and the nominal group technique.
- Problems are solved and decisions made under different conditions.
- In certain environments all alternatives are known; in risk environments information on alternatives is available but incomplete; in uncertain environments information is minimal and ambiguous.
- Criteria for evaluating alternatives include costs, benefits, timelines, and ethical soundness.

How do managers decide among alternative courses of action?

- An optimizing decision takes the absolute best or optimum alternative based on classical guidelines.
- A satisficing decision, using behavioral guidelines, takes the first satisfactory alternative to come to attention.
- Judgmental heuristics, such as the availability heuristic, the anchoring and adjustment heuristic, and the representativeness heuristic, can bias decision making.
- Management decisions can be made by individual, consultative, or group methods.
- Consultative or group decisions are preferred when the manager lacks sufficient information to make a good decision, and/or needs the support of the group to ensure implementation.

- Participation in decision making is important in planning and throughout the management process.

What must be done to implement a solution and evaluate results?

- All decisions must be implemented if their desired effects are to be achieved.
- A common impediment to implementation is the lack of participation error.
- Group forms of decision making help create the understanding, acceptance, and commitment needed to ensure implementation of decisions.
- Managerial follow-through, or control, to evaluate results achieved is necessary for effective implementation.
- Good evaluation can lead to changes that can improve the implementation of a decision.

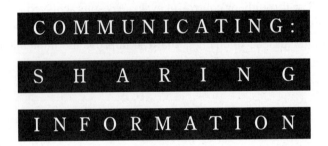

COMMUNICATING:

SHARING

INFORMATION

As you read Chapter 14, keep in mind these study questions:

- What is communication as a managerial responsibility?

- What are the major barriers to effective communication?

- How can managers improve organizational communication?

- How does perception influence communication?

- How does cultural diversity influence communication?

C ommunication is a critical managerial skill and an essential foundation for effective management. Through communication, managers establish and maintain the interpersonal relationships needed to do their jobs well on a daily basis. Through communication, managers listen to others and share the understandings and information needed to create a motivational workplace. No manager can do well without being a good communicator, and "communication skills" are often at the top of the list of the attributes employers look for in job candidates. Such skills include the ability to communicate well in face-to-face situations, on the telephone, in various forms of public speaking, in writing, and in the electronic medium of the computer. And as we have discussed at many points already in this book, they include being able to function well in an environment of workforce diversity. Indeed, the many developments in the new workplace often depend on communication as a key to unlocking the full potential of an organization's human resources.

Managers and Communication

Formally defined, **communication** is the process of sending and receiving symbols with messages attached to them.[1] This process is a foundation for all interpersonal relationships. Through communication, people exchange and share information with one another; and through communication, people influence one another's attitudes, behaviors, and understandings.

Good communication is indispensable to effective managerial leadership. Research indicates that the majority of a manager's time is spent in oral communications. Executives studied by Henry Mintzberg and others, for example, spent only about one-quarter of their time doing "desk work." The rest of their time was distributed among scheduled and unscheduled meetings (over 60 percent), telephone calls (6 to 8 percent), and walk-around tours (3 percent).[2] Indeed, one way to view the managerial role is as a nerve center of information flows. The manager serves as the center point in a complex information-processing system whose responsibilities include gathering appropriate information from sources both inside and outside the work unit (monitor role), distributing information within the work unit (disseminator role) and through external contacts (spokesperson role), and using information to solve problems and explore opportunities (decision-maker role).

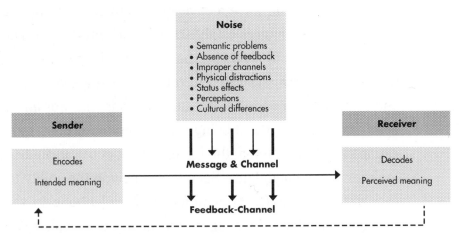

Figure 14.1   Elements in the process of interpersonal communication.

The Communication Process

The key elements in the communication process are illustrated in Figure 14.1. They include a *sender,* who is responsible for encoding an intended *message* into meaningful symbols—both verbal and nonverbal. The message is sent through a *channel,* written or oral, to a *receiver,* who then decodes or interprets its meaning—which may or may not match the sender's intentions. *Feedback,* when present, reverses the process and conveys the receiver's response back to the sender. Another way to view the communication process is as a series of questions: "Who?" (sender) "says what?" (message) "in what way?" (channel) "to whom?" (receiver) "with what result?" (interpreted meaning).

Effective communication occurs when the intended message of the sender and the interpreted meaning of the receiver are one and the same. This should be the manager's goal in any communication attempt, but it is not always achieved. Choice of communication channel is an important issue here. The opportunity to ask spontaneous questions (an important form of feedback) is a major advantage of oral, face-to-face communication. It is also something that is largely denied readers of written memos, letters, computer messages, or posted bulletins.

Efficient communication occurs at minimum cost in terms of resources expended. Time, in particular, is an important resource in the communication process. Picture an instructor taking the time to communicate individually with each student about this chapter. It would be virtually impossible—and even if it were possible, it would be costly. For similar reasons, managers often send written messages rather than visit their employees personally, and they often hold group rather than individual meetings. These channels are more efficient than one-on-one, face-to-face communications.

One of the problems managers face is that efficient communications are not always effective. A low-cost communication such as a bulletin posted in a hallway or a message sent by e-mail in a computer network may save time, but it does not always result in everyone getting the same meaning from the message. By the same token, an effective communication may not always be efficient. A manager who personally visits every employee to explain a new change in procedures can ensure that everyone fully understands the change, but such meetings are very costly in terms of the manager's time. Good managers know how to maximize the effectiveness of their communications while maintaining reasonable efficiency in the process.

Communication as Feedback

The process of telling other people how you feel about something they did or said, or about the situation in general, is called **feedback.** Giving feedback is an indispensable skill, since managers regularly give feedback to other people. Often, this takes the form of performance feedback given as evaluations and appraisals. When poorly done, such feedback can be threatening to the recipient and cause resentment. When properly done, feedback—even performance criticism—is listened to, accepted, and used to good advantage by the receiver. There are ways to help ensure that feedback is useful and constructive rather than harmful.

To begin, managers and others must learn to recognize when the feedback they are about to offer will really benefit the receiver and when it will mainly satisfy some personal need. A supervisor who berates a computer operator for data analysis errors, for example, might really be angry about personally failing to give clear instructions in the first place. In addition, a manager should make sure that any feedback is understandable, acceptable, and plausible—all from the recipient's point of view. Experts recommend the following guidelines for giving constructive feedback to others.

- Give feedback directly and with real feeling, based on trust between you and the receiver.
- Make feedback specific rather than general, using good, clear, and preferably recent examples.
- Give feedback at a time when the receiver appears to be in a condition of readiness to accept it.
- Check feedback with others to be sure they support its validity.
- Limit feedback to things the receiver might be expected to be able to do something about.
- Give feedback in small doses, and not more than the receiver can handle at any particular time.[3]

Communication Channels

A communication channel is the medium through which a message is conveyed from sender to receiver. The formal and informal structures of organizations, first discussed in Chapter 6, have their own communication patterns. *Formal communication channels* follow the chain of command established by an organization's hierarchy of authority. An organization chart, for example, indicates the proper routing for official messages passing from one level or part of the hierarchy to another. Because formal communication channels are recognized as official and authoritative, it is typical for written communications in the form of letters, memos, policy statements, and other announcements to adhere to them.

Informal communication channels develop separately from the formal structure and do not follow the chain of command; they follow the informal structures of the organization, often skipping management levels or cutting across lines of authority. An informal communication network is sometimes referred to as a *grapevine,* and grapevines are known to transmit information quickly and efficiently. Experienced managers know that a message well placed in a grapevine can travel faster—and often with greater impact—than can the same message passed along formal channels. Grapevines also help fulfill needs for the people involved in them. For example, someone can feel secure and important by being "in the know" when important things are going on. A grapevine can also provide social satisfaction through interpersonal contacts in the give and take of information.

The primary disadvantage of grapevines occurs when they transmit incorrect or untimely information. There is no doubt that rumors can be disruptive and that prematurely released information can be easily misinterpreted. Managers should get to know the grapevines and informal groups operating in their work settings and use them as complements to formal channels of communication. Instead of trying to eliminate them, the best advice is to make them work for you. After all, one of the best ways of avoiding incorrect rumors is to make sure that the key people in a grapevine get the right information to begin with. The importance of informal communication channels in organizations is highlighted in Thomas J. Peters and Robert H. Waterman Jr.'s best-selling book, *In Search of Excellence.* The authors report that successful companies "are a vast network of informal, open communications. The patterns and intensity cultivate the right people's getting into contact with each other."[4]

Barriers to Effective Communication

Effective communication is a two-way process that requires effort and skill by both the sender and the receiver. **Noise,** as shown earlier in Figure 14.1, is anything that interferes with the effectiveness of the communication process. Major sources of noise to be discussed here include poor use of communication channels, semantic problems, the absence of feedback, physical distractions, and status effects. The additional confounding influences of perceptions and cultural differences will receive separate treatment later in the chapter.

Poor Use of Communication Channels

Managers use a variety of oral, written, and nonverbal channels every day. *Oral communication* takes place via the spoken word in telephone calls, face-to-face meet-

---

THE EFFECTIVE MANAGER 14.1

How to Make a Successful Oral Presentation

- **Be prepared**—Know what you want to say; know how you want to say it; and rehearse saying it.
- **Set the right tone**—Act audience-centered; make eye contact; be pleasant and confident.
- **Sequence points**—State your purpose; make important points; follow with details; then summarize.
- **Support your points**—Give specific reasons for your points; state them in understandable terms.
- **Accent the presentation**—Use good visual aids; provide supporting handouts when possible.
- **Add the right amount of polish**—Attend to details; have the room, materials, equipment ready to go.
- **Be professional**—Be on time; wear appropriate attire; and act organized.

---

ings, formal briefings, video conferences, and the like. When it is done well, oral communication can increase effectiveness by allowing for feedback, encouraging spontaneous thinking, and conveying personal warmth. The Effective Manager 14.1 identifies guidelines for a common and important oral communication situation faced by managers—the executive briefing or formal presentation.

Written communication also takes skill. It isn't easy, for example, to write a concise letter or to express one's thoughts in a computer e-mail report. Any such message can easily be misunderstood. But when done well, written messages have the advantage of being able to reach many people in a cost-efficient manner. They also provide documents that can be filed for historical record.

Good managers choose the right communication channel, or combination of channels, to accomplish their intended purpose in a given situation. In general, written channels are acceptable for simple and easy-to-convey messages, and for those that require extensive dissemination quickly. They are also important, at least as follow-up communications, when formal policy or authoritative directives are being conveyed.[5] Oral channels work best for complex and difficult-to-convey messages where immediate feedback to the sender is valuable. They are also more personal, and are capable of creating a supportive, even inspirational, emotional climate.

Nonverbal communication takes place through such things as hand movements, facial expressions, body posture, eye contact, and use of interpersonal space. It can be a powerful means of transmitting messages. Eye contact or voice intonation can accent special parts of an oral communication. The astute manager also observes "body language" that is unknowingly expressed by others. That is, someone's body may be "talking" in a group or interpersonal situation, even as the person otherwise maintains silence. And when you speak, your body may sometimes "say" different things than your words convey.

Nonverbal channels probably play a more important part in communications than most people recognize. In fact, one potential side effect of the growing use of electronic mail, computer networking, and other communication technologies is that nonverbal signals—signals that may add important meaning to the communication event—are lost. On the other hand, a **mixed message** occurs when a person's words communicate one message while his or her actions, body language, or appearance communicate something else. Watch how people behave in a meeting. A person who feels under attack may move back in a chair or lean away from the presumed antagonist; a person pleased with what is taking place is prone to lean forward, smile, and nod in agreement. All of this is done quite unconsciously, but it sends a message to those alert enough to pick it up. Mixed messages are common in organizations, and they can cause considerable frustration and confusion for their recipients.

Another aspect of nonverbal communication involves *proxemics,* or the use of interpersonal space.[5] People can use space to increase or decrease distance between themselves and others. This distance, in turn, conveys varying intentions in terms of intimacy, openness, and status. As an everyday example, the proxemics or physical layout of an office is an often-overlooked form of nonverbal communication. But check it out. Offices with two or more chairs available for side-by-side seating, for example, convey different messages from those where the manager's chair sits behind the desk while those for visitors sit facing in front.

Semantic Problems

Communication will be effective only to the extent that the sender expresses a message in ways that can be clearly understood by the receiver. This means that verbal and/or nonverbal symbols must be well chosen and properly used to express the sender's intentions. When they are not, **semantic barriers** to communication occur as encoding and decoding errors and as mixed messages. Consider the following "bafflegab" found among some executive communications. The report said: Consumer elements are continuing to stress the fundamental necessity of a stabilization of the price structure at a lower level than exists at the present time. *Translation:* Consumers keep saying that prices must go down and stay down. The manager said: Substantial economies were effected in this division by increasing the time interval between distribution of data-eliciting forms to business entities. *Translation:* The division was saving money by sending fewer questionnaires to employers.

The Absence of Feedback

Letters, memos, e-mail, written reports, voice messages, and posted notices are examples of *one-way communications.* They do not allow for immediate feedback from receiver to source, and they may lose effectiveness as a result. But they are efficient in the use of the sender's time. In contrast, *two-way communications,* such as face-to-face conversations or group meetings, allow for spontaneous feedback. They may be less efficient for the sender, but they are usually more effective.

Physical Distractions

Any number of physical distractions can interfere with the effectiveness of a communication attempt. Some of these distractions—telephone interruptions, drop-in visitors, lack of privacy—are evident in the following (non)conversation between an employee, George, and his manager.

> Okay, George, let's hear your problem [phone rings, boss picks it up, promises to deliver a report "just as soon as I can get it done"] . . . Uh, now, where were we—oh, you're having a problem with your technician. She's [manager's secretary brings in some papers that need a signature, so he scribbles his name where indicated; secretary leaves] . . . you say she's overstressed lately, wants to leave . . . I tell you what, George, why don't you [phone rings again, and then George's lunch partner drops by] . . . uh, take a stab at handling it yourself. . . . I'll get back with you later.[7]

Besides what may have been poor intentions in the first place, the manager in this example did not do a good job of communicating with George. This problem could be corrected easily. If George has something important to say, the manager should set aside adequate time for the meeting. Additional interruptions such as telephone calls and drop-in visitors should be avoided by issuing appropriate instructions to the secretary. Many such distractions can be avoided or at least minimized through proper planning and managerial attention.

Status Effects

> "Criticize my boss? I don't have the right to."

> "I'd get fired."

> "It's her company, not mine."

As suggested in the prior comments, the hierarchy of authority in organizations creates another potential barrier to effective communication. The noise created by such *status effects* can be quite harmful. Consider the "corporate coverup" discovered, for example, at an electronics company where shipments were being predated and papers falsified to meet unrealistic sales targets set by the president. His managers knew the targets were impossible to attain, but at least twenty people in the organization cooperated in the deception. It was months before the top managers found out.[8]

What happened in the prior case is *filtering*—the intentional distortion of information to make it appear favorable to the recipient. Such filtering of information is often caused by status differences and the tendencies to create special barriers between managers and their subordinates. Tom Peters, the popular management author and consultant, calls such information distortion "Management Enemy Number 1."[9] Simply put, it most often involves "telling the boss what he or she wants to hear."

Responsibility for status effects often rests with managers who, given the authority of their positions, may be inclined to do a lot of telling, but not much listening. Subordinates, on the other hand, may be willing to communicate only what they expect the boss wants to hear. Whether the reason is a fear of retribution for bringing bad news, an unwillingness to identify personal mistakes, or just a general desire to please, the end result is the same. The manager receiving filtered communications makes poor decisions because of a biased and inaccurate information base.

THE EFFECTIVE MANAGER 14.2
Ten Rules for Good Listening
1. Stop talking.
2. Put the other person at ease.
3. Show that you want to listen.
4. Remove any potential distractions.
5. Empathize with the other person.
6. Don't respond too quickly; be patient.
7. Don't get mad; hold your temper.
8. Go easy on argument and criticism.
9. Ask questions.
10. Stop talking.

Improving Organizational Communication

Individuals and organizations can do a number of things to overcome barriers and improve organizational communication. Foremost among them is to employ the technique of active listening in all communications, to improve upward communication, and to use appropriately new development in information technology.

Better Listening

Being an effective communicator is clearly a skill, an important part of which lies in being able to encourage a flow of accurate information in your direction—that is, being a good listener as described in The Effective Manager 14.2. Managers must be sensitive to this responsibility. When people talk, they are trying to communicate something. That "something" may or may not be what they are saying.

Active listening is the process of taking action to help the source of a message say exactly what he or she really means. There are five rules for active listening.

Rule 1. *Listen for message content*—try to hear exactly what is being said in the message.

Rule 2. *Listen for feelings*—try to identify how the source feels in terms of the message content.

Rule 3. *Respond to feelings*—let the source know that the feelings are recognized.

Rule 4. *Note all cues*—be sensitive to nonverbal and verbal messages; be alert for mixed messages.

Rule 5. *Paraphrase and restate*—reflect back to the source what you think you are hearing.[10]

The following example contrasts how a "passive" listener and an "active" listener might respond in two workplace conversations.

Question Asker: "Don't you think employees should be promoted on the basis of seniority?"

Passive listener's response: "No, I don't!"

Active listener's response: "It seems to you that they should, I take it?"

Question Asker: "What does the supervisor expect us to do about these out-of-date computers?"

Passive listener's response: "Do the best you can, I guess."

Active listener's response: "You're pretty disgusted with those machines, aren't you?"

Better Upward Communication

A variety of strategies are available to avoid and otherwise minimize status effects and other problems in upward communication. One approach is called **management by wandering around,** or MBWA, for short. This means dealing directly with subordinates by regularly spending time walking around and talking with them about a variety of work-related matters. Instead of relying on formal channels to bring information to your attention, MBWA involves finding out for yourself what is going on. The basic objectives are to break down status barriers, increase the frequency of interpersonal contact, and get more and better information from lower-level sources. Of course, this requires that the manager establish trusting relationships with these employees.

There are other things managers can do to create good opportunities for upward communication. A comprehensive approach to improving upward communication often involves *open office hours,* whereby busy senior managers may set aside time in their calendars to welcome walk-in visits during certain hours each week. It often involves a program of formal *employee group meetings.* Here, a rotating schedule of "shirt-sleeve" meetings brings top managers into face-to-face contact with mixed employee groups throughout an organization. At Hewlett-Packard, "coffee talk" sessions are regularly held to bring top managers together with employees to discuss operations, strategies, and results.[11]

In some cases, a comprehensive program includes an *employee advisory council* composed of members elected by their fellow employees. Such a council may meet with top management on a regular schedule to discuss and react to new policies and programs that will affect employees. Also, there is always a place for the traditional *suggestion box* in an upward communication program. A suggestion box, electronic or other, is another way of encouraging all employees to communicate ideas or complaints. The success of any such program depends, in part, on management's willingness to address the suggestions and protect the anonymity of contributors.

One of the latest upward communication approaches is called **360-degree feedback** or *multi-rater assessment.* This typically involves upward appraisals done by a manager's subordinates, as well as additional feedback from peers, internal and external customers, and higher-ups. A self-assessment is also part of the process. Often this feedback is gathered through questionnaires in which respondents can remain anonymous. The goal of "360 feedback" is to provide the manager with information that can be used for constructive improvement. Managers who have participated in the process indicate surprise at learning they are perceived as lacking vision, having bad tempers, being bad listeners, lacking flexibility, and the like.[12] True success with the technique, however, requires follow-up communication with the "360" group to clarify expectations for future behavior.

Utilizing Information Technology

Organizational communication can benefit greatly from advancements in information technology. The nature of organizations today requires that most employees have basic computer skills and the willingness to utilize new technologies to maximum advantage. Probably the best example is the impact of e-mail and the availability of computerized information services now available. By making it easier and faster to move information from top-to-bottom in an organization, technology is contributing to the flattening of organization structures. Fewer middle managers are needed to serve information "transfer" roles when computers are able to do it for them. New information departments or centers are appearing on organization charts, and their staff experts play growing roles in day-to-day organizational affairs. And as managers adapt to the new technologies and expanded availability of information, their roles are changing as well. At the same time that computers help them to empower lower-level personnel with more and better information, they allow for improved control and accountability.

But while technology allows people to work together across great distances in real time through electronic networks, legitimate concerns may be raised over the loss of the "personal" side of group decision making and the risks of being too focused on "data" alone. Indeed, a critical test of the *new* manager may be the ability to utilize new information technology while still maintaining a motivational leadership style based on good interpersonal relationships.

Perception and Communication

The process through which people receive and interpret information from the environment is called **perception.** It is the way we form impressions about ourselves, other people, and daily life experiences, and the way we process information into the decisions that ultimately guide our actions. Perception, as shown in Figure 14.2, acts as a screen or filter through which information must pass before it has an impact on individual decisions and actions. Depending on individual values, needs, cultural background, and other circumstances of the moment, information will pass through this screen with varying interpretations.

The bottom line of the perception and communication issue is that people can perceive the same things quite differently. A manager's leadership style, as suggested in the earlier discussion of 360-degree feedback, is one area where such differences can easily arise. While we may think of ourselves as very open and democratic, our behavior may appear closed and autocratic in the eyes of others. Percep-

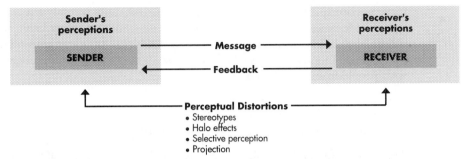

Figure 14.2 Perception as an information screen or filter that influences communication.

tual differences may also arise as multiple stakeholders in a given situation develop different impressions of a decision or series of events.

In our time of cultural and workforce diversity, great value is placed on respect for individual differences. Yet, as discussed in Chapter 9 on diversity, we also live with the daily influences of four common perceptual distortions shown in Figure 14.2: stereotypes, halo effects, selective perceptions, and projections. Each can obscure individual differences and prevent us from drawing accurate impressions of a person or situation. All such perceptual distortions can interfere with effective communication and cause problems in decision making. Thus, managers must not only be continuously on guard to make their own perceptions as accurate as possible, but they must also anticipate, recognize, and be prepared to react to the perceptions of others.

Communication and Diversity

Workforce diversity and the global economy are two of the most talked-about trends in modern society. Communicating under conditions of diversity, where the sender and receiver are part of different cultures, is certainly a significant challenge. For years, this challenge has been recognized by international travelers and businesspersons. But you don't have to travel abroad to come face-to-face with communication and cultural diversity. Just going to work is a cross-cultural journey for most of us today. The modern workplace abounds with subcultures based on gender, age, ethnicity, race, and other factors. And, as a result, the importance of cross-cultural communication skills applies at home just as well as they do in a foreign country.

Ethnocentrism and Cross-Cultural Communication

Different cultural backgrounds between senders and receivers in any situation can cause communication breakdowns. This can occur when communications involve people of different ethnic backgrounds or national origins, or even from different geographic regions within a country. A major source of difficulty in all of these cases is *ethnocentrism,* defined earlier in Chapter 9 as the tendency to consider one's culture superior to any and all others. Ethnocentrism can adversely affect communication in at least three major ways. It may cause someone to *not* listen well to what others have to say; it may cause someone to address or speak with others in ways that alienate them; and it may lead to the use of inappropriate stereotypes in dealing with people from another culture.

Communicating Across National Cultures

There is no doubt about it. Doing business in a foreign country poses a special communication challenge for the visiting businessperson. Not only must deals be negotiated, they must often be negotiated through very different ways of interacting, gesturing, entertaining, and speaking. Increasingly, business travelers are discovering that they must acquaint themselves with the cultural "rules" of the countries they visit or suffer the consequences. Behavior that is socially or professionally inappropriate—even if unintentionally so—can jeopardize a business opportunity.

Writing on a Japanese person's business card is like writing on his or her hand. Making the "OK" sign with one's fingers is an insult to a Brazilian. A nod of the head means "no" in Greece and Bulgaria. In Hong Kong, wearing blue and white indicates mourning. These examples all indicate that success in conducting business across cultural boundaries depends on the ability to understand and deal with cultural differences in a silent language that includes the languages of time, space, and things.[13]

The *language of time* must be understood for effective cross-cultural communication. Time and how it is used are viewed differently around the world. In the United States, assigning a deadline to something is accepted practice; in Southeast Asia it may convey rudeness. In Latin America, waiting in someone's office for a visit is normal; in the United States, being kept waiting is viewed as disrespect or disinterest. The *language of space* is important, too. Proxemics is an important aspect of nonverbal communications. A case in point involves cross-cultural differences in the way people use space during conversations. An American business traveler may be quite surprised at how close a counterpart from the Middle East might stand when engaged in serious business talk. The use and significance of material possessions across cultures also creates a *language of things*. A casual American visitor might be surprised to find a management consultant in Thailand very concerned about the type of watch, tie, and suit worn—and even the type of pen carried—when working with corporate clients. When questioned, however, the consultant will reply that such things are important symbols that help provide desired status in the eyes of clients.

Clearly, the emergence of the global economy and changing workforce demographics are helping to make managers increasingly more sensitive to diversity issues. But to deal with them effectively, managers must master the many complications of ethnocentrism and other influences on cross-cultural communication. And, during these dynamic and changing times, people in many work settings will still suffer the consequences of biased perceptions and ineffective communication.

In Summary

What is communication as a managerial responsibility?

- Communication is the interpersonal process of sending and receiving symbols with messages attached to them.
- Effective communication occurs when the sender and the receiver of a message both interpret it in the same way.
- Efficient communication occurs when the message is sent at low cost—time and effort—by the sender.
- Efficient communications—such as the written memo or the e-mail message— are not always effective.

What are the major barriers to effective communication?

- Noise is anything that interferes with the effectiveness of communication.
- Semantic problems, the poor choice and/or use of written or spoken words, can reduce communication effectiveness.
- Lack of feedback, failure to provide the sender with cues as to how the message is being or has been received, can reduce communication effectiveness.
- Poor use of communication channels can reduce communication effectiveness.
- Physical distractions, such as an environment with too much background noise, can reduce communication effectiveness.
- Status effects, the tendency of people in lower-level positions in organizations to filter information going to higher levels, can reduce communication effectiveness.

How can managers improve organizational communication?

- Active listening, through reflecting back and paraphrasing, can help to overcome communication barriers.
- Upward communication may be improved through techniques such as MBWA, managing by wandering around.
- Upward communication may be improved through structured meetings, suggestion systems, advisory councils, and the like.
- 360-degree feedback is a popular form of upward appraisal in today's organizations.
- Appropriate use of information technology, such as e-mail, can improve communication in organizations.

How does perception influence communication?

- Perception acts as a filter through which all communication passes as it travels from one person to the next.

- Because people tend to perceive things differently, the same message may be interpreted quite differently by different people.
- Good managers understand the perception process and are prepared to deal with differing perceptions in the workplace.
- Common perceptual distortions that may reduce communication effectiveness include stereotypes, projections, halo effects, and selective perception.

How does cultural diversity influence communication?

- The growing diversity of the workforce means that cross-cultural communication is more and more a part of everyday working life.
- People raised in different cultures often use different languages and have different ways of viewing the world and interpreting everyday events.
- Any and all cultural differences affect perceptions and have the potential to interfere with the effectiveness of communication between people of different cultural backgrounds.
- Greater cross-cultural sensitivity and an awareness of the silent languages of time, space, and things can help reduce the difficulties of communication and diversity.

15

INFLUENCING:

USING POWER

As you read Chapter 15, keep in mind these study questions:

- What is managerial power?

- How can managers gain power?

- How can managers achieve positive influence?

- Who or what sets the limits to power?

- What is the role of politics in managerial power?

R ichard S. Herlich went to the Center for Creative Leadership for training after being promoted to director of marketing for a division of American Cyanamid. "I thought I had the perfect style," he said, referring to his managerial leadership. Later, he was "devastated" to learn that other participants in the center's role-playing game viewed him as aloof and a poor communicator. But he listened to what they had to say. Back on the job, his "real" job, he held a meeting with his subordinates to discuss things. They voiced similar concerns, saying that his aloofness was even intimidating at times. After he became more involved in their projects and helped them to set deadlines, work that once took six to seven months was reduced to three.[1] It might be said that Richard learned that the popular concepts of "total quality management" and "continuous improvement" apply to more than operations—they apply equally well to individual managerial behavior. The new workplace demands that managers work with others in a way that creates sustained enthusiasm for doing a job well—time and time again. Enlightened managers know that this requires a personal commitment to the ongoing development of the talents needed to succeed in leadership situations.

What Is Managerial Power?

The foundations for effective leadership rest with the way managers use "power" to make things happen the way they want them to.[2] **Power,** simply defined, is the ability to get someone else to do something you want done. In management and organizational behavior, the sources of power are recognized in the following equation:[3]

MANAGERIAL POWER = POSITION POWER + PERSONAL POWER

Sources of Position Power

One important source of power is a manager's official status, or position, in the organization's hierarchy of authority. Whereas anyone holding a managerial position theoretically has this power, how well it is used will vary from one person to the next. Three bases of position power are reward power, coercive power, and legitimate power.

Reward power is based on the ability to control rewards or resources. It is the capability to offer something of value—a positive outcome—as a means of getting other people to do what you want them to do. Examples include pay raises, bonuses, promotions, special assignments, and verbal or written compliments. To mobilize reward power, a manager says, in effect, "If you do what I ask, I'll give you a reward."

Coercive power is based on the ability to control punishments. It is the capability to punish or withhold positive outcomes as a means of getting other people to do what you want them to do. A manager may attempt to coerce someone by threatening the person with verbal reprimands, pay penalties, or even termination. To mobilize coercive power, a manager says, in effect, "If you don't do what I want, I'll punish you."

Legitimate power is based on the control of formal **authority,** the right by virtue of one's organizational position or status to direct the activities of other people in subordinate positions. It is the ability to give orders or directives as a means of getting other people to do what you want them to do. To mobilize legitimate power, a manager says, in effect, "I am the boss and therefore you are supposed to do as I ask."

Sources of Personal Power

The second major source of power that managers may develop is personal power. This power derives from individual attributes rather than the position. It rests with the individual manager and the unique personal qualities he or she brings to a leadership situation. This is a very important source of power, one that a truly successful manager or leader cannot do without.

One base of personal power is **expert power,** the ability to control through special expertise and knowledge. It is the capability to get other people to do what you want them to do because of your recognized experience, understanding, and skills. Expertise derives from the possession of technical know-how or information pertinent to the issue at hand that others do not have.[4] This is developed by acquiring relevant skills or competencies or by gaining a central position in relevant information networks. It is maintained by protecting one's credibility and not overstepping the boundaries of true expertise or information. When a manager uses expert power, the implied message is: "You should do what I want because of my special expertise or information."

The second base of personal power is **referent power,** the ability to control through admiration and identification. It is the capability to get other people to do what you want them to do because they admire you and want to identify positively with you. Reference is a power derived from charisma or interpersonal attractiveness. It is developed and maintained through good interpersonal relations that encourage the admiration and respect of others. When a manager uses referent

Sources of power...

Power of the POSITION: Based on things managers can offer to others.	**Power of the PERSON:** Based on the ways managers are viewed by others.

Rewards: "If you do what I ask, I'll give you a reward."

Coercion: "If you *don't* do what I ask, I'll punish you."

Legitimacy: "Because I am the boss; you *must* do as I ask."

Expertise—as a source of special knowledge and information.

Reference—as a person with whom others like to identify.

Figure 15.1 The bases of managerial power.

power, the implied message is: "You should do what I want in order to maintain a positive self-defined relationship with me."

How to Gain Managerial Power

Managers need power to work successfully in a wide variety of formal and informal relationships with subordinates, peers, and higher-level executives. Ideally, their use of power in these relationships has positive results. In order to do so, managers must be continually concerned to build and maintain a substantial inventory of power from both position and personal sources, as shown in Figure 15.1.

Developing Position Power

Every manager should take steps to continuously build or enhance position power. This can be accomplished in three basic ways.[5] First, managers should strive to establish and maintain their *networking centrality*. This means becoming a part of important networks and staying intimately involved in the important information flows within them. To remain powerful, managers must avoid becoming isolated; rather, the strategy is always to become more and more a central part of all information flows. Second, *performance criticality* should always be advanced. It is essential that a manager demonstrate his or her essential importance in making sure that "high-impact" or "high value-added" tasks are accomplished. This means both supporting and taking good care of others responsible for important tasks and making sure that all significant personal tasks are done exceptionally well. Third, position power is also advanced by *personal visibility*. Managers who are adept at building position power are polite and respectful, but not shy. They are willing and able to become known as influential people. They seek out and take advantage of opportunities to make formal presentations, participate in key task forces or committees, and pursue special assignments that display their talents and capabilities to others.

Developing Personal Power

Position power alone is never enough for managers to accomplish through other people everything they need to get done. Good managers vastly expand their power by building personal power through expertise and reference. Such power derives from personal qualities that have a strong positive appeal to others.

The foundations of strong personal power are straightforward, but they must be continually nurtured and protected to ensure long-term credibility. In this respect a manager should be ever alert to gain knowledge and information. This means being willing to admit when personal expertise is insufficient and to recognize and respect the expertise of others. A manager should also respect the power of relationships. It is always easier to work with people and get them to work well with you when they like you. Interpersonal attractiveness and likability are indispensable keys to personal power. And good managers know that other people generally respect effort and hard work. The best managers are positive role models; they act in the same ways they expect others to act; they understand these personal power guidelines.

Guideline #1 There is no substitute for expertise.

Guideline #2 Likable personal qualities are very important.

Guideline #3 Effort and hard work breed respect.

Guideline #4 Personal behavior must be a model for others.[6]

Achieving Positive Influence

Whereas power is the ability to get others to do what you want them to do, **influence** is the actual outcome or behavioral response to the use of power. When managers achieve influence, it occurs in one or more of the following forms. *Compliance* is a temporary response that involves acting in a desired fashion only as long as the power source is visible. This is associated with the use of reward, coercive, and legitimate power. *Identification* is a longer-lasting response that involves acting in a desired fashion as long as the power source is viewed positively. This is associated with the use of referent power. *Internalization* is a long-lasting response that involves acting in a desired fashion because of a personal belief in its value or appropriateness. This is associated with the use of expert power. Although the influence of all three types is common in organizations, identification and internalization are more desirable outcomes that are characteristic of "positive" influence and high quality of work life.

Directions of Managerial Influence

A substantial part of any manager's time is spent working with people in formal and informal networks. These networks, furthermore, involve the manager in a variety of vertical and horizontal relationships in which the use of power to achieve positive

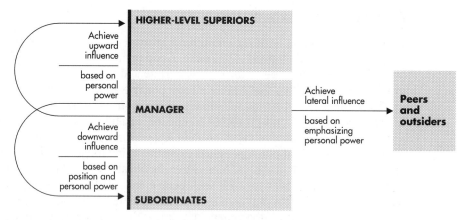

Figure 15.2   Directions of managerial influence. Source: Reprinted by permission from John R. Schermerhorn, Jr., James G. Hunt, and Richard N. Osborn, *Managing Organizational Behavior* (New York: John Wiley & Sons, 1994), p. 470.

influence is essential. Figure 15.2 shows how a manager may attempt to influence subordinates, peers, and higher-ups in the organization. Note that the power bases available for such influence attempts vary from one situation to the next.

The situation in which the manager is most commonly depicted as using power is in relationships with subordinates. In this case of *downward influence,* the full advantages of both position and personal power can be mobilized to achieve the desired impact. This contrasts markedly with the situation a manager faces when trying to influence his or her boss, for example, to gain support for a special project or to get an unfavorable decision reversed. In this *upward influence* situation the manager lacks position power; in fact, the boss has the position power in this case. Thus, when trying to influence people in higher-level positions, managers must rely solely on their personal power based on expertise and reference. A mixed situation holds in respect to lateral relations with peers and outsiders. In general, the manager does not have position power in these *horizontal influence* situations. He or she must again emphasize personal power to achieve the desired outcomes. In today's organizations with more and more emphasis on cross-functional teams and task forces, there may be cases where power is legitimated in respect to lateral relations. Although this unique aspect of position power may be helpful, the expectation is that horizontal influence will predominately be achieved through personal power bases.

Managerial Influence Strategies

It isn't enough for managers to have power; they must use it well to achieve appropriate influence over others. The Effective Manager 15.1 describes seven common managerial influence strategies, sometimes categorized into the "three Rs" of *r*etribution, *r*eciprocity, and *r*eason.[7]

Managers using **retribution strategies** rely on position power to get their ways. They can act assertive ("Everyone else is going along, why aren't you?"), appeal to higher authority ("You know I have the support of the boss."), or resort to sanctions

---
THE EFFECTIVE MANAGER 15.1

Seven Strategies of Managerial Influence

---
1. **Reason**—using facts and data to support a logical argument
2. **Friendliness**—using flattery, goodwill, and favorable impressions
3. **Coalition**—using relationships with other people for support
4. **Bargaining**—using the exchange of benefits as a basis for negotiation
5. **Assertiveness**—using a direct and forceful personal approach
6. **Higher authority**—gaining higher-level support for one's requests
7. **Sanctions**—using organizationally derived rewards and punishments

---

("If you don't do what I want, you'll regret it."). Such approaches may create resentment or intimidation, and any influence achieved may prove temporary. People respond because they feel they *have* to, not because they really *want* to.

Reason strategies, by contrast, rely more on personal power and persuasion based on data, needs, or values. They use arguments likely to appeal to another person that, once accepted, can have a lasting impact on behavior. Reason is the most commonly used influence strategy in organizations. It is accomplished by use of factual arguments and building coalitions to support a point of view.

Finally, **reciprocity strategies** use the mutual exchange of values and search for shared positive outcomes. This is an important approach for today's high-involvement workplaces because it tends to create better feelings and greater internal commitment to the desired behavior. The two most common forms of reciprocity are bargaining or negotiation to exchange benefits, and empowerment through consultation or other forms of employee participation.

Empowering Others

At many points in this book we have talked about **empowerment**—the process through which managers allow and help others to gain power and achieve influence within the organization. Good managers empower the people with whom they work. They know that when people feel powerful, they are more willing to make decisions and take the actions needed to get their jobs done. They also realize that power in organizations is a not *zero-sum* quantity—that is, for someone to gain power it isn't necessary for someone else to give it up. Indeed, to master the complexity and pace of challenges faced in today's environments, an organization's success may well depend on how much power can be mobilized throughout all ranks of employees.

The Effective Manager 15.2 offers tips on how to empower others.[8] There are many benefits for managers who are successful at doing so. On the one hand, empowerment allows people to act independently and feel more adult in their work activities. This is a form of job enrichment that should have high performance benefits as well as advance the quality of work life. On the other hand, a manager who empowers others tends to gain power, too. Having a high-performing work unit certainly helps establish the criticality, centrality, and visibility of one's position. The very act of empowering others may create a positive relationship and build reference

---

THE EFFECTIVE MANAGER 15.2

How to Empower Others

- Get others involved in selecting their work assignments and the methods for accomplishing tasks.
- Create an environment of cooperation, information sharing, discussion, and shared ownership of goals.
- Encourage others to take initiative, make decisions, and use their knowledge.
- When problems arise, find out what others think and let them help design the solutions.
- Stay out of the way; let others put their ideas and solutions into practice.
- Build high morale and confidence by recognizing successes and encouraging high performance.

---

power. And what better way to demonstrate expertise than to show that one's subordinates do great jobs?

Obedience and the Limits to Power

Some years ago a classic experiment in social psychology demonstrated an important and controversial phenomenon—human tendencies toward obedience. The issue has special relevance today as we face ever-more vocal public expectations for ethical and socially responsible behavior in and by organizations. Anyone intending to serve as a manager and leader in the new workplace should consider some tough questions: Why do some people obey directives while others do not? When do people say "no"? When will I say "no" to a directive that appears unethical, illegal, or both?

Tendencies Toward Obedience

To answer the prior questions and inquire into the nature of obedience, consider the experiment just mentioned. The situation was a Yale University laboratory and the experiment was done under the supervision of Stanley Milgram.[9] His experiment was designed to determine the extent to which forty subjects would obey the directives of an authority figure, even if by doing so it appeared that they would endanger the life of another person. The gist of the experiment follows.[10]

The subjects were falsely told that the purpose of the study was to determine the effects of punishment on "learners." The subjects were to be the "teachers," the "learner" was a confederate of Milgram's who was strapped to a chair in an adjoining room with an electrode attached to his wrist. The "teachers" were instructed to administer a shock to the "learner" each time the learner gave a wrong answer to a question. The shock was to be increased one level of intensity each time the learner made a mistake. The "teachers" controlled the switches that ostensibly administered shocks ranging from 15 to 450 volts. In reality, there was no electric current in the apparatus but the learners "erred" often and responded to each level of "shock" in progressively distressing ways.

Here are the results. A surprising twenty-six of Milgram's subjects (65 percent) stayed to the end, continuing to administer the supposed shocks to the "learners" up to the highest level (435–450 volts). This is the point at which the learners had been instructed to slump into silence! No one stopped, refused to go on, prior to reaching the "intense" (300-volt) level. This is the point at which the learners had been instructed to pound on the wall. Of the subjects in the experiment, only fourteen refused to obey the experimenter at points in between these extremes.

Milgram used these results to raise an important question: Why do some people tend to accept or comply with authoritative commands under such extreme conditions? Further experiments by Milgram showed that tendencies toward compliance with the directives of apparent authority figures were somewhat less when the experimental situation was in a rundown office rather than a prestigious university's lab, when the victim was located physically closer to the subject, when the experimenter was located farther away, and when the subject could observe the behavior of other subjects. In these experiments, however, the level of compliance by the subjects was still surprisingly high.

The Acceptance of Authority

Milgram's experiments help to highlight the potential tendencies of all of us to follow orders. Another side of this issue is raised by a classic management writer, Chester Barnard, who advanced the *acceptance theory of authority*.[11] According to Barnard, power and the extent of influence achieved by its exercise ultimately rests with the individual whose compliance is desired. That is, Barnard argued that influence is only achieved when people agree to accept it. In the organization, for example, this means that subordinates will accept or follow a boss's directive at their own discretion. When they accept, the boss has power; when they don't, he or she does not. According to Barnard's theory, these four conditions that determine whether or not a manager's directives will be followed and true influence achieved.

- The other person must truly understand the directive.
- The other person must feel capable of carrying out the directive.
- The other person must view the directive as in the organization's best interests.
- The other person must believe that the directive is consistent with personal values.

Ethics and Power

In Chapter 10 on motivating, McClelland's concept of the need for power was introduced. At the time, the important distinction was made between a need for personal power (power for self-satisfaction) and a need for social power (power to serve group or organizational goals). The need for social power and its effective utilization is the positive side of power in organizations. It is the power the managers will hopefully draw on to ethically influence others to serve organizational ends. By the same token, it must also be recognized that not everyone is ethical and that most people in organizations sooner or later must face up to ethical dilemmas (see Chapter 4). Thus, it is appropriate here to point out one final question of personal or managerial ethics that you must answer: "Where do I (or will I) draw the line, at what point do I (or will I) refuse to comply with inappropriate requests?" Someday you may face the situation of being asked by someone in authority to do something in violation of personal ethics or even the law. Can you . . . will you say "no"? As Barnard said, it is "acceptance" that establishes the limits of managerial power.

Power and Politics

Another aspect of power and influence in the workplace relates to the presence of **organizational politics,** or power-oriented behaviors that use unofficial means to try to influence other people in a manner favorable to one's personal interests. Like conflict, to be discussed in the next chapter, politics has a tendency to arise most often when people in organizations are competing for scarce resources or when important decisions are about to be made that will ultimately affect the work, status, and/or power of individuals or groups. Tendencies toward political behavior may also be more common in groups at or near the maturity stage of group development.

What Politics Can Do

Although the tendency may be to consider organizational politics as something that is bad and should be avoided, this is not always true. Like the informal aspects of communication in organizations, politics has its place and it can play a positive role in getting things done. Again similar to the impact of informal groups, politics can substitute for inadequacies in the formal systems of authority; it can help people to get legitimate things accomplished that would otherwise be very difficult or impossible to achieve.

Political Games to Watch For

It is common to describe political behavior in organizations in terms of "games" played by individuals and groups.[12] The *insurgency game* involves subterfuge and deceit in resisting directives from higher authority. Lower-level personnel, for example, may conveniently lose an important directive or new policy statement and thus fail to pass it on to their subordinates. The *counterinsurgency game,* by contrast, involves gathering unofficial information from various sources to confirm or disconfirm one's suspicions about the behavior of others. The *sponsorship game* involves one person associating himself or herself or personal preferences to another person of greater power, and then using that relationship to influence others. In the *coalition-building game,* "strength in numbers" is sought as one builds networks with others in the attempt to advance a common cause. And the *whistleblowing game* is a dramatic way to force change. Here, and as pointed out in Chapter 4, a person or a group exposes to the public some aspect of an organization that may be controversial. Given the attention and pressure, the organization may be more susceptible to change under the circumstances.

Finally, it should be recognized that organizational politics can be self-serving and directed toward the protection of individual interests.[13] The possible self-protection behaviors include *passing the buck* to avoid personal responsibility for either an action taken or not taken. Another is the well-known *memo for the record,* in which someone commits to writing a protective statement, perhaps with supporting documentation, to clarify the basis for an action taken or not taken. A *blind copy,* by contrast, is a copy of a communication sent to someone not officially entitled to receive it. Another form of self-protection occurs as *scapegoating,* where other, often less powerful, people, are conveniently blamed when things go wrong. Of course the flip side of this is *taking the credit* when things go right and downgrading or neglecting the contributions of others in making it possible.

In Summary

What is managerial power?

- Power is the ability to get other people to do what you want them to do.
- Managerial power = Position power + Personal power.
- Power in managerial positions derives from rewards, punishments, and legitimacy.
- Power of the person derives from expertise and reference.

How can managers gain power?

- Managers can and must gain and use power from both their positions in the organization and personal sources.
- Position power may be enhanced through networking centrality, high performance, and personal visibility.
- Personal power of expertise may be enhanced through information and job-relevant knowledge gained and demonstrated over time.
- Personal power of reference is gained through personal qualities and interpersonal skills that make someone attractive in the eyes of others.

How can managers achieve positive influence?

- Influence is the behavioral response of someone to the exercise of power by someone else.

- Influence may occur through temporary compliance and/or through more long-lasting identification and internalization.
- Managers and others in organizations must be prepared to exercise influence not only downward in the hierarchy, but also laterally and upward.
- The strategies of interpersonal influence include retribution, reason, and reciprocity.
- Through empowerment, enlightened managers allow others to gain power and influence in the organization.

Who and what sets the limits to power?

- Stanley Milgram's historic experiments identified tendencies toward obedience of directives from authority figures.
- Chester Barnard's acceptance theory of authority says that power rests with the target of an influence attempt; in other words, someone has power over us only because we let them.
- When applied in organizations, Barnard's theory holds that in order for a manager's directive to be accepted as authoritative by a subordinate, it must be understood, doable, identified with the best interests of the organization, and viewed as consistent with individual values.

What is the role of politics in managerial power?

- Organizational politics, the use of unofficial means to influence other people's behavior in a direction consistent with one's personal interests, is a part of organizational life.
- Managers must become comfortable with political behavior and be able to recognize its occurrence.
- Some of the political games played in organizations include the insurgency, counterinsurgency, sponsorship, coalition, and whistleblowing games.
- Some of the self-serving political behaviors of individuals include passing the buck, memos to the record, blind copies, scapegoating, and taking the credit.

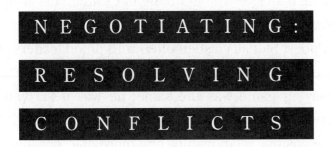

N E G O T I A T I N G :

R E S O L V I N G

C O N F L I C T S

As you read Chapter 16, keep in mind these study questions:

- How can managers negotiate successful agreements?

- What types of conflicts occur in organizations?

- How can managers deal positively with conflict?

- How can managers best deal with workplace stress?

L et's go back to the Center for Creative Leadership for another chapter opening example. The center reports that thirty percent of all managers have difficulty dealing with people; it strives to help participants in its training programs recognize this fact and do something about it. It doesn't always work. After getting a poor appraisal of his leadership performance, one participant claimed that he *was* a good manager—but all his workers were stupid. Stupid, indeed! It's the wise manager who is willing to examine his or her interpersonal skills and work to continuously improve them. Before coming to the center, Robert Siddall clashed often with union leaders and was viewed as aggressive to the point of abrasiveness. Feedback from the center's role-playing game was the same; he was described as too structured and domineering. Center instructors worked with Siddall to develop more positive relationships and more of a "coaching" style. He tried to transfer this learning back to the job and found his performance ratings went up. Regarding his relationships with co-workers, he says: "We have a lot more fun together. If I start screaming and yelling, they say, 'Old Bob, old Bob.'"[1]

Negotiating to Agreement

Put yourself in the following situations. How would you behave, and what would you do, in each case?[2]

Case 1 You have been offered a promotion and would really like to take it. However, the pay raise being offered is less than you hoped.

Case 2 You have enough money to order one new computer for your department. Two of your subordinates have each requested a new computer for their individual jobs.

The prior cases are but two examples of the many "negotiation" situations that involve managers and other people in the typical workplace. **Negotiation** is the process of making joint decisions when the parties involved have different preferences.[3] Stated a bit differently, it is a way of reaching agreement when decisions involve more than one person or group. Such situations are conflict- and stress-prone and, as just illustrated, are common facts of organizational life. People negotiate over such diverse matters as salary, merit raises and performance evaluations, job assignments, work schedules, work locations, special privileges, and many other considerations. And, as empowerment and employee involvement emerge in progressive workplaces, the requirements of teamwork and participative decision making frequently include the ability of group members to deal successfully with negotiation.

What Is Effective Negotiation?

There are two important goals in negotiation. *Substance goals* are concerned with outcomes; they are tied to the "content" issues of the negotiation. *Relationship goals* are concerned with processes; they are tied to the way people work together while negotiating and how they (and any constituencies they represent) will be able to work together in the future. Unfortunately, participants in negotiation sometimes sacrifice relationships as they pursue substance with a narrow perspective of individual self-interests. **Effective negotiation,** by contrast, occurs when both issues of substance are resolved *and* working relationships among the negotiating parties are maintained or even improved in the process. Effective negotiation meets the test of three criteria. It meets the *quality* criterion, resulting in a "wise" agreement that is truly satisfactory to all sides. It meets the *cost* criterion by using up minimum resources and time. It meets the *harmony* criterion by fostering, rather than hindering, good interpersonal relationships among negotiating parties.[4]

The way each party approaches a negotiation can have a major impact on how well these criteria of effective negotiation are met. Two alternative approaches are recognized.[5] The first is **distributive negotiation.** It focuses on "claims" made by each party for certain preferred outcomes. This can take a competitive form in which one party can gain only if the other loses. In such win–lose conditions, relationships are often sacrificed as the negotiating parties focus only on their respective self-interests. It may also become accommodative if the parties defer to one another's wishes simply "to get it over with." The second is **integrative negotiation,** often called **principled negotiation.** It is based on a win–win orientation. The focus on substance is still important, but the interests of all parties are considered. The goal is to base the final outcome on the merits of individual claims and to try to find a way for all claims to be satisfied if at all possible. No one should "lose," and relationships should be maintained in the process. Integrative negotiation is obviously a preferred negotiation approach.

Gaining Integrative Agreements

In their book *Getting to Yes,* Roger Fisher and William Ury write that truly integrative agreements are obtained by following the four negotiation rules listed in The Effective Manager 16.1.[6]

Proper attitudes and good information are important foundations for such integrative agreements. The *attitudinal foundations* of integrative agreements involve the willingness of each negotiating party to trust, share information with, and ask reasonable questions of the other party. The *information foundations* of integrative agreements involve each party knowing what is really important to him or her in the case at hand and finding out what is really important to the other party. In addition, each

---

THE EFFECTIVE MANAGER 16.1

Rules for Integrative Negotiation

1. Separate the people from the problem.
2. Focus on interests, not on positions.
3. Generate many alternatives before deciding what to do.
4. Insist that results are based on some objective standard.

---

should understand his or her personal *best alternative to a negotiated agreement*, or BATNA—that is, "What will I do if an agreement can't be reached?"

Figure 16.1 introduces a typical case of labor–management negotiations over a new contract and salary increase. This helps illustrate elements of classic two-party negotiation as they occur in many contexts.[7] To begin, look at the figure and case from the labor union's perspective. The union negotiator has told her management counterpart that the union wants a new wage of $12.00/hour. This expressed preference is the union's initial offer. However, she also has in mind a minimum reservation point of $10.75/hour. This is the lowest wage rate that she is willing to accept for the union. But the management negotiator has a different perspective. His initial offer is $9.75/hour and his maximum reservation point, the highest wage he is prepared to eventually offer to the union, is $11.25/hour.

In classic two-party negotiation of this type, the *bargaining zone* is defined as the zone between one party's minimum reservation point and the other party's maximum reservation point. The bargaining zone of $10.75/hour to $11.25/hour in this case is a "positive" one since the reservation points of the two parties overlap. If the union's minimum reservation point were greater than management's maximum reservation point, no room would exist for bargaining. Whenever a positive bargaining zone exists, there is room for true negotiation and further bargaining.

A key task for any negotiator is to discover the other party's reservation point. Until this is known and each party becomes aware that a positive bargaining zone exists, it is difficult to proceed effectively. When negotiation does proceed, each negotiator typically tries to achieve an agreement that is as close as possible to the other party's reservation point. Going back to the figure once again, the union

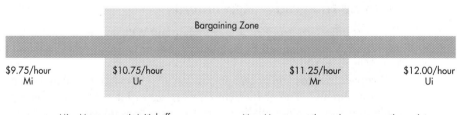

Mi = Management's initial offer   Mr = Management's maximum reservation point
Ur = Union's minimum reservation point   Ui = Union's initial offer

Figure 16.1 The bargaining zone in classic two-party negotiation between the management of a firm and a labor union.

negotiator would like to get an offer as close to $12.00/hour as possible. The management negotiator would like to get a contract for a wage as close to $9.75/hour as possible.

Avoiding Negotiation Pitfalls

The negotiation process is admittedly complex, and negotiators must guard against common mistakes. The following negotiator pitfalls can be avoided by proper discipline and personal attention. Pitfall #1 is *falling prey to the myth of the "fixed pie."* Don't act on the distributive assumption that in order for you to gain, the other party must give something up. Do accept the integrative assumption that the "pie" can sometimes be expanded and/or utilized to everyone's advantage. Pitfall #2 is *nonrational escalation of conflict.* Don't become overcommitted to your previously stated demands; don't allow concerns for ego and face-saving to exaggerate the importance of satisfying these demands. Pitfall #3 is *overconfidence and ignoring others' needs.* Don't become overconfident that your position is the only correct one; don't fail to seek out the needs and merits in the other party's position. Pitfall #4 is *too much "telling" and too little "hearing."* Don't fall prey to the telling problem, where negotiating parties don't really make themselves understood to each other. Don't fall prey to the hearing problem, where the parties don't listen well enough to understand what each other is saying.[8]

It is not always possible to achieve integrative agreements. When disputes reach the point of impasse, mediation and arbitration can be useful. *Mediation* involves a neutral third party who tries to improve communication among negotiating parties and keep them focused on relevant issues. This mediator does not issue a ruling or make a decision, but can take an active role in discussions. This may include making suggestions in an attempt to move the parties toward agreement. *Arbitration*—for example, salary arbitration in professional sports—is a stronger form of dispute resolution. It involves a neutral third party, the arbitrator, acting as a "judge" who issues a binding decision. This usually includes a formal hearing in which the arbitrator listens to both sides and reviews all facets of the case in coming to a ruling.

Some organizations formally provide for a process called *alternative dispute resolution.* This approach utilizes mediation and/or arbitration, but only after direct attempts to negotiate agreements among conflicting parties have failed. Often an *ombudsperson,* or designated neutral third party who listens to complaints and disputes, plays a key role in the process.

Ethical Aspects of Negotiation

Managers, and anyone else involved in negotiation, should maintain high standards of ethical conduct—even while personally involved in a dynamic and challenging situation. The motivation to behave unethically sometimes arises from an undue emphasis on a profit motive. This may be experienced as a desire to "get just a bit more" or to "get as much as you can" from a negotiation. The motivation to behave unethically may also result from a sense of competition. This may be experienced as a desire to win a negotiation just for the sake of it, or as a misguided belief that someone else must lose in order for you to gain.

When unethical behavior occurs in negotiation, the people involved sometimes attempt to rationalize or explain it away. We first discussed such rationalizations for unethical conduct in Chapter 4. In a negotiation situation, the following comments may be indicative of rationalizing otherwise inappropriate behavior: "It was really unavoidable," "Oh, it's harmless," "The results justify the means," or "It's really quite fair and appropriate."[9] Moral issues aside, tendencies to use or accept such explanations can be countered on a performance basis by the possibility that any short-run gains may be accompanied by long-run losses. Unethical parties should also realize they may be targeted for later revenge from those disadvantaged by their tactics. Furthermore, once people behave unethically in one situation, they have a tendency to consider such behavior acceptable in similar circumstances in the future.

Conflict in Organizations

Negotiation, like all aspects of interpersonal relations in organizations, are bound to create occasional **conflicts,** or disagreements between people on substantive or emotional issues.[10] Managers spend a lot of time dealing with conflicts of various forms. *Substantive conflicts* involve disagreements over such things as goals, the allocation of resources, distribution of rewards, policies and procedures, and job assignments. *Emotional conflicts* result from feelings of anger, distrust, dislike, fear, and resentment, as well as from personality clashes. Both forms of conflict can be destructive and cause problems in the workplace. But when managed well, they can be helpful in promoting high performance, creativity, and innovation.

Destructive and Constructive Conflict

Whether or not conflict works beneficially for the organization depends on two factors: (1) the intensity of the conflict, and (2) how well the conflict is managed. Conflict of moderate intensity can be good for the organization, whereas very low-intensity or very high-intensity conflict can be bad. Too much conflict overpowers the organization and its people. It is distracting and interferes with other more task-relevant activities. Too little conflict prevents organizations and people from achieving a creative performance edge. It offers little challenge or stimulation for change.

Destructive conflict is dysfunctional and works to the disadvantage of the people and the organization. This occurs, for example, when two employees are unable to work together because of interpersonal hostilities (a destructive emotional conflict) or when the members of a committee can't agree on group goals (a destructive substantive conflict). Any destructive conflict can reduce the effectiveness of individuals, groups, and organizations. The disadvantages may include lost productivity, lower job satisfaction, unnecessary or overpowering stress, and decreased concern for a common goal. **Constructive conflict,** by contrast, is functional. It results in benefits instead of disadvantages for the people and organization involved. The potential benefits of constructive conflict include increased creativity and innovation, greater effort, increased cohesion, and reduced tension.

Conflict Situations

Managers must be prepared to deal with various types of conflict situations that occur regularly in the workplace. *Personal conflicts,* such as self-induced role overloads, involve the individual alone. They may also develop as a conflict between personal ethics and organizational expectations. *Interpersonal conflict* occurs among two or more individuals. Everyone has experience with interpersonal conflict, and it is commonly faced by managers. Because it involves confrontation with one or more people, it is also something we try to avoid. Learning how to engage in interpersonal conflict without it becoming destructive, and being able to help others do the same, is an important managerial skill.

Intergroup conflict often occurs in two forms. First, vertical conflict involves representatives of line and staff groups. In a manufacturing firm, for example, headquarters staff might emphasize the need for detailed performance reports on a weekly basis, and might complain when the reports are submitted late and with incomplete information. Line personnel in the plant might complain that such reports are time-consuming to prepare and might fail to give an accurate picture of long-term accomplishments. Second, horizontal conflict typically arises when members of different functional departments have difficulty working with one another. Marketing's objective of customer satisfaction may lead to complaints that faster production schedules are needed, along with the ability to make design modifications to fit unique customer preferences. Manufacturing's objective of operating efficiency may lead to demands for better market forecasts and the avoidance of unnecessary design changes so that better production schedules can be set.

Interorganizational conflicts include disagreements between unions and organizations employing their members, between government regulatory agencies and organizations subject to their surveillance, and, more generally, between organizations and others that supply them with raw materials. Like the other types of conflict, interorganizational conflicts should be managed to the benefit, not the detriment, of the organizations and individuals concerned. When General Motors started its Saturn operation, for example, labor–management cooperation was considered a key to future success. Says GM's personnel vice-president during Saturn's formation: "Saturn chose to journey to Tennessee . . . with the UAW on board as a full partner committed to seeking new labor and management relationships."[11]

Conflict Sources

Conflicts of any of the prior types may arise for a variety of reasons. There are certain antecedent conditions present in most organizations most of the time, which make the eventual emergence of these conflicts very likely. *Hostile negotiations* set the stage for conflict. When negotiations focus on win–lose outcomes or end with poor relationships, conflict is likely in the future. *Role ambiguities* can create conflict.

Unclear job expectations and other task uncertainties increase the probability that some people will be working at cross-purposes at least some of the time. *Resource scarcities* make conflict likely. Having to share resources with others or to compete directly with them for resource allocations makes a situation conflict-prone, especially when resources are scarce. *Task interdependencies* create conflicts. When individuals or groups must depend on what others do in order to perform well themselves, conflicts often occur. *Competing objectives* lead to conflict. When objectives are poorly set or reward systems are poorly designed, individuals and groups may come into conflict as they work to one another's direct disadvantage. *Unresolved prior conflicts* typically lead to future conflicts. Unless a conflict is fully resolved, it may remain latent in the situation as a lingering basis for future conflicts over the same or related matters.

Managing Conflict

When any one or more of these antecedent conditions is present, an informed manager expects conflicts to occur. The resulting conflicts can be either resolved—in the sense that the sources are corrected—or suppressed—where the sources remain but the conflict behaviors are controlled. Suppressed conflicts tend to fester and recur at a later time. They can also contribute to other conflicts over the same or related issues. True **conflict resolution** eliminates the underlying causes of conflict and reduces the potential for similar conflicts in the future.[12]

Structural Approaches to Conflict Resolution

Managers can do several things to try and restructure situations in order to resolve conflicts. There are times when an *appeal to superordinate goals* can focus the attention of conflicting parties on one mutually desirable end state. The appeal to higher-level goals offers all parties a common frame of reference against which to analyze differences and reconcile disagreements. Conflicts whose antecedents lie in competition for scarce resources can also be resolved by *expanding the resources available* to everyone. Although costly, this technique removes the reasons for the continuing conflict. *Altering one or more human variables* by replacing or transferring one or more of the conflicting parties can help eliminate conflicts due to poor interpersonal relationships. The same holds true if a manager can *alter the physical environment* by rearranging facilities, workspace, or workflows to create a setting that decreases opportunities for conflict.

The use of *integrating mechanisms* is another useful approach to conflict resolution in many settings. In particular, the use of liaison personnel, special task forces and cross-functional teams, and even the matrix form of organization can change interaction patterns and assist in conflict management. *Changes in reward systems* may reduce the competition among individuals and groups for rewards. Creating systems that reward cooperation can encourage positive behaviors and attitudes that keep conflict within more constructive limits. Finally, *policies and procedures* may

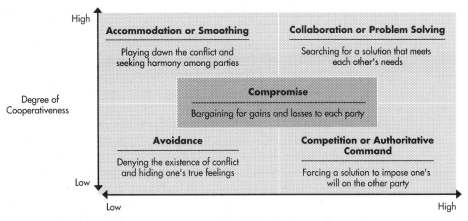

Figure 16.2 Alternative interpersonal conflict management styles.

be used to direct behavior in appropriate ways. If these plans are well conceived and followed, they can help people avoid unfortunate conflict situations.

Interpersonal Conflict Management Styles

People respond to conflict in different ways. A person's interpersonal style in conflict situations can be described on two dimensions of behavior.[13] *Cooperativeness* is the desire to satisfy another party's needs and concerns; *assertiveness* is the desire to satisfy one's own needs and concerns. Figure 16.2 shows five interpersonal styles of conflict management that result from various combinations of the two. Briefly stated, these styles involve the following behaviors:

- **Avoidance** being uncooperative and unassertive; downplaying disagreement, withdrawing from the situation, and/or staying neutral at all costs
- **Accommodation or smoothing** being cooperative but unassertive; letting others' wishes rule; smoothing over differences to maintain superficial harmony
- **Competition or authoritative command** being uncooperative but assertive; working against the wishes of the other party, engaging in win–lose competition, or forcing through the exercise of authority
- **Compromise** being moderately cooperative and assertive but not to either extreme; bargaining for "acceptable" solutions in which each party wins a bit and loses a bit
- **Collaboration or problem solving** being both cooperative and assertive; trying to fully satisfy everyone's concerns by working through differences; finding and solving problems so that everyone gains[14]

The various interpersonal styles of conflict management can create quite different outcomes.[15] Conflict management by avoidance or accommodation often creates *lose–lose outcomes.* Here, no one achieves his or her true desires, and the underlying reasons for conflict often remain unaffected. Although a lose–lose outcome might appear settled or even disappear for a while, it tends to recur in the future. Avoidance is an extreme form of nonattention. Everyone pretends that conflict doesn't really exist and hopes that it will simply go away. Accommodation or smoothing plays down differences and highlights similarities and areas of agreement. Peaceful coexistence through a recognition of common interests is the goal. In reality, smoothing may ignore the real essence of a conflict.

Competition, or authoritative command, and compromise tend to create *win–lose outcomes.* Here, each party strives to gain at the other's expense. In extreme cases, one party achieves its desires to the complete exclusion of the other party's desires. Because win–lose methods fail to address the root causes of conflict, future conflicts of the same or similar nature are likely to occur. In competition, one party wins as superior skill or outright domination allows his or her desires to be forced on the other. In authoritative command, the forcing is accomplished by a higher-level supervisor who simply dictates a solution to subordinates. Compromise occurs when trade-offs are made such that each party to the conflict gives up something and gains something of value. As a result, neither party is completely satisfied, and antecedent conditions for future conflicts are established.

Collaboration, or problem solving, tries to reconcile underlying differences; it is often the most effective conflict management style. It is a form of *win–win outcome* whereby issues are resolved to the mutual benefit of all conflicting parties. This is typically achieved by confrontation of the issues and the willingness of those involved to recognize that something is wrong and needs attention. Win–win conditions are created by eliminating the underlying causes of the conflict. All relevant issues are raised and discussed openly. Win–win methods are clearly the most preferred of the interpersonal styles of conflict management. They are also the underpinnings of successful integrative negotiation, as earlier described.

Managing Stress

When people work together in organizations—especially in situations involving conflict and negotiation—*stress* is a likely byproduct. Formally defined, it is a state of tension experienced by individuals facing extraordinary demands, constraints, or opportunities.[16] Any forward consideration of your work career would be incomplete without including the factor of stress. Job-related stress, in particular, goes hand-in-hand with the dynamic and sometimes uncertain nature of the managerial role.

Sources of Stress

Work factors have an obvious potential to create job stress. About 46 percent of workers in one survey reported that their jobs were highly stressful; 34 percent said that their jobs were *so* stressful that they were thinking of quitting.[17] Such job-related stress can result from excessively high or low task demands, role conflicts or ambiguities, poor interpersonal relations, or career progress that is too slow or too fast.

When asked what factors caused them the most stress on the job, workers in another survey identified the following: not doing the kind of work they wanted to (34%), coping with their current job (30%), working too hard (28%), colleagues at work (21%), and a difficult boss (18%).[18] Stress also tends to be high among people working for organizations with recent records of staff cutbacks and downsizing. This lack of corporate loyalty to the employee can be very threatening, especially to someone who has major financial responsibilities or is approaching retirement age.[19]

A variety of *personal factors* are also sources of potential stress for people at work. Such individual characteristics as needs, capabilities, and personality can influence how one perceives and responds to the work situation. Researchers, for example, identify a **Type A personality** of extreme achievement orientation, impatience, and perfectionism that causes people to create stress in circumstances others find relatively stress-free. Type A personalities, in this sense, bring stress on themselves. They display stressful behavior patterns that include tendencies toward always moving, walking, and eating rapidly; acting impatient, hurrying others, disliking waiting; doing, or trying to do, several things at once; feeling guilty when relaxing; trying to schedule more in less time; using nervous gestures such as a clenched fist; and hurrying or interrupting the speech of others.[20]

Finally, *nonwork factors* may spill over and influence the stress an individual experiences at work. Such things as family events (e.g., the birth of a new child), economics (e.g., a sudden loss of extra income), and personal affairs (e.g., a preoccupation with a hobby) can add to the stress otherwise associated with work and/or personal factors.

Consequences of Stress

Like conflict, stress actually has a positive side and a negative side. **Constructive stress** acts in a positive way for the individual and/or the organization. Low to moderate levels of stress can be energizing. They can encourage increased effort, stimulate creativity, and enhance diligence in one's work. Such positive outcomes can be associated with all three types of stressors just described. Individuals with a Type A personality, for example, are likely to work long hours and to be less satisfied with poor performance. High task demands imposed by a supervisor may draw forth higher levels of task accomplishment. Even nonwork stressors such as new family responsibilities may cause an individual to work harder in anticipation of greater financial rewards.

The question is: "When does a little stress become *too much* stress?" **Destructive stress** is dysfunctional for the individual and the organization. High stress can overload and break down a person's physical and mental systems. Productivity can suffer as people react to very intense stress through turnover, absenteeism, errors, accidents, dissatisfaction, and reduced performance. Medical research is also concerned that too much stress can reduce resistance to disease and increase the likelihood of physical or mental illness. It may contribute to health problems such as hypertension, ulcers, drug-alcohol-tobacco abuse, overeating, depression, and muscle aches, among others. The multiple and varied symptoms of excessive stress include changes in eating habits, restlessness, irritability, and stomach upset.

THE EFFECTIVE MANAGER 16.2

How to Cope with Workplace Stress

- **Take control of the situation**—Do your best, know your limits, and avoid unrealistic deadlines.
- **Pace yourself**—Try to plan your day to do high-priority things first. But stay flexible. Try to slow down.
- **Open up to others**—Discuss your problems, fears, and frustrations with those who care about you.
- **Do things for others**—Think about someone else's needs, and try to help satisfy those needs.
- **Exercise and work off stress**—Engage in regular physical activity as recommended by your physician.
- **Balance work and recreation**—Schedule time for recreation, including vacations from your work.

Stress Management Approaches

Managers should obviously be alert to signs of excessive stress in themselves and others with whom they work. The best stress management alternative for anyone, of course, is to prevent it from ever reaching excessive levels in the first place. Stressors emerging from personal and nonwork factors must be recognized so that action can be taken to prevent them from adversely affecting the work experience. At another level, family difficulties may be relieved by a change of work schedule, or the anxiety they cause may be reduced by knowing that one's supervisor understands the inevitable stresses of managing both work and family matters.

Among work factors with the greatest potential to cause excessive stress are role ambiguities, conflicts, and overloads. Role clarification through a management by objectives (MBO) approach can work to good advantage here. By bringing supervisor and subordinate together in face-to-face task-oriented communications, MBO is an opportunity to spot stressors and take action to reduce or eliminate them. Self-awareness and a realistic approach to one's responsibilities can also help prevent stress brought on by simply "working too much." Understanding the *survivor syndrome*—the stress experienced by people who fear for their jobs in organizations that are reducing staff through downsizing and layoffs—is also important. As more managers become aware of this phenomenon, they are developing formal programs to help those employees who remain employed better cope with the situation after major staff cut-backs have occurred.

Managers should take action when symptoms of excessive stress are recognized. Some organizations provide special assistance programs to counsel and support employees experiencing excessive stress. But it is also important to know how to help yourself. Some guidelines for coping with workplace stress are suggested in The Effective Manager 16.2.[21]

Personal wellness is a term used to describe the pursuit of one's physical and mental potential through a personal health-promotion program.[22] This concept recognizes individual responsibility to enhance personal health through a disciplined approach to such things as smoking, alcohol use, maintenance of a nutritious diet, and engaging in a regular exercise and physical-fitness program. The essence of personal wellness is a lifestyle that reflects a true commitment to health. The whole concept makes a great deal of sense, and it may be especially important for managers. Those who aggressively maintain personal wellness are better prepared to deal with the inevitable stresses of the managerial role. They may be better able to take constructive advantage of levels of workplace stress that are higher than others can tolerate; they may also have more insight into the personal wellness needs of their subordinates. Indeed, many organizations are now formally sponsoring wellness programs for employees. Among the health promotion activities typically offered are: smoking control, health risk appraisals, back care, stress management, exercise/ physical fitness, nutrition education, high-blood-pressure control, and weight control. The expectations are that investments in such programs benefit both the organization and its human resources.

In Summary

How can managers negotiate successful agreements?

- Negotiation is the process of making decisions in situations in which the participants have different preferences.
- Both substance goals—concerned with outcomes—and relationship goals—concerned with processes—are important in successful negotiation.
- Effective negotiation occurs when issues of substance are resolved and good working relationships result.
- Distributive approaches to negotiation emphasize win–lose outcomes, and are usually harmful to relationships.
- Integrative approaches to negotiation emphasize the interests of all parties and win–win outcomes.

What types of conflicts occur in organizations?

- Substantive conflicts involve disagreements over such things as goals, resources, and other work-related matters.
- Emotional conflicts result from feelings of anger, distrust, and other personality factors.
- Conflict of moderate intensity can be constructive and enhance performance.
- Conflict of too little or too much intensity can be destructive and decrease performance.
- Managers should strive for constructive conflict that facilitates a high performance edge and creativity; they should avoid the harmful effects of destructive conflict.

How can managers deal positively with conflict?

- Conflict may be managed through structural approaches that involve changing people, goals, resources, or work arrangements.
- Interpersonal conflict management "styles" are based on tendencies toward assertiveness and cooperativeness in conflict situations.
- The possible interpersonal conflict management styles include avoidance, accommodation, compromise, competition, and collaboration.
- True conflict resolution involves problem-solving through a collaborative approach.

How can managers best deal with workplace stress?

- Stress occurs as tension accompanying extraordinary demands, constraints, or opportunities.
- Stress can be destructive or constructive; a moderate level of stress typically has a positive impact on performance.
- Stressors are found in a variety of work, personal, and nonwork situations.
- For some people, having a Type A personality creates stress due to continual feelings of impatience and pressure.
- Stress can be effectively managed through prevention and coping strategies; good managers are able to manage stress in their work and personal lives and to assist others to do the same.

STRATEGIC HUMAN RESOURCE MANAGEMENT

As you read Chapter 17, keep in mind these study questions:

- Why is human resource management important?

- How do organizations attract quality workers?

- How do organizations develop quality workers?

- How do organizations maintain a quality workforce?

oday, the pressures of global competition and social change have led to what *Fortune* magazine calls "a human resources revolution" affecting organizations of all types and sizes.[1] This revolution is real and it appears here to stay. Progressive employers everywhere are taking steps to unlock the full potential of their workforces. In competitive environments people are precious; to achieve high performance on a continuing basis, no one's talents can be wasted. In principle, at least, the following organizational slogans say a lot about the demands and opportunities of the new workplace: "*People* are our most important asset"; "It's *people* who make the difference"; "It's the *people* who work for us who . . . determine whether our company thrives or languishes."[2] Such testimonials are found in newspaper and television ads, annual reports, corporate recruiting literature, executive speeches, and organizational newsletters. They make an important point. Organizations must be staffed with talented and energetic human resources to fully accomplish their objectives.

Essentials of Human Resource Management

The term **human resource management** describes the wide variety of activities involved in staffing organizations with capable workers and ensuring that their performance potential is fully utilized. *Staffing,* in turn, is the process of filling jobs with talented people. The basic objective of human resource management is to make sure that an organization always has the right people on the job to achieve consistent high performance outcomes. Success with this critical responsibility is one of the most basic foundations of effective management. Says a marketing manager at Ideo, a Palo-Alto–based industrial design firm: "If you hire the right people—if you've got the right fit—then everything will take care of itself."[3] The major elements in the human resource management process are:

- **Attracting a quality workforce** managing human resource planning, recruitment, and selection
- **Developing a quality workforce** managing employee orientation, training and development, and career planning and development.
- **Maintaining a quality workforce** managing retention and turnover, performance appraisal, compensation and benefits, and labor-management relations.

Influences of the Legal Environment

Human resource management must be accomplished within the framework of government regulations and laws. This legal environment of management grows increasingly complex as old laws are modified, new ones are added, and changes occur among the agencies that monitor them. In the United States, the legal and regulatory environment of human resource management covers activities related to pay, employment rights, occupational health and safety, retirement, privacy, vocational rehabilitation, and related areas. Earlier, in Chapter 9, a core set of laws relating to equal employment opportunity was described (the *Civil Rights Act of 1964,* the *Civil Rights Act Amendments of 1991,* and the *Equal Employment Opportunity Act of 1972*). Figure 17.1 further highlights a number of important federal employment laws that apply to organizations employing fifteen or more people.[4]

Human Resource Planning

To achieve its full potential, any organization must at all times have the right people available to do the required work. In practical terms, this means that *all* managers must make sure that *all* jobs in their responsibility areas are always staffed with capable people who can best perform them. To do so, furthermore, managers must be good at **human resource planning,** the process of analyzing staffing needs and identifying actions to satisfy these needs over time.[5]

Human resource planning begins with a review of organizational strategies and objectives. This is followed by forecasts of personnel needs and labor supplies, both within and outside the organization. Ultimately, the process should produce action plans to correct any actual or projected staffing surpluses or shortages. This may include a formal *human resource audit* or systematic inventory of the strengths and weaknesses of existing personnel. A good audit helps managers pinpoint and plan for dealing with very specific staffing needs. These may include promotions, transfers, training and development programs, other types of career enhancement activities, and even personnel replacement where weaknesses exist.

The foundations for human resource planning are set by *job analysis*—the orderly study of just *what* is done, when, where, how, why, and by whom in jobs.[6] The job analysis provides useful information that can then be used to develop *job descriptions*—written statements of job duties and responsibilities. The information can also be used to create minimum *job specifications*—lists of the education, experience, and skill requirements for someone to be given the job.

Attracting a Quality Workforce

This excerpt from an advertisement once run by the Motorola Corporation sets a clear human resource management challenge: "Productivity is learning how to hire the person who is *right* for the job." To attract such high-quality workers, an organization needs good employee recruitment and selection systems.

Equal Pay Act of 1963	Prohibits pay differences for men and women doing equal work.
Title VII *of the Civil Rights Act of* 1964 (as amended)	Prohibits discrimination in employment based on race, color, religion, sex, or national origin.
Age Discrimination Employment Act of 1967 (as amended)	Prohibits discrimination in employment against persons over 40; restricts mandatory retirement.
Occupational Safety and Health Act of 1970 (OSHA)	Establishes mandatory safety and health standards in workplaces.
Vocational Rehabilitation Act of 1973	Prohibits discrimination in employment based on physical or mental disability.
Pregnancy Discrimination Act of 1978	Prohibits employment discrimination against pregnant workers.
Immigration Reform and Control Act of 1986	Prohibits knowing employment of illegal aliens.
Americans with Disabilities Act of 1990	Prohibits discrimination against a qualified individual on the basis of disability.
Civil Rights Act of 1991	Reaffirms Title VII of the 1964 Civil Rights Act; reinstates burden of proof by employer; and allows for punitive and compensatory damages.
Family and Medical Leave Act of 1993	Allows employees up to 12 weeks of unpaid leave with job guarantees for childbirth, adoption, or family illness.

Figure 17.1   A selection of federal laws with human resource management implications.

The Recruiting Process

Recruitment is a set of activities designed to attract a *qualified* pool of job applicants to an organization. Emphasis on the word *qualified* is important. Effective recruiting should bring employment opportunities to the attention of people whose abilities and skills meet job specifications.

The three steps in a typical recruitment process are: (1) advertisement of a job vacancy, (2) preliminary contact with potential job candidates, and (3) initial screening to create a pool of qualified applicants. In collegiate recruiting, for example, *advertising* is done by the firm posting short job descriptions at the campus placement center and/or in the campus newspaper. *Preliminary contact* is made after candidates register for interviews with company recruiters on campus. This typically involves a short (20- to 30-minute) interview, during which the candidate presents a written résumé and briefly explains job qualifications. As part of the *initial screening,* the recruiter shares interview results and résumés from the campus visits with appropriate line managers. Decisions will then be made on who to include in the final pool of candidates to be invited for further interviews during a formal visit to the organization.

This case is an example of **external recruitment**—the attraction of job candidates from sources outside the organization. Newspapers, employment agencies, colleges, technical training centers, personal contacts, walk-ins, employee referrals, and even people in competing organizations are all sources of external recruits. The advantages of external recruiting include bringing in outsiders with fresh perspectives. It also provides access to specialized expertise or work experience not otherwise available from insiders.

Internal recruitment, by contrast, involves notifying existing employees of job vacancies through job posting and personal recommendations. Most organizations have a procedure for announcing vacancies through newsletters, bulletin boards, and the like. They also rely on managers to recommend subordinates who are good candidates for advancement. Internal recruitment also offers advantages. It is usually less expensive than external recruitment. It also deals with people of known performance records who are already familiar with the organization. A history of serious internal recruitment can also be encouraging to employees. It shows that one can advance in a career by working hard and achieving high performance at each point of responsibility.

Effective Recruiting Practices

In what may be called *traditional recruitment,* the emphasis is on selling the organization to job applicants.[7] In this case, only the most positive features of the job and organization are communicated to potential candidates. Bias may even be introduced as these features are exaggerated while negative features are concealed. This form of recruitment is designed to attract as many candidates as possible. The problem is that it may create unrealistic expectations. Premature turnover in the early resignation of new hires often occurs in these circumstances.

Realistic job previews, by contrast, try to provide the candidate with *all* pertinent information about the job and organization without distortion and *before* the job is accepted. Instead of selling only positive features of a job, this approach tries to be realistic and balanced in the information provided. It tries to be fair in depicting actual job and organizational features. With a more complete view of the job and organization, new employees should have more realistic job expectations. A healthy psychological contract, higher levels of early job satisfaction, and less premature turnover are the anticipated benefits.

Making Selection Decisions

Selection is the process of choosing from a pool of applicants the person or persons who offer the greatest performance potential. Steps in a typical selection process include (1) completion of a formal application form, (2) interviewing, (3) testing, (4) reference checks, (5) physical examination, and (6) final analysis and decision to hire or reject.

THE EFFECTIVE MANAGER 17.1

How to Conduct Job Interviews

- **Plan ahead**—Review the job specifications and job description, as well as the candidate's application.
- **Create a good interview climate**—Allow sufficient time; choose a quiet place; act open and friendly; show interest and give the candidate your sincere attention.
- **Conduct a goal-oriented interview**—Know what information you need, and get it; don't forget to look for creativity, independence, and a high energy level.
- **Avoid questions that may imply discrimination**—Focus all questioning on the job applied for and the candidate's *bona fide* qualifications for it.
- **Answer the questions asked of you . . . and even some that may not be asked**—Do your part to create a realistic job preview.
- **Write notes on the interview immediately upon completion**—Document details and impressions for later deliberation and decision making.

Application Forms   The application form declares the individual a formal candidate for a job. It documents the applicant's personal history and qualifications. The personal résumé is often included with the job application. This important document should accurately summarize an applicant's special qualifications. As a job applicant, you should exercise great care in preparing your résumé for job searches. As a manager, you should also learn how to screen applications and résumés for insights that can help you make good selection decisions.

Interviews   Interviews are extremely important in the selection process because of the information exchange they allow.[8] Six things to remember when you are the one conducting the interview are shown in The Effective Manager 17.1.

Employment Tests   Testing is often used in the screening of job applicants. Some common employment tests are designed to identify intelligence, aptitudes, personality, and interests. Whenever tests are used and in whatever forms, however, the goal should be to gather information that will help predict the applicant's eventual performance success. To do so, they must meet two important criteria: (1) a *valid test* measures exactly what it intends relative to the job specification; (2) a *reliable test* yields approximately the same results over time if taken by the same person. Invalid or unreliable employment tests can bias selection decisions. This is one reason why the process is subject to legal constraints. Under Equal Employment Opportunity legislation, any employment test used as a criterion of selection must be defensible on the grounds that it actually measures an ability required to perform the job.

New developments in testing extend the process into actual demonstrations of job-relevant skills and personal characteristics. *Computerized testing* is becoming more common today, aided by specialized software that includes interactive and multimedia approaches. Such computerized tests often ask the applicant to indicate how he or she would respond to a series of job-relevant situations. Another form of this testing approach is *work-sampling* that directly assesses a person's performance on a set of tasks that directly replicate those required in the job under consideration. Here, applicants are asked to work on actual job tasks while being graded by observers on their performance. An *assessment center* evaluates a person's potential by observing performance in experiential activities designed to simulate daily work. When Mitsubishi was staffing a new plant in the United States, for example, prospective group leaders were required to pass through a sophisticated assessment. It included group and individual exercises that simulated situations requiring them to counsel troubled workers, teach workers how to handle equipment, and show organizational abilities by processing an in-basket full of paperwork.[9]

Reference Checks Reference checks are inquiries to prior employers, academic advisors, co-workers, and/or acquaintances regarding the qualifications, experience, and past work records of a job applicant. Although they might be biased if friends are prearranged "to say the right things if called," reference checks can be helpful. They may reveal important information on the applicant that was not discovered elsewhere in the selection process. The references given by a job applicant can also add credibility to an application if they include a legitimate and even prestigious list of persons.

Physical Examinations Some organizations ask job applicants to take a physical examination. This health check helps ensure that the person is physically capable of fulfilling job requirements. It may also be used as a basis for enrolling the applicant in health-related fringe benefits such as life-, health-, and disability-insurance programs. A recent and controversial development in this area is the emerging use of drug testing. This has become part of pre-employment health screening and a basis for continued employment at some organizations.

Final Analysis and Decisions to Hire or Reject Final responsibility for the decision to hire or reject a job applicant usually rests with the manager. But the best selection decisions are likely to be ones made in consultation with others, including potential co-workers, and ones based on information obtained from a variety of screening devices. And importantly, the emphasis in selection must always be on someone's capacity to perform in the new job. At Stew Leonard's innovative dairy store, for example, the emphasis in any job is always on customer service and the firm looks above all else for a good attitude in new employees. Owner Stew Leonard says: "If applicants have a good attitude, we can do the rest . . . but if they have a bad attitude to start with, everything we do seems to fail."[10]

Developing a Quality Workforce

When people join an organization, they must "learn the ropes" and become familiar with the way things are done. **Socialization** is the process of influencing the expectations, behavior, and attitudes of a new employee in a manner considered desirable by the organization.[11] The intent, consistent with the staffing process, is to achieve the best possible match between the individual, the job, and the organization.

Employee Orientation

Socialization of newcomers begins with **orientation**—a set of activities designed to familiarize new employees with their jobs, co-workers, and key aspects of the organization as a whole. This includes clarifying the organizational mission and culture, explaining operating objectives and job expectations, communicating policies and procedures, and identifying key personnel.

The first six months of employment are often crucial in determining how well someone is going to perform over the long run. It is a time when attitudes and work patterns are subject to influence. Unfortunately, orientation is often neglected and newcomers are left to fend for themselves. They may learn job and organizational routines on their own or through casual interactions with co-workers, and they may acquire job attitudes the same way.[12] The end result is that too many otherwise well-intentioned and capable people may learn inappropriate attitudes and/or behaviors. Good orientation, by contrast, enhances a person's understanding of the organization and adds purpose to their daily job activities. Increased performance, greater job satisfaction, and greater commitment to the job and organizational culture are the desired results.

Training and Development Alternatives

Training is a set of activities that provides the opportunity to acquire and improve job-related skills. This applies both to the initial training of an employee and to upgrading or improving someone's skills to meet changing job requirements. A major concern of some American employers is the lack of educational preparation of some workers for jobs, often high-technology jobs, in the new workplace. These concerns sometimes extend to basic skills of reading, writing, and arithmetic.[13] The more progressive organizations are implementing major training programs to ensure that their workers have the basic skills needed to learn and perform in new jobs.

Among the possible training methods, **on-the-job training** is done in the work setting while someone is doing a job. Some of the approaches include job rotation, formal and informal coaching, apprenticeship, and modeling. *Job rotation,* discussed in Chapter 11, allows people to spend time working in different jobs and thus expand the range of their job capabilities. *Coaching* occurs when an experienced person gives specific technical advice to someone else. This can be done on a formal and planned basis by a supervisor or co-workers. It can also occur more informally as help spontaneously offered when the need arises. *Apprenticeship* involves a formal work assignment where a person serves as understudy or assistant to someone who already has the desired job skills. Through this relationship, an apprentice learns a job over time and eventually becomes fully qualified to perform it. *Mentoring,* the act of informally sharing experiences and insights between a seasoned worker and a junior worker, can be another important form of personal development. And *modeling* is the process through which one person demonstrates through personal behavior what is expected of others. When people in supervisory capacities work for good managers, for example, their managerial skills can be enhanced simply by practicing the techniques of their managers.

Off-the-job training is accomplished outside the work setting. It may be done within the organization at a separate training room or facility, or at an off-site location. Examples of the latter include attendance at special training programs sponsored by universities, trade or professional associations, or consultants. *Management development workshops* are special forms of off-the-job training to improve a person's knowledge and skill in the fundamentals of management. If you are truly serious about a managerial career, management development activities should be an important part of your continuing personal agenda.

The Role of Performance Appraisal

The process of formally assessing someone's work and providing feedback on his or her performance is **performance appraisal.**[14] This should serve two purposes. The *evaluation purpose* of performance appraisal is to let people know where they stand relative to performance objectives and standards. Here, the appraisal focuses on past performance and measurements of results against standards. Performance is documented for the record, establishing a basis for allocating performance rewards. Consequently, the manager acts in the *judgmental role* of giving a direct evaluation of another person's performance accomplishments.

The *development purpose* of performance appraisal is to assist in the training and continued personal development of people. Here, the appraisal focuses on future performance and the clarification of success standards. It is a way of discovering performance obstacles and identifying training and development opportunities. The manager acts in a *counseling role,* focusing on a subordinate's developmental needs. This aspect of performance appraisal contributes most positively to training and development as a human resource management function.

Performance Appraisal Methods

Like employment tests, any performance appraisal method should meet the criteria of reliability and validity. To be reliable, the method should be consistent in yielding the same result over time and for different raters; to be valid, it should be unbiased and measure only factors directly relevant to job performance. In today's complex legal environment, any manager who hires, fires, or promotes someone is increasingly called upon to defend such actions—sometimes in specific response to lawsuits alleging that the actions were discriminatory. At a minimum, written documentation of performance appraisals and a record of consistent past actions will be required to back up any contested evaluations.

Graphic rating scales list a variety of characteristics thought to be important in a given job—work quantity, work quality, cooperativeness, punctuality, enthusiasm, and the like. A manager rates the individual on each characteristic using a summary numerical rating, such as "excellent," "good," "fair," "poor." The primary appeal of graphic rating scales is that they are relatively quick and easy to complete. Their

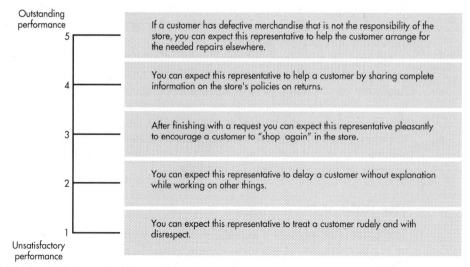

Figure 17.2 Sample behaviorally anchored rating scale (BARS) for a customer service representative.

reliability and validity are questionable, however, since the categories and rating levels are subject to varying interpretations.

The *free-form narrative* is a written essay description of a person's job performance. The commentary typically includes actual descriptions of performance, discusses an individual's strengths and weaknesses, and provides an overall evaluation. Free-form narratives are sometimes used in combination with other performance appraisal methods, such as the graphic rating scale. Because of their essay character, free-form narratives require good written communication skills on the part of the person doing the evaluation.

A *behaviorally anchored rating scale* (BARS) is based on explicit descriptions of actual behaviors that exemplify various levels of performance achievement. Look at the case of a customer-service representative in Figure 17.2. "Extremely poor" performance is clearly defined as rude or disrespectful treatment of a customer. Because performance assessments are anchored to specific descriptions of work behavior, a BARS is more reliable and valid than a graphic rating scale. The behavioral anchors can also be helpful in training people to master job skills of demonstrated performance importance. Even though somewhat complex to develop and administer, the BARS method of performance appraisal is gaining in popularity.

The *critical-incident technique* involves keeping a running log or inventory of effective and ineffective job behaviors. Creating a written record of positive and negative performance examples provides documented success or failure patterns that can be specifically discussed with the individual. A good critical-incident log is complete and unbiased. Thus, a manager must be observant, diligent, and fair when selecting incidents for the record. Using the case of the customer service representative again, a critical-incidents log might contain the following types of entries:

Positive example "Took extraordinary care of a customer who had purchased a defective item from a company store in another city."

Negative example "Acted rudely in dismissing the complaint of a customer who felt that a 'sale' item was erroneously advertised."

An increasingly popular approach to performance appraisal involves the use of *multiperson comparisons,* which formally compare one person's performance with that of one or more others. Such comparisons can be used on their own or in combination with some other method. They can also be done in different ways. In *rank ordering,* everyone being rated is ranked in order of performance achievement, with the best performer at the top of the list, the worst performer at the bottom; no ties are allowed. In *paired comparisons,* each person is formally compared to every other person and rated as either the superior or the weaker member of the pair. After all paired comparisons are made, each person is assigned a summary ranking based on the number of superior scores achieved. In *forced distribution,* each person is placed into a frequency distribution that requires a certain percentage of people to fall into specific performance classifications, such as top 10 percent, next 40 percent, next 40 percent, and bottom 10 percent.

Maintaining a Quality Workforce

An effective staffing process results in the presence of a qualified workforce at all times, even in the face of a dynamic and changing environment with shifting work demands. It is not enough to attract and develop a qualified workforce; this workforce must be successfully maintained as well. Important here are issues of retention and turnover, compensation and benefits, and labor–management relations.

Managing Retention and Turnover

The several steps in the staffing process both conclude and recycle with **replacement,** the management of promotions, transfers, terminations, layoffs, and retirements. Any replacement situation is an opportunity to review human resource plans, update job analyses, rewrite job descriptions and job specifications, and make sure that the best people are selected to perform the required tasks.

Some replacement decisions shift people among positions within the organization. *Promotion* is movement to a higher-level position; *transfer* is movement to a different job at the same or similar level of responsibility. Both are key to succession planning, as described earlier. Well-managed organizations combine appropriate training and development activities with planned promotions and transfers. This ensures that a talented pool of people are always ready to move into advanced responsibilities as needed.

Transfers may be especially important in organizations undergoing downsizing (reducing costs by eliminating workers). Fewer promotions are available in such settings and more people hit *career plateaus.* These are positions from which a person is unlikely to advance.[15] The existence of career plateaus increases the importance of handling job transfers as growth and development opportunities. They offer chances to broaden experience, learn new skills, and become more familiar with other areas—things that can benefit the individual as well as the organization.

Another set of replacement decisions relates to the termination of employment. Retirement is something most people look forward to, until it is close at hand. Then the prospect of being retired often raises fears and apprehensions. Many organizations try to manage this aspect of replacement by offering special counseling and other forms of support for pre-retirement employees. Recommending seminars that assist workers with company benefits, money management, estate planning, and use of leisure time, as well as just being a good listener, are among the things managers can do to assist retiring workers. Downsizing is sometimes accompanied by special offers of early retirement—retirement before formal retirement age but with special financial incentives. Where this is not possible, a growing number of organizations provide outplacement services to help terminated employees find other jobs.

The most extreme form of termination is the involuntary and permanent dismissal of an employee. For the person being dismissed, accepting the fact of being terminated is difficult. The termination notice might come by surprise and without the benefit of advance preparation for either the personal or the financial shock. The experts' advice, though, is for the dismissed employee to brace up and stay rational. It is time to ask at least three tough questions of the ex-boss: "Why am I being fired?" "What are my termination benefits?" "Can I have a good reference?"

Managing Labor–Management Relations

Labor unions, organizations to which workers belong and that collectively deal with employers on their behalf, are important forces in the workplace.[16] Whereas they used to be associated primarily with industrial and business occupations, labor unions also represent such public-sector employees as teachers, police officers, and government workers. Any manager in any organization—small or large, public or private—must be prepared to deal successfully with them. Unions act as bargaining agents who negotiate legal contracts that affect many aspects of human resource management. These **labor contracts** specify the rights and obligations of employees and management in respect to wages, work hours, work rules, and other conditions of employment. They typically include the items referenced in The Effective Manager 17.2.

The foundation for any labor–management relationship is **collective bargaining**—the process of negotiating, administering, and interpreting labor contracts. Labor contracts and the collective bargaining process—from negotiating a new contract to resolving disputes under an existing one—are major influences on human resource management in unionized work settings. They are also governed closely in the United States by a strict legal framework. For example, the Wagner Act of 1935 protects employees by recognizing their rights to join unions and engage in union activities; the Taft–Hartley Act of 1947 protects employers from unfair labor practices by unions and allows workers to decertify unions; and the Civil Service

---

THE EFFECTIVE MANAGER 17.2

Things to Look for in a Labor Contract

- Job specifications regarding what workers are allowed to do.
- Seniority rules for changing jobs, advancing in pay, and choosing work shifts.
- Compensation plans covering wage rates and benefits.
- Grievance mechanisms for handling worker and management complaints.
- Procedures for hiring, promoting, transferring, and dismissing workers.

Reform Act Title VII of 1978 clarifies the rights of government employees to join and be represented by labor unions.

The collective bargaining process typically occurs in face-to-face meetings between labor and management representatives. During this time a variety of demands, proposals, and counterproposals are exchanged. Several rounds of bargaining may be required before a contract is reached or a dispute over a contract issue is resolved. As you might expect, the process can lead to adversarial relationships. But when they do, the resulting conflicts can be costly in money, time, and emotional energies to both sides. Take the case of the U.S. automobile industry, which is still struggling to meet the challenges of global competition. For years, the bargaining between Ford, General Motors, Chrysler, and the strong, demanding leadership of the United Auto Workers (UAW) had an adversarial character. Unions perceived management as aloof and uncaring in dealing with the needs of auto workers. The resulting labor contracts tried to protect worker interests through complex work rules and expensive compensation packages. While all this was happening, the competitiveness of the automakers was eroding. Many layoffs and plant closings occurred.

Fortunately, the traditional adversarial model of labor–management relations seems to be giving way to a new and more progressive era. Going back to the prior example, the automakers and the UAW have tried to work more closely together to reduce production costs while maintaining basic worker rights and benefits. Each side seems more willing to recognize that the productivity and future survival of the industry depend on cooperation and mutual adjustment to new and challenging times. The same positive, albeit tentative, move toward greater cooperation is seen in other organizational settings. Many unions and employers are now trying to work together for the common good. Today's union leaders appear to recognize that unions must adapt to changing conditions if they are to survive and prosper in the years ahead.[17] By the same token, modern managers seem more willing to view labor leaders as equal partners in human resource management.

In Summary

Why is human resource management important?

- The purpose of human resource management is to make sure the organization always has people with the right abilities available to do the required work.

- Human resource management is the process of attracting, developing, and maintaining a quality workforce.
- Good human resource management respects the complex legal environment governing fair employment practices, including those relating to equal employment opportunity.
- Human resource planning helps managers formally assess personnel needs and develop action plans for dealing with them over time.

How do organizations attract quality workers?

- To attract high-quality workers, managers must first do a good job of recruiting qualified job applicants and selecting from this pool the most talented people to fill open positions.
- Recruitment can be both internal and external to the organization, and should involve realistic job previews that provide job candidates with accurate information on the job and organization.
- Managers should use interviews, tests, and reference checks to help make selection decisions; more in-depth analysis of job candidates through assessment center and work sampling approaches are gaining popularity.

How do organizations develop quality workers?

- Socialization is the process of influencing the attitudes and behaviors of a new organizational member.
- Orientation is the process of formally introducing new hires to their jobs, performance requirements, and the organization.
- A variety of on-the-job and off-the-job training and development opportunities is essential for long-term performance success in most jobs.
- Performance appraisal should serve both evaluation and development purposes; it is a means of not only evaluating employee performance, but also of identifying important training and development needs.

How do organizations maintain a quality workforce?

- To maintain a high-quality workforce, staff retention and turnover must be managed well.
- Workers must be replaced over time due to promotions, transfers, retirements, and terminations.
- The goal in managing replacement should always be to treat people fairly while ensuring that jobs are filled with the best personnel available.
- Where labor unions exist, labor–management relations should be positively approached, and should be handled in all due consideration of applicable laws.

18

PLANNED CHANGE

AND CONTINUOUS

IMPROVEMENT

As you read Chapter 18, keep in mind these study questions:

- What are learning organizations?

- What are the components of organizational change?

- How can planned change be managed?

- How can organization development help in continuous improvement?

The New Realities, The Age of Unreason, The Age of Paradox—these titles of popular books communicate the urgency of dealing with our dynamic society in creative and progressive ways.[1] Read the newspapers and magazines to get a greater feel for the issue. Even some of the terms used to describe organizational responses to new and demanding circumstances have a sensational quality: *rightsizing, restructuring,* and *reengineering* are just a few. The more mundane descriptions of *plant closings, mergers, acquisitions,* and the like are just as significant in their impact on the organizations and people involved. The very nature of the dynamic, complex, and sometimes unpredictable environment in which we live demands a commitment to continuous improvement. People change, their tastes and values change, governments and laws change, technologies change, and knowledge changes. Unless organizations also change, they risk stagnation, decline, and even death. Enlightened managers help their organizations keep pace with these and other challenges. They help people and organizations learn and renew themselves continuously.

Learning Organizations

This is the age of the *learning organization,* where members at all levels commit to set aside old ways of thinking and search for ways to best work together to accomplish plans.[2] The watchwords of the day are *innovation* and *change.* Organizations and their members must continually adapt to survive and prosper over time. To do this, they must be capable of managing in a progressive way. Max DePree, chairperson and CEO of Herman Miller Company, is known for his creativity and leadership accomplishments. He says: "You have to have an environment where the body of people are really amenable to change and can deal with the conflicts that arise out of change and innovation."[3] Consultant Peter Senge, author of *The Fifth Discipline,* says that managers must stimulate and lead change in order to create learning organizations with these core ingredients:[4]

1. **Mental models** Everyone sets aside old ways of thinking.
2. **Personal mastery** Everyone becomes self-aware and open to others.
3. **Systems thinking** Everyone learns how the whole organization works.

4. **Shared vision** Everyone understands and agrees to a plan of action.

5. **Team learning** Everyone works together to accomplish the plan.

Creativity and Innovation

Creativity, as noted in Chapter 13, is the use of ingenuity and imagination to create a novel approach to things or a unique solution to a problem. It is obviously very important to organizations struggling to meet the demands of a complex, ever-changing environment. Good managers should be interested in stimulating individual and group creativity in their work settings. Yet people's creative abilities are too often blocked by poor management and organizational practices. Consider these words penned by a Unilever executive trying to put his frustrations into rhyme.

Along this tree
From root to crown
Ideas flow up
And vetoes down.[5]

This verse leaves the impression of an organization that has the advantages of alertness and imagination at its lower levels but is suffering from rigidity, resistance to change, and a lack of foresight at the top. Whereas Unilever had the internal resources for creativity, top management was apparently discouraging instead of encouraging it. The ability to both encourage and tolerate creativity is among the most basic of a manager's work responsibilities.

The Innovation Process

Formally defined, **innovation** is the process of creating new ideas and putting them into practice.[6] It is the act of converting new ideas into usable applications. In organizations, these applications occur in the form of *process innovations,* which result in better ways of doing things, and *product innovations,* which result in the creation of new or improved goods and services. The management of innovation includes supporting both invention—the act of discovery—and application—the act of use. *Invention* relates to the development of new ideas. Here, managers need to be concerned about creating new work environments that stimulate creativity and an ongoing stream of new ideas. *Application,* on the other hand, deals with the utilization of inventions to take best advantage of their value. Here, managers must make sure that good ideas for new or modified work processes are actually implemented. They must also make sure that the commercial potential of ideas for new products or services is fully realized.

Innovation in Organizations

While creativity and innovation are key operating objectives for progressive organizations like 3M, maker of the well-known Post-it notes, there are many organizations that should be innovating but fail to do so. Dramatic technological, economic, political, and social changes continue to characterize the world at large, and managers in these organizations must stimulate, support, and achieve innovation. We can describe four basic elements in organizational innovation as follows:

1. **Idea creation** New knowledge forms around basic discoveries, extensions of existing understandings, or spontaneous creativity made possible by individual ingenuity and communication with others.
2. **Initial experimentation** Ideas are initially tested in concept by discussions with others, referrals to customers, clients, or technical experts, and/or in the form of prototypes or samples.
3. **Feasibility determination** Practicality and financial value are examined in formal feasibility studies, which also identify potential costs and benefits as well as potential markets or applications.
4. **Final application** A new product is finally commercialized or put on sale in the open market, or a new process is implemented as part of normal operating routines.[7]

Each of these steps is especially relevant to an important business activity called *commercializing innovations*. This is the process of turning new ideas into products or processes that can make a difference in sales, profits, or costs. One of the major features of organizational innovation is that the entire process must be related to the needs of the organization and its marketplace. New ideas alone are not sufficient to guarantee success in this setting; they must be implemented effectively in order to contribute to organizational performance. At Rubbermaid, one of America's most-admired corporations, the goal is at least one new product idea every day.[8]

Characteristics of Innovative Organizations

Innovative organizations are mobilized to support creativity and entrepreneurship, and their managers take active roles in leading the innovation process.[9] In highly innovative organizations, the *culture and corporate strategy* support innovation. The strategies of the organization, visions and values of senior management, and the framework of policies and expectations emphasize an innovative spirit. But even with such directions in place, failure is accepted and the organization is willing to take risk. For example, Johnson & Johnson CEO James Burke says: "I try to give people the feeling that it's okay to fail, that it's important to fail."[10] The key here is for managers to eliminate risk-averse climates and replace them with organizational cultures in which innovation is expected and failure is accepted.

In highly innovative organizations, *organization structures* also support innovation. More and more large organizations are trying to capture the structural flexibility of smaller ones. That is, they are striving for more organic operations with a strong emphasis on lateral communications and cross-functional teams and task forces. In particular, research and development, historically a separate and isolated function, is being integrated into a team setting. As Peter Drucker points out, "Successful innovations . . . are now being turned out by cross-functional teams with people from marketing, manufacturing, and finance participating in research work from the very beginning."[11] Innovative organizations are also reorganizing to create many smaller

THE EFFECTIVE MANAGER 18.1

Spotting Barriers to Innovation

- **Top management isolation**—fosters misunderstandings and contributes to a "risk-averse" climate
- **Intolerance of differences**—denies uniqueness, creates homogeneity, and brands as "troublemakers" those who question the status quo
- **Vested interests**—focuses on the parts rather than the whole and emphasizes the defense of one's "turf" against the encroachment of outsiders
- **Short time horizons**—emphasizes short-term goals rather than the potential for new ideas to generate long-term gains
- **Overly rational thinking**—tries to put creative and sometimes chaotic processes into systematic and rational sequences, and may emphasize schedules over development needs
- **Inappropriate incentives**—uses reward and control systems to reinforce regularity and routines, and discourages surprises and differences linked to innovation
- **Excessive bureaucracy**—gives allegiance to rules, procedures, and efficiency that frustrate creativity and innovation

divisions to allow creative teams, or *skunkworks,* to operate and encourage intrapreneurial new ventures.

In highly innovative organizations, the organization's *staffing* supports innovation as well. Organizations need different kinds of people to succeed in all steps of the innovation process: idea generators who create new insights; information gatekeepers linked with knowledge sources; product champions who advocate adoption of new practices; project managers who perform the technical functions needed to keep an innovative project on track; and leaders who actively encourage, sponsor, and coach others to pursue innovation.[12]

Finally, in highly innovative organizations, *top management* supports innovation. In the case of 3M, for example, many top managers have been the innovators and product champions of the past. They understand the innovation process, are tolerant of criticisms and differences of opinion, take all possible steps to keep the pressure on, and remove the obstacles to success. The key, once again, is to allow the creative potential of people to operate fully. As Max DePree of Herman Miller again states: "If you want the best things to happen in corporate life, you have to find ways to be hospitable to the unusual person."[13]

In contrast to the positive characteristics just identified, other forces sometimes limit innovation in organizations. A number of common barriers to innovation in organizations are listed in The Effective Manager 18.1.[14]

Organizational Change

Some say that change is inevitable, but is it? Consider what happened, for example, at BankAmerica after the company announced a large quarterly operating loss. New

CEO Samuel Armacost complained about the lack of "agents of change" among his top managers, who seemed more interested in taking orders than initiating change. "I came away quite distressed from my first couple of management meetings," he said. "Not only couldn't I get conflict, I couldn't even get comment. They were all waiting to see which way the wind blew."[15]

The Manager as Change Agent

A **change agent** is a person or group who takes responsibility for changing the existing pattern of behavior of another person or social system. Change agents make things happen, and part of every manager's job is to act as a change agent in the work setting. This requires being alert to situations or people needing change, open to good ideas, and able to support the implementation of new ideas in actual practice.

Change occurs in different ways in organizations. *Top-down change* is initiated and directed by top management. Strategic and comprehensive changes typically follow this pattern. When done well, top-down change can occur rather rapidly and with a comprehensive impact on the organization. It runs the risk of being perceived as insensitive to the needs of lower-level personnel, however, and can suffer from implementation problems brought on by resistance and a lack of organization-wide commitment to change. Part of the success of top-down change, as with top-down planning discussed in Chapter 5, is usually determined by the willingness of middle and lower-level managers to actively support top-management initiatives.

Bottom-up change is also important in organizations. In such cases, the initiatives for change come from people throughout an organization and are supported by the efforts of middle- and lower-level managers acting as change agents. Bottom-up change is essential to organizational innovation and is useful in terms of adapting operations and technologies to the changing requirements of work. It is especially strong in creating the advantages of empowerment and participation, discussed in earlier chapters. Indeed, innovation-oriented companies such as Rubbermaid and 3M are organized and managed to facilitate bottom-up change.

We are particularly interested in planned change that happens as a result of specific efforts by a change agent. Planned change is a direct response to a person's perception of a *performance gap,* or discrepancy between the desired and actual state of affairs. As you should recall from the discussion of planning in Chapter 5, performance gaps may represent problems to be resolved or opportunities to be explored. In each case, managers as change agents should be ever alert to spot performance gaps and take action to initiate planned changes in dealing with them.

Forces and Targets for Change

Performance gaps and the impetus for change in any one or more of these targets can arise from the variety of *external forces* for change. These include the global economy and market competition, local economic conditions, government laws and regulations, technological developments, market trends, and social forces, among others. As things develop and change over time in an organization's general and specific environments, the organization must adapt as well.

Internal forces for changes are important, too. Indeed, any change in one part of the organization as a complex system—perhaps a change initiated in response to one or more of the external forces just identified—can often create the need for change in another part of the system. The many organizational targets for planned change include all the aspects of organizations already discussed in this book—tasks, people, culture, structure, technology, and strategy, among other possibilities.

Managed Planned Change

Change is a complicated phenomenon in any setting, and people always stand at the heart of it. But people tend to act habitually and in stable ways over time; that is, they may tend not to change even when circumstances warrant it. Any manager needs to recognize and deal with such inertia in the work setting. To begin, it helps to understand the phases of planned change and their managerial implications.

The Phases of Planned Change

Kurt Lewin, a noted psychologist, recommends that any planned-change effort be viewed as the three-phase process shown in Figure 18.1.[16] Lewin's three phases of planned change are: (1) *unfreezing,* preparing a system for change, (2) *changing,* making actual changes in the system, and (3) *refreezing,* stabilizing the system after change.

In order for change to be successful, Lewin points out, the system to be changed—individual, group, or organization—must be ready for it to occur. **Unfreezing** is the stage of preparing a situation for change. This requires that a manager establish a good relationship with the people involved and help them develop a felt need for change. Planned change has little chance for long-term success unless existing attitudes and behaviors are disconfirmed and people become open to doing things differently. Unfreezing can be assisted through environmental pressures for change, declining performance, recognizing that problems or opportunities exist, and observing behavioral models that display alternative approaches. When handled well, conflict can be an important unfreezing force in organizations. It often helps people break old habits and recognize alternative ways of thinking about or doing things.

In the **changing** phase, something new takes place in a system and change is actually implemented. This is the point at which managers initiate changes in the organizational targets of tasks, people, culture, technology, and structure. All such change is done ideally in response to good problem diagnosis and a careful examination of alternatives. However, Lewin believes that many change agents enter the changing phase prematurely, are too quick to change things, and therefore end up creating resistance to change. When managers implement change before the people involved feel a need for it, there is an increased likelihood of failure.

The final stage in the planned-change process is **refreezing.** Here, the manager is concerned about stabilizing the change and creating the conditions for its long-

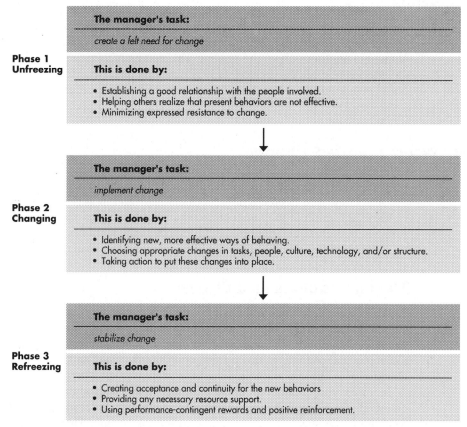

**Phase 1
Unfreezing**

The manager's task:

create a felt need for change

This is done by:

- Establishing a good relationship with the people involved.
- Helping others realize that present behaviors are not effective.
- Minimizing expressed resistance to change.

**Phase 2
Changing**

The manager's task:

implement change

This is done by:

- Identifying new, more effective ways of behaving.
- Choosing appropriate changes in tasks, people, culture, technology, and/or structure.
- Taking action to put these changes into place.

**Phase 3
Refreezing**

The manager's task:

stabilize change

This is done by:

- Creating acceptance and continuity for the new behaviors
- Providing any necessary resource support.
- Using performance-contingent rewards and positive reinforcement.

Figure 18.1   Lewin's three phases of planned organizational change: unfreezing, changing, and refreezing.

term continuity. Refreezing is accomplished by providing appropriate rewards for performance, positive reinforcement, and necessary resource support. It is also important to evaluate results carefully, provide feedback to the people involved, and make any required modifications in the original change. When refreezing is done poorly, changes are too easily forgotten or abandoned with the passage of time. When it is done well, the benefits of more long-lasting change can be realized.

Choosing a Change Strategy

Managers use various approaches when attempting to get others to adopt a desired change.[17] As shown in Figure 18.2, a **force–coercion strategy** uses the power bases of legitimacy, rewards, and punishments as primary inducements to change. The likely outcomes are immediate compliance but little commitment. In *direct forcing* the change agent takes direct and unilateral action to "command" that change take place. This involves the exercise of formal authority or legitimate power, offering special rewards, and/or threatening punishment. In *political maneuvering,* the

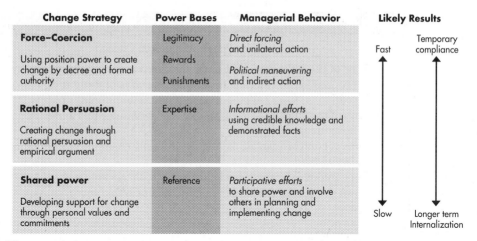

Change Strategy	Power Bases	Managerial Behavior	Likely Results	
Force–Coercion Using position power to create change by decree and formal authority	Legitimacy Rewards Punishments	*Direct forcing and unilateral action* *Political maneuvering and indirect action*	Fast	Temporary compliance
Rational Persuasion Creating change through rational persuasion and empirical argument	Expertise	*Informational efforts using credible knowledge and demonstrated facts*		
Shared power Developing support for change through personal values and commitments	Reference	*Participative efforts to share power and involve others in planning and implementing change*	Slow	Longer term Internalization

Figure 18.2   Three change strategies and their managerial implications: force–coercion, rational persuasion, and shared power.

change agent works indirectly to gain special advantage over other people and thereby make them change. This involves bargaining, obtaining control of important resources, or granting small favors in return.

In both versions, the force–coercion strategy has limited results. Although it can be done rather quickly, most people respond to this strategy out of fear of punishment or desire for reward. This usually results in only temporary compliance with the change agent's desires. The new behavior continues only as long as the opportunity for rewards and punishments is present. For this reason, force–coercion is most useful as an unfreezing device that helps people break old patterns of behavior and gain initial impetus to try new ones.

Change agents using a **rational persuasion strategy** attempt to bring about change through persuasion backed by special knowledge, empirical data, and rational argument. The likely outcomes are eventual compliance with reasonable commitment. This is an *informational* strategy that assumes that rational people will be guided by facts, reason, and self-interest in deciding whether or not to support a change. A manager using this approach must convince others that the cost–benefit value of a planned change is high and that it will leave them better off than before. Accomplishing this depends to a large extent on the presence of expert power. This can come directly from the change agent if he or she has personal credibility as an "expert." If not, it can be obtained in the form of consultants and other "outside experts" or from demonstration projects. When successful, a rational persuasion strategy helps unfreeze and refreeze a change situation. While slower than force–coercion, it tends to result in longer-lasting and internalized change.

A **shared power strategy** identifies or establishes values and assumptions from which support for a proposed change will naturally emerge. The process is slow but it is likely to yield high commitment. This approach is based on *empowerment* and is highly *participative* in nature. It relies on involving others in examining personal needs and values, group norms, and operating goals as they relate to the issues at

---

THE EFFECTIVE MANAGER 18.2

Why People May Resist Change

- **Fear of the unknown**—not understanding what is happening or why
- **Disrupted habits**—feeling upset when old ways of doing things can't be followed
- **Loss of confidence**—feeling incapable of performing well under the new ways of doing things
- **Loss of control**—feeling that things are being done "to" you rather than "by" or "with" you
- **Poor timing**—feeling overwhelmed or that things are moving too fast
- **Work overload**—not having the physical or psychic energy to commit to the change
- **Loss of face**—feeling inadequate or humiliated because the "old" ways weren't "good" ways
- **Lack of purpose**—not seeing a reason for the change or not understanding its benefits

---

hand. Power is shared by the change agent and other people as they work together to develop new consensus to support needed change.

Managers using shared power as an approach to planned change need reference power and the skills to work effectively with other people in group situations. They must be comfortable allowing others to participate in making decisions affecting the nature of the planned change and its manner of implementation. Because it entails a high level of involvement, a normative-reeducation strategy is often quite time-consuming, but it is likely to result in a longer-lasting and internalized change.

Dealing with Resistance to Change

When people resist change, they are defending something important—something that appears threatened, to them at least, by the attempted change. Such resistance is often viewed by change agents and managers as something that must be overcome in order for change to be successful. This is not necessarily true. Resistance is really a type of feedback that the informed change agent can use constructively to modify a planned change. When encountered, it usually means that something can be done to achieve a better "fit" between the planned change, the situation, and the people involved. Some of the common reasons why people in organizations resist planned change are shown in The Effective Manager 18.2.

Once resistance to change is recognized and understood, it can be dealt with in positive ways. This is especially true if the manager has been alert and identified resistance early in the planned change process.[18] Among the alternatives for effectively managing resistance, *education and communication* uses discussions, presentations, and demonstrations to educate people beforehand about a change. *Participation and involvement* allows others to contribute ideas and help design and implement the change. *Facilitation and support* provides encouragement and training, actively listens to problems and complaints, and helps to overcome performance pressures. *Facilitation and agreement* provides incentives that appeal to actual or potential resistors, making trade-offs in exchange for assurances that change will not be blocked. *Manipulation and cooptation* tries to covertly influence others; providing information selectively and structuring events in favor of the desired change. *Explicit and implicit coercion* forces people to accept change, threatening resistors with a variety of undesirable consequences if they do not go along as planned. Among these strategies, the last two alternatives listed are very common in organizations. They are also the least desirable of any on the list.

Organization Development

"OD," standing for *organization development,* is recognized as a special and comprehensive approach to planned organizational change. It is a change approach that lends itself especially well to the "continuous improvement" concept that is part of the current emphasis on total quality management and learning organizations. Formally defined, *OD* is the application of behavioral science knowledge in a systematic and long-range effort to improve organizational effectiveness.[19] In particular, organization development should help organizations cope with forces of change in their environments while simultaneously improving their internal problem-solving capabilities. Thus, it has both "outcome" goals and "process" goals. The *outcome goals* of OD focus on task accomplishments, while the *process goals* focus on the way people work together.

You may want to think of OD as "planned change *plus*," with the "plus" being the creation of change in such a way that organization members develop a capacity for continued self-renewal. That is, OD tries to achieve change in such a way that organization members become more active and self-reliant in the future when making changes as needed to maintain longer-run organizational effectiveness. What also makes OD unique as a planned change approach is its allegiance to strong humanistic values and several established behavioral science principles. OD is committed to improving organizations through freedom of choice, shared power, and self-reliance.

A General Model of Organization Development

The process of OD is based on a working relationship between a "facilitator," who may be a trained consultant, staff specialist, or actual manager, and a "client system" with whom he or she works with the goal of improving organizational effectiveness. The approach requires that the facilitator first *establish a working relationship* with members of the client system. The next step is *diagnosis*—gathering and analyzing data to assess the situation and set appropriate change objectives. This helps unfreeze an existing situation as well as pinpoint appropriate action directions. Diagnosis leads to active *intervention,* wherein change objectives are pursued through a variety of specific interventions, a number of which will be discussed shortly.

Essential to any OD effort is *evaluation.* This is the examination of the process to determine if things are proceeding smoothly and in a desired direction, and if further action is needed. Eventually, the goals of OD are for the consultant or facilitator to *achieve a terminal relationship* with the client system, that is, to leave the client able to function on its own. If OD has been done well, the system and its members should be prepared to better manage their continuing needs for self-renewal and development.

The success or failure of any OD program rests in part on the strength of its action research foundations. **Action research** is a process of systematically collecting data on an organization, feeding the data back to the members for action planning, and evaluating results by collecting more data and repeating the process as necessary. Action research is initiated when someone senses a performance gap and decides to analyze the situation systematically for the problems and opportunities it represents. Data gathering can be done in several ways. Interviews are common means of gathering data in action research. Formal written surveys of employee attitudes and needs are also growing in popularity. Many such climate, attitude, or morale questionnaires have been tested for reliability and validity. Some have even been used to the extent that "norms" are available so that one organization can compare its results with those from a broad sample of counterparts.

Types of Organization Development Interventions

Many different *OD interventions* can be used as foundations for formal organization development programs. These interventions seek to change and develop systems effectiveness at the level of individual, group, or system-wide action.

In respect to individuals, OD generally recognizes that needs for personal growth and development are most likely to be satisfied in a supportive and challenging work environment. It also accepts the premise that most people are capable of assuming responsibility for their own actions and of making positive contributions to organizational performance. Based on these principles, some of the more popular OD interventions designed to help improve individual effectiveness include:

- **Sensitivity training (T-groups)** unstructured group sessions where participants learn interpersonal skills and increased sensitivity to other persons
- **Management training** structured educational opportunities for developing important managerial skills and competencies
- **Role negotiation** structured interactions to clarify and negotiate role expectations among people who work together
- **Job redesign** realigning task components to better fit the needs and capabilities of the individual
- **Career planning** structured advice and discussion sessions to help individuals plan career paths and programs of personal development

The group plays a very important role in organization development. OD generally recognizes two principles regarding groups. First, groups are viewed as important vehicles for helping people satisfy important needs. Second, it is believed that better collaboration within groups can help them better serve individual and organizational needs. Selected OD interventions designed to improve group effectiveness include:

- **Team building** structured experiences to help group members set goals, improve interpersonal relations, and become a better-functioning team

- **Process consultation** third-party observation of critical group processes (e.g., communication, conflict, and decision making) and giving advice on how to improve these processes

- **Intergroup team building** structured experiences to help two or more groups set shared goals, improve intergroup relations, and become better coordinated and mutually supportive

At the level of the total organization OD operates with the premise that any changes in one part of the system will also affect other parts. The organization's culture is considered to have an important impact on member attitudes and morale. And it is believed that structures and jobs can be designed to bring together people, technology, and systems in highly productive—and satisfying—combinations. Some of the OD interventions designed to improve organizational effectiveness include:

- **Survey feedback** comprehensive and systematic data collection to identify attitudes and needs, analyze results, and plan for constructive action

- **Confrontation meeting** one-day intensive, structured meeting of a cross-section of organization members, held to gather data on workplace problems, analyze results, and plan for constructive actions.

- **Structural redesign** realigning the organization structure to meet the needs of environmental and contextual forces

- **Management by objectives** formalizing an MBO framework throughout the organization so that individual (subunit) organizational objectives are clearly linked to one another in means–end chains.

Organization Development and Continuous Improvement

OD is an exciting application of behavioral science theory to management practice. It often involves the assistance of an external consultant or an internal staff person with special training. But a manager with appropriate skills and understanding can and should utilize elements of OD in ongoing development efforts with a work unit. As a comprehensive and systematic approach to planned change, OD can and should be used routinely by managers to help achieve and maintain high levels of effectiveness in their areas of performance responsibility.

The imperatives of total quality management and continuous improvement have been themes throughout this book. They apply to all aspects of management and organizational behavior. At all times, in all organizations, and by all managers, strengths and weaknesses as well as problems and opportunities must be constructively addressed. Organization development is one more approach that informed managers may use as they try to introduce planned changes, foster creativity and innovation, and generally improve the performance of organizations and the quality of working lives for their members.

In Summary

What are learning organizations?

- Learning organizations operate with a commitment by people at all levels to set aside old ways of thinking and continually search for ways to best work together to accomplish plans.
- The innovation process involves idea creation, initial experimentation, feasibility determination, and final application.
- Innovation allows creative ideas to be turned into products and/or processes that benefit the organization and its customers.
- Highly innovative organizations tend to have supportive strategies, structures, staffing, and top management.
- The possible barriers to successful innovation in organizations include a lack of top management support for the process, excessive bureaucracy, short time horizons, and vested interests.

What are the components of organizational change?

- Managers acting as change agents help organizations meet the day-to-day challenges of change.
- Organizational change occurs from both the top-down and bottom-up perspectives.
- A manager's responsibility for leading planned change involves being aware of external and internal forces for change.
- The manager's responsibility for leading planned change also involves selecting proper targets for change—including structures, tasks, technology, people, and culture, among others.

How can planned change be managed?

- Lewin identified three phases of planned change as unfreezing (preparing a system for change), changing (making a change), and refreezing (stabilizing the system with a new change in place).
- Managers as change agents must understand the differences among the force–coercion, rational persuasion, and shared power change strategies.
- Resistance to change should always be anticipated, understood, and respected by a change agent.
- People resist change for a variety of reasons, including fear of the unknown and force of habit.

- Good change agents deal with resistance positively and in a manner that best supports the long-term success of a planned change.

How can organization development help in continuous improvement?

- Organization development (OD) is a comprehensive approach to planned organization change that uses behavioral science principles to improve organizational effectiveness over the long term.
- OD has both outcome goals—with a focus on improved task accomplishment—and process goals—with a focus on improvements in the way people work together to accomplish important tasks.
- The organization development process involves action research wherein people work together to collect and analyze data on system performance and decide what actions to take in order to improve things.
- OD interventions to support an OD program may be implemented at the individual, group, and/or organizational levels.
- Organization development can be used regularly to assist in the creation of a self-sustained and ongoing process of organizational renewal devoted to both high performance systems and high quality-of-work-life environments.

N O T E S

CHAPTER 1

[1] *Fortune* (February 10, 1992), pp. 40–70.

[2] For a complete introduction to the study of management see John R. Schermerhorn, Jr., *Management,* fifth edition (New York: John Wiley & Sons, 1996).

[3] Henry Mintzberg, "The Manager's Job: Folklore and Fact." *Harvard Business Review,* vol. 53 (July–August 1975), p. 61.

[4] Information on this series of examples from "Consciousness-Raising among 'Plain Old White Boys,'" *Business Week* (October 28, 1991), p. 32.

[5] Mintzberg (1973), op. cit., p. 46.

[6] Mintzberg (1973), op. cit.; Morgan W. McCall, Jr., Ann M. Morrison, and Robert L. Hannan, *Studies of Managerial Work: Results and Methods.* Technical Report #9 (Greensboro, NC: Center for Creative Leadership, 1978), pp. 7–9. See also John P. Kotter, "What Effective General Managers Really Do," *Harvard Business Review,* vol. 60 (November–December 1982), pp. 156–157.

[7] Kotter, op. cit., p. 164; also his book *The General Managers* (New York: Free Press, 1982).

[8] Robert L. Katz, "Skills of an Effective Administrator," *Harvard Business Review,* vol. 52 (September–October 1974), p. 94.

[9] Richard E. Boyatzis, *The Competent Manager: A Model for Effective Performance* (New York: Wiley: 1982). See also Edward A. Powers, "Enhancing Managerial Competence: The American Management Association Competency Program," *Journal of Management Development,* vol. 6 (1987), pp. 7–18.

[10] Developed from the *Outcome Measurement Project of the Accreditation Research Committee, Phase II* (St. Louis: American Assembly of Collegiate Schools of Business, 1984, pp. 15–18.

[11] For a full treatment of organizational behavior see John R. Schermerhorn, Jr., James G. Hunt, and Richard N. Osborn, *Managing Organizational Behavior,* 5th ed. (New York: John Wiley & Sons, 1994). This section based with permission on John R. Schermerhorn, Jr., James G. Hunt, and Richard N. Osborn, *Basic Organizational Behavior* (New York: John Wiley & Sons, 1995), pp. 3–6.

[12] Tom Peters, "Managing in a World Gone Bonkers," *World Executive Digest* (February 1993), pp. 26–29.

[13] Adapted by permission from Schermerhorn, et al., 1995, pp. 2–3.

[14] See John P. Fernandez, *Managing a Diverse Workforce* (Lexington, Mass.: D.C. Heath, 1991); and Julie O'Mara, *Managing Workplace 2000* (San Francisco: Jossey-Bass, 1991).

[15] See Walter Kiechel III, "How We Will Work in the Year 2000," *Fortune* (May 17, 1993), pp. 38–52.

[16] John Gardner, *No Easy Victories* (New York: Harper & Row, 1968).

[17] See Charles Handy, *The Age of Unreason* (Cambridge, Mass.: Harvard University Press, 1991).

[18] Ralph Sorenson, "A Lifetime of Learning to Manage Effectively," *The Wall Street Journal* (February 28, 1983), p. 18.

CHAPTER 2

[1] Michael Porter's books include *Competitive Strategy: Techniques for Analyzing Industries and Competitors* (New York: Free Press, 1980), *Competitive Advantage: Creating and Sustaining Superior Performance* (New York: Free Press, 1986), and *The Competitive Advantage of Nations* (New York: Free Press, 1989).

[2] Joseph M. Juran, "Made in U.S.A.: A Renaissance in Quality," *Harvard Business Review* (July–August 1993), pp. 42–50.

[3] Roosevelt Thomas, "From 'Affirmative Action' to 'Affirming Diversity.'" *Harvard Business Review* (November–December 1990), pp. 107–117.

[4] Taylor Cox, Jr., *Cultural Diversity in Organizations* (San Francisco: Berrett-Koehler Publishers, Inc., 1994). See also William Johnson and Arnold Packer, *Workforce 2000: Work and Workers for the Twenty-first Century* (Indianapolis: Hudson Institute, 1987; tenth printing, 1991).

[5] Rosabeth Moss Kanter, "Transcending Business Boundaries: 12,000 World Managers View

Change," *Harvard Business Review* (May–June 1991), pp. 151–164.

[6] Survey reported in *Business Week* (January 13, 1992), p. 39.

[7] See Paul Shrivastava, "Greening Business Education: Toward an Ecocentric Pedagogy," *Journal of Management Inquiry,* Vol. 3 (1994), pp. 235–243.

[8] Shrivastava, op. cit.

[9] Gene Bylinsky, "Manufacturing for Reuse," *Fortune* (February 6, 1995), pp. 102–112.

[10] See Joseph M. Juran, *Quality Control Handbook,* 3rd ed. (New York: McGraw-Hill, 1979); "Deming's Quality Manifesto," *Best of Business Quarterly,* vol. 12 (Winter 1990–1991), pp. 6–10. See also W. Edwards Deming, *Quality, Productivity, and Competitive Position* (Cambridge, MA: MIT Center for Advanced Engineering Study, 1982), and *Out of Crisis* (Cambridge, MA: MIT Center for Advanced Engineering Study, 1986). See also Howard S. Gitlow and Shelly J. Gitlow, *The Deming Guide to Quality and Competitive Position* (Englewood Cliffs, NJ: Prentice Hall, 1987): Juran, op. cit., 1993.

[11] "The Quality Imperative," special issue of Business Week (October 25, 1991), p. 58; "Does the Baldrige Award Really Work?" *Harvard Business Review* (January–February 1992), pp. 126–147.

[12] Author's adaptation of W. Edwards Deming Institute, *Out of the Crisis.* Copyright © 1986 by W. Edwards Deming Institute. Reprinted with the permission of MIT Center for Advanced Engineering Study and The W. Edwards Deming Institute.

[13] See Edward E. Lawler III, Susan Albers Mohrman, Gerald E. Ledford, Jr., *Employee Involvement and Total Quality Management: Practices and Results in Fortune 1000 Companies* (San Francisco: Jossey-Bass, 1992).

[14] See Edward E. Lawler III and Susan A. Mohrman, "Quality Circles After the Fad," *Harvard Business Review* (January–February 1985), pp. 65–71.

[15] Quotes from Arnold Kanarick, "The Far Side of Quality Circles," *Management Review,* vol. 70 (October 1981), pp. 16–17.

[16] William M. Bulkeley, "Pushing the Pace: The Latest Big Thing at Many Companies Is Speed, Speed, Speed," *The Wall Street Journal* (December 23, 1994), pp. A1, A5.

[17] Richard J. Shonberger and Edward M. Knod, Jr., *Operations Management: Serving the Customer,* 3rd ed. (Plano, TX: Business Publications, 1988), p. 4.

[18] Kanter, op. cit., 1991.

[19] *Business Week,* special issue, op. cit. (1991), p. 14.

[20] See Wickham Skinner, "Manufacturing—Missing Link in Corporate Strategy," *Harvard Business Review* (May–June 1969), pp. 136–145; Wickham Skinner, *Manufacturing in the Corporate Strategy* (New York: Wiley, 1978).

[21] See B. Joseph Pine II, Bart Victor and Andrew C. Boynton, "Making Mass Customization Work," *Harvard Business Review* (September–October 1993), pp. 108–119; and "The Agile Factory: Custom-made, Direct from the Plant," *Business Week,* special report on "21st Century Capitalism" (January 23, 1995), pp. 158–159.

[22] Information from Gene Bylinsky, "The Virtual Factory," *Fortune* (November 14, 1994), pp. 92–110.

[23] David Woodruff, "Miles Traveled, More to Go," *Business Week* (October 25, 1991), pp. 70–73.

[24] For a report on Motorola see Ronald Henkoff, "Keeping Motorola on a Roll," *Business Week* (April 18, 1994), pp. 67–78.

CHAPTER 3

[1] See, for example, Jeremy Main, "How Latin America Is Opening Up," *Fortune* (April 8, 1991), pp. 84–89; "Free-Market Mexico," *The Economist* (December 14, 1991), pp. 19–21; "We Have to Get Together," *Business Week* (February 3, 1992), p. 41.

[2] Reported in Main, op. cit., p. 84.

[3] "Special Report: The Growing Power of Asia," *Fortune* (October 7, 1991), pp. 118–160; "Special Report: Asia—The Next Era of Growth," *Business Week* (November 11, 1991), pp. 56–68.

[4] See for example, "Into Africa," *Fortune* (September 19, 1994), pp. 17–18.

[5] See Helene Cooper, "Sub-Saharan Africa Is Seen as Big Loser in GATT New World Trade Accord," *The Wall Street Journal* (August 15, 1994), p. A7.

[6] Udayan Gupta, "African-American Firms Gain Foothold in South Africa," *The Wall Street Journal* (October 6, 1994), p. B2; Ken Wells, "U.S. Investment in South Africa Quickens," *The Wall Street Journal* (October 6, 1994), p. A14.

[7] Anthony J. F. O'Reilly, "Establishing Successful Joint Ventures in Developing Nations: A CEO's Perspective," *The Columbia Journal of World Business* (Spring 1988), pp. 65–71.

[8] Data reported in "Multinational Firms Tighten Control Over World Economy," *New Straits Times* (August 31, 1993), p. 16.

[9] R. Hall Mason, "Conflicts Between Host Countries and Multinational Enterprise," vol. XVII, *California Management Review* (1974), pp. 6, 7.

[10] See Randall E. Stross, *Bulls in the China Shop: And Other Sino-American Business Encounters* (New York: Pantheon, 1991).

[11] For a recent discussion see "Why Sweet Deals are Going Sour in China," *Business Week* (December 19, 1994), pp. 50–51; and Jet Maqsaysay, "Managing in China: The Toughest Test," *World Executive's Digest* (May 1994), pp. 14–25.

[12] For an interesting discussion see George F. Kennan, *Around the Cragged Hill* (New York: W. W. Norton, 1993).

[13] Sylvia Ann Hewlett, "The Boundaries of Business: The Human Resource Deficit," *Harvard Business Review* (July–August 1991), pp. 131–133. See also William B. Johnston, "Global Workforce 2000: The New World Labor Market," *Harvard Business Review* (March–April 1991), pp. 115–127.

[14] Examples reported in Neil Chesanow, *The World-Class Executive* (New York: Rawson Associates, 1985).

[15] Based on Barbara Benedict Bunker, "Appreciating Diversity and Modifying Organizational Cultures: Men and Women at Work," pp. 127–149 in Suresh Srivastva, David L. Cooperrider, et al., *Appreciative Management and Leadership: The Power of Positive Thought and Action in Organizations* (San Francisco: Jossey-Bass, 1990).

[16] For a good overview of the practical issues, see Philip R. Harris and Robert T. Moran, *Managing Cultural Differences,* 2nd ed. (Houston: Gulf Publishing, 1987); and, Martin J. Gannon, *Understanding Global Cultures* (Thousand Oaks, Calif.: Sage, 1994).

[17] Edward T. Hall, *Hidden Differences* (New York: Doubleday, 1990).

[18] Geert Hofstede's research is summarized in this article, "Motivation, Leadership, and Organization: Do American Theories Apply Abroad?" *Organizational Dynamics,* vol. 9 (Summer 1980), p. 43. It is presented in detail in his book *Culture's Consequences* (Beverly Hills: Sage, 1984). Hofstede and Michael H. Bond further explore Eastern and Western perspectives on national culture in their article, "The Confucious Connection: From Cultural Roots to Economic Growth," *Organizational Dynamics,* vol. 16 (1988), pp. 4–21, which presents comparative data from Bond's "Chinese Values Survey."

[19] For reports on the new fifth dimension, see Geert Hofstede and Michael H. Bond, "The Confucious Connection: From Cultural Roots to Economic Growth," *Organizational Dynamics,* vol. 16 (1988), pp. 4–21.

[20] For a good discussion see Chapters 4 and 5 in Miriam Erez and P. Christopher Early, *Culture, Self-Identity, and Work* (New York: Oxford University Press, 1993). See also J. Bernard Keys, Luther Trey Denton, and Thomas R. Miller, "The Japanese Management Theory Jungle—Revisited," *Journal of Management,* Vol. 20 (1994), pp. 373–402.

[21] Hofstede (1980), op cit.

[22] William Ouchi, *Theory Z: How American Businesses Can Meet the Japanese Challenge* (Reading: Mass.: Addison-Wesley, 1981); and Richard Tanner Pascale and Anthony G. Athos, *The Art of Japanese Management: Applications for American Executives* (New York: Simon & Schuster, 1981).

[23] A useful perspective on Japanese management practices is the teaching note by Stephen E. Marsland, Bert Spector, and Michael Beer, "Note on Japanese Management and Employment Systems," #481-009 (Boston: HBS Case Services, 1980). See also Shoichi Suzaqa, "How the Japanese Achieve Excellence," *Training & Development Journal,* vol. 39 (1985), pp. 110–114; J. Bernard Keys, Luther Trey Denton, and Thomas R. Miller, "The Japanese Management Theory Jungle—Revisited," *Journal of Management,* Vol. 20 (1994), pp. 373–402.

[24] "Free, Young, and Japanese," *The Economist* (December 21, 1991), p. 38.

[25] Carla Rapoport, "Why Japan Keeps on Winning," *Fortune* (July 15, 1991), pp. 76–85.

[26] Quote from Kenichi Ohmae, "Japan's Admiration for U.S. Methods Is an Open Book," *Wall Street Journal* (October 10, 1983), p. 21. See also his book

The Borderless World: Power and Strategy in the Interlinked Economy (New York: Harper, 1989).

[27] Geert Hofstede, "A Reply to Goodstein and Hunt," *Organizational Dynamics,* vol. 10 (Summer 1981), p. 68.

CHAPTER 4

[1] Desmond Tutu, "Do More Than Win," *Fortune* (December 30, 1991), p. 59.

[2] For an overview, see Francis Joseph Aguilar, *Managing Corporate Ethics: Learning from America's Ethical Companies How to Supercharge Business Performance* (New York: Oxford, 1994).

[3] See Gerald F. Cavanagh, Dennis J. Moberg, and Manuel Velasquez, "The Ethics of Organizational Politics," *Academy of Management Review,* vol. 6 (1981), pp. 363–374; Justin G. Longnecker, Joseph A. McKinney, and Carlos W. Moore, "Egoism and Independence; Entrepreneurial Ethics," *Organizational Dynamics* (Winter 1988), pp. 64–72; Justin G. Longnecker, Joseph A. McKinney, and Carlos W. Moore, "The Generation Gap in Business Ethics," *Business Horizons* (September–October 1989), pp. 9–14.

[4] Raymond L. Hilgert, "What Ever Happened to Ethics in Business and in Business Schools," *The Diary of Alpha Kappa Psi* (April 1989), pp. 4–8.

[5] Clarence C. Walton, *The Moral Manager* (New York: Harper Business, 1990).

[6] Reported in Barbara Ley Toffler, "Tough Choices: Managers Talk Ethics," *New Management,* vol. 4 (1987), pp. 34–39. See also Barbara Ley Toffler, *Tough Choices: Managers Talk Ethics* (New York: Wiley, 1986).

[7] The case and subsequent discussion are developed from Steven N. Brenner and Earl A. Mollander, "Is the Ethics of Business Changing?" *Harvard Business Review,* vol. 55 (January–February 1977), p. 57.

[8] Saul W. Gellerman, "Why 'Good' Managers Make Bad Ethical Choices," *Harvard Business Review,* vol. 64 (July–August 1986), pp. 85–90.

[9] *The Economist* (November 2, 1991), p. 68.

[10] The Body Shop has come under recent scrutiny on the degree to which its business practices actually live up to this charter and the company's self-promoted green image. See for example,

John Entine, "Shattered Image," *Business Ethics* (September/October 1994), pp. 23–28.

[11] William M. Carley, "Antitrust Chief says CEOs Should Tape All Phone Calls to Each Other," *The Wall Street Journal* (February 12, 1983), p. 23; "American Air, Chief End Antitrust Suit, Agree Not to Discuss Fares With Rivals," *The Wall Street Journal* (July 15, 1985), p. 4.

[12] Both consulting approaches reported in Alan L. Otten, "Ethics on the Job: Companies Alert Employees to Potential Dilemmas," *The Wall Street Journal* (July 14, 1986), p. 17.

[13] See Otten, op cit.

[14] For a good review of whistleblowing, see Marcia P. Micelli and Janet P. Near, *Blowing the Whistle* (Lexington, MA: Lexington Books, 1992); see also Micelli and Near, "Whistleblowing: Reaping the Benefits," *Academy of Management Executive,* Vol. VIII (August 1994), pp. 65–72.

[15] See "Blowing the Whistle Without Paying the Piper," *Business Week* (June 3, 1991), pp. 138–140; Daniel Wesman, *Whistleblowing: The Law of Retaliatory Discharge* (New York: BNA Books).

[16] Information from James A. Waters, "Catch 20.5: Morality as an Organizational Phenomenon," *Organizational Dynamics,* vol. 6 (Spring 1978), pp. 3–15.

[17] "Robert D. Gilbreath, "The Hollow Executive," *New Management,* vol. 4 (1987), pp. 24–28.

[18] Developed from recommendations of the Government Accountability Project reported in "Blowing the Whistle Without Paying the Piper," *Business Week* (June 3, 1991), pp. 138–140.

[19] All reported in Charles D. Pringle and Justin G. Longnecker, "The Ethics of MBO," *Academy of Management Review,* vol. 7 (April 1982), p. 309. See also Barry Z. Posner and Warren H. Schmidt, "Values and the American Manager: An Update," *California Management Review,* vol. 26 (Spring 1984), pp. 202–216.

[20] David B. Hilder, "Accountants' Code Calls Whistle-Blowing Inappropriate Unless the Law Requires It," *The Wall Street Journal* (July 21, 1983), p. 6.

[21] See Rick Wartzman, "Nature or Nurture? Study Blames Ethical Lapses on Corporate Goals," *The Wall Street Journal* (October 9, 1987), p. 21; Amanda Bennett, "Ethics Codes Spread Despite

Criticism," *The Wall Street Journal* (July 15, 1988), p. 13.

[22] This discussion is developed from Keith Davis, "The Case for and Against Business Assumption of Social Responsibility," *Academy of Management Journal* (June 1973), pp. 312–322; Keith Davis and William Frederick, *Business and Society: Management: Public Policy, Ethics,* 5th ed. (New York: McGraw-Hill, 1984).

[23] The Friedman quote is from Milton Friedman, *Capitalism and Freedom* (Chicago: University of Chicago Press, 1962); Samuelson quote is from Paul A. Samuelson, "Love That Corporation," *Mountain Bell Magazine* (Spring 1971). Both are cited in Davis, op. cit.

[24] Davis and Frederick, op. cit.

[25] Davis, op. cit.

[26] Elizabeth Gatewood and Archie B. Carroll, "The Anatomy of Corporate Social Response," *Business Horizons,* vol. 24 (September/October 1981), pp. 9–16.

CHAPTER 5

[1] See Romuald A. Stone, "AIDS in the Workplace: An Executive Update," *Academy of Management Executive,* vol. VIII (August 1994), pp. 52–64.

[2] See Dick Levin, *The Executive's Illustrated Primer of Long Range Planning* (Englewood Cliffs, NJ: Prentice Hall, 1981).

[3] For a thorough review of forecasting see J. Scott Armstrong, *Long-Range Forecasting,* 2nd ed. (New York: Wiley, 1985).

[4] The scenario planning approach is described in Peter Schwartz, *The Art of the Long View* (New York: Doubleday/Currency, 1991).

[5] T. Mack, "Time, Money and Patience," *Forbes* (August 21, 1989), pp. 60–62; *Fortune* (December 31, 1990), pp. 70–78.

[6] Jack Welch, "Create a Company of Ideas," *Fortune* (December 30, 1991), p. 25.

[7] The four grand strategies were originally described by William F. Glueck, *Business Policy: Strategy Formulation and Management Action,* 2nd ed. (New York: McGraw-Hill, 1976).

[8] "Reckitt to Pay $1.6 billion for Kodak Unit," *International Herald Tribune* (September 27, 1994), p.

13; and, "Kodak's New Focus," *Business Week* (January 30, 1995), pp. 62–66.

[9] F. Colin, "Second Thoughts on Growth," *Inc.* (March 1991), pp. 60–66.

[10] See Arthur A. Thompson, Jr. and A. J. Strickland III, *Strategic Management: Concepts and Cases,* 5th ed. (Homewood, IL: BPI/Irwin, 1990).

[11] See Laura Nash, "Mission Statements—Mirrors and Windows," *Harvard Business Review* (March–April 1988), pp. 155–156. Russell L. Ackoff, *Management in Small Doses* (New York: Wiley, 1986), pp. 38–42, offers additional thoughts on the purposes served by corporate mission statements.

[12] See Peter F. Drucker, *The Practice of Management* (New York: Harper & Row, 1954); and *Management: Tasks, Responsibilities, Practices* (New York: Harper & Row, 1973).

[13] Richard G. Hammermesh, "Making Planning Strategic," *Harvard Business Review,* vol. 64 (July–August 1986), pp. 115–120.

[14] See Gerald B. Allan, "A Note on the Boston Consulting Group Concept of Competitive Analysis and Corporate Strategy," Harvard Business School, Intercollegiate Case Clearing House, ICCH9-175-175 (June 1976).

[15] For a discussion of Michael Porter's approach to strategic planning see his books *Competitive Strategy: Techniques for Analyzing Industries and Competitors* (New York: Free Press, 1980) and *Competitive Advantage: Creating and Sustaining Superior Performance* (New York: Free Press, 1986); and his *Harvard Business Review* article, op. cit., 1987.

[16] Information from Suzanne Steel, "Quality in Bloom," *Business Today* (August 22, 1994), pp. 1–2.

[17] James Brian Quinn, "Strategic Change: Logical Incrementalism," *Sloan Management Review,* vol. 20 (Fall 1978), pp. 7–21.

[18] Daniel J. Isenberg, "The Tactics of Strategic Opportunism," *Harvard Business Review,* vol. 65 (March–April 1987), pp. 92–97.

[19] Robert H. Waterman, Jr., *The Renewal Factor* (New York: Bantam Books, 1987).

[20] Henry Mintzberg, "Planning on the Left Side and Managing on the Right," *Harvard Business Review,* vol. 54 (July–August 1976), pp. 46–55; Henry

Mintzberg and James A. Waters, "Of Strategies, Deliberate and Emergent," *Strategic Management Journal,* vol. 6 (1985), pp. 257–272; Henry Mintzberg, "Crafting Strategy," *Harvard Business Review,* vol. 65 (July–August 1987), pp. 66–75.

[21] Developed from Dick Levin, *The Executive's Illustrated Primer of Long Range Planning* (Englewood Cliffs, NJ: Prentice Hall, 1981), pp. 98–100; David A. Aaker, "How to Select a Business Strategy," *California Management Review,* vol. 26 (Spring 1984), pp. 167–175.

[22] Information from "Kodak's New Focus," *Business Week* (January 30, 1995), pp. 62–66.

CHAPTER 6

[1] The classic work is Alfred D. Chandler, *Strategy and Structure* (Cambridge, MA: MIT Press, 1962).

[2] See Alfred D. Chandler, Jr., "Origins of the Organization Chart," *Harvard Business Review* (March–April 1988), pp. 156–157.

[3] See David Krackhardt and Jeffrey R. Hanson, "Informal Networks: The Company Behind the Chart," *Harvard Business Review* (July–August 1993), pp. 104–111.

[4] See Kenneth Noble, "A Clash of Styles: Japanese Companies in the U.S." *New York Times* (January 25, 1988), p. 7.

[5] Excellent reviews of matrix concepts are found in Stanley M. Davis and Paul R. Lawrence, *Matrix* (Reading, MA: Addison-Wesley, 1977); Paul R. Lawrence, Harvey F. Kolodny, and Stanley M. Davis, "The Human Side of the Matrix," *Organizational Dynamics,* vol. 6 (1977), pp. 43–61; Harvey F. Kolodny, "Evolution to a Matrix Organization," *Academy of Management Review,* vol. 4 (1979), pp. 543–553.

[6] See Rahul Jacob, "The Struggle to Create an Organization for the 21st Century," *Fortune* (April 3, 1995), pp. 90–100.

[7] Information from William Bridges, "The End of the Job," *Fortune* (September 19, 1994), pp. 62–74; Alan Deutschman, "The Managing Wisdom of High-Tech Superstars," *Fortune* (October 17, 1994), pp. 197–206.

[8] Michael Selz, "Small Companies Thrive by Taking Over Some Specialized Tasks for Big Concerns," *The Wall Street Journal* (September 11, 1991), pp.

B1, B2, and *Business Week* (October 17, 1994), p. 85.

[9] See for example, David Van Fleet, "Span of Management Research and Issues," *Academy of Management Journal,* vol. 26 (1983), pp. 546–552.

[10] Developed from Roger Fritz, *Rate Your Executive Potential* (New York: Wiley, 1988), pp. 185–186; Roy J. Lewicki, Donald D. Bowen, Douglas T. Hall, and Francine S. Hall, *Experiences in Management and Organizational Behavior,* 3rd ed. (New York: Wiley, 1988), p. 144.

[11] See George P. Huber, "A Theory of Effects of Advanced Information Technologies on Organizational Design, Intelligence, and Decision Making," *Academy of Management Review,* vol. 15 (1990), pp. 67–71.

[12] Max Weber, *The Theory of Social and Economic Organization,* translated by A. M. Henderson and H. T. Parsons (New York: Free Press, 1947).

[13] For classic discussions of bureaucracy, see Alvin Gouldner, *Patterns of Industrial Bureaucracy* (New York: Free Press, 1954); Robert K. Merton, *Social Theory and Social Structure* (New York: Free Press, 1957).

[14] Tom Burns and George M. Stalker, *The Management of Innovation* (London: Tavistock, 1961). Republished by Oxford University Press (London: 1994).

[15] See Rosabeth Moss Kanter, *The Change Masters* (New York: Simon & Schuster, 1983). Quote from Rosabeth Moss Kanter and John D. Buck, "Reorganizing Part of Honeywell: From Strategy to Structure," *Organizational Dynamics,* vol. 13 (Winter 1985), p. 6.

[16] See Jay R. Galbraith, Edward E. Lawler III, and Associates, *Organizing for the Future* (San Francisco: Jossey-Bass Publishers, 1993).

[17] Edgar H. Schein, "Organizational Culture," *American Psychologist,* vol. 45 (1990), pp. 109–119.

[18] Peter F. Drucker, "Don't Change Corporate Culture—Use It!" *The Wall Street Journal* (March 28, 1991), p. A14.

[19] Edgar H. Schein, *Organizational Culture and Leadership* (Reading, MA: Addison-Wesley, 1985); Terrence E. Deal and Alan A. Kennedy, *Corporate Cultures: The Rites and Rituals of Corporate Life* (Reading, MA: Addison-Wesley, 1982); Ralph Kil-

mann, *Beyond the Quick Fix* (San Francisco: Jossey-Bass, 1984).

[20] See John P. Kotter and James L. Heskett, *Corporate Culture and Performance* (New York: Free Press, 1992),

[21] This is a simplified model developed from Schein (1985), op. cit.

[22] Deal and Kennedy, op. cit.

CHAPTER 7

[1] Quotes from Marshall Loeb, "Where Leaders Come From," *Fortune* (September 19, 1994), pp. 241–242; Genevieve Capowski, "Anatomy of a Leader: Where are the Leaders of Tomorrow?" *Management Review* (March 1994), pp. 10–17.

[2] James M. Kouzes and Barry Z. Posner, *The Leadership Challenge: How to Get Extraordinary Things Done in Organizations,* second edition (San Francisco: Jossey-Bass, 1995).

[3] Max DePree, "An Old Pro's Wisdom: It Begins with a Belief in People," *The New York Times* (September 10, 1989), p. F2; Max DePree, *Leadership Is an Art* (New York: Doubleday, 1989); David Woodruff, "Herman Miller: How Green Is My Factory," *Business Week* (September 16, 1991), pp. 54–56.

[4] The early work on leader traits is well represented in Ralph M. Stogdill, "Personal Factors Associated with Leadership: A Survey of the Literature," *Journal of Psychology,* vol. 25 (1948), pp. 35–71. Another well-respected empirical study is Edwin E. Ghiselli, *Explorations in Management Talent* (Santa Monica, CA: Goodyear, 1971).

[5] See also John W. Gardner's article, "The Context and Attributes of Leadership," *New Management,* vol. 5 (1988), pp. 18–22; John P. Kotter, *The Leadership Factor* (New York: Free Press, 1988); and Bernard M. Bass, *Stogdill's Handbook of Leadership* (New York: Free Press, 1990).

[6] Shirley A. Kirkpatrick and Edwin A. Locke, "Leadership: Do Traits Matter?" *Academy of Management Executive,* vol. 5 (May 1991), pp. 48–60.

[7] See Bernard Bass, *Stogdill's Handbook of Leadership,* op. cit.

[8] Robert R. Blake and Jane Srygley Mouton, *The New Managerial Grid III* (Houston: Gulf Publishing, 1985).

[9] For a good discussion of this theory, see Fred E. Fiedler, Martin M. Chemers, and Linda Mahar, *The Leadership Match Concept* (New York: Wiley, 1978); Fiedler's current contingency research with the cognitive resource theory is summarized in Fred E. Fiedler and Joseph E. Garcia, *New Approaches to Effective Leadership* (New York: Wiley, 1987).

[10] Paul Hersey and Kenneth H. Blanchard, *Management and Organizational Behavior* (Englewood Cliffs, NJ: Prentice Hall, 1988).

[11] See Robert J. House, "A Path–Goal Theory of Leader Effectiveness," *Administrative Sciences Quarterly,* vol. 16 (1971), pp. 321–338; Robert J. House and Terrence R. Mitchell, "Path–Goal Theory of Leadership," *Journal of Contemporary Business* (Autumn 1974), pp. 81–97; the path–goal theory is reviewed by Bernard M. Bass in *Stogdill's Handbook of Leadership,* op. cit., and Yukl in *Leadership in Organizations,* op cit.

[12] Julie Indvik, "Path–Goal Theory of Leadership: A Meta-Analysis," in John A. Pearce II and Richard B. Robinson, Jr., eds., *Academy of Management Best Paper Proceedings* 1986, pp. 189–192.

[13] See Steven Kerr and John Jermier, "Substitutes for Leadership: Their Meaning and Measurement," *Organizational Behavior and Human Performance,* vol. 22 (1978), pp. 375–403; Jon P. Howell and Peter W. Dorfman, "Leadership and Substitutes for Leadership Among Professional and Nonprofessional Workers," *Journal of Applied Behavioral Science,* vol. 22 (1986), pp. 29–46.

[14] Victor H. Vroom and Arthur G. Jago, *The New Leadership: Managing Participation in Organizations* (Englewood Cliffs, NJ: Prentice Hall, 1988); Victor H. Vroom, "A New Look in Managerial Decision-Making," *Organizational Dynamics* (Spring 1973), pp. 66–80; Victor H. Vroom and Phillip Yetton, *Leadership and Decision-Making* (Pittsburgh: University of Pittsburgh Press, 1973).

[15] Suggested by Jay Hall, "Decisions, Decisions, Decisions," *Psychology Today* (November 1971), pp. 55–66.

[16] Edgar H. Schein, *Process Consultation Volume I: Its Role in Organization Development,* 2nd ed. (Reading, MA: Addison-Wesley, 1988), p. 73.

[17] The distinction was originally made by James McGregor Burns, *Leadership* (New York: Harper & Row, 1978), and was further developed by Bernard

Bass, *Leadership and Performance Beyond Expectations* (New York: Free Press, 1985).

[18] Among the popular books addressing this point of view are Warren Bennis and Burt Nanus, *Leaders* (New York: Harper & Row, 1985); Max DePree, *Leadership Is an Art* (Lansing: The Michigan State University Press, 1987); Kotter, op. cit.; Kouzes and Posner, op. cit. A number of the issues are well summarized in James O'Toole, ed., "Special Section on Leadership," *New Management: The Magazine for Innovative Managers,* vol. 5 (1988), pp. 2–31.

[19] See for example, Jay A. Conger, "Inspiring Others: The Language of Leadership," *Academy of Management Executive,* Vol. 5 (1991), pp. 31–45.

[20] See Burns, op. cit.: Bass, op. cit., 1985; Bernard M. Bass, "Leadership: Good, Better, Best," *Organizational Dynamics,* vol. 13 (Winter 1985), pp. 26–40.

[21] This list is based on Kouzes and Posner, op. cit.; Gardner, op. cit.

[22] Research on gender issues in leadership is reported in Sally Helgesen, *The Female Advantage: Women's Ways of Leadership* (New York: Doubleday, 1990); Judith B. Rosener, "Ways Women Lead," *Harvard Business Review* (November–December 1990), pp. 150–160; and Alice H. Eagly, Steven J. Karau, and Blair T. Johnson, "Gender and Leadership Style Among School Principals: A Meta Analysis," *Administrative Science Quarterly,* vol. 27 (1992), pp. 76–102.

[23] Peter F. Drucker, "Leadership: More Doing than Dash," *The Wall Street Journal* (January 6, 1988), p. 16.

[24] Drucker, op cit.

[25] Gardner, op. cit., 1988.

[26] For an interesting view of the "Spiritual" aspects of leadership see Lee G. Bolman and Terrence E. Deal, *Leading with Soul* (San Francisco: Jossey-Bass, 1995).

CHAPTER 8

[1] Alvin Toffler, "Toffler's Next Shock," *World Monitor* (November 1990), pp. 34–44. See also Toffler's book *Powershift* (New York: Bantam Books, 1990).

[2] See Dale D. McConkey, *How to Manage by Results,* 3rd ed. (New York: AMACOM, 1976); Stephen J. Carroll, Jr., and Henry J. Tosi, Jr., *Management by Objectives: Applications and Research* (New York: Macmillan, 1973); Anthony P. Raia, *Managing by Objectives* (Glenview, IL: Scott, Foresman, 1974). For criticisms, see Steven Kerr, "Overcoming the Dysfunctions of MBO," *Management by Objectives,* vol. 5, no. 1 (1976).

[3] See William Newman, *Constructive Control: Design and Use of Control Systems* (Englewood Cliffs, NJ: Prentice-Hall, 1975).

[4] For this and following examples see John F. Love, *McDonald's: Behind the Arches* (New York: Bantam Books), November 1986.

[5] For a good discussion, see Cortlandt Cammann and David A. Nadler, "Fit Control Systems to Your Management Style," *Harvard Business Review,* vol. 54 (January–February 1976), pp. 65–72.

[6] See Jeremy Main, "The Battle over Benefits," *Fortune* (December 16, 1991), pp. 91–96.

[7] Eric L. Harvey, "Discipline vs. Punishment," *Management Review,* vol. 76 (March 1987), pp. 25–29; Joshua Hyatt, "Easy Money," *Inc.* (February 1988), pp. 91–99.

[8] The "hot-stove rules" are developed from R. Bruch McAfee and William Poffenberger, *Productivity Strategies: Enhancing Employee Job Performance* (Englewood Cliffs, NJ: Prentice Hall, 1982), pp. 54–55. They are originally attributed to Douglas McGregor, "Hot Stove Rules of Discipline," in *Personnel: The Human Problems of Management* (G. Strauss and L. Sayles, eds., (Englewood Cliffs, NJ: Prentice-Hall, 1967).

[9] Information from Jacyln Fierman, "Winning Ideas from Maverick Managers," *Fortune* (February 6, 1995), pp. 66–80.

[10] The article by Dorothy Leonard-Barton and John J. Sviokla, "Putting Expert Systems to Work," *Harvard Business Review,* vol. 66 (March–April 1988), pp. 91–98, provides a practical overview of expert systems and their management applications.

[11] Barbara Garson, *The Electronic Sweatshop* (New York: Viking Penguin, 1989); see also, Tony Horwitz, "Mr. Edeas Profits by Watching His Employees' Every Move," *The Wall Street Journal* (December 14, 1994) p. A9.

[12] See Shoshana Zuboff's book, *In the Age of the Smart Machine: The Future of Work and Power* (New York: Basic Books, 1988).

[13] Shawn Tully, "Purchasing's New Muscle," *Fortune* (February 20, 1995), p. 75.

[14]Information from Myron Magnet, "The New Golden Rule of Business," *Fortune* (February 21, 1994), pp. 60–64.

[15]Richard J. Schonberger, "A Revolutionary Way to Streamline the Factory," *The Wall Street Journal* (November 15, 1982), p. 24.

CHAPTER 9

[1]Information from "Woman Executive Hopes to Improve Diversity at Ford," *Columbus Dispatch* (September 17, 1994), p. E1.

[2]*Workforce 2000: Work and Workers for the 21st Century* (Indianapolis: Towers Perrin/Hudson Institute, 1987).

[3]Ibid.

[4]*Opportunity 2000: Creative Affirmative Action Strategies for a Changing Workforce* (Indianapolis: Hudson Institute, 1988). *Workforce 2000: Competing in a Seller's Market: Is Corporate America Prepared?* (Indianapolis: Towers Perrin/Hudson Institute, 1990).

[5]R. Roosevelt Thomas, Jr., "From Affirmative Action to Affirming Diversity," *Harvard Business Review* (March–April 1990), pp. 107–117.

[6]Information from *Business Week* (June 24, 1991), pp. 62–63; *Diversity, a Source of Strength* (Dupont, n.d.), pp. 5–9.

[7]Taylor Cox, Jr., "The Multicultural Organization," *Academy of Management Executive,* vol. 5 (1991), pp. 34–47.

[8]Ann M. Morrison, Randall P. White, and Ellen Van Velso, *Breaking the Glass Ceiling* (Reading, MA: Addison-Wesley, 1987).

[9]Information from Michael S. Malone, "Translating Diversity Into High-Tech Gains," *The New York Times* (July 18, 1993).

[10]Thomas, op. cit. (1990), p. 112.

[11]Developed from the *Outcome Measurement Project of the Accreditation Research Committee Phase II* (St. Louis: American Assembly of Collegiate Schools of Business, 1984), pp. 15–18.

[12]*The Wall Street Journal* (May 16, 1991), p. B6.

[13]The MBTI is published by Consulting Psychologists, Inc., Palo Alto, California, 94306.

[14]The classic work is by Julian B. Rotter, "Generalized Expectancies for Internal versus External Locus of Control of Reinforcement," *Psychological Monographs,* 1 (1966), pp. 1–28.

[15]Niccolò Machiavelli, *The Prince,* Translated by George Bull (Middlesex, England: Penguin, 1961).

[16]See R. G. Vleeming, "Machiavellianism: A Preliminary Review," *Psychological Reports* (1979), pp. 295–310.

[17]For classic studies of values see Milton Rokeach, *The Nature of Human Values* (New York: Free Press, 1973); and Gordon Allport, Philip E. Vernon, and Gardner Lindzey, *Study of Values* (Boston: Houghton Mifflin, 1931).

[18]See John R. Schermerhorn, Jr., James G. Hunt, and Richard N. Osborn, *Managing Organizational Behavior,* 5th ed. (New York: John Wiley & Sons, 1994), p. 137.

[19]Morrison, White, and Velsor (1987), op cit.

[20]These examples are from Natasha Josefowitz, *Paths to Power* (Reading, MA: Addison-Wesley, 1980), p. 60.

[21]Ibid.

[22]Taylor Cox, Jr., "The Multicultural Organization," *Academy of Management Executive,* vol. 5 (May 1991), pp. 34–47.

[23]Joseph A. Raelin, *Clash of Cultures* (Cambridge, MA: Harvard Business School Press, 1986).

[24]Geert Hofstede, *Cultures Consequences* (Beverly Hills: Sage, 1982).

[25]See Suneel Ratan, "Generational Tension in the Office: Why Buster's Hate Boomers," *Fortune* (October 4, 1993), pp. 56–70; and Faye Rice, "Making Generational Marketing Come of Age," *Fortune* (June 26, 1995), pp. 110–115.

[26]Barbara Benedict Bunker, "Appreciating Diversity and Modifying Organizational Cultures: Men and Women at Work," Chapter 5 in Suresh Srivastva, David L. Cooperrider, et al., *Appreciative Management and Leadership* (San Francisco: Jossey-Bass, 1990).

CHAPTER 10

[1]Thomas J. Peters and Robert H. Waterman, Jr., *In Search of Excellence* (New York: Warner Books, 1982).

[2]For a comprehensive treatment of extrinsic re-

wards see Bob Nelson, *1001 Ways to Reward Employees* (New York: Workman Publishing, 1994).

[3] For a research perspective, see Edward Deci, *Intrinsic Motivation* (New York: Plenum, 1975); Edward E. Lawler III, "The Design of Effective Reward Systems" in Jay W. Lorsch, ed., *Handbook of Organizational Behavior* (Englewood Cliffs, NJ: Prentice Hall, 1987), pp. 255–271.

[4] Michael Maccoby's book *Why Work: Leading the New Generation* (New York: Simon & Schuster, 1988) deals extensively with this point of view.

[5] See Abraham H. Maslow, *Eupsychian Management* (Homewood, IL: Richard D. Irwin, 1965); Abraham H. Maslow, *Motivation and Personality,* 2nd ed. (New York: Harper & Row, 1970). For a research perspective see Mahmoud A. Wahba and Lawrence G. Bridwell, "Maslow Reconsidered: A Review of Research on the Need Hierarchy," *Organizational Behavior and Human Performance,* vol. 16 (1976), pp. 212–240.

[6] See Clayton P. Alderfer, *Existence, Relatedness and Growth* (New York: Free Press, 1972).

[7] The complete two-factor theory is in Frederick Herzberg, Bernard Mausner, and Barbara Block Snyderman, *The Motivation to Work,* 2nd ed. (New York: Wiley, 1967): Frederick Herzberg, "One More Time: How Do You Motivate Employees?" *Harvard Business Review,* vol. 47 (January–February 1968), pp. 53–62, and reprinted as an HBR classic in vol. 65 (September–October 1987), pp. 109–120.

[8] Critical reviews are provided by Robert J. House and Lawrence A. Wigdor, "Herzberg's Dual-Factor Theory of Job Satisfaction and Motivation: A Review of the Evidence and a Criticism," *Personnel Psychology,* vol. 20 (Winter 1967), pp. 369–389; Steven Kerr, Anne Harlan, and Ralph Stogdill, "Preference for Motivator and Hygiene Factors in a Hypothetical Interview Situation," *Personnel Psychology,* vol. 27 (Winter 1974), pp. 109–124.

[9] For a collection of McClelland's work, see David C. McClelland, *The Achieving Society* (New York: Van Nostrand, 1961); "Business Drive and National Achievement," *Harvard Business Review,* vol. 40 (July–August 1962), pp. 99–112; David C. McClelland and David H. Burnham, "Power Is the Great Motivator," *Harvard Business Review,* vol. 54 (March–April 1976), pp. 100–110; David C. McClel-

land, *Human Motivation* (Glenview, IL: Scott, Foresman, 1985); David C. McClelland and Richard E. Boyatsis, "The Leadership Motive Pattern and Long Term Success in Management," *Journal of Applied Psychology,* vol. 67 (1982), pp. 737–743.

[10] Developed from Edward E. Lawler III, *Motivation in Work Organizations* (Monterey, CA: Brooks/Cole Publishing, 1973), pp. 30–36.

[11] See, for example, J. Stacy Adams, "Toward an Understanding of Inequity," *Journal of Abnormal and Social Psychology,* vol. 67 (1963), pp. 422–436; J. Stacy Adams, "Inequity in Social Exchange," in L. Berkowitz, ed., *Advances in Experimental Social Psychology,* vol. 2 (New York: Academic Press, 1965), pp. 267–300.

[12] Victor H. Vroom, *Work and Motivation* (New York: Wiley, 1964); republished by Jossey-Bass, 1994.

[13] The work on goal-setting theory is well summarized in Edwin A. Locke and Gary P. Latham, *Goal Setting: A Motivational Technique That Works!* (Englewood Cliffs, NJ: Prentice Hall, 1984). See also Edwin A. Locke, Kenneth N. Shaw, Lisa A. Saari and Gary P. Latham, "Goal Setting and Task Performance 1969–1980," *Psychological Bulletin,* vol. 90 (1981), pp. 125–152; Mark E. Tubbs, "Goal Setting: A Meta-Analytic Examination of the Empirical Evidence," *Journal of Applied Psychology,* vol. 71 (1986), pp. 474–483.

[14] Portions of this presentation of motivation theories originally adapted from John R. Schermerhorn, Jr., James G. Hunt, and Richard N. Osborn, *Managing Organizational Behavior* (New York: Wiley, 1982), pp. 107–126, 138–156. Used by permission.

[15] E. L. Thorndike, *Animal Intelligence* (New York: Macmillan, 1911), p. 244.

[16] See B. F. Skinner, *Walden Two* (New York: Macmillan, 1948); *Science and Human Behavior* (New York: Macmillan, 1953); *Contingencies of Reinforcement* (New York: Appleton-Century-Crofts, 1969).

[17] OB mod is clearly explained in Fred Luthans and Robert Kreitner, *Organizational Behavior Modification* (Glenview, IL: Scott, Foresman, 1975); Luthans and Kreitner, op. cit., 1985.

[18] Keith L. Miller, *Principles of Everyday Behavior Analysis* (Monterey, CA: Brooks/Cole Publishing, 1975), p. 122.

[19] For a good review see Lee W. Frederickson, ed., *Handbook of Organizational Behavior Management* (New York: Wiley-Interscience, 1982); Luthans and Kreitner, op. cit., 1985.

[20] Edwin A. Locke, "The Myths of Behavior Mod in Organizations," *Academy of Management Review,* vol. 2 (October 1977), pp. 543–553.

[21] For an excellent discussion of compensation and performance, see Rosabeth Moss Kanter, "The Attack on Pay," *Harvard Business Review,* vol. 65 (March–April 1987), pp. 60–67; Edward E. Lawler III, *Strategic Pay* (San Francisco: Jossey-Bass, Inc., 1990).

[22] See Tove Helland Hammer, "New Developments in Profit Sharing, Gain Sharing, and Employee Ownership," Chapter 12 in John P. Campbell, Richard J. Campbell, et al., *Productivity in Organizations: New Perspectives from Industrial and Organizational Psychology* (San Francisco: Jossey-Bass, 1988).

[23] Amanda Bennett, "Paying Workers to Meet Goals Spreads, but Gauging Performance Proves Tough," *The Wall Street Journal* (September 10, 1991), p. B1.

[24] *Business Ethics,* vol. 5, no. 4 (1991), pp. 12–13.

[25] See "How to Not Ask the Boss for a Raise," *Fortune* (June 26, 1995), p. 76.

CHAPTER 11
[1] Portions of the description of job design alternatives based by permission on Schermerhorn, Hunt, and Osborn, op. cit. (1994), pp. 228–231, 238–239.

[2] John P. Kotter, "The Psychological Contract: Managing the Joining Up Process," *California Management Review,* vol. 15 (Spring 1973), pp. 91–99.

[3] Developed from an example in Edward E. Lawler III, *Motivation in Work Organizations* (Monterey, CA: Brooks-Cole, 1973), pp. 154–155.

[4] For an interesting report on automation, see "When GM's Robots Ran Amok," *The Economist* (August 10, 1991), pp. 64–65.

[5] Frederick Herzberg, "One More Time: How do You Motivate Employees?" *Harvard Business Review,* vol. 47 (January–February 1968), pp. 53–62, and reprinted as an HBR classic in vol. 65 (September–October 1987), pp. 109–120.

[6] For a complete description of the job characteristics model, see J. Richard Hackman and Greg R. Oldham, *Work Redesign* (Reading, MA: Addison-Wesley, 1980); additional descriptions of directions in job design research and practice are available in Ramon J. Aldag and Arthur P. Brief, *Task Design and Employee Motivation* (Glenview, IL: Scott, Foresman, 1979); and Ricky W. Griffin, *Task Design: An Integrative Approach* (Glenview, IL: Scott, Foresman, 1982).

[7] Paul J. Champagne and Curt Tausky, "When Job Enrichment Doesn't Pay," *Personnel,* vol. 3 (January–February 1978), pp. 30–40.

[8] William W. Winipsinger, "Job Enrichment: A Union View," in Karl O. Magnusen, ed., *Organizational Design, Development and Behavior: A Situational View* (Glenview, IL: Scott, Foresman, 1977), p. 22.

[9] See Richard E. Walton, *Up and Running: Integrating Information Technology and the Organization* (Boston, MA: Harvard Business School Press, 1989).

[10] Recent developments are described in Richard Walton, "From Control to Commitment in the Workplace," *Harvard Business Review,* vol. 64 (March–April 1985), pp. 77–94. A comprehensive review is provided by William A. Pasmore, *Designing Effective Organizations; A Sociotechnical Systems Perspective* (New York: Wiley, 1988).

[11] Ben Hamper, *Rivethead: Tales from the Assembly Line* (New York: Warner, 1991).

[12] Paul S. Goodman, Rukmini Devadas, and Terri L. Griffith Hughson, "Groups and Productivity: Analyzing the Effectiveness of Self-Managing Teams," Chapter 11 in John R. Campbell, Richard J. Campbell, et al., *Productivity in Organizations* (San Francisco: Jossey-Bass, 1988).

[13] Information from "Team Player: No More 'same-ol'-same-ol'," *Business Week* (October 17, 1994), pp. 95–97.

[14] See Barney Olmsted and Suzanne Smith, *Creating a Flexible Workplace: How to Select and Manage Alternative Work Options* (New York: American Management Association, 1989).

[15] See Allen R. Cohen and Herman Gadon, *Alternative Work Schedules: Integrating Individual and Organizational Needs* (Reading, MA: Addison-Wesley, 1978), p. 125; Simcha Ronen and Sophia B. Primps, "The Compressed Work Week as Organizational Change: Behavioral and Attitudinal Outcomes,"

Academy of Management Review, vol. 6 (1981), pp. 61–74.

[16] Information from Lesli Hicks, "Workers, Employers Praise Their Four-Day Workweek," *The Columbus Dispatch* (August 22, 1994), p. 6.

[17] *The Columbus Dispatch* (June 23, 1991), pp. 1G–2G.

[18] This survey is reported in *The Wall Street Journal* (January 20, 1988), p. 31.

[19] See Sue Shellenbarger, "Overwork, Low Morale Vex the Mobile Office," *The Wall Street Journal* (August 17, 1994), pp. B1, B7.

CHAPTER 12

[1] See Marvin E. Shaw, *Group Dynamics: The Psychology of Small Group Behavior,* 2nd ed. (New York: McGraw-Hill, 1976).

[2] Harold J. Leavitt, "Suppose We Took Groups More Seriously," in Eugene L. Cass and Frederick G. Zimmer, eds., *Man and Work in Society* (New York: Van Nostrand Reinhold, 1975), pp. 67–77.

[3] Jon R. Katzenbach and Douglas K. Smith, *The Wisdom of Teams: Creating the High Performance Organization* (Boston: Harvard Business School Press, 1993).

[4] The "linking pin" concept is introduced in Rensis Likert, *New Patterns of Management* (New York: McGraw-Hill, 1962).

[5] See Jack Orsbrun, Linda Moran, Ed Musslewhite, John H. Zenger, with Craig Perrin, *Self-Directed Work Teams: The New American Challenge* (Homewood, IL: Business One Irwin, 1990).

[6] See Susan D. Van Raalte, "Preparing the Task Force to Get Good Results," S.A.M. *Advanced Management Journal,* vol. 47 (Winter 1982), pp. 11–16; Walter Kiechel III, "The Art of the Corporate Task Force," *Fortune* (January 28, 1991), pp. 104–106.

[7] See, for example, Edward E. Lawler III, Susan Albers Mohrman, and Gerald E. Ledford, Jr., *Employee Involvement and Total Quality Management: Practices and Results in Fortune 1000 Companies* (San Francisco: Jossey-Bass, 1992).

[8] Information from Aimee L. Stern, "Managing by Team Is Not Always as Easy as It Looks," *The New York Times* (July 18, 1994), p. 5.

[9] For a good discussion of quality circles see Edward E. Lawler III and Susan A. Mohrman, "Quality Circles After the Fad," *Harvard Business Review,* vol. 63 (January–February 1985), pp. 65–71; Gerald E. Ledford, Jr., Edward E. Lawler III, and Susan A. Mohrman, "The Quality Circle and Its Variations," Chapter 10 in John R. Campbell, Richard J. Campbell and associates, *Productivity in Organizations* (San Francisco: Jossey-Bass, 1988); and Lawler, Mohrman and Ledford, 1992, op cit.

[10] See W. Jack Duncan, "Why Some People Loaf in Groups While Others Loaf Alone," *Academy of Management Review,* vol. 8 (1004), pp. 79–80.

[11] For insights on how to run an effective meeting see Mary A. De Vries, *How to Run a Meeting* (New York: Penguin, 1994).

[12] For a review of research on group effectiveness see J. Richard Hackman, "The Design of Work Teams," pp. 315–342, in Jay W. Lorsch, ed., *Handbook of Organizational Behavior* (Englewood Cliffs, NJ: Prentice-Hall, 1987).

[13] See Warren Watson, "Cultural Diversity's Impact on Interaction Process and Performance," *Academy of Management Journal,* vol. 16 (1993).

[14] A classic model of group dynamics is found in George C. Homans, *The Human Group* (New York: Harcourt, Brace, and World, 1950).

[15] Bruce W. Tuckman, "Developmental Sequence in Small Groups," *Psychological Bulletin,* vol. 63 (1965), pp. 384–399; Bruce W. Tuckman and Mary Ann C. Jensen, "Stages of Small-Group Development Revisited," *Group & Organization Studies,* vol. 2 (1977), pp. 419–427; J. Steven Heinen and Eugene Jacobson, "A Model of Task Group Development in Complex Organizations and a Strategy of Implementation," *Academy of Management Review,* vol. 1 (1976), pp. 98–111. Discussion based by permission on Schermerhorn, Hunt and Osborn, op. cit. (1994), pp. 298–300.

[16] For a good discussion see Robert F. Allen and Saul Pilnick, "Confronting the Shadow Organization: How to Detect and Defeat Negative Norms," *Organizational Dynamics* (Spring 1973), pp. 13–17.

[17] See Edgar Schein, *Process Consultation: Its Role in Organization Development* (Reading, MA: Addison-Wesley, 1988), pp. 76–79.

[18] See Irving L. Janis, "Groupthink," *Psychology Today* (November 1971), pp. 43–46; *Victims of Groupthink,* 2nd ed. (Boston: Houghton Mifflin, 1982).

[19] A classic work in this area is the 1948 article in

the *Journal of Social Issues,* vol. 2, pp. 42–47, by K. Benne and P. Sheets. See also Rensis Likert, op. cit., pp. 166–169; Schein, op. cit., pp. 49–56.

[20] Katzenbach and Smith (1993), op. cit.

[21] William D. Dyer, *Team-Building* (Reading, MA: Addison-Wesley, 1977).

[22] Carl E. Larson and Frank M.J. LaFasto, *Team Work: What Must Go Right/What Can Go Wrong* (Newbury Park, CA: Sage, 1990), p. 118.

CHAPTER 13

[1] Information from "Chrysler Pleads No Contest to Suit," appearing in the *Southern Illinoisian* (December 15, 1987).

[2] See George P. Huber, *Managerial Decision Making* (Glenview, IL: Scott, Foresman, 1975).

[3] For a good discussion, see Weston H. Agor, *Intuition in Organizations: Leading and Managing Productively* (Newbury Park, CA: Sage, 1989); Herbert A. Simon, "Making Management Decisions: The Role of Intuition and Emotion," *Academy of Management Executive,* Vol. 1 (1987), pp. 57–64; Orlando Behling and Norman L. Eckel, "Making Sense Out of Intuition," *Academy of Management Executive,* vol. 5 (1991), pp. 46–54.

[4] Trish Hall, "When Budding MBAs Try to Save Kool-Aid, Original Ideas Are Scarce," *The Wall Street Journal* (November 26, 1986), p. 31.

[5] Daniel J. Isenberg, "How Senior Managers Think," *Harvard Business Review,* vol. 62 (November–December 1984), pp. 81–90.

[6] Daniel J. Isenberg, "The Tactics of Strategic Opportunism," *Harvard Business Review,* vol. 65 (March–April 1987), pp. 92–97.

[7] Peter F. Drucker, "Marketing for a Fast-Changing Decade," *The Wall Street Journal* (November 20, 1990), p. A20.

[8] For scholarly reviews see Dean Tjosvold, "Effects of Crisis Orientation on Managers' Approach to Controversy in Decision Making," *Academy of Management Journal,* vol. 27 (1984), pp. 130–138; Ian I. Mitroff, Paul Shrivastava, and Firdaus E. Udwadia, "Effective Crisis Management," *Academy of Management Executive,* vol. 1 (1987), pp. 283–292.

[9] For many insights on creativity, see Roger von Oech, *A Whack on the Side of the Head* (New York: Warner Books, 1983), and *A Kick on the Seat of the Pants* (New York: Harper & Row, 1986).

[10] These techniques are well described in Andre L. Delbecq, Andrew H. Van de Ven, and David H. Gustafson, *Group Techniques for Program Planning* (Glenview, IL: Scott, Foresman, 1975).

[11] Barry M. Staw, "The Escalation of Commitment to a Course of Action," *Academy of Management Review,* vol. 6 (1981), pp. 577–587; Barry M. Staw and Jerry Ross, "Knowing When to Pull the Plug," *Harvard Business Review,* vol. 65 (March–April 1987), pp. 68–74.

[12] For a sample of Simon's work, see Herbert A. Simon, *Administrative Behavior* (New York: Free Press, 1947); James G. March and Herbert A. Simon, *Organizations* (New York: Wiley, 1958); Herbert A. Simon, *The New Science of Management Decision* (New York: Harper, 1960).

[13] This presentation is based on the work of R. H. Hogarth, D. Kahneman, A. Tversky, and others, as discussed in Max H. Bazerman, *Judgment in Managerial Decision Making,* 3rd ed. (New York: Wiley, 1994).

[14] The classic work on this topic is Norman R. F. Maier's "Assets and Liabilities in Group Problem Solving: The Need for an Integrative Function," *Psychological Review,* vol. 4 (1967), pp. 239–249.

CHAPTER 14

[1] Portions of the discussion of communication based by permission on John R. Schermerhorn, Jr., James G. Hunt and Richard N. Osborn, *Managing Organizational Behavior,* Fifth Edition (New York: Wiley, 1994), pp. 565–574.

[2] Henry Mintzberg, *The Nature of Managerial Work* (New York: Harper & Row, 1973); Lance B. Kurke and Howard Aldrich, "Mintzberg Was Right! A Replication and Extension of *The Nature of Managerial Work, Management Science,* vol. 29 (1983), pp. 975–984.

[3] Developed from John Anderson, "Giving and Receiving Feedback," in Paul R. Lawrence, Louis B. Barnes, and Jay W. Lorsch, *Organizational Behavior and Administration.* 3rd ed. (Homewood, IL: Richard D. Irwin, 1976), p. 109.

[4] Thomas J. Peters and Robert H. Waterman, Jr., *In Search of Excellence* (New York: Harper & Row, 1983).

[5] See Robert H. Lengel and Richard L. Daft, "The Selection of Communication Media as an Executive

Skill," *Academy of Management Executive,* vol. 2 (August 1988), pp. 225–232.

[6] A classic work on proxemics is Edward T. Hall's book *The Hidden Dimension* (Garden City, NY: Doubleday, 1986).

[7] Adapted from Richard V. Farace, Peter R. Monge, and Hamish M. Russell, *Communicating and Organizing* (Reading, MA: Addison-Wesley, 1977), pp. 97–98.

[8] John and Mark Arnold, "Corporation Coverups," *The Wall Street Journal* (June 5, 1978), p. 18.

[9] Tom Peters and Nancy Austin, *A Passion for Excellence* (New York: Random House, 1985).

[10] Based on Carl R. Rogers and Richard E. Farson, "Active Listening" (Chicago: Industrial Relations Center of the University of Chicago), n.c.

[11] Information from Raju Narisetti, "Executive Suites' Walls Come Tumbling Down," *The Wall Street Journal* (June 29, 1994), pp. B1, B12.

[12] Brian O'Reilly, "360 Feedback Can Change Your Life," *Fortune* (October 17, 1994), pp. 93–100.

[13] See Edward T. Hall, *The Silent Language* (New York: Doubleday, 1973).

CHAPTER 15

[1] Dana Milbank, "Managers Are Sent to 'Charm Schools' to Discover How to Polish Up Their Acts," *The Wall Street Journal* (December 14, 1990), pp. B1, B3.

[2] Rosabeth Moss Kanter, "Power Failure in Management Circuits, *Harvard Business Review,* vol. 47 (July–August 1979), pp. 65–75.

[3] See John R. P. French, Jr., and Bertram Raven, "The Bases of Social Power," in Darwin Cartwright, ed., *Group Dynamics: Research and Theory* (Evanston, IL: Row, Peterson, 1962), pp. 607–613. For managerial applications of this basic framework, see Gary Yukl and Tom Taber, "The Effective Use of Managerial Power," *Personnel,* vol. 60 (1983), pp. 37–49; Robert C. Benfari, Harry E. Wilkinson and Charles D. Orth, "The Effective Use of Power," *Business Horizons,* vol. 29 (1986), pp. 12–16.

[4] Gary A. Yukl, *Leadership in Organizations,* 2nd ed. (Englewood Cliffs, NJ: Prentice Hall, 1989), includes "information" as a separate, but related, power source.

[5] Based on David A. Whetten and Kim S. Cameron, *Developing Management Skills,* 2nd ed. (New York: HarperCollins, 1991), pp. 281–297.

[6] Developed from Whetten and Cameron, op. cit., p. 282.

[7] Ibid, pp. 297–305.

[8] Jay A. Conger, "Leadership: The Art of Empowering Others," *The Academy of Management Executive,* vol. 3 (1989), pp. 17–24.

[9] Stanley Milgram, "Behavioral Study of Obedience," *Journal of Abnormal and Social Psychology,* vol. 67 (1963), pp. 371–378.

[10] Summarized by permission from John R. Schermerhorn, Jr., James G. Hunt, and Richard W. Osborn, *Managing Organizational Behavior,* fifth edition (New York: John Wiley & Sons, 1994), p. 467.

[11] Chester A. Barnard, *Functions of the Executive* (Cambridge, MA: Harvard University Press, 1938).

[12] See Henry Mintzberg, *Power in and Around Organizations* (Englewood Cliffs, N.J.: Prentice-Hall, 1983).

[13] See John R. Schermerhorn, Jr., James G. Hunt, and Richard N. Osborn, *Basic Organizational Behavior* (New York: John Wiley & Sons, 1995), pp. 153–54.

CHAPTER 16

[1] Dana Milbank, "Managers Are Sent to 'Charm Schools' to Discover How to Polish Up Their Acts," *The Wall Street Journal* (December 14, 1990), pp. B1, B3.

[2] Portions of this treatment of negotiation are adapted from John R. Schermerhorn, Jr., James G. Hunt, and Richard N. Osborn, *Managing Organizational Behavior,* 4th ed. (New York: Wiley, 1991), pp. 382–387. Used by permission.

[3] For excellent overview see Roger Fisher and William Ury, *Getting to Yes: Negotiating Agreement Without Giving in* (New York: Penguin, 1983).

[4] Fisher and Ury, op. cit.

[5] Fisher & Ury, op. cit.; and, James A. Wall, Jr., *Negotiation: Theory and Practice* (Glenview, IL: Scott, Foresman, 1985).

[6] Based on a discussion in Robert E. Quinn, Sue R. Faerman, Michael P. Thompson, and Michael R. McGrath, *Becoming a Master Manager* (New York: Wiley, 1990), pp. 289–294.

[7] Developed from Max H. Bazerman, *Judgment in Managerial Decision Making,* 3rd ed. (New York: Wiley, 1994), Chap. 7.

[8] Ibid; and Fisher and Ury, op. cit., pp. 10–14.

[9] Roy J. Lewicki and Joseph A. Litterer, *Negotiation* (Homewood, IL: Irwin, 1985).

[10] Richard E. Walton, *Interpersonal Peacemaking: Confrontations and Third-Party Consultation* (Reading, MA: Addison-Wesley, 1969), p. 2.

[11] James L. Lewnadowski and William P. MacKinnon, "What We Learned at Saturn," *Personnel Journal* (December 1992), pp. 22–24.

[12] For a good overview see Roger Fisther, Elizabeth Kpelman and Andrea Kupfer Schneider, *Beyond Machiavelli: Tools for Coping with Conflict* (Cambridge, Mass.: Harvard University Press, 1994).

[13] See Kenneth W. Thomas, "Conflict and Conflict Management," in M.D. Dunnett, ed., *Handbook of Industrial and Organizational Behavior* (Chicago: Rand McNally, 1976), pp. 889–935.

[14] See also Robert R. Blake and Jane Strygley Mouton, "The Fifth Achievement," *Journal of Applied Behavioral Science,* vol. 6 (1970), pp. 413–427; Alan C. Filley, *Interpersonal Conflict Resolution* (Glenview, IL: Scott, Foresman, 1975).

[15] This discussion is based on Filley, op. cit.; and, Vincent L. Ferraro and Sheila A. Adams, "Interdepartmental Conflict: Practical Ways to Prevent and Reduce It," *Personnel,* vol. 61 (1984), pp. 12–23.

[16] Arthur P. Brief, Randall S. Schuler, and Mary Van Sell, *Managing Job Stress* (Boston: Little, Brown, 1981), pp. 7, 8.

[17] Alan Farnham, "Who Beats Stress Best—and How," *Fortune* (October 7, 1991), pp. 71–86.

[18] Worries at Work," *The Wall Street Journal* (April 7, 1988), p. 31.

[19] See "Stress on the Job," *Newsweek* (April 25, 1988) pp. 40–45; Brian Dumaine, "Cool Cures for Burnout," *Fortune* (June 20, 1988), pp. 78–84.

[20] Meyer Friedman and Ray Roseman, *Type A Behavior and Your Heart* (New York: Knopf, 1974). See also Jerry E. Bishop, "Prognosis for the 'Type A' Personality Improves in a New Heart Disease Study," *The Wall Street Journal* (January 14, 1988), p. 29.

[21] See Robert Kreitner, "Personal Wellness: It's Just Good Business," *Business Horizons,* vol. 25 (May–June 1982), pp. 28–35.

[22] Kreitner, op. cit., and "Plain Talk about Stress," National Institute of Mental Health Publication (Rockville, MD: U.S. Department of Health and Human Services).

CHAPTER 17

[1] Quote from William Bridges, "The End of the Job," *Fortune* (September 19, 1994), p. 68.

[2] See, for example, "Rethinking Work," Special Report, *Business Week* (October 17, 1994), pp. 74–87.

[3] *HRM Magazine* (April 1991), pp. 42–43.

[4] Information from *The Wall Street Journal* (August 10, 1994), p. A10.

[5] Boris Yavitz, "Human Resources in Strategic Planning," in Eli Ginzberg (ed.), *Executive Talent: Developing and Keeping the Best People* (New York: Wiley, 1988), p. 34.

[6] See Ernest McCormick, "Job and Task Analysis," in Marvin Dunnette, ed., *Handbook of Industrial and Organizational Psychology* (Chicago: Rand McNally, 1976), pp. 651–696.

[7] See John P. Wanous, *Organizational Entry: Recruitment, Selection, and Socialization of Newcomers* (Reading, MA: Addison-Wesley, 1980), pp. 34–44.

[8] See Dale Yoder and Herbert G. Heneman, eds., *ASPA Handbook of Personnel and Industrial Relations,* vol. 1 (Washington: Bureau of National Affairs, 1974), pp. 152–154; Walter Kiechel III, "How to Pick Talent," *Fortune* (December 8, 1986), pp. 201–203.

[9] *Southern Illinoisan* (January 31, 1988), p. 9; W. J. Holstein, "Why Mitsubishi Is Right at Home in Illinois," *Business Week* (May 30, 1988), p. 45; company information letter (September 4, 1991).

[10] Information from William M. Bulkeley, "Replaced by Technology: Job Interviews," *The Wall Street Journal* (August 22, 1994), pp. B1, B4.

[11] For a scholarly review see John Van Maanen and Edgar H. Schein, "Toward a Theory of Socialization," in Barry M. Staw, ed., *Research in Organizational Behavior,* vol. 1 (Greenwich, CT: JAI Press, 1979), pp. 209–264; for a practitioner view, see Richard Pascale, "Fitting New Employees into the Company Culture," *Fortune* (May 28, 1984), pp. 28–42.

[12] This involves the social information processing

concept as discussed in Gerald R. Salancik and Jeffrey Pfeffer, "A Social Information Processing Approach to Job Attitudes and Task Design," *Administrative Science Quarterly,* vol. 23 (June 1978), pp. 224–253.

[13] Occasional reports on this issue appear in the business press. See, for example, "Education: The Wall Street Journal Reports," *The Wall Street Journal* (February 9, 1990); "A Shortage of Basic Skills," *Business Week* (January 13, 1991), p. 39.

[14] Developed in part from Larry L. Cummings and Donald P. Schwab, *Performance in Organizations; Determinants and Appraisal* (Glenview, IL: Scott, Foresman, 1973).

[15] See Thomas P. Ference, James A. F. Stoner, and E. Kirby Warren, "Managing the Career Plateau," *Academy of Management Review,* Vol. 2 (October 1977), pp. 602–612; and, Julie Connelly, "Have You Gone as Far as You Can Go? *Fortune* (December 26, 1994), pp. 231–232.

[16] See Richard B. Freeman and James L. Medoff, *What Do Unions Do?* (New York: Basic Books, 1984): Charles C. Heckscher, *The New Unionism* (New York: Basic Books, 1988).

[17] See "Reinventing Labor: An Interview with Union President Lynn Williams," *Harvard Business Review* (July–August 1993), pp. 115–125.

CHAPTER 18

[1] Peter F. Drucker, *The New Realities* (New York: Harper & Row, 1990); Charles Handy, *The Age of Unreason* (Cambridge, MA: Harvard University Press, 1990); Charles Handy, *The Age of Paradox* (Boston: Harvard University Press, 1994).

[2] Peter Senge, *The Fifth Discipline* (New York: Harper, 1990).

[3] George Melloan, "Herman Miller's Secrets of Creativity," *The Wall Street Journal* (May 3, 1988), p. 23.

[4] Senge op. cit.; see also Brian Dumaine, "Mr. Learning Organization," *Fortune* (October 17, 1994), pp. 147–157.

[5] Cited in Peter F. Drucker, *Management: Tasks, Responsibilities, and Practices* (New York: Harper & Row, 1973), p. 797.

[6] This discussion is based on the thorough review of the concept of innovation provided by Edward B. Roberts, "Managing Invention and Innovation," *Research Technology Management* (January–February 1988), pp. 1–19.

[7] This model of the innovation process is adapted from Roberts, op. cit.

[8] *Fortune* (December 1991), pp. 56–62.

[9] This discussion is stimulated by James Brian Quinn, "Managing Innovation Controlled Chaos," *Harvard Business Review,* vol. 63 (May–June 1985). Selected quotes and examples from Kenneth Labich, "The Innovators," *Fortune* (June 6, 1988), pp. 49–64.

[10] Ibid.

[11] Peter F. Drucker, "Best R&D Is Business Driven," *The Wall Street Journal* (February 10, 1988), p. 11.

[12] See Roberts, op. cit., 1988.

[13] *The Wall Street Journal* (May 3, 1988), p. 23.

[14] Developed in part from Quinn, op. cit., 1984.

[15] G. Christian Hill and Mike Tharp, "Stumbling Giant Big Quarterly Deficit Stuns BankAmerica. Adds Pressure on Chief," *The Wall Street Journal* (July 18, 1985), pp. 1, 16.

[16] Kurt Lewin, "Group Decision and Social Change," in G. E. Swanson, T. M. Newcomb and E. L. Hartley, eds., *Readings in Social Psychology* (New York: Holt Rinehart, 1952), pp. 459–473.

[17] This discussion is based on Robert Chin and Kenneth D. Benne, "General Strategies for Effecting Changes in Human Systems," in Warren G. Bennis, Kenneth D. Benne, Robert Chin and Kenneth E. Corey, eds., *The Planning of Change,* 3rd ed. (New York: Holt, Rinehart, 1969), pp. 22–45; Patrick E. Connor, "Strategies for Managing Technological Change," *Harvard International Review,* vol. X (1988), pp. 10–13.

[18] John P. Kotter and Leonard A. Schlesinger, "Choosing Strategies for Change," *Harvard Business Review,* vol. 57 (March–April 1979), pp. 109–112.

[19] Two good overviews of organization development are provided by W. Warner Burke, *Organization Development: A Normative View* (Reading, MA: Addison-Wesley, 1987); and, Wendell L. French and Cecil H. Bell, Jr., *Organization Development,* 5th ed. (Englewood Cliffs, NJ: Prentice Hall, 1995).

GLOSSARY

A

Ability   is the capacity to do a particular task well.

Accommodation or **smoothing**   involves playing down differences among conflicting parties and highlighting similarities and areas of agreement.

An **accommodating strategy**   accepts social responsibilities and tries to satisfy prevailing economic, legal, and ethical performance criteria.

Action research   is a collaborative process of systematically collecting data on an organization, feeding it back for action planning, and evaluating results.

Active listening   involves taking action to help the source of a message say what he or she really means.

An **adaptive organization**   operates with a minimum of bureaucratic features and encourages worker empowerment and participation through teamwork and network structuring.

An **administrator**   is a manager who works in a public or nonprofit organization

Attitudes   are specific "likes" and "dislikes" that result in predispositions to behave in certain ways toward other people, objects and events.

Attribution error   is the tendency to make judgments based upon incomplete information or limited perceptions.

An **authority decision**   is a decision made by the manager and then communicated to the group.

Avoidance   involves pretending that a conflict doesn't really exist or hoping that a conflict will simply go away.

B

A **BCG matrix**   is a portfolio planning approach, developed by the Boston Consulting Group, that ties strategy formulation to an analysis of business opportunities according to market growth rate and market share.

Behavioral decision theory   assumes that people act only in terms of what they perceive about a given situation.

Benchmarking   is the use of external comparisons to gain added perspective on current performance and help initiate the planning process; a process of comparing operations and performance with other organizations known for excellence.

A **bonus pay plan**   provides cash bonuses to employees based on the achievement of specific performance targets.

Brainstorming   is a group technique for generating a large quantity of ideas by freewheeling contributions made without criticism.

A **budget**   is a plan that commits resources to projects or programs; a formalized way of allocating resources to specific activities.

A **business strategy**   identifies the intentions of a division or strategic business unit to compete in its special product and/or service domain.

Bureaucracy   is an intentionally rational and efficient form of organization founded on principles of logic, order, and legitimate authority.

C

Central-planning economies   are those in which the central government makes basic economic decisions for an entire nation.

Chain of command   is an unbroken line of authority that vertically links all persons in an organization with successively higher levels of authority.

A **change agent**   is a person or group that takes leadership responsibility for changing the existing pattern of behavior of another person or social system.

Changing   is the central phase in the planned-change process in which the manager actually implements the change.

A **charismatic leader**   is a leader who develops special leader-follower relationships and truly inspires his or her followers in extraordinary ways.

The **classical decision theory**   describes how managers ideally should make decisions using complete information.

A **code of ethics** is a written document that states values and ethical standards to guide the behavior of employees.

Coercive power is the capability to punish or withhold positive outcomes as a means of influencing other people.

Cognitive style deals with the way people gather, process and interpret information for decision-making purposes.

Collaboration or **problem solving** involves working through conflict differences and solving problems so everyone wins as a result.

Collective bargaining is the process of negotiating, administering, and interpreting a labor contract.

A **combination strategy** involves stability, growth, and retrenchment in one or more combinations.

A **committee** is a formal group designated to work on a special task on a continuing basis.

Communication is an interpersonal process of sending and receiving symbols with meanings attached to them.

Comparative management is the study of how management practices systematically differ from one country and/or culture to the next.

Competition or **authoritative command** occurs when a conflict victory is achieved through force, superior skill, or domination of one party by another.

A **competitive advantage** is a special edge that allows an organization to deal with market and environmental forces better than its competitors.

Competitors are specific organizations that offer the same or similar goods and services to the same consumer or client groups.

A **compressed workweek** is any work schedule that allows a full-time job to be completed in less than the standard 5 days of 8-hour shifts.

Compromise occurs when accommodations are made such that each party to the conflict gives up something of value to the other.

A **conceptual skill** is the ability to think analytically and solve complex problems to the benefit of everyone involved.

A **concurrent control** or **steering control** is a control that acts in anticipation of problems and focuses primarily on what happens during the work process.

Conflict is a disagreement over issues of substance and/or emotional antagonism.

Conflict resolution is the removal of the reasons—substantial and/or emotional—for a conflict.

Constructive stress is stress that acts in a positive or energizing way to increase effort, stimulate creativity, and encourage diligence in one's work.

A **consultative decision** is a decision made by a manager after receiving information, advice, or opinion from group members.

Contingency planning is the process of identifying alternative courses of action that can be used to modify an original plan if and when circumstances change with the passage of time.

Continuous improvement involves searching for new ways to incrementally improve operations quality and performance.

Controlling is the process of measuring performance and taking action to ensure desired results.

Corporate social responsibility is an obligation of an organization to act in ways that serve both its own interests and the interests of its many external publics.

A **corporate strategy** sets the direction of and serves as a resource allocation guide for the total enterprise.

Cost-benefit analysis involves comparing the costs and benefits of each potential course of action.

A **cost leadership strategy** is a corporate competitive strategy that seeks to achieve lower costs than competitors by improving efficiency of production, distribution, and other organizational systems.

Creativity is an application of ingenuity and imagination that results in a novel approach or unique solution to a problem.

Culture is a shared set of beliefs, values, and patterns of behavior common to a group of people.

Culture shock is the confusion and discomfort a person experiences when in an unfamiliar culture.

Customers are specific consumer or client groups, individuals, and organizations that purchase the organization's goods and/or use its services.

Cycle time is the elapsed time between receipt of an order and delivery of a finished good or service.

D

Decentralization is the dispersion of authority to make decisions throughout all levels of management by extensive delegation.

A **decision** is a choice among alternative courses of action for dealing with a "problem."

Decision making involves the identification of a problem and the choice of preferred problem-solving alternatives.

A **defensive strategy** seeks to protect the organization by doing the minimum legally required to satisfy social expectations.

Delegation is the process of distributing and entrusting work to other persons.

Democratic systems establish government with open participation by the society as a whole through free elections and representative assemblies.

Design for disassembly is the design of products with attention to how their component parts will be used when the product life cycle ends.

Design for manufacturing involves creating a design that lowers production costs and improves quality in all stages of production.

Destructive stress is stress that is dysfunctional for the individual and/or the organization.

Differentiation is the degree of differences that exists among people, departments, or other internal components of an organization.

Discipline is the act of influencing behavior through reprimand.

Discrimination is an active form of prejudice that disadvantages people by denying them full benefits of organizational membership.

Distributive negotiation is negotiation that focuses on "claims" made by each party for certain preferred outcomes.

A **divisional structure** is an organizational structure that groups together people with diverse skills and tasks but who work on the same product, with similar customers or clients, in the same geographical region, or on the same time schedule.

E

Economic condition is the general state of the economy in terms of inflation, income levels, gross domestic product, unemployment, and related indicators of economic health.

Economic order quantity (EOQ) is a method of inventory control that involves ordering a fixed number of items every time an inventory level falls to a predetermined point.

Effective communication occurs when the intended meaning of the source and the perceived meaning of the receiver are identical.

An **effective group** is a group that achieves and maintains high levels of both task performance and membership satisfaction over time.

Effective negotiation occurs when both issues of substance are resolved and working relationships among the negotiating parties are maintained or improved in the process.

Efficient communication is communication that occurs at minimum cost in terms of resources expended.

An **employee involvement group** meets on a regular basis with the goal of applying members' expertise to solve problems and achieve continuous improvement.

An **employee stock ownership plan** allows employees to share ownership of their employing organization through the purchase of stock.

Empowerment is the process through which managers allow and help others to gain power and achieve influence within the organization.

Entrepreneurial pay involves workers putting part of their compensation at risk in return for the right to pursue entrepreneurial ideas and share in any resulting profits.

Environmentalism is the expression and demonstration of public concern for conditions of the natural or physical environment.

Equity theory is based on the phenomenon of social comparison and posits that people gauge the fairness of their work outcomes compared to others.

Escalating commitment is the tendency to continue to pursue a course of action, even though it is not working.

Ethical behavior is behavior that is accepted as "right" or "good" in the context of a governing moral code.

An **ethical dilemma** is a situation proposing a potential course of action that, although offering potential benefit or gain, is also unethical and/or illegal in the broader social context.

Ethics are the code of morals of a person or group that sets standards as to what is good or bad, or right or wrong in one's conduct.

Ethics training seeks to help people better understand the ethical aspects of decision making and to incorporate high ethical standards into their daily behavior.

Ethnocentrism is the tendency to consider one's culture as superior to all others.

Equal employment opportunity is the right of people to employment and advancement without regard to race, sex, religion, color, or national origin.

Expectancy is a person's belief that working hard will enable various levels of task performance to be achieved.

Expert power is the capability to influence other people because of specialized knowledge.

Exporting is the process of producing products locally and selling them abroad in foreign markets.

An **external customer** is the customer or client who buys or uses the organization's goods and/or services.

External recruitment is the attraction of job candidates from sources outside the organization.

Extinction discourages a behavior by making the removal of a desirable consequence contingent on the occurrence of the behavior.

An **extrinsic reward** is a reward given as a motivational stimulus to a person, usually by a superior.

F

Feedback is the process of telling someone else how you feel about something that person did or said or about the situation in general.

A **feedback control** or **postaction control** is a control that takes place after an action is completed.

A **feedforward control** or **preliminary control** ensures that proper directions are set and that the right resources are available to accomplish them before the work activity begins.

First-line managers oversee single units and pursue short-term performance objectives consistent with the plans of middle and top management levels.

Flexible working hours are work schedules that give employees some choice in the pattern of daily work hours.

A **focus strategy** is a corporate competitive strategy that concentrates attention on a special market segment to serve its needs better than the competition.

A **force-coercion strategy** attempts to bring about change through formal authority and/or the use of rewards or punishments.

A **forecast** is an attempt to predict outcomes; it is a projection into the future based on historical data combined in some scientific manner.

A **formal group** is a group created by the formal authority within the organization.

Formal structure is the structure of the organization in its pure or ideal state.

Franchising is a form of licensing in which the licensee buys the complete "package" of support needed to open a particular business.

Free-market economies are those which operate under capitalism and laws of supply and demand.

Functional managers are responsible for one area of activity, such as finance, marketing, production, personnel, accounting, or sales.

A **functional strategy** guides the activities within various functional areas or organizational operations.

A **functional structure** is an organizational structure that groups together people with similar skills who perform similar tasks.

G

A **gain-sharing plan** allows employees to share in any savings or "gains" realized through their efforts to reduce costs and increase productivity.

The **General Agreement on Trade and Tariffs (GATT)** is an international accord in which member nations agree to ongoing negotiations and the reduction of tariffs and trade restrictions.

The **general environment** is comprised of the cultural, economic, legal-political, and educational conditions in the locality in which an organization operates.

General managers are responsible for complex organizational units that include many areas of functional activity.

A **geographical structure** is a divisional structure that groups together jobs and activities being performed in the same location or geographical region.

The **glass ceiling effect** is an invisible barrier that limits the advancement of women and minorities to higher level responsibilities in organizations.

The **global economy** is an economic perspective based on worldwide interdependence of resource supplies, product markets, and business competition.

A **global manager** works successfully across international boundaries.

Global sourcing is a process of purchasing materials or components in various parts of the world and then assembling them at home into a final product.

A **group** is a collection of people who regularly interact with one another over time and in respect to the pursuit of one or more common goals.

Group cohesiveness is the degree to which members are attracted to and motivated to remain part of a group.

A **group decision** is a decision made with the full participation of all group members.

A **group norm** is a behavior, rule, or standard expected to be followed by group members.

Group process is the way group members work together to accomplish tasks.

Groupthink is a tendency for highly cohesive groups to lose their critical evaluative capabilities.

Growth-need strength is an individual's desire to achieve a sense of psychological growth in her or his work.

A **growth strategy** involves expansion of the organization's current operations.

H

A **halo effect** occurs when one attribute is used to develop an overall impression of a person or situation.

Heuristics are strategies for simplifying decision making.

Higher order needs, in Maslow's hierarchy, are esteem and self-actualization needs.

Human resource management is the process of attracting, developing, and maintaining a qualified workforce.

Human resource planning is the process of analyzing staffing needs and identifying actions to fill those needs over time.

Human resources are the people, individuals, and groups that help organizations produce goods or services.

A **human skill** is the ability to work well in cooperation with other people.

I

Importing is the process of acquiring products abroad and selling them in domestic markets.

Individual differences are the demographic, competency, and personality characteristics that make each person a unique human being.

The **individualism view** is a view of ethical behavior based on the belief that one's primary commitment is to the advancement of long-term self-interests.

Influence is the actual outcome of behavioral response to the use of power.

An **informal group** is not officially created and emerges based on relationships and shared interests among members.

Informal structure is the undocumented and officially unrecognized structure that coexists with the formal structure of an organization.

Innovation is the process of taking a new idea and putting it into practice as part of the organization's normal operating routines.

Instrumentality is a person's belief that various work-related outcomes will occur as a result of task performance.

Integrative negotiation see principled negotiation.

An **internal customer** is someone who uses or depends on the work of another person or group within the same organization.

Internal recruitment involves notifying existing employees of job vacancies through job posting and personal recommendations.

International business is the conduct of for-profit transactions of goods and/or services across national boundaries.

An **intrinsic** or **natural reward** is a reward that occurs naturally as a person performs a task or job.

ISO 9000 certification is granted by the International Standards Organization to indicate that a business meets a rigorous set of quality standards.

J

A **job** is the collection of tasks a person performs in support of organizational objectives.

Job design is the allocation of specific work tasks to individuals and groups.

Job enlargement is a job-design strategy that increases task variety by combining into one job two or more tasks that were previously assigned to separate workers.

Job enrichment is a job-design strategy that increases job depth by adding to a job some of the planning and evaluating duties normally performed by the supervisor.

Job performance is the quantity and quality of task accomplishment by an individual or group at work.

Job rotation is a job-design strategy that increases task variety by periodically shifting workers among jobs involving different tasks.

Job satisfaction is the degree to which an individual feels positively or negatively about various aspects of the job, including assigned tasks, work setting, and relationships with coworkers.

Job sharing is an arrangement that splits one job between two people.

Job simplification is a job-design strategy that involves standardizing work procedures and employing people in clearly defined and very specialized tasks.

A **joint venture** is a form of international business that establishes operations in a foreign country through joint ownership with local partners.

The **justice view** is a view of ethical behavior based on the belief that ethical decisions treat people impartially and fairly according to guiding rules and standards.

Just-in-time scheduling (JIT) is a system, popularized by the productivity of Japanese industry, that attempts to reduce costs and improve workflows by scheduling materials to arrive at a work station or facility "just in time" to be used.

K

Keiretsu is a Japanese term describing alliances or business groups that link together various businesses, manufacturers, suppliers, and finance companies for common interests.

L

A **labor union** is an organization to which workers belong that collectively deals with employers on their behalf.

Leadership is the process of inspiring others to work hard to accomplish important tasks.

Leadership style is the recurring pattern of behaviors exhibited by a leader.

Leading is the process of arousing enthusiasm and directing human-resource efforts toward organizational goals.

Legal-political condition is the general state of the prevailing philosophy and objectives of the political party or parties running the government, as well as laws and government regulations.

Legitimate power is the capability to influence other people by virtue of formal authority or the rights of office.

Licensing agreement is an international business approach giving a foreign firm the rights to make or sell another company's products, usually upon payment of a fee.

Life-long learning is the process of continuously learning from work experiences.

Line managers have direct responsibility for activities making direct contributions to the production of the organization's basic goods or services.

Locus of control is the internal-external orientation, that is, the extent to which people feel able to affect their lives.

Lower order needs, in Maslow's hierarchy, are physiological, safety, and social needs.

M

Machiavellianism describes the personality of someone inclined toward manipulation and political control of other people.

A **maintenance activity** is an action taken by a group member that supports the emotional life of the group as a social system.

A **manager** is a person in an organization who is responsible for the work performance of one or more other persons.

Management is the process of planning, organizing, leading, and controlling the use of resources to accomplish performance goals.

Management by exception focuses managerial attention on situations in which differences between actual and desired performance are substantial.

Management by objectives (MBO) is a process of joint objective setting between a superior and subordinate that can be done on an organization-wide basis.

Management by wandering around involves dealing directly with subordinates by regularly walking around and talking with them about a variety of work-related matters.

A **management information system (MIS)** collects, organizes, and distributes data in such a way that the information meets managers' needs.

Managerial competency is a skill or personal characteristic that contributes to high performance in a management job.

Manufacturing resources planning (MRPII) is an operations planning and control system that extends MRP to include the control of all organizational resources.

Materials requirements planning (MRP) is an operations planning and control system for ensuring that the right materials and parts are always available at each stage of production.

A **matrix structure** is an organizational form that combines functional and divisional departmentation to take best advantage of each.

Merit pay is a system of awarding pay increases in proportion to performance contributions.

Middle managers report to top-level management, oversee the work of several units, and implement plans consistent with higher level objectives.

The **mission** of an organization is its reason for existing as a supplier of goods and/or services to society.

Monochronic culture is a culture in which people tend to do one thing at a time.

The **moral-rights view** is a view of ethical behavior that seeks to respect and protect the fundamental rights of people.

Motivation is a term used in management theory to describe forces within the individual that account for the level, direction, and persistence of effort expended at work.

A **multicultural organization** is one that is internally rich in diversity and operates every way in full respect for individual differences and subcultural differences.

A **multinational corporation (MNC)** is a business firm with extensive international operations in more than one foreign country.

A **multinational organization (MNO)** is a non-profit organization whose mission and operation span the globe.

N

Natural environment condition is the general state of nature and conditions of the natural or physical environment, including levels of environmentalism.

A **need** is a physiological or psychological deficiency a person feels the compulsion to satisfy.

Need for Achievement (nAch) is the desire to do something better or more efficiently, to solve problems, or to master complex tasks.

Need for Affiliation (nAff) is the desire to establish and maintain friendly and warm relations with other people.

Need for Power (nPower) is the desire to control, influence, or be responsible for other people.

Negative reinforcement strengthens a behavior by making the avoidance of an undesirable consequence contingent on the occurrence of the behavior.

Negotiation is the process of making joint decisions when the parties involved have different preferences.

A **network structure** is an organizational structure that consists of a central core with "networks" of outside suppliers of essential business services.

Noise is anything that interferes with the effectiveness of the communication process.

The **nominal group technique** is a group technique for generating ideas by following a structured format of individual response, group sharing without criticism, and written balloting.

Nonverbal communication is communication that takes place through channels such as body language and the use of interpersonal space.

North American Free Trade Agreement (NAFTA) is a free trade agreement among the United States, Canada, and Mexico.

O

An **obstructionist strategy** avoids social responsibility and reflects mainly economic priorities.

Off-the-job training is a set of activities done outside the work setting which provide the opportunity to acquire and improve job related skills.

On-the-job training is a set of activities done in the work setting which provide the opportunity to acquire and improve job related skills.

An **open system** is one that interacts with its environment and transforms resource inputs into outputs.

Operant conditioning is the process of controlling behavior by manipulating its consequences.

Operating objectives are the specific ends toward which organizational resources are actually allocated.

An **operational plan** is a plan of limited scope that addresses those activities and resources required to implement strategic plans.

Operations management is a branch of management theory that studies how organizations transform resource inputs into product and service outputs.

An **organization** is a collection of people working together in a division of labor to achieve a common purpose.

Organizational behavior is the study of individuals and groups in organizations.

Organizational behavior modification is the application of operant conditioning techniques to influence human behavior in work settings.

Organizational culture is the system of shared beliefs and values that develops within an organization and guides the behavior of its members.

Organizational design is the process of choosing the implementing structures that best organize resources to serve mission and objectives.

Organizational politics are power oriented behaviors that use unofficial means to try to influence other people in a manner favorable to one's personal interest.

Organizing is the process of assuming tasks, allocating resources, and arranging coordinated activities to implement plans; the process of mobilizing people and other resources to accomplish tasks that serve a common purpose.

Orientation consists of activities through which new employees are made familiar with their jobs, their co-workers, and the policies, rules, objectives, and services of the organization as a whole.

P

Participative planning is the inclusion in the planning process of as many people as possible from among those who will be affected by plans and/or asked to help implement them.

Part-time work is work done on a basis that classifies the employee as "temporary" and requires less than the standard 40-hour workweek.

Perception is the process through which people receive, organize, and interpret information from the environment.

Performance appraisal is a process of formally evaluating performance and providing feedback on which performance adjustments can be made.

Performance effectiveness is an output measure of a task or goal accomplishment.

Performance efficiency is a measure of the resource cost associated with goal accomplishment.

A **performance norm** identifies the level of work effort and performance expected of group members.

Personality is the enduring and relatively stable profile of traits that make each person unique in the eyes of others.

Planning is the process of setting objectives and determining what should be done to accomplish them.

A **policy** is a standing plan that communicates broad guidelines for making decisions and taking action.

Political risk is the risk of losing one's investment in or managerial control over a foreign asset due to political changes in the host country.

Polychronic culture is a culture in which people tend to do more than one thing at a time.

Positive reinforcement strengthens a behavior by making a desirable consequence contingent on the occurrence of the behavior.

Power is the ability to get someone else to do something you want done or to make things happen the way you want.

Prejudice is the holding of negative, irrational attitudes toward individuals because of their group identity.

Principled/integrative negotiation is a negotiation process that seeks a way for all claims to be satisfied if at all possible.

Privatization is the selling of state-owned enterprises into private ownership.

A **proactive strategy** meets all the criteria of social performance, including discretionary performance.

A **problem** is a difference between an actual situation and a desired situation.

Problem solving is the process of identifying a discrepancy between an actual and a desired state of affairs and then taking action to resolve the discrepancy.

A **procedure** or **rule** is a standing plan that precisely describes what actions are to be taken in specific situations.

Productivity is a summary measure of the quantity and quality of work performance with resource utilization considered.

A **profit-sharing plan** distributes a proportion of net profits to employees during a stated performance period.

The **program evaluation and review technique (PERT)** is a means for identifying and controlling the many separate events involved in the completion of projects.

Progressive discipline is the process of tying reprimands in the form of penalties or punishments to the severity of the employee's infractions.

Projection is the assignment of personal attributes to other individuals.

A **psychological contract** is the shared set of expectations held by an individual and the organization, specifying what each expects to give and receive from the other in the course of their working relationship.

Punishment discourages a behavior by making an unpleasant consequence contingent on the occurrence of that behavior.

Q

Quality is a degree of excellence, often defined in managerial terms as the ability to meet customer needs 100 percent of the time.

A **quality circle** is a group of employees who meet periodically to discuss ways of improving the quality of their products or services.

Quality control is the process of checking products or services to ensure that they meet certain standards.

Quality of work life (QWL) is the overall quality of human experiences in the workplace.

R

A **rational persuasion strategy** attempts to bring about change through persuasion backed by special knowledge, empirical data, and rational argument.

Realistic job previews are attempts by the job interviewer to provide the job candidate with all pertinent information about a prospective job and the employing organization, without distortion and before a job offer is accepted.

A **reason strategy** of influence relies on personal power and persuasion based on data, needs, and/or values.

A **reciprocity strategy** of influence involves the mutual exchange of values and a search for shared positive outcomes.

Recruitment is a set of activities designed to attract a qualified pool of job applicants to an organization.

Referent power is the capability to influence other people because of their desires to identify personally and positively with the power source.

Refreezing is the final stage in the planned-change process during which the manager is concerned with stabilizing the change and creating the conditions for its long-term continuity.

Regulators are specific government agencies and representatives, at the local, state, and national levels, that enforce laws and regulations affecting the organization's operations.

A **retrenchment strategy** involves slowing down, cutting back, and seeking performance improvement through greater efficiencies in operations.

A **retribution strategy** of influence relies on position power and results in feelings of coercion or intimidation.

A **reward** is a work outcome of positive value to the individual.

Reward power is the capability to offer something of value—a positive outcome—as a means of influencing other people.

S

A **satisfier factor** is a factor in job content, such as a sense of achievement, recognition, responsibility, advancement, or personal growth, experienced as a result of task performance.

Scenario planning involves identifying several alternative future scenarios or states of affairs that may occur as well as making plans to deal with each, should they occur.

Selection is the process of choosing from a pool of applicants the person or persons who best meet job specifications.

Selective perception is the tendency to define problems from one's own point of view or to single out for attention things consistent with one's existing beliefs, values, or needs.

A **self-managing work team,** sometimes called an autonomous work group, is a group of workers whose jobs have been redesigned to create a high degree of task interdependence and who have been given authority to make decisions about how they go about the required work.

Semantic barriers are verbal and nonverbal symbols that are poorly chosen and expressed, creating barriers to successful communication.

Shaping is positive reinforcement of successive approximations to the desired behavior.

A **shared power strategy** is a participative change strategy that relies on involving others to examine values, needs, and goals in relationship to an issue at hand.

A **skill** is the ability to translate knowledge into action that results in the desired performance.

Skills-based pay is a system of paying workers according to the number of job-relevant skills they master.

A **social audit** is a systematic assessment and reporting of an organization's commitments and accomplishments in areas of social responsibility.

Socialization is the process of systematically changing the expectations, behavior, and attitudes of a new employee in a manner considered desirable by the organization.

Sociocultural condition is the general state of prevailing social values on such matters as human rights and environment, trends in education and related social institutions, as well as demographic patterns.

A **specific environment** is comprised of the actual organizations and persons with whom the focal organization must interact in order to survive and prosper.

A **stability strategy** maintains the present course of action.

Staff managers use special technical expertise to advise and support the efforts of line workers.

A **strategic business unit (SBU)** is a separate operating division that represents a major business area and operates with some autonomy vis-à-vis other similar units in the organization.

Strategic management is the managerial responsibility for leading the process of formulating and implementing strategies that lead to longer term organizational success.

Strategic opportunism is the ability to remain focused on long-term objectives by being flexible in dealing with short-term problems and opportunity as they occur.

A **strategy** is a comprehensive plan or action orientation that sets critical direction and guides the allocation of resources for an organization to achieve long-term objectives.

A **stereotype** is the identification of an individual with a group or category, and the associating of oversimplified attributes of the group or category to the individual.

Stock option is the right to buy stock at a future date at a fixed price.

Stress is a state of tension experienced by individuals facing extraordinary demands, constraints, or opportunities.

Structure is the system of networks of communication and authority that links people and groups together as they perform important tasks.

Substitutes for leadership are factors in the work setting that move work efforts toward organizational objectives without the direct involvement of a leader.

Suppliers are specific providers of the human, information, and financial resources and raw materials needed by the organization to operate.

A **SWOT analysis** sets the stage for strategy formulation by analyzing organizational strengths and weaknesses and environmental opportunities and threats.

A **symbolic manager** is a manager who uses symbols well to establish and maintain a desired organizational culture.

Synergy is the creation of a whole that is greater than the sum of its individual parts.

T

A **task activity** is an action taken by a group member that contributes directly to the group's performance purpose.

A **task force** is a formal group convened for a specific purpose and expected to disband when that purpose is achieved.

Task goals are performance targets for individuals and/or groups.

Team building is a sequence of planned activities to gather and analyze data on the functioning of a group and implement constructive changes to increase its operating effectiveness.

A **team structure** is an organizational structure through which permanent and temporary teams are created to improve lateral relations and solve problems throughout an organization.

Teamwork is the process of people working together in groups to accomplish common goals.

A **technical skill** is the ability to use a special proficiency or expertise in one's work.

Technological condition is the general state of the development and availability of technology in the environment, including scientific advancements.

Telecommuting involves working at home using a computer terminal with links to the office or other places of work.

Theory X is a set of managerial assumptions that people in general dislike work, lack ambition, are irresponsible and resistant to change, and prefer to be led than to lead.

Theory Y is a set of managerial assumptions that people in general are willing to work and accept responsibility and are capable of self-direction, self-control, and creativity.

Theory Z is a term that describes a management framework used by American firms following Japanese examples.

360-degree feedback is an upward communication approach that involves upward appraisals done by a manager's subordinates, as well as additional feedback from peers, internal and external customers, and higher ups.

Top managers are the highest level managers and work to ensure that major plans and objectives are set and accomplished in accord with the organization's purpose.

Total quality management (TQM) is managing with an organization-wide commitment to continuous work improvement, product quality, and totally meeting customer needs.

Totalitarian systems restrict representation in government through dictatorship or single-party rule.

Training involves a set of activities that provide learning opportunities through which people can acquire and improve job-related skills.

A **trait** is a relatively stable and enduring personal characteristic of an individual.

Transactional leadership is leadership that orchestrates and directs the efforts of others through tasks, rewards, and structures.

Transformational leadership is the ability of a leader to get people to do more than they originally expected to do in support of large-scale innovation and change.

A **type A personality** is a person oriented toward extreme achievement, impatience, and perfectionism and who may find stress in circumstances others find relatively stress-free.

U

Unfreezing is the initial phase in the planned-change process during which the manager prepares a situation for change.

Utilitarian view is a view of ethical behavior based on delivering the greatest good to the greatest number of people.

V

Valence is the value a person assigns to work-related outcomes.

Values are the broad underlying beliefs, attitudes, preferences, and inclinations forming a person's approach to the surrounding world that help determine individual behavior.

A **virtual team** is a group of people who work together and solve problems through computer-based rather than face-to-face interactions.

Vision is a term used to describe a clear sense of the future.

W

Whistle blowers are people who expose the misdeeds of others in an organization as an attempt to preserve ethical standards.

Wholly owned subsidiary is an operation completely owned by another firm.

Workforce diversity is a term used to describe demographic differences (age, gender, race and ethnicity, and able-bodiedness) among members of the workforce.

I N D E X